the Roy conceptual model applied

ADAPTATION NURSING
the Roy conceptual model applied

BROOKE RANDELL, R.N., M.N.

Visiting Lecturer in Nursing,
University of California, Los Angeles;
Formerly Assistant Professor of Nursing,
Mount St. Mary's College,
Los Angeles, California

MARY POUSH TEDROW, R.N., M.S.

Assistant Professor of Nursing, Mount St. Mary's College;
Consultant, Adaptation Nursing Curriculum,
Los Angeles, California

JOYCE VAN LANDINGHAM, R.N., B.S.N., M.S.N.

Instructor, California State University;
Formerly Associate Professor of Nursing, Mount St. Mary's College,
Los Angeles, California

Illustrated

LIBRARY
COLBY-SAWYER COLLEGE
NEW LONDON, NH 03257

The C. V. Mosby Company

ST. LOUIS · TORONTO · LONDON   1982

MOSBY

A TRADITION OF PUBLISHING EXCELLENCE

Editor: Pamela Swearingen
Assistant editor: Bess Arends
Manuscript editor: Laura Kaye McNeive
Book design: Susan Trail
Cover design: Diane Beasley
Production: Kathleen Teal

#7998406

Printed in the United States of America

The C.V. Mosby Company
11830 Westline Industrial Drive, St. Louis, Missouri 63141

Library of Congress Cataloging in Publication Data

Randell, Brooke.
    Adaptation nursing.

    Bibliography: p.
    Includes index.
    1. Nursing.   2. Nursing—Philosophy.
3. Adaptation (Physiology).   4. Adjustment (Psychology).   I. Tedrow, Mary Poush.   II. Van Landingham,
Joyce.   III. Title.   IV. Title: Roy conceptual
model applied.
RT41.R35   610.73   81-18844
ISBN 0-8016-4024-5   AACR2

GW/VH/VH   9 8 7 6 5 4 3 2 1   01/A/047

To the Randell boys
John, Jedd, Seth
who shared their time, love, and caring.
BPR

To my daughter, **Becky**
who made new friends while I wrote.
To my **parents**
who helped me begin my nursing venture.
To my dear friend, **Joyce**
mentor, catalyst, and colleague
MPT

To my loving **parents** *and beloved* **family**
who always believed it was possible.
JVL

Foreword

The decade of the 1970s produced great growth in the development and use of conceptual models for nursing practice. Efforts have been directed toward identifying the phenomena that nurses deal with and the specific approaches that nurses take in dealing with those phenomena. A number of nursing theorists have focused on various descriptions of the person who acts holistically to cope with situations of wellness and illness. In addition to a view of the person, the other two important elements of nursing conceptual models are how the model describes the goal of nursing and nursing intervention.

The Roy adaptation model is one of the most commonly used models in this country and increasingly abroad. The Roy model had its beginning when I worked under Dorothy E. Johnson while earning my Master of Science degree at the University of California, Los Angeles, during the years 1964 to 1966. The model basically describes persons as adaptive systems who use cognator and regulator activity to cope with the stimuli that affect them during situations of wellness and illness. The nursing goal is to promote adaptation in regard to the four modes of physiological needs, self-concept, role function, and interdependence. Nurses intervene by changing internal and external stimuli so that the stimuli come within the range of the person's ability to cope and adapt.

The Roy adaptation model was implemented in the baccalaureate curriculum at Mount St. Mary's College in Los Angeles in the spring of 1970. At the same time, the first published articles on the model began to appear in the literature. Faculty members at the college, and eventually those from other institutions, as well as Master's and doctoral level students, have contributed greatly to the further development of the Roy adaptation model. To date nearly 20 publications have appeared showing this continuing development. The three authors of this book were all faculty members at the college in the 1970s. They participated in the initial stages of the model's development and made significant contributions, particularly in explicating the adaptive modes and the nursing process.

The present textbook is an important contribution to the continuing growth of the Roy adaptation model. In the process of developing nursing models, it is important to identify basic assumptions, concepts, and propositions, at the same time that this theoretical basis is made practical for use by nurses in the daily role of patient care. The authors have taken a fresh approach to concepts of the model previously not sufficiently explicated, for example, the focal stimulus as the triggering event and coping stance and coping strategy. They have added relevant concepts that expand the model, for example, dealing with the environment in terms of transaction and perception* and describing wellness and illness in terms of disruption in adaptive modes with efforts to quantify diagnostic levels. In addition to this creative theoretical work, they have made real efforts to reach the practicing nurse with many examples of the use of conceptual models and the Roy adaptation model in particular.

The authors are to be commended for undertaking this difficult dual task and presenting one of the first works of its kind, that is, a text expanding upon and applying the work of another theorist in the field. It is through these cumulative efforts that the science of nursing will continue to grow.

Sister Callista Roy

Mount St. Mary's College,
Los Angeles, California

---

*It is interesting to note that these authors independently identified these concepts with their own meaning and definitions, but they are surprisingly related to the work of other nurse theorists, for example, Imogene King.

Preface

The 1980s will be the decade of the nurse. This text is prepared for the nurse who wishes to be a practitioner of this decade. The adaptation nurse of the 1980s will be a thinker, a facilitator, and an independent practitioner. *Adaptation Nursing: the Roy Conceptual Model Applied* will contribute to the preparation of the 1980s nurse by teaching process: the adaptive coping process, the process of becoming an adaptation nurse, and the process of adaptation nursing. Process means a natural progression of changes that lead toward a particular result, a series of actions or operations conducting to an end. Process means growth. The reader of this text will grow.

The decade of the 1970s saw a revolution in the development and implementation of conceptual models. Mount St. Mary's College was one of the front-runners in that revolution, utilizing the Roy conceptual model to structure a nursing curriculum. Lured by offers of challenge and professional growth, we joined the faculty of Mount St. Mary's College and participated in the operationalization of a conceptual model. We were indeed challenged, and we experienced professional growth. Because of our experience at Mount St. Mary's College, hours of clinical practice, and thousands of student experiences and consultations with faculties all over the United States, we have expanded our perspective of the Roy adaptation model and developed a method of instruction especially suited to this type of conceptual thinking. In this textbook we will share the Roy adaptation model and our process of thinking so that you, too, may be challenged and grow.

Adaptation Nursing: the Roy Conceptual Model Applied demonstrates how the Roy adaptation model is applied to the interaction between adaptation nurses and clients who are experiencing wellness, disrupted wellness, and illness. The book is designed to teach a process of thinking that will allow the adaptation nurse to understand, organize, and utilize the complex relationship that exists between the adapting person and the environment to help the person to cope effectively. The text is divided into four sections. Section One deals with the essential components of adaptation nursing practice: the adapting person, the adaptation nurse, and the adaptation nursing process. The adaptive person and the coping process are examined, and then the process of becoming an adaptation nurse is described. Finally, the adaptation nursing process and the health/illness continuum are discussed in detail. Chapter 1 investigates the unique internal transaction that determines the person's coping response. Chapter 2 describes the role change that occurs when an adapting person becomes an adaptation nurse, and Chapter 3 explores the adaptation nursing process in depth.

Section Two is devoted to an expansion of adaptation theory with special emphasis on the concepts of health and illness and the professional role. Chapter 4 develops the concept of the health/illness continuum, demonstrating the relationships that exist between adaptation nursing diagnoses, health care facilities, and common medical conditions. Chapter 5 studies the adaptation nurse's evolution from recent graduate in her first nursing staff position to advanced practitioner.

Section Three is devoted to a demonstration of the complex cognitive process that underlies adaptation nursing practice and contains a detailed analysis of three case studies that illustrate significant aspects of this process. Chapter 6 focuses on adapting persons who are experiencing disrupted wellness as they might typically interact with nurses in the adolescent stage of development. Chapter 7 describes adapting persons who are experiencing illness as they interact with adaptation nurses in the young adult stage of development. Chapter 8 illustrates the interaction between adapting persons who are experiencing wellness and adaptation nurses in the generative stage of development.

Finally, some prospects for the future of adaptation nursing practice are explored in Section Four, Chapter 9.

The format of this textbook is designed to provide the reader with a process for learning the concepts presented in each section. Chapters are preceded by objectives and definitions for essential terms; exercises intended to test the reader's mastery of content are provided at the end of each chapter. This is a process text; therefore, it is hoped that, having utilized this book to acquire the tools of the adaptation nurse, the reader will be able to provide the adapting person with the unique experience of interacting with an adaptation nurse.

This book represents insights we have gained about adaptation theory and nursing practice. The synthesis of our shared perceptions evolved over the past 12 years as we worked with students and faculty in implementing the Roy adaptation model in a variety of curricula. Although this text is a finished product in one sense, our ideas are still in the process of change and growth. Even at the time of printing we recognize the need to explore and develop new theoretical issues and potential implications for practice that have arisen from the writing of this book. We wish, however, to share the collaborative effort this text represents with other faculty and students with the hope of expanding our thinking and enhancing the practice of nursing. We look forward to receiving responses concerning the effectiveness of our approach to adaptation nursing practice.

The ideas set forth in this text represent our combined backgrounds and interests. Each of us has a strong commitment to education, and the text reflects this conviction in its structure, which is designed to facilitate learning. Our primarily developmental and psychosocial perspective has evolved from our beliefs about and practice of adaptation nursing in maternal-child, medical-surgical, and psychiatric clinical settings. It would be impossible to delineate all the personal and theoretical sources that have influenced our knowledge and perceptions about the person and the practice of nursing. However, certain people merit special acknowledgment.

Special thanks go to the students at Mount St. Mary's College and the UCLA School of Nursing for their excitement in learning, prolific assessment guides, and sound critical attitudes, which helped us to clarify and distill many concepts. We also wish to thank our colleagues for their encouragement and support during the past years. In particular we are deeply indebted to Marie Driever, Janet Dunning, and Sue Ann Brown for their critical thinking and stimulating participation in our early development as well as for their specific insights and perceptions about adaptation nursing, which are incorporated in this text.

These acknowledgments would not be complete without reference to the work of Sister Callista Roy and Sister Rebecca Doan. We thank Sister Callista for her model as well as for her support and encouragement of our work in expanding the conceptual model. And we acknowledge that many of our efforts could not have progressed without Sister Rebecca's support of our creative approaches to curriculum development.

We also wish to express deep appreciation for the conscientious, efficient, and tireless efforts of our typist, Ruth Garrick, and our editor, Catherine Edwards, without whose efforts this manuscript would never have been brought to completion. In addition we extend special thanks to Pamela Swearingen, our patient and tolerant editor.

Finally, we most gratefully acknowledge the forbearance, good humor, and support of our families throughout this endeavor.

Brooke Randell
Mary Poush Tedrow
Joyce Van Landingham

Contents

The big picture
an adaptation perspective

CHAPTER 1

The adapting person: biopsychosociospiritual being

OBJECTIVES

Describe how the adaptation nurse will use her knowledge of the internal transaction.
List and define the essential terms related to the adaptation process.
Describe the adaptation process.
Explain the five-phase process involved in adaptation.
Show the relationship between coping stance and strategies, and describe the effects of this relationship on the person's behavioral outcome.
List and describe the factors that influence the person's adaptive response.
Show the relationship between the transaction and influencing factors, and explain the effect this relationship has on the person's behavioral outcome.

Adaptation is what you and I do. We have been adapting since conception and will continue to adapt until the moment we die. It is the way we respond to and reach out into the world. It is the way we make sense of the complex interaction between ourselves and our environment. An understanding of this adaptation process and the adapting person is essential to the practice of adaptation nursing. The Roy Adaptation Model views each adapting person as unique. Each adapting person sees and experiences the world in a different way. If the adaptation nurse hopes to interact effectively with the adapting person, she must be able to see and feel, at least in part, as he does. In this text we will explore in depth the mechanisms the nurse can use to facilitate effectiveness with the adapting person. The initial focus will be on the unique internal process each adapting person uses to experience his world. If the adaptation nurse can understand and interpret this process, she will often perceive the world from the perspective of the adapting person.

When you have completed this chapter, you should have a clear understanding of the ways in which a person interacts with the environment. In addition, you should be able to explain the internal transaction the person uses to sift and sort the personal internal and environmental stimuli that influence his behavior. Finally, you will be able to recognize the relationship between the adaptation process and the behavioral responses that are an expression of the person's adaptation. To begin with, let's look at the definitions that are critical to your understanding of this chapter. You will need to master these terms before proceeding with Chapter 1.

ESSENTIAL TERMS

Person   The person is an *open*, living system who uses *adaptive mechanisms to meet needs* for biological, psychological, and social *adequacy*. This level of adequacy is influenced by the person's unique physiological makeup, maturational level, and perceptions.

Adequacy   Adequacy is the *state of balance* or equality *between the person and the environment*, which he constantly strives to achieve and maintain. This state of balance is experienced as a feeling of competence in relationship to stress.

Regulator   The regulator is the person's *physiological adaptive mechanism* for responding to an environmental impact. This mechanism *alerts* and *mobilizes* the neural and hormonal systems to produce a *continuous, universal physiological response*. It is also responsible for the body's specific physiological response to a physical, chemical, or infectious triggering event.

Cognator   The cognator is the person's *conscious* and *unconscious adaptive mechanism* that, when signalled by the regulator, *labels, clarifies, defines*, and *initiates* a *behavioral response*. This mechanism *alters the stress experience* and terminates the activity of the regulatory mechanism by affecting the relationship between the person and the environment.

Influencing stimuli   Influencing stimuli are those *elements* that affect the person's *ability to achieve adequacy*. These stimuli include the person's *internal state* and the *environment*.

Internal state   The internal state consists of the person's *physiological makeup, maturational level*, and *unique perceptions*.

Environment   The environment is the *constantly changing* but often *predictable* composition of *people, places, and objects* that surround the person.

Triggering event   A triggering event occurs whenever the *environment* touches or penetrates the person and *causes a change* in his *level of adequacy*.

Change   Change is the process of altering, varying, or modifying. When a person or situation is changed, the difference may be perceived as positive or negative and is evaluated according to the person's sense of comfort or discomfort.

Stress   Stress is any *change in the level of adequacy* experienced by the person any time he is touched by the environment.

Transaction   Transaction is the *process whereby the person alters the stress experience*. This alteration, expressed as a behavioral response, is achieved by the regulator and cognator and may be said to have maintained, increased, or decreased the level of adequacy.

Behavioral responses   Behavioral responses are *observable* or *measurable activities* in which the person engages in an attempt to achieve or maintain physiological, psychological, and social adequacy.

Coping stance   Coping stance is the intellectual or emotional posture assumed by the adapting person when he transacts to process a triggering event.

Coping strategy   Coping strategy represents the careful method the person behaviorally employs to master the relationship with the triggering event.

Adaptation process   The adaptation process encompasses *all the activities* engaged in by the person while *striving for adequacy*. This process is represented by the *give-and-take relationship between the transaction and the influencing stimuli*. The ultimate effect of this process may be to maintain, increase, or decrease the level of adequacy.

When you believe you understand the essential terms, continue with the chapter.

THE PERSON AND THE ENVIRONMENT

The adapting person is a constantly vigilant, open, living system striving for adequacy. By definition an open, living system is an organism that strives for survival, growth, reproduction, mastery, and autonomy in a give-and-take relationship with the environment. The person is vigilant because he must constantly *scan* the ever-changing but often predictable environment. This environment brings the person in contact with people, places, and objects that influence his ability to achieve the level of adequacy for which he strives. In addition, this level of adequacy is influenced by the person's unique internal state, which includes his physiological makeup, maturational level, and perceptions.

The point at which the person and the environment come together is called a triggering event. This event produces a change in the person's level of adequacy. He experiences the change as a stress and begins the transaction in an effort to maintain the level of adequacy. If the transaction is effective, he will either maintain or increase the level of adequacy; if it is ineffective, that level will decrease.

In the adaptation process the person utilizes a five-phase internal transaction in order to produce behavior that will bring about a reduction in stress and a stabilization in his level of adequacy. Initially the internal transaction is expressed physiologically. As Hans Selye (1959) indicates, this physiological alarm reaction places the person on physiological alert and also signals the need to process the experience cognitively. The person exhibits a behavioral response based on his cognitive interpretation. If the transaction is effective, stress is reduced, and the system returns to its previous level or a higher level of adequacy. If the transaction is ineffective, the person may experience a drop in the level of adequacy. Adaptation, then, is the give-and-take relationship between the person and the environment. This relationship, or adaptation, is mediated by the internal transaction.

It is obvious from this description that the critical issue is the internal transaction that processes the relationship between the person's internal state and the external environment. Stress reduction is dependent on an effective transaction, which results in the correct selection of a behavioral response. An incorrect internal process results in behavioral responses that increase stress, and it further decreases the level of adequacy. Adaptation theory labels these critical transacting elements as the regulator and the cognator. It is essential to understand the adapting person's unique regulator/cognator transaction process if one wishes to practice adaptation nursing.

The *regulator* is the physiological response to the interaction between the person and the environment. It is an alarm reaction that mobilizes the neural and hormonal systems. This alarm has three functions in stress: to initiate the automatic response essential to the maintenance of life; to stimulate defensive responses to physical, chemical, or infectious triggering events; and to alert the cognator that a triggering event has occurred.

The *cognator*, or conscious and unconscious thinking process, then, evaluates the physiological experience in order to label, clarify, define, and initiate a behavioral response to stress. The regulator is the source of information for the cognator; it calls the person's attention to the contact with the environment and continues signaling as a constant source of feedback for the duration of the experience. The cognator is the mechanism by which the person interprets or makes sense of the environmental experience.

Example

Using a typical interaction between a mother and child, let's look at the adaptation process. In this example, there is a mother and a 2-year-old child in a kitchen. The mother is cooking, and the child is playing nearby. The child begins to cry, stating, "I'm hungry." The child's cry is an example of a triggering event: it causes a change in the environment that affects the mother. She then experiences stress, a change in the level of adequacy. The regulator puts the mother on physiological alert and signals her cognator to process the child's statement. She considers many factors: whether she can stop cooking to prepare a snack, the time of the child's previous meal, how she feels about the child eating between meals, the time of the next meal, and her current level of tolerance for crying behavior. The cognator processes all these possibilities and selects a behavioral response to cope with the stress. In this instance the mother sees an apple nearby, and because dinner will not be ready for 2 hours, she prepares the apple for the child. The environmental change results in the child quietly returning to play activities and the mother experiencing a decrease in stress and a return to her previous level of adequacy.

Obviously, each person engages in many similar transactions each day; often such transactions occur simultaneously. One cannot consciously be aware of all these simultaneous interactions without being overwhelmed; therefore, the regulator and cognator are constantly vigilant yet selectively responsive to triggering events.

Now that you have an overview of the adaptation process, you are ready to explore the two major elements in this process: the transaction and the stimuli that influence the transaction.

THE TRANSACTION

The transaction is represented by the activities of the regulator and the cognator and is described in five phases.

Phase I

The first phase is represented by the person's state of constant vigilance as well as the initial contact with the triggering event. As an open, living system residing in an ever-changing yet often predictable environment, the adapting person must at all times be aware of himself and the surroundings. The person constantly *scans* so that he can anticipate contact and make the most appropriate response when he

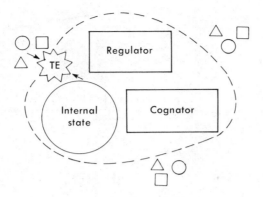

FIGURE 1-1
The person in a constant state of vigilance. The broken line represents the open, living system transacting with the ever-changing environment; the circles represent people; the squares indicate objects; and the triangles symbolize place. The jagged line represents the impact of the triggering event.

touches or is touched by someone or something in the environment. Also, during this first phase, the initial contact between the environment and the person occurs. In adaptation theory this contact is called the triggering event, which is anything that can be considered an interaction between the person and the environment. It can be as simple as a change in the weather or as complex as an automobile accident involving the person and family members. This phase is represented in Figure 1-1. Simply stated, the first phase involves a constantly vigilant person interacting with an ever-changing yet often predictable environment. This interaction is set in motion by a *triggering event*, which in turn starts or triggers this complex, five-phase internal transaction.

Phase II

In the second phase both the regulator and cognator are activated. Stress, brought about by an interaction between the person and the environment, is experienced by the person as a change in the level of adequacy. The regulator responds to this change by performing three functions. First, the regulator stimulates the protective behaviors associated with physiological readiness. This stimulation of the neural and hormonal systems results in observable changes in blood pressure, pulse, respiration, and heart rate. Second, when the triggering event is a physical, chemical, or infectious assault on the adapting person, the second stage of the body's defense system is activated. The person may experience a variety of physiological changes depending upon the nature of the assault. These changes might include nausea and vomiting, elevated temperature, and an increase in the white blood cell count. Finally, the regulator flashes a message to the cognator, signaling that a triggering event has

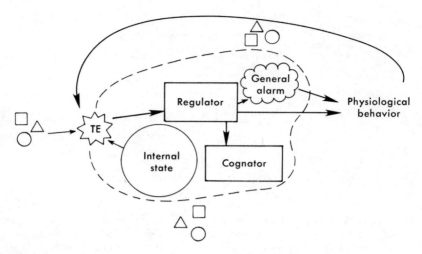

FIGURE 1-2
The person begins to process the interaction with the environment. The regulator is signaled, a general alarm produces physiological behavior, additional physiological behaviors are generated to protect the person, and the cognator is alerted. The behavioral response impacts on the environment and influences the triggering events. The directional arrows represent the sequence of the second phase of transaction.

occurred and that the body is on physiological alert. All of these functions occur automatically without conscious or cognative processing by the adapting person. The functions are presented graphically in Figure 1-2. In phase II, then, the regulator sounds the alarm, which results in a state of physiological readiness; initiates a defensive response in interactions involving a physical, chemical, or infectious triggering event; and alerts the cognator to the fact that the person needs assistance.

Phase III

The third phase represents the beginning work of the cognator. In this phase all triggering events are processed. The cognator interprets the data received from the regulator and selects the most appropriate coping stance (an intellectual or emotional posture). When the triggering event is a physical, chemical, or infectious assault on the person, the cognator does not affect the physiological behavioral response previously initiated by the regulator. In this instance the cognator allows the person to assess this assaulting triggering event and assume an initial coping stance that will hopefully terminate the noxious interaction. In all interactions the alerted cognator has four coping stances or postures from which to choose: approach/avoidance, compromise, self-enhancement, and inaction. The cognator makes a choice based upon the assessment of the internal state and the external environment, taking into account the person's need for biological, psychological, and social adequacy.

Approach/avoidance. The cognator chooses approach/avoidance as a coping stance when the assessment process indicates that the person is in imminent danger, such as when there is an extreme threat to survival, growth, mastery, or autonomy. This stance is frequently chosen when the triggering event is a physical, chemical, or infectious assault on the person. The cognator communicates to the person that the triggering event must be terminated immediately. When this coping stance is taken, the behavior is generally motivated by fear, and little cognitive activity is initiated by the adapting person.

Compromise. The cognator chooses compromise as a coping stance when the assessment process reveals stress but no immediate danger for the person. This stance tends to be selected when the triggering event is social or intrapersonal. In the compromise stance the cognator initiates a problem-solving process because stress, not fear, is the motivation for action. The person has time to choose the approach most likely to maintain the level of adequacy. This coping stance is very commonly used. As Robert White (1974) states, "Adaptation does not mean a total triumph over the environment or a total surrender to it, but rather a striving toward an acceptable compromise, the maintenance of integrity being a relative notion." The cognator assesses the stress, then sifts and sorts the data to select a solution. The solution allows the person to maintain the sense of adequacy for which he strives without undue harm.

Self-enhancement. When the cognator chooses the third coping stance, self-enhancement, it means that the cognator has assessed the potential for more self-directed functioning. Certain triggering events prompt the cognator to select this problem-solving process to alter certain types of stress experiences. A self-enhancing coping stance may be chosen at some risk and may produce additional stress for the person, but this striving is also compatible with the constant need for biological, psychological, and social adequacy. Few people are satisfied with simply maintaining adequacy and will seek mastery and self-autonomy at some personal cost.

Inaction. The final coping stance, like the first, is motivated by fear. Inaction differs from approach/avoidance because it is the least effective means for coping with stress. In this stance a triggering event occurs, and the regulator sounds the alarm; but the interpretation is so threatening that the cognator fails to process the experience. This coping stance denies the stress resulting from the triggering event. Thus, it places the person in a position in which the level of adequacy is severely threatened, for the person's compatibility with the environment is limited. The adapting person is an open, living system in constant interaction with the environment. If the person consistently blocks the environment, the system becomes closed and unresponsive, therefore decreasing the level of adequacy.

In summary, then, during the third phase of the transaction the cognator interprets the input from the regulator and selects the optimal coping stance (Figure 1-3). Thus, the cognator selects a coping stance from the following four options: ap-

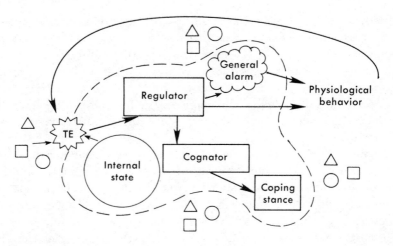

FIGURE 1-3
The person continues the adaptive response. The cognator mechanism processes the interaction and selects a coping stance to deal with the triggering event. The arrows represent the sequence of the third phase of the transaction.

proach/avoidance, compromise, self-enhancement, and inaction. This selection sets the stage for the fourth phase in the transaction process, in which the cognator assists the person to make a plan for implementing the appropriate coping stance.

Phase IV

The fourth phase represents the cognator's development of coping strategies, which reflect the cognator's careful plan or method for implementing the coping stance. In order to formulate this plan, the cognator must again evaluate the person's internal state and external environment, constantly evaluating options against the individual's need for biological, psychological, and social adequacy. In order to examine this process, the four possible coping stances should be reviewed so that the major strategies can be identified.

Common coping strategies associated with approach/avoidance

Fight or flight. The first and most straightforward coping stance is approach/avoidance. This stance is based on the cognator's warning that failure to act will result in significant damage to the person's level of adequacy. The cognator continues to assess the danger and signals the person to take direct action to destroy the environmental stimulus or withdraw from it immediately. The strategy in this coping stance, then, is to stop the interaction between the person and the environment by either distorting the internal state or destroying the external environment by force or withdrawal.

The first coping strategy associated with this stance is fight. The adapting person adopts this strategy based on the belief that he is more powerful than the triggering event. The cognator's assessment reveals that direct action will terminate the triggering event and bring about a stabilization in the level of adequacy.

The second coping strategy associated with the stance of approach/avoidance is flight. In this situation the adapting person believes that the triggering event is more powerful than himself. The cognator's assessment reveals that the person must remove himself from the proximity of the triggering event if he wishes to prevent a severe and/or permanent decline in the level of adequacy.

These strategies generally occur in situations of extreme stress and are usually motivated by fear of destruction. The person has a characteristic response pattern to fear-producing situations. Once the cognator takes a stance of approach/avoidance, the person acts automatically with little problem solving regarding alternatives. The major concern is the person's safety, and this goal is pursued at any cost. This can be a highly effective coping strategy, because it assists the person to terminate life-threatening interactions. It also has the potential to be destructive to the person's maintenance of the level of adequacy for several reasons.

If the fight or flight coping strategies are used too often, they will serve to isolate the person from the environment. As an open, living system the person is dependent on the environment for survival, growth, reproduction, mastery, and adequacy. If the person repeatedly destroys part of the environment or regularly flees from interaction, the environment will become increasingly less accessible, and the person's level of adequacy will decline. The fight or flight coping strategy is an automatic response to a stress associated with fear. It is highly effective when used sparingly, but it can be destructive when utilized excessively or to the exclusion of more appropriate strategies.

Common coping strategies associated with compromise. One of the most commonly used and most effective stances is compromise. This stance is an appropriate alternative to the approach/avoidance stance. It can be described as *defensive reappraisal,* a term used by Richard Lazarus (1966). Defensive reappraisal involves psychological maneuvers in which the individual deceives himself about the actual conditions of the threat. Essentially, the cognator allows the person to reevaluate the stress provoked by the triggering event. In the reevaluation the cognator denies or distorts the stimulus. The process prevents the person from being overwhelmed and maintains the level of adequacy so that the person can deal with at least a portion of the stress. It seems obvious from the volumes of psychological literature on the subject of defense mechanisms that a multitude of strategies could be listed. For the sake of simplification, the three major defense mechanisms can be described as suppression/repression, projection, and substitution. These mechanisms seem to operate most frequently when the person assumes the coping stance of compromise.

Suppression/repression. Suppression/repression is a mechanism by which the cognator stimulates the person to forget. Stress-producing interactions that threaten adequacy are blocked, allowing the person to continue functioning. Suppression is the conscious process that the person utilizes to control or inhibit unacceptable impulses, emotions, or ideas. Repression is the unconscious process by which the person removes from consciousness the ideas, impulses, and affects that are unacceptable to him. Suppression and repression are often seen in combination, with the conscious preceding the unconscious.

These mechanisms are not totally successful, and the stress tends to recur; therefore, the person has many opportunities to deal with the interaction and perhaps resolve it more completely. In addition, suppression/repression may be utilized for only a portion of the stress, thereby maintaining the level of adequacy and leaving the person the necessary energy to complete the interaction effectively.

Projection. Projection is another commonly used defense that allows the person to rid the self of incompatible feelings and thoughts by ascribing them to other people or objects in the environment. The person denies the existence of certain feelings or emotions within himself, while declaring that these feelings or emotions are present in another person or persons. The individual may even maintain that these feelings or emotions are present in certain people, objects, or places. Frequently, interactions between the person and the environment result in emotionally unacceptable feelings, which lower the level of adequacy. If the person can project these emotions into the environment, his level of adequacy can be maintained.

Substitution. Finally, in substitution, the cognator allows the person to choose alternate people, places, and objects for interacting. When the person interacts with another person, place, or object, he invests energy into them. Should a particular person, place, or object be unavailable to the person, he must be able to find a substitute for the invested energy. When the individual's energy has no object, he experiences stress. This stress can be reduced when the person substitutes another person, place, or object as a recipient of the energy. In this way transactions are made with more readily attainable objects within the environment, and the unattainable or unacceptable goals are made compatible with the environment. This particular defense is very successful because it serves to make the self more compatible with others in the environment.

In summary, the coping stance is translated into a coping strategy, which is designed to facilitate the interaction between the person and the environment, allowing him to maintain a functional level of adequacy. In compromise, the strategies are commmonly called defense mechanisms and include suppression/repression, projection, and substitution. Generally, these mechanisms serve to distort or deny the relationship between the person and the environment; they can be considered successful as long as the distortion of reality is minimal. As soon as the person begins to use these mechanisms exclusively or in the extreme, however, they cease to maintain the level of adequacy effectively; in fact, they severely limit it. Therefore, defense mechanisms of repression, projection, and substitution can successfully facilitate a compromise between the person and the environment. If, on the other hand, these mechanisms are used too frequently, the compromise will fail, and the level of adequacy will fall below the level acceptable to the person.

Common coping strategies associated with self-enhancement. Another group of commonly used coping strategies is included in the self-enhancement stance. As in the compromise stance, the cognator communicates the stress but does not signal imminent danger. This signal indicates to the person that certain behavioral patterns will result in growth or increased autonomy. The process that operates here is problem solving.

Although a variety of strategies reflect the problem-solving stance, three occur most frequently: confrontation, manipulation, and negotiation.

Confrontation. In confrontation, as the word implies, the cognator suggests that the person meet the environment head on. The stress is assessed as a significant one, and considerable conflict exists; however, the person feels that if he approaches the problem directly, he will not only experience a stabilization in the level of adequacy but will be challenged and feel more autonomous following his action. Confrontation usually occurs when the person assesses less than optimal conditions, but rather than hesitate (as occurs in manipulation or negotiation), he acts immediately. Hesitating to act and waiting for an alteration in the environment or the internal state might bring about a more optimal circumstance but could also result in a less than optimal or even negative response. Therefore, when the person engages in confrontation, he bases his selection on the belief that acting immediately in a potentially risky situation is the optimal response, as waiting would prove much less effective. This selection is usually made for one of two reasons: because of a belief that the time is right and that the oppportunity may never again arise or because there exists a lack of knowledge, skill, or potential to impact on the environment or the internal state.

Manipulation. The problem-solving approach of manipulation involves the person's expending considerable energy to reach his goal. The cognator signals the person that the transaction is potentially self-enhancing but that there are environmental ingredients missing. If the person wants to achieve increased adequacy, he needs to supply those missing ingredients. He accomplishes this by managing the environment in such a way that the essential elements become available. In this strategy the person delays his response until all the influencing stimuli are available to provide an optimal outcome.

Negotiation. In negotiation the person transacts with the environment in an attempt to clarify the stress and bargain with the environment so that he achieves a greater share of the positive response. The cognator communicates that, if the person is willing to compromise in a certain area, the responses from the environment will be greater, and the person will experience an increased sense of mastery and autonomy. The compromise usually involves a change in the person's internal state.

The environment, or set of circumstances, is optimal and cannot be altered further. The message from the cognator clearly indicates that if one is willing to take the risk of changing or altering one's knowledge, beliefs, or values, one can achieve a greater level of adequacy.

When the person adopts the coping stance of self-enhancement, he can choose an immediate response calculated to beat the odds, or he can choose to wait, and in waiting manipulate the environment or alter the internal state to achieve an optimal response. The coping strategies of manipulation and negotiation can also be used in combination. This is very effective when changes are necessary in the environment as well as the internal state. Additionally, these self-enhancing strategies can be used in combination with the compromise stance. For example, a person may repress a portion of the stress, which allows him to maintain the level of adequacy. This in turn provides the necessary energy to respond to the remainder of the stressful transaction with a self-enhancing strategy.

Common coping strategies associated with inaction. The least successful strategy arises from a coping stance of inaction. Like the compromise stance, inaction involves the use of defense mechanisms; however, in this instance, the mechanisms are used to distort reality to a nonfunctional degree. Mechanisms are used to maintain the level of adequacy, but in the stance of inaction the strategies tend to immobilize the person, resulting in a rapid drop in the level of adequacy. This may occur when certain mechanisms are used to excess or to the exclusion of other mechanisms or when the chosen defenses are extremely distorting, as occurs with inaction. Three frequently used strategies in this stance are denial, reaction formation, and dissociation. The goal of these coping strategies is to decrease or obliterate the person's awareness of a triggering event and the consequent stress experience.

Denial. The most common coping strategy used in inaction is denial, which is the unconscious blocking out of emotional experiences. When the regulator signals the triggering event and the person experiences stress, the cognator should begin the assessment process. However, when the triggering event produces an extreme stress response, the cognator signals that it is overwhelmed and will not respond. Denial is used to block the message from the regulator, keeping the stress out of awareness.

Reaction formation. Another coping strategy is reaction formation. In this response the person replaces a painful or unacceptable interaction with an acceptable opposite interaction and develops a socialized attitude or interest that is the direct antithesis of some infantile wish or impulse. This defensive maneuver is often used when the person experiences a conflict between feelings and behavioral responses. The triggering event occurs, the regulator signals stress, and the cognator chooses a behavioral response that conflicts with the person's feelings, such as laughing at a tragic event or speaking unkindly of someone who is secretly admired. Reaction formation is used to disregard the feeling signaled by the regulator, and stress is temporarily reduced by the person exhibiting opposing behaviors. The person believes the opposing behaviors are expected by the environment. If the person were to express the actual response he anticipates, he would experience a decline in the level of adequacy.

Dissociation. In the coping strategy of inaction the cognator employs dissociation, which is used to separate the person from interaction with the environment. This maneuver involves a group of mental processes that are split off from the rest of the person's thinking. This results in an independent functioning of the group of processes and a loss of the usual interrelationships. The cognator allows the person to deny the triggering event, the stress, and the regulator's signal. Thus, the person separates himself from the interaction. The person essentially says, "It didn't happen."

In summary, all the strategies of inaction are designed to maintain the level of adequacy by denying or distorting the interaction between the person and the environment. In the defenses of denial, reaction formation, and dissociation, the distortions of reality are so great that the mechanisms are only functional for a very short period of time. Then the mechanisms make the person so estranged from others that his level of adequacy begins to decline. Therefore, these are the least effective coping strategies and provide only a temporary experience of adequacy.

Coping strategies, then, are the plans that a person makes once the cognator has assumed a coping stance. Figure 1-4 portrays this concept. The common coping

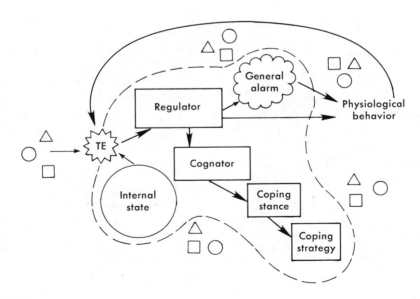

FIGURE 1-4
The person continues to attend to the environmental encounter. The cognator selects strategies that will most meaningfully help the person transact with the triggering event. The arrows continue to plot the course of the adapting person's coping process.

strategies include *fight, flight, suppression/repression, projection, substitution, confrontation, manipulation, negotiation, denial, reaction formation,* and *dissociation*. The most successful strategies are those that protect the person, maintain or enhance adequacy and minimally distort reality.

Phase V

The fifth phase of the transaction involves the person's behavioral response to the triggering event. The person channels his coping energy in an attempt to achieve or maintain the level of physiological, psychological, and/or sociological adequacy. These responses, which represent the culmination of the work of the regulator and the cognator, operate on the components of the interaction to facilitate an adaptive interaction. All physiological behaviors are automatically stimulated by the regulator and represent the person's striving for physiological adequacy. Psychological and sociological behaviors are mediated by the cognator and represent the person's striving for psychological and social adequacy. The channeling of coping energy is shown in Figure 1-5. It is important to recall that the adapting person is a whole and that these segments represent arbitrary divisions for the purpose of organizing one's thinking. Therefore, remember that psychological and social responses, mediated

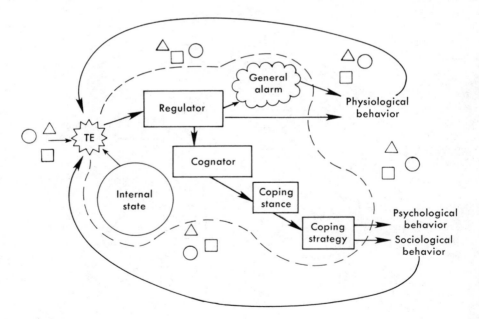

FIGURE 1-5
The person, through the work of the regulator/cognator process, channels his coping energy and demonstrates physiological and sociological behavior to influence his level of adequacy. In phase 5 the directional arrows impact on the environment and alter the experience of the triggering event.

by the cognator, accompany the physiological response. Likewise, physiological responses, initiated by the regulator, have psychological and social components. Based on the coping stance and strategies selected by the cognator, the person will demonstrate behavior in at least one of these three areas. The goal of this behavior is to alter the relationship between the person and the environment so that the person achieves survival, reproduction, growth, mastery, and autonomy. He acts on the environment to reduce stress and to increase the level of adequacy.

Five phases in review

Before studying a behavioral example, one should review the five phases that reflect the dynamic interaction between a constantly vigilant, open, living system and an ever-changing but predictable environment. When the person and the environment touch or penetrate, a *triggering event* occurs. The regulator then sounds an alarm, creating a state of *physiological alert,* stimulating a physiological behavioral response, and *activating the cognator*. Once activated, the cognator functions in two ways: by selecting a *coping stance* and by selecting the appropriate *strategy* to accompany that stance. These coping strategies are then *expressed behaviorally* when energy is channeled to the environment. This process, which includes five phases, recurs many times each hour and is the major mechanism by which the person and the environment interact. Each behavioral response has impact and produces a new triggering event, which in turn triggers a new process that functions as a constant source of feedback regarding the relationship between the person and the environment.

Example

Let us examine a typical interaction between the person and the environment to illustrate further each of the five phases. In this example the person is sleeping soundly in a warm bed in a dark room with a telephone sitting on a table beside the bed.

In the first phase of the transaction the triggering event is the ringing of the phone; the environment has touched the person. In the second phase a state of physiological alert begins, the person's heart rate and blood pressure increase, and since the triggering event is physiological, the auditory response and the associated physical movements toward the source of the noise are automatically initiated by the regulator. Additionally, the cognator is signaled and begins processing the interaction. Then the cognator, in the third phase, chooses a coping stance, in this case compromise. This stance is selected based on the assessment that stress is present but that the self is in no immediate danger. In the fourth phase the cognator selects a coping strategy compatible with the compromise stance. In response to the ringing telephone the cognator chooses substitution as the appropriate defensive response. The cognator has helped the person to understand that even though he wishes to continue sleeping in the warm bed, the only way he can terminate the noise is to answer the telephone. The cognator helps the person choose an alternate object for his behavior—the ringing telephone instead of the comfortable self. The rationale offered to the person by the cognator indicates that a change in the level of adequacy will result if the phone continues to ring and he misses the message the phone might convey. Finally, in the fifth phase, the behavioral output is expressed by the person answering the phone. The adapting person demonstrates two types of behavioral response: physiological, in the form of arousal, and sociological, in the form of pre-scribed behaviors in answering the phone.

In this example it is evident that the regulator and the cognator immediately process the interaction between the person and the environment. Notice also how the behavior has an effect on the environment that often produces additional trig-gering events. The five phases are recycled when the person says "Hello," producing a triggering event for someone else, and this in turn produces a triggering event for the person in the warm bed. The second triggering event must be processed in the same manner as the first. Thus begins a new day for this person, who will constantly interact with the environment to maintain or elevate that level of adequacy for which all people strive.

INFLUENCING STIMULI

The influencing stimuli include the person's internal state and the external en-vironment. The internal state is what makes up the adapting person and influences his transactional process and behavioral responses: physiological structure, matura-tional level, and unique perceptions. The environment refers to the adapting person's surroundings: the people, places, and objects that exist outside the person and influence how he transacts and behaves. Therefore, the influencing stimuli consist of the person's internal state, which is a unique personal experience, and the external environment, which is a physical space shared by others.

Internal state

Physiological makeup. The term *internal state* refers to several sets of stimuli. First, it refers to the person's biological systems. For a person's biological internal state to be intact, he must have all the structures associated with the human body. These structures must be functioning at a level adequate to maintain life, and the body must have the regulatory mechanisms necessary for the operation of these various bodily functions.

Maturational level. The internal state also refers to the level of maturation of the adapting person. This maturation is expressed physiologically, psychologically, and sociologically and implies the adapting person's position in the aging process. Re-stated, the maturational level reflects the complex set of stimuli and behaviors as-sociated with the stages of development. Many theorists have postulated the steps or progression associated with maturation. Any of these theories will provide a framework for establishing the adapting person's level of maturity, which, combined with associated behaviors, constantly influences the adapting person's transactions. The work of Erik Erikson (1963) has been employed extensively in the development and implementation of the Roy model. The reader might find it helpful to review Erikson's developmental stages on completion of this chapter.

Perceptions. The internal state also includes a complex collection of perceptions that the person internalizes and stores in the brain. These perceptions arise from the person's experience as the biological system matures and constantly interacts with the environment. These perceptions are coded and stored and become part of the unique inner world of the adapting person. They have labels such as beliefs, attitudes, ideas, myths, and knowledge, and they significantly influence the process of adaptation.

The person has an internal state that consists of his biological systems, level of maturation, and his internalized perceptions. Because the person is an open, living system, this internal state is in constant interaction with the environment.

Environment

The environment is the collection of persons, places, and objects that surround the physical space occupied by the adapting person. This space is filled with a variety of physical and interactional objects. The *physical environment* includes the geographical location and all the other places and conditions that can be associated with it, such as climate, nutritional substances, natural resources, shelter, and harmful or dangerous substances. The *interactional environment* is composed of people (and their presence or absence) within physical nearness of the adapting person. These people can be further categorized to represent the cultural, religious, political, and philosophical notions prevalent in the physical space.

Summary

The adapting person, then, is an open, living system whose internal state is composed of a physical structure, maturational level, and a vast collection of perceptions that constantly interact with the environment, both physical and interactional. The person's internal state openly responds to the constantly changing collection of people, places, and objects that make up the environment.

The adapting person and the external environment come together constantly. This produces a triggering event, which signals the regulator and the cognator that the internal state and environment are interacting, and a change in the level of adequacy results. The regulator initiates the physiological alarm and alerts the cognator, which then begins to process the interaction between the internal state and the environment. The cognator must take into account the person's physical structure, functioning, regulatory assets, the level of maturation, and the perceptions relevant to this particular experience. In addition, the cognator must scan the environment, making decisions regarding the importance of people, places, and objects in relation to the person's internal stimuli. The cognator functions like a minicomputer, constantly making decisions based on input both from the person's internal state and from the external influencing factors. It is the regulator/cognator process that makes the person unique. Many people will experience similar interactions between themselves and the environment, but the cognator makes the experience and the behavioral response uniquely personal. When the environment is combined with the adapting person's internal state, the coping stance and strategy reflect the person's interpretation and response to the environment.

Example

Using the example of the sleeping person being awakened by a ringing telephone, we will review the adaptation process and take a closer look at the internal and external influencing stimuli. Again we have a person sleeping soundly in a warm bed with a telephone nearby. Let us further relate that it is 10:00 A.M. on a Monday morning in Los Angeles. The sleeping person resides alone in an apartment and is employed as a junior executive at a bank. Now let us examine the behavioral responses of two different sleepers with similar environments but different internal states.

When the phone rings, the regulator goes into operation, a state of physiological alert is induced, and the cognator is signaled. The uniqueness of the experience begins when the cognators of the two bank employees begin categorizing this experience. Bank employee number one, Fred, sits up in bed, looks at the clock, falls back, covers his head, and ignores the phone. Bank employee number two, Bill, sits up in bed, looks at the clock, and immediately answers the phone. What happened in the cognator processing that can account for the different behavioral responses? We will examine the internal influencing stimuli to see how the cognators arrived at alternate coping stances and strategies.

Both Bill and Fred are healthy young men in their late twenties. Both have all biological structures, which are functioning optimally with necessary regulatory control. Bill and Fred are developmentally at the same level, dealing with the tasks of young adulthood, striving for intimacy with a significant other, and attempting to achieve independent support. On the surface the two sleepers seem very similar; but closer observation of the two reveals some differences. Fred has several girlfriends; one whom he likes considerably more than the others has recently begun to pressure him for more commitment than he feels ready to give. He spent much of the past weekend trying to maintain this significant relationship without committing himself to a more permanent arrangement. In addition, Fred has held his position at the bank for only 3 months; he has not completed the training program and is considerably ambivalent about the position. He took the job at the insistence of his parents, who were fearful he would not be able to support himself as a carpenter working on custom cabinets. In fact, Fred's father arranged this job with a fellow banker. Prior to this time Fred had stayed with no job longer than 6 months, with the exception of woodworking, which he had done sporadically since high school.

Bill, on the other hand, has been seeing several girls socially, has many friends, but is not actively pursuing or being pursued in any relationships. He had a relaxing weekend with friends but spent Sunday evening at home because he thought he might be getting a cold. Bill has been at the bank for 18 months; he is currently being considered for a promotion and feels confident he will receive it. A math and business major in college, he has been single minded about a career in banking since adolescence. His upwardly mobile middle-class family actively supports his career choice.

Bill and Fred have similar physiological states and maturational levels. Bill seems to be having more success than Fred in mastering the tasks of his developmental stage. In addition to differences in maturational level, there is an indication that different perceptual experiences might be occurring.

Fred is ambivalent about his job and seems to definitely prefer a different occupation. He is feeling pressure from both his family and a girlfriend to do things that make him uncomfortable. In addition, we might learn from talking to Fred that he opposes today's economy and philosophically supports a society that values the sufficiency of individuals instead of large groups. We also learn that Fred has made the decision to finish the training program in another month and then take his small savings and move to a small northern California community to start a custom cabinetry business. Bill, on the other hand, hopes to be a bank president one day. He finds the economy and its manipulation fascinating and hopes to be making enough money in the next year to begin investing, perhaps even buying some property. In the meantime, he would like to meet and marry the "right girl" and begin acquiring those possessions he associates with the "good life." Obviously, there are differences in Fred and Bill that result in one's answering the phone and the other's letting it ring.

Both men assume, because it is 10:00 A.M. on a working day, that the phone call is from their respective bosses; each, however, chooses a different option. Fred selects the coping stance of compromise, deciding on a strategy that appears to be a combination of repression and projection. He chooses not to answer the phone and to stay in bed, using repression to block the stress he feels about his job being threatened. He thinks, "I was going to quit anyway," and uses projection to deal with the anger he feels with himself by placing blame on his father and the bank for the faulty state of the world today. His sense of adequacy is maintained, and for the present he is free from the stress associated with the conflict between the internal world of his maturational level and perceptions and the external work of his job.

Bill, on the other hand, chooses to implement the coping stance of self-enhancement by utilizing the coping strategy of confrontation. The cognator tells him there is considerable risk in this approach: "You've been irresponsible, and you don't have the promotion yet"; but the cognator also tells him, "If you're able to accept the challenge, the odds are in your favor—you have a good relationship with your boss, and your record is exemplary." Bill receives the message that he can choose a defensive maneuver, or he can meet the stress head on. He chooses to meet the environment directly, believing that his good record, honesty, and contriteness will result in an increased sense of adequacy.

In both cases Fred and Bill, who share similar physiological makeups, experienced similar environments; nevertheless, both are at different levels in their developmental stages and have vastly different perceptions of their environment. Therefore, when the regulator and cognator went into operation in this instance, the behavioral responses of the adapting persons were different.

Like Fred and Bill, we are all open, living systems in constant interaction with a somewhat predictable but ever-changing environment. When there is a contact between ourselves and the environment, a triggering event occurs. We experience stress and utilize the internal process of the regulator and the cognator to interact with the environment. The goal of this interaction is to maintain or improve one's level of adequacy. This is achieved by taking a particular coping stance and implementing a coping strategy, a combination of defensive maneuvers and problem solving. The resultant behavioral response produces a change in the relationship between the person and the environment. This change reduces stress and returns adequacy to a more desirable level. When adaptation is successful, the behavioral response has a positive impact on the environment. If the behavioral response has a negative impact on the environment and stress continues or is increased, additional triggering events occur, and the entire adaptation process is reinitiated.

CONCLUSION

In this chapter the adapting person has been described as an open, living system constantly interacting with an ever-changing yet often predictable environment. The critical elements of the chapter include (1) the five-phase internal process for transacting with the environment and (2) the stimuli that influence this process—the internal state and the environment.

Now that you have completed this chapter, you should be able to list and define essential terms, describe the adaptation process, and explain the relationship between the person's coping and behavioral output. This can be demonstrated by completing the following exercises.

LEARNING EXPERIENCE

1 An understanding of the adapting person's internal transaction is essential to the practice of adaptation nursing for two reasons. List those two reasons.

2 Describe your understanding of the following concepts.

The person	Regulator	Transaction
Adequacy	Stress	Adaptation
Cognator		

3 Without referring to the chapter, complete the following outline by giving the appropriate definitions.

The transaction

a Phase I: _____

b Phase II: Regulator sounds alarm and alerts cognator

c Phase III: _____

d Phase IV: _____

e Phase V: _____
f Complete the following for phases III and IV.
   1. Approach/avoidance
      a. _____
      b. _____
   2. Compromise
      a. Suppression/repression
      b. _____
   3. Self-enhancement
      a. Confrontation
      b. _____
      c. _____
   4. Inaction
      a. _____
      b. _____
      c. _____
g Influencing stimuli
   1. Internal state
      a. _____
      b. _____
      c. _____
   2. Environment
      a. _____
      b. _____

If you could not complete this outline, review the relevant sections in Chapter 1 before you proceed to exercises 4 and 5.

4 Describe a situation you have observed that represents the adaptive process.

5 Using your example, identify the triggering event, the coping stance and strategies, the relevant influencing factors, and the person's behavioral outcome.

REFERENCES

Branden, N.: The psychology of self-esteem, New York, 1979, Bantam Books, Inc.

Brown, E.L.: Nursing reconsidered: a study of change. I. The professional role in institutional nursing, Philadelphia, 1970, J.B. Lippincott Co.

Brown, E.L.: Nursing reconsidered: a study of change. II. The professional role in community nursing, Philadelphia, 1971, J.B. Lippincott Co.

Combs, A.W., and Snygg, D.: Individual behavior: a perceptual approach to behavior, New York, 1959, Harper & Row, Publishers, Inc.

Dohrenwend, B.P.: The social psychological nature of stress: a framework for causal inquiry, Journal of Abnormal Social Psychology, 62(2):294-302, 1961.

Engel, G.L.: Psychological development in health and disease, Philadelphia, 1962, W.B. Saunders Co.

Erickson, E.H.: Childhood and society, ed. 2, New York, 1963, Norton & Co., Inc.

Helson, H.: Adaptation level theory, New York, 1964, Harper & Row, Publishers, Inc.

Jourard, S.M.: The transparent self, New York, 1964, D. Van Nostrand Co.

Jourard, S.M.: Healthy personality, New York, 1974, Macmillan Inc.

Lazarus, R. Psychological stress and the coping process, New York, 1966, McGraw-Hill Book Co., pp. 266-267.

Lazarus, R., Lazarus, S., Averill, J.K., and Opton, E.R.: The psychology of coping: issues of research and assessment. In Coleho, G.V., Hamburd, D.A., and Adams, J.E.: Coping and adaptation, New York, 1974, Basic Books, Inc.

Maslow, A.H.: Toward a psychology of being, New York, 1968, D. Van Nostrand Co.

Nightingale, F.: Notes on nursing: what it is; what it is not. A facsimile of the first edition printed in London, 1859, with a foreword by A.W. Goodrich, Philadelphia, 1966, J.B. Lippincott Co.

Roy, C.: Introduction to nursing: an adaptation model, Englewood Cliffs, N.J., 1976, Prentice-Hall, Inc.

Selye, H.: The stress of life, New York, 1956, McGraw-Hill Book Co.

Selye, H.: The physiopathology of stress, Postgraduate Medicine, vol. 25, June 1959.

Selye, H.: Stress without distress, New York, 1974, New American Library, Inc.

Smith, M., and Selye, H.: Reducing the negative effects of stress, American Journal of Nursing, 79(19):1953-1957, 1979.

Valetti, R.: Self actualization, Niles, Ill., 1974, Argus Communications.

White, R.W.: Strategies of adaptation: an attempt at systematic description. In Coleho, G.V., Hamburd, D.A., and Adams, J.E.: Coping and adaptation, New York, 1974, Basic Books, Inc.

CHAPTER 2

The adaptation nurse:
what you will feel, do, and become

OBJECTIVES

Define role prescription.
Describe role change.
List two of three factors that facilitate role change.
Define adaptation nursing.
List and describe five of the influencing factors in this chapter.
Show the relationship between influencing factors in the environment and your own nurse-role
    behaviors.
Describe the (five-step) adaptation process as you experience it in the student-nurse role.

This chapter is for you—the adaptive person who is in the process of becoming an adaptation nurse. Its purpose is to facilitate your personal adaptation during the process of role change, and it is designed to guide and encourage you.

The chapter begins with a review of the characteristics of the adapting person. The five-step adaptation process and stimuli that will influence you as you become an adaptation nurse will also be explored. Finally, a case study will be developed that illustrates the process of role change from lay person to adaptation nurse.

The essential concepts that follow should be mastered before proceeding with the chapter.

ESSENTIAL TERMS

Role prescription The actions that society ascribes to a role.

Role change The process a person goes through in order to enter a new or previously relinquished role. This process involves incorporating society's role prescriptions and the environmental influencing stimuli with a person's unique self.

Student nurse role All the activities engaged in by the student nurse while striving for personal and professional adequacy. This adaptive process is represented by a give-and-take relationship between oneself and the environment, which includes classroom and clinical settings, persons who direct one's learning experiences, and persons who need one's professional service.

Reality shock Intrarole conflict experienced when there are contradictory expectations (role prescriptions) from the profession and the institution that employs the person.

Adaptation nurse A person who uses specialized knowledge and intervention strategies to help the client/patient maintain or enhance a sense of adequacy and security while striving for survival, growth, reproduction, mastery, and autonomy.

THE ADAPTING PERSON AND PROCESS

As defined in Chapter 1, the adapting person is an open, living system in constant interaction with a predictable but ever-changing environment. *A specific occurrence or incident in the environment that causes the person to experience stress is called a triggering event.* The transaction process utilized to process the triggering event involves the *regulator*, which *recognizes* and *records* the triggering event and then transmits the data to the cognator. The *cognator assesses* the data received from the regulator and makes a decision of how to proceed. This decision includes a *coping stance* and then a *coping strategy*. The person responds to the triggering event through one of four energy channels to maintain or enhance a sense of adequacy. This chapter focuses on the social, behavioral channels called role and interdependence. You, the student nurse, are experiencing repeated triggering events with which you choose to transact via the role mode because you are involved in a role change—that of lay person to adaptation nurse.

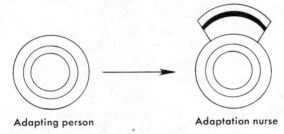

Adapting person　　　　　　Adaptation nurse

LEARNING EXPERIENCE

1 Before you continue this chapter, it is important for you to reflect on your perceptions of the nursing profession. Define nursing by completing this statement: A nurse is _____ and "should" do (tasks, jobs) _____

As you, the adapting person, strive to become an adaptation nurse, you experience the process of role change. This role change involves the process of integrating society's role prescription of the nurse with the specific environmental influencing factors that affect the nurse and her own unique, internal influencing factors. Role change proceeds most smoothly when the adapting person is *clear about role prescription* (expected behaviors, knowledge, and skills, which come from many sources) and has *adequate time* and a *safe place to learn* the knowledge and skills involved in implementing the role. The feelings you experience as you make the role change are usually those of gratification or frustration. The feelings that accompany the student nurse role are manifested in interdependence behaviors.

THE ADAPTATION NURSE

The role prescription or definition of an adaptation nurse describes the professional person you will become as you put adaptation theory into practice.

The adaptation nurse enters into a partnership with a person for the purpose of helping the person maintain or achieve a sense of adequacy and security. She believes that people are constantly vigilant, open, living systems constantly striving for survival, growth, reproduction, mastery, and autonomy in a give-and-take relationship with the environment. She also believes that people utilize the adaptive process to transact with the environment. The adaptation nurse interacts with people for the purpose of facilitating the interaction between the person's internal state and the environment. She utilizes a specialized body of knowledge in combination with specific strategies for intervention and a variety of nursing skills.

You will begin to understand the role of an adaptation nurse as you experience the influencing stimuli discussed in this chapter and complete a nursing curriculum based on the adaptation conceptual model of nursing.

There are many stimuli that will influence you as you become an adaptation nurse. Stimuli explored in this chapter are the nursing curriculum, faculty, and philosophy; the nursing profession; the consumer; the physician; the bureaucracy; and the internal stimuli that specifically influence you. Each of these stimuli will, at one time or another, become a triggering event for you, causing stress. Your resolution of that stress as you utilize the five-step adaptation process will move you toward becoming an adaptation nurse. You will sometimes experience triggering events from these influencing factors hundreds of times each day. At other times you may not experience any of these stimuli as triggering events. Some of these influencing stimuli are illustrated in the following story.

You are a nursing student, and this is your seventh week of clinical practice. You are assigned to be the nurse for Mr. Reynolds, a 49-year-old man who had an appendectomy yesterday. The physician had ordered a chest x-ray film to be taken at 8:00 A.M. today to assess the condition of the lungs postoperatively.

It is now 10:00 A.M., the x-ray film has not been taken, and the physician is angry. Mr. Reynolds is concerned that he is not getting "good" care. You recall a discussion from a clinical conference regarding your status in the hospital; i.e., student nurses are guests covered by a contract and are not of employee status. In this situation the influencing stimuli represent the consumer (Mr. Reynolds); the bureaucracy (the x-ray department and your status as a student nurse); and the physician. Each of these stimuli can be a triggering event to begin the five-phase adaptation process.

In the following pages the frequently occurring stimuli of the nursing curriculum, the nursing profession, the consumer, the physician, the bureaucracy, and the person's internal state will be discussed at an introductory level. As you proceed through your nursing program you will study in theory and practice each of these influencing stimuli in depth.

EXTERNAL INFLUENCING STIMULI
The nursing curriculum

The philosophy on which your educational program is based is one of the most important factors in your environment as a nursing student. Nursing curricula based on conceptual models strive for effective nursing care founded on scientific rationale. An adaptation model–based curriculum, therefore, is concerned with facilitating the student's learning concepts, attitudes, and techniques rather than the acquisition of a multiplicity of facts. The nursing faculty is responsible for implementing an educational program that clearly defines the basic knowledge and skills you need to become an adaptation nurse. You will learn to problem solve very effectively in the nursing curriculum. You have learned coping mechanisms from your families and during your educational process. The nursing curriculum and planned learning experiences will help you become more aware of the coping mechanisms and strategies you have learned. There will be opportunities for you to increase your skill at developing and implementing problem-solving and self-enhancing coping strategies. As you acquire more effective coping strategies, you will experience a greater sense of adequacy.

A basic assumption inherent in a nursing curriculum is that you, the student nurse, must become an independent learner. Many of your previous learning experiences may not have encouraged you to become an independent learner. Nursing practice, on the other hand, is at the application and synthesis level of learning. This means you will gather information that you must learn to incorporate into effective nursing practice. An independent learner is one who believes that learning is a self-initiated, lifelong process manifested by a change or reorganization of behavior. As you become an adaptation nurse, you will become a lifelong, independent learner.

The faculty members who implement a nursing curriculum are influencing stimuli. Faculty effectivity directly parallels (1) how clear they are regarding the role of nursing faculty as opposed to that of nursing practitioners; (2) their belief about the colleagueship of faculty and students; and (3) their understanding of learning and evaluation periods.

The nursing profession

Another influencing stimulus in your environment is the nursing profession itself. Both as a group and as individuals, nursing professionals influence you in many ways as you define the role prescription of nurse. While you are a student, registered nurses will serve as role models for you. You will relate especially well to a particular team leader and find yourself adopting some of her nurse role behaviors. You will work with another nurse and note how effective she is in communicating with her client, and you will incorporate some of her words into your nursing role. After you become an adaptation nurse, the colleagues you select as a peer/support group will probably share a common philosophy of nursing with you. The individual nurse is an important influencing factor, but so is the corporate body of nurses.

The American Nurses Association (ANA) is the official organization for the registered nurse. As such, it can be a triggering event in various ways. It has been active in defining nursing practice. It formulated a Code of Ethics for nurses in 1950, and Standards of Nursing Practice were published in 1973. A 1980 ANA definition of nursing is as follows: "Nursing is the diagnosis and treatment of *human responses* to actual or potential health problems."

The ANA has the power to become a triggering event because it leads the profession of nursing in areas of consumer accountability, economic security, legislative lobbying, and liaison with other health care disciplines and organizations. The ANA is a triggering event for the nurse when major decisions are made that affect the practice of nursing. It affects the nurse's practice as she reads articles published in the *American Journal of Nursing* and modifies her practice. As a student you may join and be involved with a student branch of ANA, which serves as a representative of the parent organization and which will influence you in similar ways.

The consumer

The consumer of nursing actions can also be a triggering event in many ways. First of all, as a client, the consumer expects the nurse to be competent in the areas of health care, the treatment of illness, and the treatment of response to illness. Furthermore, he expects the nurse to be caring and supportive as he experiences crisis, illness, or imminent death. In another role the consumer, because he is represented by membership on most state boards of nursing, can also affect nursing education and practice. Thus, the consumer of nursing services places a number of expectations on the individual nurse as well as the profession as a whole.

The physician

At times the physician is also a triggering event for the nurse. The physician's expectations of the nurse usually are that the nurse will augment the task of diagnosing and treating a medical problem. The doctor/nurse relationship is becoming a colleague relationship as the nurse's skills of assessment, decision making, and intervention continue to increase. Collaboration between the nurse and doctor is essential if the client is to experience good health care and be able to maintain or enhance a sense of adequacy and security.

The bureaucracy

Most nurses work in health care institutions; thus, the institutional structure is a constant influencing stimulus. Marlene Kramer (1974) is a nurse researcher who has explored some of the reasons why nurses leave nursing practice. She discusses the inherent conflict between the characteristics of the profession and those of health care institutions. Institutional bureaucracy is characterized as being specialized into many tasks and identified with the institutional goals (not the individuals). Kramer names the intrarole conflict experienced by the nurse as reality shock. The triggering event is the conflicting expectations of the bureaucracy and the profession, which are both influencing the nurse simultaneously and constantly. The nursing profession is exploring ways of decreasing the reality shock experienced by nurses. Areas that are being explored are the factors that influence a person's ability to practice effective nursing.

In summary, many different influencing stimuli become triggering events as you become an adaptation nurse. These external influencing stimuli, which include the role prescription of an adaptation nurse, impact on the unique you. The unique you is composed of internal influencing stimuli. When the external influencing stimuli become meshed with your internal influencing stimuli, you are on the way to becoming an adaptation nurse.

INTERNAL INFLUENCING STIMULI

The internal stimuli that influence the student nurse include her physiological make-up, maturational level, and individual perceptions.

Physiological make-up

Most nursing students have biological systems that are intact and functioning adequately; thus, triggering events are usually processed without difficulty. As a student nurse who is facing the uncertainties that accompany role change, you may at times experience decreased physiological adequacy. You may become excessively fatigued, be more susceptible than usual to infections, and experience a change in weight and changes in exercise and rest patterns. These physiological behaviors are directly related to the many influencing stimuli in your environment as well as your internal state, genetic state, and usual health patterns.

Maturational level

A person's maturational level is a constant influencing stimulus because it affects everything one does. The 40-year-old generative adult who has, for instance, lived in four states and experienced illness in the family, the joys of sharing achievements with family and loved ones, and loss, divorce, or death of significant people is at one maturational level. On the other hand, the 20-year-old woman who has lived with her intact family in two states is at a different maturational level. The younger woman simply has not had time to accumulate the life experiences of the older adult.

Because student nurses are usually older adolescents or young adults, they are influenced by the developmental tasks of these respective ages. The developmental tasks are discussed throughout this text. The reader might choose to turn to Chapter 5 and read the section that relates to the adolescent, young adult, and generative adult stages of development. The reader might also choose to explore the concepts of developmental psychology.

Perceptions

The final influencing stimuli to be addressed are the individual's perceptions. Perceptions arise out of life experiences, beliefs, attitudes, ideas, myths, and knowledge. Your perceptions make up, to a great extent, the unique person you are. They influence the kind of nurse behavior that you will choose to incorporate from nurse role models. Your beliefs about pain and why people suffer, about death, about life after death, and about illness and why illness is a part of the life story all shape the kind of nurse you will become.

The nurse who values the humanist philosophy and believes she can provide an environment that is conducive to wellness will practice the arts and skills of nursing differently from the nurse who "treats" illnesses and feels her tasks are directed by the medical problems. The nurse who believes that each person is responsible for his own behavior will negotiate or contract with the client, accepting the fact that final accountability for wellness lies within the client.

Perceptions are a vital part of each person's reality; they will influence the person's choice of coping stance and strategies. The self-enhancing coping strategies demand a degree of risk taking. The person who has a high level of self-esteem, and therefore feels good about himself, can take greater risks. Thus, the level of a person's self-esteem is an internal influencing factor.

The preceding has shown how role prescriptions for the adaptation nurse are influenced by many triggering events, some internal and some external. The process of incorporating the external triggering events with the unique internal influencing stimuli is role change. For you, the present role change is from lay person to adaptation nurse. The following paragraphs present a case study of a young woman, Lynda Clark, who goes through this role change and becomes an adaptation nurse. A period of Lynda's life will be described; then an analysis of her situation will follow. The analysis will focus on Lynda's use of the adaptation process to transact with a triggering event and show how certain influencing stimuli become part of Lynda's environment and role change.

CASE STUDY—LYNDA CLARK
High school senior

As we meet Lynda Clark, she is a 17-year-old high school senior. Lynda attended a career day at school and is giving serious thought to what she wants to do with her life. She makes an appointment with her high school counselor, Ms. Fran Jacobi. During the interview, Ms. Jacobi listens as Lynda explains her reasons for believing she wants to be a nurse and looks at Lynda's transcript in relation to the requirements of the local junior college as well as a nearby college that has a baccalaureate nursing program. A few weeks later, Lynda, with her parents, decides she should apply to both colleges; Lynda hopes she will be accepted for the baccalaureate program.

First day of clinical practice

Lynda was accepted by both schools and chose the baccalaureate program. Tomorrow is her first day of clinical practicum; she anticipates the day with excitement and puts on her freshly ironed student uniform. She knows that today she will be assigned to give patient care to someone who is hospitalized and moderately ill. Later Lynda shares her thoughts about this day.

> I was worried that I wouldn't do anything correctly. I lacked confidence until I walked into my first room and saw that the client didn't have terror in his eyes. After that I enjoyed doing the tasks I was assigned to do. It was exciting to take a *real* client's vital signs, give him a partial bath, and make the bed. Granted, I felt clumsy all morning. I think I was afraid that I might not like nursing, but when I realized what it felt like to be a part of the nursing team and to actually have a patient depend on me as a nurse . . . well, I felt a boost of confidence and assurance. I was nervous today, but not the kind of nervous that made me wish I was elsewhere; instead, it was the kind that made me want to hurry up and *know* what I'm supposed to *learn* . . . it's a feeling that's hard to explain. I'm really glad I had my patient assignment yesterday, so I could read about the disease and nursing care and come to the hospital prepared. As I think back about today, I realize so many of my emotions are jammed together. On the whole, I was excited and felt good about myself, yet I don't feel like a nurse.

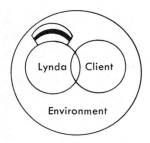

In applying the adaptation process to this first clinical day, we see Lynda in the nurse role interacting with a client. Lynda experiences many triggering events. The client and Lynda share an environment of a medical-surgical unit in a local hospital. The environment on this day is composed of a patient, faculty, a nursing team leader, team members, five other student nurses, the physician, and all the other hospital staff. The environment also includes the clinical learning objectives of the nursing curriculum, the bureaucracy (hospital), and the student's own maturational level.

The triggering event is Lynda's assignment to provide the patient with safe, effective care. She carefully listens to the morning report given by her team leader to plan the care for each client for the day. As she listens, the regulator is processing the triggering event, recording it, and sending the data to the cognator. Lynda processes the data through her cognator. Even though gathering data and planning patient care were taught in the theory course, Lynda knows she needs help to make sense out of the report. She chooses a coping stance of self-enhancement and the coping strategy of confrontation. She then approaches her instructor and expressses a need to meet to discuss the plan for patient care.

Lynda is resolving the stress caused by the triggering event by manifesting behaviors in the role mode. She specifically takes the secondary role of *student nurse:* taking vital signs, giving a partial bath, making the client's bed, taking a report, and planning nursing care with her instructor. The interdependence behaviors associated with student nurse role are reflected in her comments: "I was nervous today," "I was excited today and felt good about myself," "I don't *feel* like a nurse." The influencing stimulus that is causing and contributing to Lynda's role behavior is the triggering event, i.e., the expectation that she will act like a member of the health care team and provide safe, effective care for this patient. Other influencing stimuli are (1) the patient and the faculty, who are both consumers of the student nurse role behaviors; (2) the physician managing the medical treatment regimen; (3) the role prescription of the nurse role that Lynda is evolving; (4) the busy medical-surgical unit in the hospital bureaucracy; (5) Lynda's maturational level; and (6) Lynda's feeling that she has made good decisions. The behaviors and influencing stimuli that Lynda is experiencing are listed below.

BEHAVIORS	INFLUENCING STIMULI
1. Took report. 2. Planned nursing care with her instructor. 3. Took vital signs. 4. Gave a partial bath. 5. Made the client's bed. 6. "I was nervous and excited today." 7. "I felt good about myself." 8. "I don't feel like a nurse."	1. Lynda is assigned to provide safe, effective nursing care to one patient. 2. Patient, faculty and clinical objectives, physician, Lynda's role prescription for nurses, medical-surgical unit with its team members, Lynda's maturational level, perceptions, first clinical day.

As reflected by her thoughts on the day, Lynda is able to resolve positively the stress caused by the triggering event. She experiences a higher level of adequacy in the student nurse role by using a coping stance of self-enhancement and a coping strategy of confrontation.

Ill student nurse

As we next meet Lynda, she is ending her first year in the nursing program. It is a clinical practice day, and Lynda is absent. She has a temperature of 102° F and a sore throat and is spending the day resting in her room. She has made an appointment at the student health service. The nurse at the health service is a graduate of the same nursing program in which Lynda is currently enrolled. The nurse assesses Lynda in the following way: she inquires about her physical health, examines her throat and does throat culture and sensitivity tests, and records Lynda's vital signs (temperature 102.5° F, pulse 88, respirations 18). Lynda's cervical lymph nodes are enlarged, and she reports that her throat is very sore. She is drinking 10 to 12 glasses of fluid per day, including juices, water, sodas, and hot tea. She doesn't feel hungry and is eating "very little" solid food. The nurse asks Lynda about her sleep and activity in general. Lynda states that she has a lot of studying to do, has to get up early for clinical practice, and rarely gets to bed before midnight. She says, "I still have trouble sleeping the night before clinical." The nurse asks her how school is going and how she feels about becoming a nurse. Lynda comments that she is getting B's in her nursing courses; although she studies hard, she just can't get A's. She states, "I got a lot of A's in high school without studying, but this is really different; there is so much material to study." Lynda also confides that this is the third clinical practice day she has missed this semester and that she can't miss any more. She states, "I've never been sick so much in my life; I don't understand it. I've had the flu and diarrhea once this semester. I had a bad cold and now this sore throat. What's the matter with me? I'm supposed to be a nurse and I can't even keep myself well. How can I help others?" The nurse responds by being supportive and exploring with Lynda the influencing stimuli in her environment that might be causing this increased incidence of illness. Together, they conclude that (1) Lynda's most important goal right now is getting through the nursing program; (2) she sleeps 6 hours most nights; (3) she eats meals in the cafeteria, and because she is tired, she eats desserts and drinks beverages with caffeine for energy; (4) she has gained 10 pounds since September; (5) she has not been swimming, biking, or horseback riding since October; and (6) she escapes the pressures by watching television on weekends for 12 to 15 hours. The behaviors Lynda is expressing as well as the stimuli are illustrated below.

BEHAVIORS	INFLUENCING STIMULI
1. Throat (nasopharyngeal area) very red; cervical lymph nodes swollen. T 102.5° F, P 88, R 18. Drinking 10 to 12 glasses of liquid per day.	1. Pathogenic organism, probably *Streptococcus*.
2. Throat hurts.	2. Sleeps 6 hours per night, eats meals in cafeteria (lots of sweets and caffeine).
3. "I've been sick so much this year." Went to student health service.	3. No planned physical activity.
	4. Resting in bed, T 102.5° F.
	5. Cervical lymph nodes enlarged.

Lynda and the nurse set some goals that should increase Lynda's level of phsyiological adequacy and thus decrease the frequency of illness. At the same time, Lynda should experience an increased sense of adequacy in the student nurse role. The goals set by Lynda and the nurse are that she will (1) go to bed one night per week by 10:00 P.M. and sleep until she awakens the next morning, (2) increase the amount of complex carbohydrates and protein in her diet and decrease the amount of desserts and caffeine, (3) exercise with a friend after clinical practice instead of taking 3-hour naps, and (4) make out a weekly general schedule for managing her time more effectively. The physician has prescribed erythromycin (250 mg q.i.d.) and gargling with saline solution and has told Lynda she can return to the clinical area after she has taken erythromycin for 72 hours. Lynda states, "'I'm glad today is Friday and I'll be able to go back to clinical on Monday." She also thanks the nurse and expresses how difficult it is to be the patient and how good it feels to have the nurse help her look at her life and find some ways to improve her level of health.

In applying the adaptation process to Lynda, it is clear that the triggering event was another illness; this time it was a sore throat. Lynda processed the triggering event by noting via her regulator that her throat was very sore, she felt very warm, the glands in her neck were sore, and she felt ill. The cognator received the data from the regulator and processed it with the additional data that Lynda believed she should not expose sick people to her illness, that she had already missed 2 clinical practice days and 3 is the maximum number she can miss, that there were 3 weeks remaining in clinical practice, and that she could not afford to become ill again within this 3-week period. She then chose a coping stance of self-enhancement and a combined coping strategy of confrontation and negotiation. Lynda was using confrontation when she called her instructor to report her illness and went to the student health service. She and the nurse established goals that would require a coping strategy of negotiation (i.e., clarifying the stress and compromising and managing the environment). The behavioral outcome will be manifested in the energy channels of the physiological mode, the role performance mode, and the interdependence mode.

Lynda is taking on the nurse role. When we met Lynda on her first clinical practice day she "didn't feel like a nurse." Progress regarding the role change from lay person to adaptation nurse is manifested by the behaviors that Lynda shares with us: her ethical self, protecting the patient from her own pathogenic organisms; her awareness that she should apply her knowledge of nursing to herself as well as to her clients; her encounter with the client role and recognition of how much it helps to have a professional nurse intervene to increase the level of adequacy.

Senior nursing student

Some time later Lynda is sharing this story.

I'm a senior now. Today, when I was team leading, I had beginning student nurses as team members on my team. It really made me stop and think about how much I have grown since I became a nursing student. Last year I was so anxious, and there seemed to be so much to learn. Everything I studied seemed so fragmented. I feel like a nurse now. I'm no longer afraid to touch a patient or to ask questions that used to seem so personal. I have confidence in myself this year. I know how to problem solve effectively and how to ask for help when I need it. I can take responsibility now. Last year I would think "You want *me* to do that?" Now I know it's up to me.

I found myself systematically assessing a patient the other day and I didn't even have to do it. Not only that—I went way beyond what is usually expected of a student nurse, or anything I had to do. I'm really interested now, and I'll pick up a nursing book to acquire more knowledge or understanding of something I've seen clinically. I even went to the library to read the AJN when I didn't have an assignment to do! I've really changed and grown up a lot. I still have some trouble working effectively with the psychosocial mode. I find it difficult to talk with a patient about his or her feelings. I hope I'll get more comfortable and better at it as I work with more clients. Oh, I have some frustrations. I'm up to my eyeballs in studying, and I never get enough sleep. I'm impatient with being "just" a student. Other staff members sometimes think that, because I'm wearing this blue uniform, I am unable to do some things, but I often prove them wrong. There are some skills I really need to do—like catheterizing a patient and putting in a nasogastric tube. Nursing is pretty much what I thought it would be. I didn't know when I began that the easy part of nursing is the skills and treatments and the hard part is making decisions and helping people deal with their illnesses and life changes.

I really feel less stressed this year. Last year I either had a cold, an upset GI tract, or headaches. This year I've learned some new coping mechanisms. I especially wish I had understood how helpful my faculty meant to be last year. I thought that they were checking up on me, or my not knowing the answer!! Now I know all those questions were to help me think through and put together the whole picture of patient care. I really missed out on a lot of learning because I was so paranoid and insecure. I am more active physically than I've ever been, and it feels good. I'm clear about who I am as a nurse and what I should do. A nurse where I worked last summer really helped me. She was so knowledgeable and competent and really cared for her patients and what they were experiencing. She treated every patient like an important human being. She taught me so much, I find that I assess a lot like she does, and I interact with patients the way she does. She really became a part of me. But I'm ready to turn in this blue uniform for a white one.

As we look at Lynda, a senior nursing student nearing the completion of her basic nursing education, we note the following student nurse role/adaptation nurse role behaviors and influencing stimuli. The assessment of the senior nurse role for Lynda is shown below.

ROLE PERFORMANCE MODE

Senior student nurse role

BEHAVIORS

"I'm comfortable assessing patients physically and verbally."

"I know how to ask for help when I need it."

"I can take responsibility now."

"Everything makes sense."

"I read professional materials."

"I still find it hard to talk to a client about his/her feelings."

"There are some skills I've never done."

INFLUENCING STIMULI

Senior in a team-leading environment. Faculty expects independent behavior. Adaptation nursing curriculum. Nursing team leader gives positive feedback.

Perception of nursing role

High-level of self-esteem.

From this assessment it is clear that Lynda is becoming an adaptation nurse, because she is demonstrating behaviors that are congruent with the definition of an adaptation nurse. We can conclude that Lynda is indeed incorporating the definition of an adaptation nurse and is combining it with her unique self.

ROLE CONGRUENCE

ADAPTATION NURSE	LYNDA	INFLUENCING STIMULI
The adaptation nurse believes that the nurse and client are partners.	"I really involve the client in discharge planning."	Adaptation nursing curriculum.
The purpose of nursing is to help the client feel adequate and secure in the areas of survival, growth, reproduction, mastery, and autonomy.	"I can take responsibility now." "There are some skills I've never practiced."	Faculty expects independent behavior. Adaptation nursing curriculum.
The person is in constant interaction with the environment.	"I still find it hard to talk to clients about their feelings."	Adaptation nursing curriculum. Team leading, meets many clients.
The person uses the adaptation process to transact with the environment.	"I still find it hard to talk to clients about their feelings."	Adaptation nursing curriculum.
The nurse interacts with clients to facilitate the interaction between the internal state and the environment.	"Everything makes sense." "I really involve the client in discharge planning."	Nursing team leader. Adaptation nursing curriculum.
She utilizes a specialized body of knowledge, specific intervention strategies, and nursing skills.	"I feel like a nurse now." "I'm comfortable assessing patients physically and verbally." "I read professional materials."	Adaptation nursing curriculum.

Some of the behaviors that Lynda demonstrates so securely will probably be threatened as shes moves out of the protected student nurse role and into a position of registered nurse in a hospital. With any role change there is a period of taking on the role and internalizing the role prescription. The process that an adaptation nurse experiences as she moves from a beginning adaptation nurse to a higher level of practice is explored in Chapter 5.

Beginning adaptation nurse

It is 2 years later. Lynda has passed the state board examination and is a staff nurse at a local hospital. She has been working with adult patients in a medical-surgical unit. She is sharing her perceptions of nursing practice and nursing education with a class of nursing students who are focusing on the various areas of nursing practice.

I remember when I was a new graduate and was working as a team leader on a busy medical-surgical unit at the hospital. I wanted to work days but ended up working a rotating shift, same days and same evenings each week. I found it really difficult to be a nurse for the first few months. I had so much to do as a team leader. I was only able to complete the medication and treatments, charting, and essential physiological assessment at first. I can recall thinking, "How can I possibly find time to devise two patient care plans this week?" There was an inservice program that I really wanted to attend, and I couldn't find the time. And the only patients I talked to about their illnesses were those who were very overt and persistent. I remember thinking, "I'll never be able to practice nursing the way I did as a student." About 6 months after I had been working, I found everything falling into place. I had become organized about the routine tasks and technical skills. I found myself listening for cues that the client needed help coping with his illness. I was taking care of a 36-year-old woman who had ulcerative colitis. She had a temporary colostomy, and I found myself intervening and helping her resolve the threats to her adequacy as a person, as a woman, and as a businesswoman. I was delighted with my intervention skills and with the fact that I was providing nursing care to the whole client by doing so much health teaching. I reread our nursing practice act a few days ago in preparing to spend time with you. The exciting part of nursing for me now is the part defined in the act as "helping people cope . . . with actual or potential health or illness problems or the treatment thereof." Because I believe in living life to the fullest and believe in the sanctity of each human being, I found I was ready to take workshops to learn more about nursing. I've especially focused on the client and how much health teaching they need. We have a liaison nurse where I work, and working with her I've learned a lot about discharge planning.

Recently I worked with a 76-year-old woman who had congestive heart failure and diabetes. Her diabetes had been controlled by oral hypoglycemic drugs, but now she needed to use insulin. She was experiencing failing eyesight; her husband was an alcoholic and was not helpful as a support system. I helped her with the liaison nurse to problem solve in order to meet her needs for survival. Her goal was to continue living in her home with her husband. We were able to reach this goal by utilizing a community support system. A retired next door neighbor was available to give the daily insulin; a homemaker aide cooked two meals a day that were within the 1 gm sodium, 1600 calorie American Diabetic Association diet regimen and also did two tests for urine sugar and acetone each day. The client and her husband were able to meet most of their other needs. This part of nursing, doing the health teaching and becoming aware of resources in the hospital and the community, has really been rewarding to me. I'm really growing; I'm able to use most of my knowledge from my educational program. I found working with the feelings of the person so difficult when I was a nursing student. Now I find it easy. I'm very clear about who I am as a nurse and what I am to do with a client. I'm also beginning to realize that I probably need to go to graduate school.

As we leave Lynda to reflect on her role performance as an adaptation nurse, we see that she has intentionally chosen an environment in which to practice that is congruent with her philosophy of nursing. Her job is in the institutional bureaucracy but does not suffer too much specialization; i.e., Lynda is part of a team that is accountable for the whole process of preparing the client to return to the community. She is able to use her specialized nursing knowledge and to practice at the level of the state nurse practice act's definition of nursing. In addition, she is able to work with the client's physician on a colleague basis. She also finds contracting with the patient/client rewarding. Being a patient advocate, health educator, and facilitator of an individual's adaptation process is very rewarding to Lynda.

Lynda's performance as an adaptation nurse parallels the definition of an adaptation nurse. The definition, Lynda's behavior, and the influencing stimuli are charted below.

ROLE CONGRUENCE

ADAPTATION NURSE	LYNDA	INFLUENCING STIMULI
The nurse believes that the nurse and client are partners.	Lynda contracts with the client for a specific purpose.	
The purpose of nursing is to help the client feel adequate and secure in the areas of survival, growth, reproduction, mastery, and autonomy.	"I helped him problem solve in order to meet his needs for survival."	Institutional definition of the job is not fragmented. The job is defined within the state's nurse practice act.
The person is in constant interaction with the environment.	She understands the patient's wish to live in her own home with her husband, using the community as a support system.	Physician is colleague.
The person uses the adaptation process to transact with the environment.	"I help a person reach his or her highest level of adequacy."	Her philosophy of nursing parallels how she practices as a nurse.
The nurse interacts with the client to facilitate the interaction between the internal state and the environment.	"I find it easy to talk with a client about his feelings."	Two years of practice as a nurse. Went to a workshop on communication.
She utilizes a specialized body of knowledge, specific intervention strategies, and nursing skills.	"I use the knowledge and skills from my nursing program."	Graduated from an adaptation nursing curriculum.

As you become an adaptation nurse, you will become clear about who you are. You will master a specialized body of knowledge and intervention skills; you will be committed to the whole person as an advocate to facilitate his moving to higher levels of adequacy; and you will be committed to lifelong independent learning.

CONCLUSION

This chapter has focused on you, the person, as you become an adaptation nurse. You have looked at the process of role change, the definition of the adaptation nurse, and several environmental stimuli. We have attempted to help you recognize the unique you and show, through a longitudinal case study, how the unique you and the environment become interwoven to evolve into you, the adaptation nurse.

LEARNING EXPERIENCE

1 Write the definition of the nurse you want to become.
2 Compare and contrast the definition of the nurse in item 1 with the definition of an adaptation nurse.
3 Compare and contrast the definition of the nurse in item 1 with the definition of nursing you wrote at the beginning of this chapter. Has your definition changed? If so, how?
4 Read your state's nurse practice act. Does it define nursing the way you do? If not, how does it differ?
5 List the stimuli in your current environment that may become triggering events as you go through the process of becoming an adaptation nurse.

REFERENCES

American Nurses Association: Nursing: a social policy statement, Kansas City, Mo., 1980, American Nurses Association.

Benner, P., and Benner, R.V.: The new nurse's work entry: a troubled sponsorship, New York, 1979, Tirias Press.

Folta, J.R., and Deck, E.S.: A sociological framework for patient care, New York, 1979, John Wiley & Sons, Inc.

Guinee, K.K.: Teaching and learning in nursing, New York, 1978, Macmillan Inc.

Kramer, M.: Reality shock: why nurses leave nursing, St. Louis, 1974, The C.V. Mosby Co.

Kramer, M., and Schmalenberg, C.: Path to biculturalism, Wakefield, Mass., 1977, Contemporary Publications, Inc.

Olesen, V.L., and Whittaker, E.W.: The silent dialogue: a study in the social psychology of professional socialization, San Francisco, 1968, Jossey-Bass, Inc., Publishers.

Simms, L.M., and Lindberg, J.B.: The nurse person, New York, 1978, Harper & Row, Publishers, Inc.

Simpson, I.: From student to nurse, New York, 1980, Cambridge University Press.

CHAPTER 3

The adaptation nursing process: a case study

OBJECTIVES
Overall

List and define the essential terms related to the adaptation nursing process.

Describe the three-step adaptation nursing process.

Complete a nursing care guide on one mode when presented with a client situation; illustrate the steps of the nursing process in the guide.

Step I: data collection

Explain the process involved in classifying behavior according to the four adaptive modes and label the components of each mode.

Describe the relationship between the three types of influencing stimuli and explain the rationale for classifying stimuli according to one of these three categories.

Classify behavior and stimuli according to adaptation criteria when presented with a case study.

Step II: judgments and diagnosis

Define the two kinds of judgments the nurse makes regarding each cluster of meaningful behavior and stimuli.

List the two judgments and describe the relationship between them in each of the three diagnostic categories.

Formulate two judgments, assign them to the appropriate diagnostic category, write a nursing diagnosis, and establish a priority nursing action, when presented with a sample case study.

Step III: intervention and evaluation

Describe the process and rationale for goal setting.

Explain the relationship between nursing diagnosis, goal, intervention and the diagnostic category.

Describe the relationship between the evaluative criteria and the diagnostic category.

Formulate a goal, nursing intervention, and evaluative criteria when presented with step I and step II of a sample case study.

An understanding of the interaction between the nurse and the adapting person in a shared environment is essential if one is to apply the adaptation nursing process. In Chapter 1, the person is described as an organism striving for survival, growth, reproduction, mastery, and autonomy in a give-and-take relationship with the environment. Add to this concept the idea that the nurse, who is herself an open, living system with a unique internal state, is striving for the same goals in a give-and-take relationship with her environment. The adapting person and the nurse share this environment, including the physical space of a health care agency or system. They interact within this shared environment, using the adaptation nursing process to maintain or enhance their mutual levels of adequacy.

The adaptation nursing process can be compared, in some ways, with assembling the pieces of a jigsaw puzzle. Each interaction between the person and the environment represents a section of the puzzle that the nurse must first combine to interact effectively with the person. As the nurse completes parts of the puzzle, she begins to have a clearer understanding of the person's coping style, effective or ineffective behavior, and adaptive needs. The nurse, using the adaptation process, then interacts with the person as together they assemble the remaining parts of the puzzle. If they have interacted successfully in this give-and-take relationship, the puzzle pieces will interlock to form the satisfying picture of a person who has significantly improved his level of adequacy.

Chapter 3 will describe this adaptation process. Upon completing this chapter, you should be able to classify behavioral observations according to the four adaptive modes and to label stimuli, showing the relationship to behavioral responses. If you have mastered the material, you should also have the background to make judgments regarding the adapting person's coping pattern and level of adequacy. Utilizing these judgments, you will then be able to assign them to a diagnostic category, formulate nursing diagnoses that define the adaptation needs, and suggest nursing actions. Finally, you will be able to identify goals, select appropriate nursing interventions from the four categories of nursing actions, and evaluate behavioral responses. You will have the theoretical background necessary for utilizing the adaptation nursing process. To begin this critical examination of the adaptation process, review and master the following definitions, which are essential to an understanding of this chapter.

ESSENTIAL TERMS
Step I

Problem-solving process Is based on the scientific method developed for the purpose of logically and systematically searching for the cause-and-effect relationships in specific or predetermined situations. The elements of this process include data collection, problem identification, formulation of a hypothesis (cause-and-effect relationship), validation of the hypothesis, and the actions taken to solve the problem.

Adaptation nursing process A three-step problem-solving process applied to nursing situations. This process includes data collection, judgments and diagnosis, and interventions and evaluation.

Adaptive mode The channel of energy for the behavioral activity or response in which a person engages to maintain or enhance the level of adequacy.

Physiological mode The channel of energy for the behavioral activities that the person uses to maintain or enhance biological adequacy. This adequacy depends on the person's biological function and regulatory behavior necessary to maintain life. The regulator is the source of this behavioral response.

Self-concept mode   The channel of energy for the behavioral activities that the person employs to maintain or enhance psychological adequacy. This adequacy depends on the person's sense of self so that he can know *who he is in order to be* or exist. The cognator is the mediator of this behavioral response.

Role performance mode   The channel of energy for the behavioral activities in which the person engages to maintain or enhance social adequacy. This adequacy depends on the person's knowledge of who he is in relation to others so that he can act. The cognator mediates these behavioral responses.

Interdependence mode   The channel of energy for the behavioral activities that the person also employs to maintain or enhance social adequacy. This adequacy depends on the person's nurturing and supportive relationships with others that provide meaning to his being and acting. The cognator mediates these behavioral responses.

Behavioral assessment   The systematic gathering of information about the person's observable or measurable activities or actions. These actions are assigned meaning and classified according to the adaptive mode.

Stimuli   Internal and external factors that provoke or influence a person's behavioral response.

Focal stimulus   Any environmental stimulus that provokes the person's behavioral response and causes a change in the level of adequacy. In this text a triggering event is always a focal stimulus.

Contextual stimuli   Identifiable internal or external stimuli that noticeably influence the person's behavioral response to a triggering event.

Residual stimuli   Internal or external stimuli that appear to influence the person's behavioral response to a triggering event. These stimuli require validation as to their actual level of influence.

Stimuli assessment   The systematic gathering of information or observations concerning the internal and external stimuli that provoke and influence a person's adaptive response to a triggering event. Once the information is gathered, these stimuli are evaluated and classified according to their level of influence on the behavioral response.

Step II

Nursing judgment   The sound and considered conclusion the nurse reaches after assessing, analyzing, and integrating the cause-and-effect relationship between behavior and stimuli.

Nursing diagnosis   The summary statement of nursing judgments. It clearly indicates the cause-and-effect relationship between the person's behavioral response and the influencing stimuli. This summary statement must reflect the relationship between the person's level of adequacy and the triggering event as well as the relationship between his cognator response and coping strategy.

Diagnostic category   The organized grouping of nursing judgments. This grouping must reflect the degree of disruption in the person's level of adequacy and the quality and quantity of nursing interventions required.

Priority setting   The ongoing process the nurse uses to make critical decisions about the timing of her interactions with the adapting person as well as the immediacy and importance of her nursing intervention.

Step III

Goal A precise and positive statement about the adaptive person's behavioral activities in which he must engage to reestablish, maintain, or enhance personal adequacy. The goal statement must reflect the cause-and-effect relationship defined in the nursing diagnosis.

Intervention A specific behavioral activity a person engages in to achieve a previously stated goal. There are four methods of nursing intervention that help maintain or increase the person's level of adequacy. These methods are support, teaching, collaboration, and enabling.

Support The behavioral activity the nurse uses to approve, sanction, or validate the person's adaptive behavior.

Teaching The behavioral activity the nurse utilizes to impart or clarify knowledge, information, and cognitive or psychomotor skills.

Collaboration The behavioral activity the nurse employs in cooperation with other caregivers to maintain the person's physiological adequacy.

Enabling The set of complex behaviors in which the nurse engages to strengthen, maintain, or give power to the adapting person.

Evaluation The judgment process the nurse uses to reassess the person's behavioral response to nursing interactions and methods of intervention. This judgment process is based on evaluative criteria reflective of the diagnostic categories and the goal statement.

Evaluation criterion Reflects the goal of the adapting person to achieve an optimal level of adequacy. Therefore, the criterion for effective nursing intervention is whether or not the adapting person maintains or achieves a higher level of adequacy.

The adaptation nursing process is not a unique process; it utilizes the same procedures nursing has used for years to assess, diagnose, and intervene with adapting persons. These elements include the problem-solving process in which data is gathered, judgments and evaluations are made, a diagnosis is formulated, action is taken, and an evaluation is completed. The adaptation nursing process, however, is unique in its philosophical view. Simply stated, this view asserts that the adapting person and the adaptation nurse significantly affect the manner in which the elements of the process are assembled and utilized. The adaptation nurse and the adapting person occupy complementary roles, and together they interact to maintain or enhance their adequacy.

The adaptation nursing process is divided into three distinct steps. In step I behavioral observations are made and related influencing stimuli are identified. The relationship between the behavioral responses and the stimuli are hypothesized by classifying the behavior and identifying the causal significance of the stimuli. The adapting person is an active participant in the first step of this process. The person validates or invalidates the nurse's perceptions. In step II, the adaptation nurse engages in a variety of internal operations. Based on her assessment, which includes an understanding of the person's regulator/cognator process, she formulates judgments, formulates diagnostic categories and diagnoses, and sets priorities. The adaptation nurse clearly expresses her understanding of the person's interaction with the environment. Finally, in step III the adaptation nurse and the adapting person set goals, plan and initiate interventions, and evaluate the effectiveness of these interventions in the maintenance or enhancement of the person's adequacy. The nurse and the person use the judgments and the diagnosis formulated in step II as a basis for action in step III.

In summary, the nurse, in concert with the person, categorizes behavior and stimuli, groups this information according to the appropriate adaptive mode, defines relationships, formulates judgments, makes a diagnosis, and evaluates the consequences of the interaction and interventions. The nurse and the person, in effect, assemble the puzzle pieces to form a meaningful picture. The adaptation nurse then interacts with the person to facilitate his adaptation in such a way that his level of adequacy will be maintained or improved.

We will now discuss each of the three steps in the adaptation process. It is recommended that the reader review the objectives and terms before proceeding.

STEP I: DATA COLLECTION

As the nurse and the adapting person interact in their shared environment, a number of behaviors are generated, and many stimuli impinge on both of them. Application of the adaptation nursing process allows the nurse to organize and make sense of this complex combination of behaviors and stimuli. She categorizes her observations of the person's behaviors according to one of the four modes and identifies the relationship between these behaviors and the influencing stimuli.

The four adaptive modes

Behavior. In adaptation theory the adapting person's regulator and cognator channel coping energy in an attempt to maintain or enhance the person's adequacy. These channels, through which coping energy is expressed, are called adaptive modes. Roy (1976) defines a mode as being a way or method of doing or acting and an adaptive mode as being a way of adapting. An adaptive mode, then, is the source of behavioral responses used by the adapting person to maintain or enhance the level of adequacy.

The adaptive modes represent four aspects of the adaptive person as he or she strives to maintain a level of adequacy in response to the stress experienced when interacting with the environment. The *physiological adaptive mode* includes the behaviors that represent the person's attempt to maintain or enhance biological adequacy. This adequacy depends on the person's biological function and regulatory behaviors necessary to maintain life. The *self-concept mode* includes the behaviors that represent the person's attempt to maintain or enhance psychological adequacy. This adequacy depends on the person's sense of self that he may know who he is in order to be or exist. The *role performance mode* includes the behaviors that represent the person's attempt to maintain or enhance social adequacy. This adequacy depends on the person's knowledge of who he is in relation to others so that he can act.

Finally, the *interdependence mode* includes the behaviors that represent an additional attempt by the person to maintain or enhance social adequacy. This adequacy depends on the person's nurturing relationships with others that provide meaning for his being and acting.

In summary, the four modes represent the means whereby the person acts on the environment, seeking to maintain or improve his level of adequacy as a physiological, psychological, and sociological system. He strives for a body that is functioning and regulated properly, an awareness of self in relation to others so that he can meet role expectations, and love and support so that his being and performance have meaning.

Because the person's environment includes the external and internal stimuli that affect his behavior, it is important next to consider the relationship between behavior and the influencing stimuli.

Influencing stimuli. The person's internal state and the environment are the sources of triggering events for the adapting person. The adaptive response results when the regulator and cognator transact within a unique set of circumstances. This unique set of circumstances, which includes the triggering event, is composed of influencing stimuli. The significance of the triggering event to the person and relevant influencing stimuli will then become the focus of the adaptation nurse's interaction. To alter a behavioral response, additional triggering events must be produced, and supportive influencing stimuli must be generated. The adaptation nurse must therefore assess influencing stimuli as well as the person's response to the stimuli. Internal influencing stimuli include the person's physiological makeup, maturational level, and perceptions; external influencing stimuli include physical and interactional environments. These stimuli can be further categorized based on their relationship to the observed behavior.

Roy (1976) has identified three types of influencing stimuli: focal, contextual, and residual. The focal stimulus is the influencing stimulus immediately confronting the person, a stimulus that demands an adaptive response. The nurse can make either a situational or a modal assessment of the focal stimulus. If the nurse is making a situational assessment, the focal stimulus is that stimulus immediately confronting the person, the predominant cause of the behavior. However, if the nurse is assessing the person's level of adequacy in a particular mode or the person's overall perception of himself or his usual performance, the focal stimulus may be a historical event or a theoretical concept. For example, if the person's level of adequacy in the self-concept mode was chronically low and declining, the nurse might be unable to identify an immediate or current influencing stimulus. Using knowledge of the person's history and theoretical understanding, she may, however, be able to identify a focal stimulus such as multiple losses of significant relationships over the past 10 years. The focal stimulus may be an immediately identifiable event or may be a combination of stimuli that can be documented as theoretically influential.

Contextual stimuli are those additional influencing stimuli that can be validated and affect the behavior precipitated by the focal stimulus. The adapting person and the environment are extremely complex. As a result, any number of stimuli may influence his behavior. Contextual stimuli are all stimuli other than focal that appear to be influencing the person's behavior.

Residual stimuli are the stimuli that seem to be influencing the behavior but will require further validation to determine the relationship between the behavior and the influencing stimuli. These stimuli are often more obscure or global, such as a feeling or an attitude. Residual stimuli also include hunches, postulations, ideas, or events the adaptation nurse believes may be influencing behavior but for a variety of reasons has yet to validate.

Influencing stimuli are both internal and external and have varying degrees of impact on the behavioral response. The impact on behavior is ascribed by classifying a stimulus as focal, contextual, or residual.

The *focal stimulus* has particular significance for the adaptation nurse's interaction with the person. In order to alter or correct a behavioral response, a change needs to occur in the focal stimulus. In planning nursing interventions, the nurse and the person must pay particular attention to the focal influencing stimulus. Very often intervention in this area will bring about an immediate, desired change in behavior. When the focal stimulus is irreversible or ongoing, it adds significance to the other categories of stimuli and focuses the nurse and the person on contextual stimuli. Whether the focus of nursing intervention is on the focal or contextual stimuli, the purpose is to assist the adapting person in coping with the focal stimulus, the triggering event.

Contextual stimuli, by definition, are stimuli that are also influencing the person's behavior but that do not represent the triggering event. Much nursing intervention is developed by the nurse and the person based on their assessment of which external and internal stimuli (contextual stimuli) are significantly contributing to the behavioral response. For example, should the triggering event be irreversible, the nurse and the person need to interact so that the person can alter his internal state or add supports to the external environment. In this way more adaptive behavioral responses can occur despite the focal stimulus.

Finally, *residual stimuli* represent areas for further assessment. The nurse rarely uses stimuli in this category to intervene actively, because this information is generally unvalidated and has an uncertain or even unknown relationship to the person's behavior. The adaptation nurse uses these stimuli when discussing with the person the effectiveness of possible intervention. As soon as a residual stimulus is validated, it assumes significance as either a focal or contextual stimulus and can then be used actively in the intervention.

To review, in step I of the adaptation nursing process the person's behavior is classified according to one of four adaptive modes, and stimuli are classified according to the relationship between the behavior and stimuli. The behavioral response from each mode represents the person's attempt to maintain or enhance physiological, psychological, and social adequacy. Influencing stimuli affect the person's adequacy as a focal stimulus, a contextual stimulus, or a residual stimulus. The relationship between behavior and stimuli is continuous and rather circular, forming the basis for the nurse's understanding of the adapting person and the mutual planning and implementation of nursing intervention. To facilitate the implementation of step I in the adaptation nursing process, each mode and the associated behavioral categories will be examined in detail. At the same time, stimuli that commonly influence behavioral response in this mode will be reviewed. Following the theoretical discussion, an example will be used to demonstrate the process and its application.

Physiological mode

Behavior. Each adaptive mode can be further divided into segments that represent more specific functions for the adapting person. There are a wide variety of theoretical frameworks effective in the assessment of the physiological mode. Recent alterations in the Roy model suggest categorizing physiological behavior according to the adapting person's needs: musculoskeletal, respiratory, circulatory, neurological, ingestive, eliminative, protective, reproductive, and endocrine. Physiological behavior, then, can be classified in one of the nine categories based on the function it appears to serve for the adapting person's maintenance of physical adequacy.

In examining these categories more closely, let us consider the behaviors commonly associated with each physiological category. Behaviors appropriately categorized under *musculoskeletal* include posture, mobility, activity, sleep patterns, and sleep disruptions. In evaluating *ingestive* behaviors, consideration should include appetite, food intake, weight, allergies, teeth, and senses of taste and smell. *Eliminative* behaviors are associated with the elimination of body wastes by the urinary tract, gastrointestinal tract, and the skin. In this category behaviors represent the relationship between intake and output, weight, and physiological status. *Circulatory* behaviors involve skin color, pulse, blood pressure, respiration, and physiological status as determined by laboratory tests (e.g., hemoglobin level, white blood cell count). When assessing *neurological* behavior, observations regarding body temperature, reflexes, level of consciousness, and orientation to time, place, and person should be noted. The *respiratory* category comprises behaviors that represent the transfer of oxygen, such as chest movement and size, patency of airways, secretions, and rate, depth, and rhythm of breathing. The *protective* category includes behaviors indicative of the condition of the skin, hair, and nails. *Reproductive* behaviors involve the structure and level of function of both external and internal reproductive organs and include menses, menopause, and the presence or absence of essential organs. Finally, the *endocrine* behaviors concern size, weight, and hormonal level. All physiological behaviors can be included in one of the nine categories, reflecting the function they appear to serve in the maintenance of physiological adequacy. Physiological adequacy, then, is dependent on the presence of behaviors in each of the categories that will reduce the stress experienced when the person interacts with the environment.

Influencing stimuli. Each mode is influenced by the external environment and the internal state of the person. The environment includes the adapting person's surroundings—people, places, and objects that exist outside the person and influence how he transacts and behaves. The *internal state* consists of the person's physiological structure, maturational level, and unique perceptions. The physiological mode is most frequently affected by the person's physical makeup or an external disease producing a traumatizing event.

When examining the relationships between physiological behavior and stimuli, the nurse must have an awareness of the person's physical makeup. Physical structure and the presence or absence of adequate functions and regulatory mechanisms are stimuli that must be reviewed. In addition, the person's level of maturation must be considered. For example, is the person fully mature or still in the process of physical growth? Finally, the nurse should consider his attitude toward health care and his beliefs regarding such aspects of his physical structure as ability to function and wellness or illness.

External influencing stimuli include substances that are essential or threatening to life, including oxygen, water, nutritional substance, and minerals and noxious or harmful substances such as smog, fire, and certain chemicals. Interactional stimuli involve the presence or absence of people who provide physiological necessities such as food or water or substances essential to health maintenance or restoration.

Focal stimuli commonly associated with a threat to physiological adequacy would include (1) internal structural changes, (2) the presence of an organism or substance that is physically harmful, (3) the absence of some essential substance, and (4) prolonged, unresolved stress experiences. Whenever one of these influencing stimuli is present, the person experiences a decrease in the level of adequacy, and illness usually follows. Stimuli that have the potential to become focal include an attitude about health or death and the person's stage of development. However, most commonly the behavior in this mode is directly related to an internal structural or functional change or the presence or absence of some external stimulus.

In step I of the adaptation nursing process the nurse examines the regulator/cognator process and *categorizes physiological behavior* under one of the nine categories: musculoskeletal, respiratory, circulatory, neurological, ingestive, eliminative, protective, reproductive, and endocrine. At the same time, she scans the external environment and makes a judgment about the person's internal state to identify focal, contextual, and residual stimuli. In the physiological mode she pays special attention to *physical makeup and the presence or absence of essential or potentially harmful stimuli*.

Case study—Carol Mackie. We will examine how a nurse using the adaptation nursing process might categorize physiological behavior and label influencing stimuli in a clinical situation. The adapting person in this situation is Carol Mackie, a 27-year-old married woman who works as an assistant manager of a savings and loan company. She is hospitalized for the surgical repair of a torn ligament that she sustained on her honeymoon while skiing. Carol had surgery 2 days ago and now wears a leg cast that extends from just below her hip to her ankle.

Regulator/cognator transaction. The regulator/cognator transaction is inferred based on the behavioral observations and knowledge of the stimuli that influence the adapting person. When this knowledge and these observations are validated, the nurse and the person can examine the regulator/cognator process. This examination gives the nurse and the person information essential for formulating judgments, setting goals, and planning interventions. For this reason this transaction process is of major significance during the second step of the adaptation nursing process. However, to facilitate learning, a summary of the regulator/cognator process will be presented, preceding the examination of the behavioral response and the influencing stimuli. In actual practice the adaptation nurse acquires information regarding stimuli influencing the person, observes behavioral responses, and simultaneously begins to hypothesize about the person's coping abilities as she continues to collect data.

First, we will review Carol's probable transaction when she experiences the internal triggering event associated with her second postoperative day and the wearing of a full leg cast. Carol's regulator is activated, stimulating the general alarm reaction; the physical sensations associated with pain and exhaustion are transmitted, and the cognator is alerted. The physiological behavior occurs automatically and is not mediated by the cognitive process. At the same time the cognator assumes the coping stance of approach and the associated coping strategy of fight; the behavioral expression of the cognator's operations will be described in the role performance mode. Carol has realized that the physiological triggering event she experienced is normal; her physiological responses are described below.

Behavioral response. In making a physiological assessment of Carol on her second postoperative day, the adaptation nurse would review the need areas associated with the physiological mode. For the *musculoskeletal* category the nurse would note that Carol is able to walk with the aid of crutches for 15- to 20-minute periods three times per day. She cannot bear weight on her injured right leg, and she moves slowly and with some difficulty on the crutches. In addition, Carol reports that she has difficulty sleeping through the night; she awakens every 2 to 3 hours and asks to be repositioned. In assessing Carol's *ingestive* needs, the adaptation nurse notes that Carol is eating well. She orders meals containing all elements from the basic food groups with emphasis on protein items, fruits, and vegetables. Carol is 5 feet 7 inches tall, weighs 127 pounds, and is well proportioned. On her first postoperative day she had one episode of vomiting. Carol's *eliminative* behaviors represent physiological adequacy. She has been voiding six times per day since surgery and has had a formed stool daily. Carol received 2000 ml of fluid by mouth and intravenously yesterday and had an output of 2200 ml. Her sodium level was 140 mEq/ml, and her potassium level was 3.8 mEq/ml. Carol's respiratory and circulatory behaviors are adequate. Her pulse is 82; her blood pressure is 120/76; her respirations are 16; and her toes are warm and pink. Her complete blood cell count is within normal limits. Finally, Carol's *neurological* function reflects that she has periodic pain in her right leg that increases when she is walking with the crutches. Carol's morning temperature was 98° F, and she has usual feeling in the toes of her right foot. Finally, Carol's *protective* behavior indicates adequacy in that her incision is clean and dry (as viewed through the window in her cast).

Influencing stimuli. In completing this review of the physiological mode, the adaptation nurse concludes that Carol is experiencing physiological adequacy in most areas. The nurse will continue to focus her observations and activities on Carol's difficulties with mobility, sleep, and pain. In order to understand Carol's behavior, the adaptation nurse must simultaneously review and classify relevant stimuli that are affecting Carol's adaptation.

To assess these influencing stimuli, the nurse must collect additional data. From the chart, the morning report, conversations with Carol, and theoretical knowledge regarding this type of surgery, the nurse has a great deal of information. She knows that Carol pulled the ligament while skiing in Utah and has learned that Carol is very active physically: she jogs, plays tennis, and skis regularly. The adaptation nurse also knows that the surgical procedure involved in repairing Carol's ligament is a relatively simple one that is followed by moderate to severe pain for a period of several days and will require Carol to wear a cast for the next 6 weeks. In addition, the nurse has learned that Carol has been married for 2 weeks and was enjoying her honeymoon at the time of her accident. She has also learned that despite Carol's involvement in sports for the last 20 years, she has never had an injury, and this is her first experience with surgery and hospitalization. Carol's chart indicates that she will have a physical therapist to help her with crutch walking. In addition, she may have meperidine (50 mg every 4 hours) for pain, aspirin (10 grains) for a temperature above 99.5° F, and secobarbital (100 mg orally) at night for sleep.

In classifying all the stimuli that influence Carol's physiological behavior, the nurse first scans her data to identify the focal stimulus for the physiological mode. The behaviors indicative of stress are related to the musculoskeletal and neurological categories. For Carol's decreased mobility, sleeplessness, and pain, the focal stimuli are the surgical repair of the torn ligament 2 days ago and the application of a full leg cast. Contextual stimuli in this situation would include the fact that this is Carol's second postoperative day, the medications she has ordered for pain and sleep, and the expectation that she practice crutch walking with the physical therapist at least twice per day. Residual stimuli that might also be affecting Carol's physiological behavior include the fact that she is newly married, is a considerable distance from home, and lacks experience with surgery and hospitals.

In summary, Carol's behavior (difficulty moving about, lack of sleep, and pain) indicates that her level of physiological adequacy has been disrupted. Her behavior is directly related to her recent surgery and the application of a full leg cast. A nursing assessment guide for Carol's physiological mode is shown below.

NURSING CARE GUIDE—Carol Mackie

PHYSIOLOGICAL MODE

MUSCULOSKELETAL BEHAVIORS

1. Right leg in extension from hip to ankle with slight flexion at the knee.
2. "I'm exhausted after walking a few feet."
3. "How do I get this thing out of bed?"
4. "I hardly slept at all last night. I looked at the clock every 2 hours."
5. "I kept calling the night nurse to re-do these pillows."

NEUROLOGICAL BEHAVIORS

1. "This thing really throbs, especially at night."
2. "Can I have a shot now?"

INFLUENCING STIMULI

Focal: Surgical repair of torn ligament and application of full cast.

Contextual: Second postoperative day. Eliminative, ingestive, respiratory, circulatory, and protective components of mode demonstrate adequacy (e.g., eating three high-protein meals daily; intake 2000 ml, output 2200 ml; Na 140 mEq/ml, K 3.8 mEq/ml, P 82, B 120/76, R 16; toes warm and pink; T 98° F; skin at incision clean and dry).

In the guide Carol's behavior has been categorized according to the components of the physiological mode, and a clear relationship has been identified between behaviors and stimuli. This completes the first step in the adaptation nursing process for the physiological mode. Now let us examine the components of the self-concept mode and the commonly occurring stimuli.

Self-concept mode

Behavior. The self-concept mode represents the continuous striving to achieve adequacy by increasing self-awareness, autonomy, and self-actualization. This adequacy depends on the person's sense of self, that he may know who he is in order to be or exist. According to Combs and Snygg (1959) the self-concept is the more or less organized perceptual object resulting from present or past self-observation. It is what the person believes about himself. These beliefs arise from perception and are a product of social interaction. Behaviors categorized here represent the adapting person's struggle to maintain his perception of himself or increase his perceptions by increasing autonomy or self-actualization. Roy (1976) identifies two components of the self-concept, the physical self and the personal self.

The *physical self* refers to the person's perception of himself as a physical being, his body image. Behaviors in this category manifest the adapting person's striving to maintain adequacy by demonstrating that he can accomplish what he wishes when and where he wishes. The adapting person is concerned with the function and control of his physical being. Behaviors commonly seen in this category would include statements or actions reflecting the control and manipulation of the body. In addition, observations should be included regarding physical appearance and posture.

The *personal self* is divided into three additional categories: self-consistency, moral and ethical self, and self-ideal. These categories encompass separate areas of self-appraisal. *Self-consistency*, a concept developed by Combs and Snygg, represents the person's desire for sameness, his need to present himself to the environment in a manner consistent with environmental expectations. Behaviors in this category evince the person's attempt to maintain his perceptions of others' perceptions of himself. The *moral and ethical self* relates to the person's evaluation of himself in relation to a value system. This category comprises the person's efforts to measure himself against an internal set of values he has acquired through experience. Finally, the *self-ideal* is the person's desire for autonomy and self-actualization, the self's striving to become that which it wishes to be. Behaviors in this category include acts or statements that reflect the person's belief about his capacity or ultimate potential.

All behaviors in the self-concept mode are classified according to the particular level of adequacy they maintain. In this mode the person strives to maintain his self-perception as well as the perceptions he believes others have of him. In addition, he continually strives for increased autonomy and self-actualization. Adequacy in the self-concept mode, then, is reflected in behaviors designed to reduce stress experienced in the physical and personal self.

Influencing stimuli. The relationship between behavior and influencing stimuli in the self-concept mode is somewhat more complex than that in the physiological mode. Threats to adequacy in this mode are generally associated with major physiological changes, movement from one developmental level to the next, attitudes, and beliefs, or an alteration in a significant relationship. Focal stimuli that frequently affect the behavioral response in the self-concept mode include sudden loss or change in physiological function or structure, such as an amputation or reconstructive surgery. Major developmental transitions, such as the progression from childhood to adolescence or from generative adulthood to old age, may place significant stress on the person's feelings of adequacy. Religious and cultural beliefs may significantly influence self-concept behaviors. Finally, the loss or gain of a significant relationship may alter one's perception of psychological adequacy.

As is the case in the physiological mode, any one of these stimuli may become focal. However, based on the interactional nature of the self-concept and the reflected appraisal of others, the interaction of significant people in the person's environment is the most common focal stimulus associated with psychological adequacy. Perhaps even more significant than an actual change in a relationship are the person's perceptions, attitudes, and beliefs about himself in relation to others. Major physiological changes or developmental crises are the next most frequently observed stimuli that alter behavioral responses in the self-concept mode.

In step I of the adaptation nursing process the nurse examines the regulator/cognator process and categorizes psychological behavior under one of the following categories: physical self, self-consistency, moral and ethical self, and self-ideal. At the same time the nurse scans the environment and the person's internal state to identify focal, contextual, and residual stimuli that influence behavior. In the self-concept mode she is especially attentive to the *adapting person's relationships, developmental level,* and *attitudes and beliefs about himself*.

Case study
Regulator/cognator transaction. Again to facilitate learning, the regulator/cognator process for the self-concept mode will be summarized prior to the presentation of the behavioral observations and influencing stimuli. Remember, in actual practice the nurse's knowledge of this transaction is gained by examining behavior and stimuli.

Recalling the case study, let us examine Carol's regulator/cognator process when she is confronted with the triggering event of confinement in a full leg cast for 6 weeks. The regulator signals a general alarm; there are no other overt physiological behaviors triggered; and the cognator is alerted. In this transaction Carol has identified that she can cope with this triggering event by assuming the coping stances of compromise and self-enhancement. She will utilize the coping strategies of suppression and manipulation to deal with her immobilization. Essentially, Carol's cognator allows her to block out some of her feelings resulting from not being able to engage in her usual activities. Additionally, Carol views learning to overcome the obstacles as another challenge that she will have to take on. The behavioral response that Carol exhibits and the stimuli that influence that response follow.

Behavioral response. To assess Carol Mackie's self-concept on her second postoperative day, the adaptation nurse would review the areas associated with psychological adequacy. Regarding the physical self, the nurse would discover that Carol sees herself as strong and physically capable. She states that she has never had a sports-related injury; she feels bad that she will miss the remainder of the ski season and is concerned that she will be out of condition in the 6 weeks that she must wear the cast. Carol also expresses frustration at not being agile on crutches: "You'd think that, if I could compete in a downhill race, I could get to the bathroom on my own." Carol also talks frequently about the loss of possible social contacts that will result from her immobilization: "Who's going to want to jog or play tennis with somebody on crutches?" Concerning the *personal self*, Carol's behavior represents adequacy in all four categories. In *self-consistency* Carol often refers to her positive attributes and her ability to maintain her attitudes and beliefs despite temporary disability. She frequently states, "I'm a fighter. If I worked like I did to make it to the Olympic swimming trials, I guess I can handle these crutches." Carol occasionally expresses regret (the *moral and ethical self*) at having disrupted her honeymoon: "I guess Jeff knows I would not do this purposely. I guess you can't cry over spilled milk." Discussing personal goals, Carol expresses her wish to achieve a few more promotions before taking time to raise a family. "We want two children, and I intend to continue working. I'm going to be a bank president within the next 6 years." Carol's *self-ideal* represents a high level of adequacy.

Reviewing the self-concept behaviors, the adaptation nurse concludes that Carol feels psychologically adequate in most areas. The nurse will continue to focus her attention on Carol's temporary change in her body image. A review and classification of relevant stimuli will provide meaningful information about Carol's behavior in the physical self category.

Influencing stimuli. To assess the influencing stimuli the nurse must continue to collect additional data. From conversations with Carol, observations of her interactions, information shared by Carol's husband, and the nurse's knowledge of psychological principles, the adaptation nurse can make assessments about the relationships between Carol's behavior and the stimuli. She has learned that Carol is accustomed to succeeding, likes a challenge, and is very competitive. As an adolescent, Carol was an alternate for the U.S. Olympic Team. She now swims for pleasure but frequently enters local 10-km runs. Carol also skis for pleasure but often rises to the challenge of a downhill race. In addition to an active sports life, she has a responsible position in a savings and loan institution and is actively pursuing an advanced degree in business administration. Her husband states, "The company she works for is very staid; they've never had a woman executive. Carol plans to be the first." Carol talks frequently about her family and confides that she has been surrounded by supporters all her life. "When you have two parents and three sisters and brothers, you always feel there's someone on your side." Carol also believes Jeff has a positive influence on her life and that their goals are compatible. "He doesn't like competitive women, and he doesn't think I'm too aggressive. Not everyone would marry a 'jock' who wants to be a bank president."

To identify a focal stimulus for the behaviors observed in the physical self category, the nurse must determine which stimulus is the most significant. For Carol, 6 weeks in a full leg cast seems to be the most significant stimulus. Contextual stimuli influencing her behavior would include Carol's successful participation in athletics, her career, her support system, the temporary nature of her disability, and her inexperience with illness. Residual stimuli requiring further validation comprise Carol's professional goals, her values and beliefs, and her recent marriage.

In summary, Carol's behavior manifests the disruption in her level of psychological adequacy as evidenced by a change in her body image. Her behavior is directly related to the fact that she must wear a full leg cast and that this alteration is disrupting her usual activity pattern. A nursing care guide using all the information about Carol's self-concept mode is presented on p. 55.

NURSING CARE GUIDE—Carol Mackie

SELF-CONCEPT MODE

PHYSICAL SELF BEHAVIORS

1. "You'd think I could at least get to the bathroom on these crutches."
2. "Who's going to want to play tennis or jog with someone on crutches?"
3. "When he takes this cast off, I'll have to go to the gym every day to get back in shape."
4. "I guess I'm not such a 'klutz'—this is my first sports injury in a very competitive 20 years."

INFLUENCING STIMULI

Focal: Carol will be in a full leg cast for 6 weeks.

Contextual: Alternate for the Olympic swim team 10 years ago. Currently jogs in 10-km runs. Skis for recreation. Is a junior executive at a savings and loan and will be able to return to work and her studies in about 10 days. Has concerned family members who call daily and a husband who has been supportive and consistently available. Will be out of the cast in 6 weeks and able to return gradually to all of her activities. Is successfully mastering the tasks of young adulthood. First experience with injury or pain—is accustomed to her body performing adequately.

Residual: Carol's beliefs about her body and her worth. Her 2-week-old marriage. Her career goals.

The regulator/cognator transaction has been reviewed, behavior has been categorized according to the components of the self-concept mode, and a clear relationship has been identified between behaviors and stimuli. This completes the first step in the adaptation nursing process for the self-concept mode. Next, the adaptation nurse should examine the components of the role-performance mode and commonly occurring stimuli.

Role performance mode

Behavior. The role function mode is the adapting person's expression of his social function. Behaviors categorized here represent the person's attempt to maintain or enhance social adequacy and depend on the person's knowledge of who he is in relation to others so that he can act. In adaptation theory the works of Banton and Erikson have been used to provide a framework that assists the nurse in ascribing meaning to the person's social behavior.

Banton (1965) introduces the concept of the role tree, identifying three major roles that all people assume: primary, secondary, and tertiary. A *primary role* represents the major psychosocial task of the person at his particular developmental stage. The person assumes *secondary roles* to complete the tasks associated with his primary role. Finally, *tertiary roles* are generally temporary and voluntarily assumed, representing a specialized role often associated with a secondary role. This category is of particular importance in adaptation nursing, because the illness role or client role is considered tertiary.

In classifying behavioral responses in the role performance mode, the adaptation nurse is concerned primarily with the tertiary role of illness or client. However, the adaptation nurse must first identify the person's developmental stage and label his primary role. Any developmental theory is adequate for this purpose. The theory of Eric Erikson (1963) has been used with the Roy model. According to Erikson, the schoolage child or generative adult stage might be identified and then utilized to identify the primary role. The adaptation nurse would then identify secondary roles by listing the tasks associated with the adapting person's developmental stage. For example, the primary role of the schoolage child would probably be associated with the secondary roles of child, student, and sibling. The adaptation nurse, then, assesses the secondary roles that she observes to have a direct influence on the person's current level of adequacy. Common secondary roles the adaptation nurse might see manifested behaviorally include student role, parent role, and spouse role. Additionally, the adaptation nurse may observe that the person occupies a role that reflects his spirituality. Depending on the personal significance of religion or a belief in a supreme power, this role may be secondary or tertiary. In classifying the behaviors in the role performance mode, the nurse should include observations of instrumental role behaviors. Instrumental behaviors (Parsons and Shils, 1951) are long-term, goal-directed, action-oriented behaviors and might be comparable to behaviors identified in a job description. These behaviors represent the person's attempt to maintain or enhance social adequacy by engaging in the tasks society has assigned him. Such behaviors associated with the sick role might include the person's seeking and following appropriate regimens. Parent role behaviors would include appropriate care-taking responses toward children. The spiritual role would be reflected in reading religious literature, talking with spiritual advisors, making statements about beliefs, or requesting that someone pray with them.

Role performance mode behavior, then, includes the nurse's observations of the person's behavior as he strives for social adequacy. The nurse focuses her attention on the tertiary role that brings the person into contact with the health care system and relevant secondary roles.

Influencing stimuli. Adequacy in role performance is also closely related to interactions with significant people in the environment. Threats to adequacy in this mode are usually the result of changes in personal relationships or developmental changes. Attitudes and beliefs, especially religious and cultural, have an impact on social adequacy. In addition, an intellectual knowledge of the prescribed behavior for a role is essential for adequate role performance. Physiological changes may affect social adequacy. Changes in the physical environment, such as geographical or nutritional changes, may result less frequently in an alteration in the level of adequacy in the role performance mode.

Focal stimuli commonly associated with threats to adequacy in role performance are losses or additions of persons with complementary roles. For example, stress occurs when parents and children are separated, when spouses are separated, when bosses have no employees, or when pupils have no teachers. Adequacy in role performance is very dependent on the presence of complementary role figures. Adequacy is also strongly influenced by maturational level. The person's primary role is based on his developmental stage. The tasks associated with the developmental stage define the secondary roles assumed by the adapting person. Changes in developmental stage affect both the primary and the secondary roles and thus have impact on the person's behavior in the role performance mode.

Physiological changes that alter the person's capabilities also frequently affect adequacy in role performance. Loss of a limb may affect the person's job performance, or a series of infections may result in a child's lack of success as a student. Changes in locale often affect social adequacy. A new physical environment often alters friendships and occupations.

Social adequacy is affected by many stimuli. The most common focal stimuli associated with role performance are changes in significant relationships, maturational changes, or physiological changes.

In step I of the adaptation nursing process the nurse examines the regulator/cognator process and categorizes role performance behaviors under the *tertiary role* of illness or client and *secondary roles* that influence this tertiary role performance. At the same time, the nurse collects data regarding the stimuli in the environment and the person's internal state that affect role performance. In the role performance mode, *complementary role figures,* the *developmental stage,* and the *physiological status of the adapting person* are of primary significance.

Case study

Regulator/cognator transaction. Let us return to Carol Mackie and again look at the regulator/cognator transaction with yet another triggering event. In examining Carol's client role behavior, we see that Carol is responding to an internal stimulus—her perception of herself as a well-coordinated, athletic woman. The regulator signals the change, a general alarm reaction occurs, no other overt physiological behaviors are evident, and the cognator is alerted. In this transaction Carol realizes that her body has changed and does not meet her usual expectations. She therefore needs to assume a more dependent position and take on the role of client or injured person. Carol again decides that she can handle this situation and assumes a coping stance of compromise. She uses the strategy of suppression to block some of her feelings and limitations and engages in a few expected client behaviors. Her behavioral response and the influencing stimuli are detailed in the following section.

Behavioral response. In order to complete a behavioral assessment in the role performance mode, the adaptation nurse would first review Carol's response in her client role. She would then examine Carol's secondary role performance. Under her *client role performance* the nurse notes that Carol walks with the crutches whenever requested to do so by the physical therapist. In addition, Carol has requested medication for pain every 6 hours but has said she would like to wait a bit longer today. Although Carol is to remain in bed except for her crutch-walking activities, the nurses frequently find her up, hopping to the bathroom. On one occasion she lost her balance and attempted to stabilize herself with her right leg. An orthopedic technician, who was just leaving the room, saved her from a dangerous fall by quickly catching her. Carol continues to suggest that she leave the hospital tomorrow, stating, "I can just as easily lie in bed at home. I don't want Jeff to lose his job because he has to take time to fly home with me." The only secondary role behavior the adaptation nurse has observed has been Carol's behavior as a wife. Her responses are adequate, and she appears to be experiencing little stress in this area. She has few opportunities to engage in goal-directed instrumental behaviors because of her immobilization and the restrictions imposed by the hospital environment. Carol orders meals for Jeff daily, and they have been having meals together at her bedside. Carol has also made lists of activities such as telephoning and shopping for Jeff to do. Jeff and Carol have long daily conversations regarding their shortened honeymoon, their waiting jobs, and their isolation from family and friends. Carol's behavior expresses adequacy in the secondary role of spouse, but she appears to be having some difficulty fully assuming the tertiary role of client.

Influencing stimuli. When assessing the stimuli that influence role behavior, the presence of complementary role figures should be assessed first. As a measure of social adequacy, role performance demands reciprocal relationships. In the client role Carol has nurses, doctors, and other health care providers as well as support from her husband. Another significant stimulus would be knowledge regarding the expected role performance. Carol seems to have general knowledge about her hospitalization and expected behaviors, but she has no first-hand experience with a disabling surgery and the healing process. Attitudes and beliefs also affect Carol's client role performance. She is accustomed to overcoming physical obstacles and having control over her body; her normally healthy body image makes it difficult for her to assume the role of client. In addition, Carol is away from home and only recently has taken on the role of wife. These factors may limit the amount of energy she can focus on the client role. In addition, her pain is decreasing, and as she becomes more agile with crutches, she will feel less like restricting her activity. Finally, Carol is working with a doctor assigned to her in the emergency room. She has had few opportunities to develop the relationship necessary for a positive client/physician relationship.

In reviewing all these contributory stimuli, the nurse needs to select the most significant stimulus influencing Carol's client role performance. The focal stimulus in this situation would be Carol's positive body image and athletic successes. Contextual stimuli include the presence of appropriate health care providers, the lack of a strong relationship with her physician, and her limited knowledge about her surgery, recovery time, and expected client behaviors. Carol's recent marriage and her separation from other significant people may also be affecting her desire to leave the hospital soon.

In summary, Carol's behavior indicates that she is fulfilling her role as a wife adequately but that her role as a client has been somewhat disrupted. This seems directly related to Carol's perception of herself as a healthy, physically capable person. A nursing care guide based on the role performance mode is outlined below.

NURSING CARE GUIDE—Carol Mackie

ROLE PERFORMANCE MODE

CLIENT ROLE BEHAVIORS

1. Demerol, 50 mg intramuscularly for pain every 6 hours. Wishes to wait longer today.
2. Gets up and hops on her left leg to the bathroom without assistance.
3. Loses balance and tries to support herself on her right leg.
4. Talks about immediate discharge: "I can just as easily lie in bed at home. I don't want Jeff to lose his job because he has to take time to fly home with me."
5. Walks on crutches whenever requested to do so.

INFLUENCING STIMULI

Focal: Positive body image and athletic successes.

Contextual: Limited knowledge of surgery, recovery time, and expected client behaviors. Nurses, doctors, and other health care workers providing needed services. Supportive, available husband. Lack of a strong relationship with her physician because of the emergency nature of her hospitalization.

Residual: Developmentally, Carol has taken on a new role recently and needs to devote a great deal of her energy to being a wife. Considerable distance from home, separated from family members.

Behavior has been categorized according to the components of the role performance mode, and a clear relationship has been identified between behavior and stimuli. This completes step I in the adaptation nursing process for the role performance mode.

Interdependence mode

Behavior. The interdependence mode, like the role performance mode, is an expression of the person's social function and is based on the need for nurturing relationships. Behavioral responses in this mode represent the person's attempts to maintain or enhance adequacy in relation to significant people in the environment. These behaviors are often considered emotional and are engaged in to gain direct responses that offer self-gratification and immediate feedback. The interdependence mode represents the person's striving for love and support as well as his offering of love and support to others. Roy (1976) states that the goal of the interdependence mode of acting is to live successfully in a world of other people.

In recent years the development of the concept of the interdependence mode has undergone many changes. Previously there were many conflicts between this mode and the role performance mode. Although this difficulty can never be totally resolved because of the holistic nature of the adapting person, it is hoped that recent alterations, reflected in this section, will eliminate some of the previous concerns. Because both interdependence and role performance are measures of social adequacy and because both modes are dependent on the presence of another significant relationship for behavior to occur, a parallel assessment process was developed. In assessment and classification of both behavioral responses and the influencing stimuli, the adaptation nurse will utilize the person's roles for both interdependence and role performance. The focus of the behavioral assessment will be different. In interdependence the nurse will be concerned with the expressive role behaviors (Parsons and Shils, 1951) as opposed to the goal-directed instrumental behaviors associated with role performance. These role behaviors, which are often considered emotional, manifest the person's striving for immediate feedback and self-gratification, thus offering the nurturance and support required by the adapting person.

In categorizing behavior in the interdependence mode, the adaptation nurse identifies the adapting person's primary role. She then lists the secondary roles the person occupies and observes for expressive behaviors associated with each of these roles. Additionally, she looks for expressive behaviors in the client role and the spiritual role. The adaptation nurse is also concerned with two types of expressive behavior when she assesses each of these roles. The first group of behaviors describe the person as a *recipient* of love and support. The second group of behaviors describe the person as the *contributor* of love and support. The interdependence mode, then, reflects the reciprocal relationship implied in the word *interdependence*. There is a circular relationship that involves giving and receiving between the adapting person and at least one other person in the external environment. Observations in these two categories would include nurturing behaviors that occur between the person and other significant persons. Recipient behaviors would include the person's response to physical demonstrations of affection, protection, caring, recognition, or offers of help from caregivers. Contributive behaviors are the types of physical demonstrations of affection the person initiates, methods of praise and approval, and the ways in which the person asks for help.

The interdependence mode behavioral responses reflect the person's level of adequacy in relationship to the sources of support in the environment. The person continually strives to be nurtured and provide nurturance by engaging in behaviors that provide immediate, self-gratifying feedback. Various stimuli influence the person's behavior in the interdependence mode.

Influencing stimuli. Like role performance, the interdependence mode is a measure of social adequacy. Social function in the areas of nurturance and support is highly dependent on experience, knowledge, and significant people in the adapting person's environment. The most common focal stimulus for the interdependence mode is a change in a relationship (individual, family, or social).

Attitudes and beliefs about love, nurturance, and support may influence interdependence behavior. Experience as a recipient, especially in infancy and childhood, and the presence or absence of role models for interdependence behavior affect behavioral response in this area. A physiological change or a change in location may likewise alter interdependent behavioral response. Maturational changes may affect the adapting person's approach to seeking and receiving help and support. For example, in the transition from childhood to adolescence there are many alterations in interdependent behavior.

Since interdependence, like role performance, is a measure of social adequacy, interpersonal relationships are the most important influencing stimuli. Therefore, the alteration in a significant relationship or the availability of a relationship affects behavioral responses in this mode. Maturational changes may significantly alter affectional relationships; attitudes and beliefs, cultural as well as religious, may also produce a meaningful behavioral response in the interdependence mode.

A change in an interpersonal relationship or the person's attitudes is the most significant influencing stimulus affecting behavior and is usually focal.

In step I of the adaptation nursing process the nurse categorizes interdependent behavior according to secondary and tertiary roles and according to *contributive* and *recipient* categories. At the same time, the nurse must identify focal, contextual, and residual stimuli that influence interdependent behavior. In this mode these stimuli characteristically include *significant relationships, attitudes, knowledge, beliefs, and maturational changes*.

Case study
Regulator/cognator transaction. Returning to the case study, Carol Mackie, we will discuss the triggering event that has stimulated Carol's interdependence behavior. Carol appears to be responding to a change in her environment that diminishes the number of supportive, nurturing people usually available to her. This triggering event stimulates the regulator's general alarm reaction; no other overt physiological behavior is triggered; and the cognator is alerted. Carol again has decided that since she has Jeff, a usual source of love and support, she can cope with this triggering event maximally. Carol selects the coping stance of self-enhancement and uses manipulation to make a nurturing environment more readily available. In the following section Carol's behavioral response and the significant influencing stimuli will be presented.

Behavior. As the adaptation nurse reviews Carol's chart, she observes Carol's interactions with significant others and utilizes theoretical knowledge to classify her receptive and contributory interdependent behavior. On the second postoperative day the nurse notes that Carol exhibits many receptive and contributive interdependent behaviors in the roles of client, spouse, daughter, and religious person. Carol asks for medication for pain, requests that her doctor be contacted to facilitate her early discharge, and asks Jeff to purchase toilet articles and a new nightgown for her. Carol responds positively to Jeff's affection. They are frequently observed holding hands, and they kiss at all arrivals and departures. Carol is excited and enthusiastic about phone calls from family and friends. Carol makes frequent statements about God's will and His gifts to her in the past. In addition to these receptive behaviors, Carol exhibits many contributive behaviors. She offers reassurance and positive statements about her recovery whenever her parents call. In addition, she is very appreciative of any help offered and always praises the work and attention of her health care providers. She expresses concern about how Jeff is managing on his own in a strange city. Carol exhibits regular physical contact with Jeff, requesting that he sit on her bed, rub her back, and read to her. In the interdependence mode both receptive and contributive behaviors represent social adequacy in all roles, especially spouse and client roles.

Influencing stimuli. Carol's major source of input is Jeff. His availability and receptiveness allow Carol to function optimally in the interdependence mode. Carol also has phone contact with her family and friends despite her hospitalization several thousand miles from home. This contact also allows Carol to maintain adequacy. Her belief about her own worth as the recipient of care and her attitudes toward health care professionals also facilitate behavior in this area. The physiological change Carol has undergone and her subsequent disability increase her behavioral response in the recipient category. In addition, Carol's religious beliefs provide support and nurturance during this time of stress.

In assessing all these contributing stimuli, the nurse determines that the focal stimuli for Carol's expressive wife role behavior are Jeff's availability and responsiveness. Contextually, Carol's behavior is supported by her frequent family contact, her religious beliefs, her attitudes about health care, and the nature of her illness and immobilization. Residual stimuli that may be affecting her behavior include the fact that she is a 27-year-old middle-class white woman. The focal stimulus for Carol's expressive client role behavior is the presence of caregivers. Contextually, her behavior is supported by the environment, which supplies the medications and other resources necessary for her care; by her lack of experience in the role; and by her belief that caregivers are helpful and effective. Finally, residual stimuli might include Carol's middle-class upbringing, which taught her to be respectful and show appreciation. In Carol's expressive role of religious person the focal stimulus seems to be Carol's belief in God. Contextually, Carol is influenced by her Bible study experiences and the fact that she is a born-again Christian. Residual stimuli might include Carol's belief in her own abilities as well as the absence of other usual sources of support. A nursing care guide for Carol's interdependence behavior could be diagramed as shown on p. 63.

NURSING CARE GUIDE—Carol Mackie

INTERDEPENDENCE MODE

WIFE ROLE BEHAVIORS

Receptive
1. Holds hands with and kisses Jeff frequently.
2. "Should I take offense when my groom brings me a toothbrush?"
3. "Oh, will you bring me some of that chocolate I like?"

Contributive
1. "Here, sit by me. Thanks so much for spending all this time here."
2. "You look so tired. Go back to the hotel and sleep. You don't have to watch this dumb movie with me."

INFLUENCING STIMULI

Focal: Jeff's presence and receptive behavior.

Contextual: Phone calls from family and friends. Religious beliefs. Born-again Christian. Attends church regularly and is a member of a Bible study class.

Residual: White middle-class woman, 27 years of age.

CLIENT ROLE BEHAVIORS

Receptive
1. "Can I have my shot now?"
2. "Would you please call my doctor? I really need to talk to him about my discharge."

Contributive
1. "Thanks so much. Those pillows really help."

Focal: Presence of caregivers (nurse, doctor, physical therapist).

Contextual: Jeff's support. Hospitalized for 3 days for first time. Has never had to assume this role before. Belief that health care professionals help you and provide a valuable service. Hospital environment that supplies needs and equipment.

Residual: Cultural background and upbringing (taught to be respectful and show appreciation). Is used to being well cared for and believes she deserves such care.

SPIRITUAL ROLE BEHAVIORS

Receptive
1. "It's God's will. He has been good to me in the past. I've had many gifts."
2. "Oh, I believe what it says in the Bible. God has a plan for us all, and he won't ask anything that you can't give."

Focal: Belief in God.

Contextual: Is a born-again Christian. Raised as a Presbyterian, but when in college became involved with a Christian group. Has participated in many Bible study groups and uses the Bible teachings to guide her behavior and help her cope with stressful situations.

Residual: Belief in her own abilities. Absence of other sources of support.

Behavior has been categorized according to the components of the interdependence mode, and a clear relationship has been identified between behavior and stimuli.

Summary

When interacting with the adapting person, the nurse must process an enormous amount of data, organizing it in a meaningful way to interact effectively with the adapting person. Step I is the data collection phase of the adaptation nursing process in which the nurse begins to assemble the puzzle presented by the interaction. By examining the regulator/cognator process and organizing the data according to behavioral categories and types of stimuli, the nurse begins to sort the puzzle pieces into related groups. In adaptation theory the four modes (physiological, self-concept, role performance, and interdependence) and the three types of stimuli (focal, contextual, and residual) are like the piles of sorted puzzle pieces. Once the pieces are sorted, they must be assembled into meaningful groups or relationships. Only then can you begin to feel you have a good understanding of step I in the adaptation nursing process.

Now we will study judgment and diagnosis formation—the process in which the puzzle pieces are grouped and sections are assembled. The reader is advised to begin this examination by reviewing the objectives and the essential terms associated with the adaptation nursing process (see pp. 40-43).

STEP II: FORMULATION OF JUDGMENTS AND DIAGNOSIS

In step II of the adaptation nursing process the nurse uses her knowledge of the regulator/cognator process, her own internal state, her clinical experience, and her theoretical background in pathophysiology, psychology, and sociology to set priorities. The judgments are formulated based on the assessment of behavior and influencing stimuli. These judgments reflect coping behavior and the effectiveness of the behavior in relationship to the triggering event. The nursing diagnosis is formulated from the two judgments and reflects the adaptive needs of the person and a clear statement of the necessary nursing action. Nursing priorities are established by reviewing the judgments and the diagnosis and establishing a timetable for nursing action. Based on her assessment, the adaptation nurse gives precedence to certain nursing actions: the greatest threats to adequacy warrant immediate intervention. Based on her theoretical knowledge and the judgments and diagnosis she has formulated, the adaptation nurse ranks her nursing actions according to the severity and acuteness of the adapting person's needs. Priorities concerning these needs range from emergent to optional.

Judgments

After completing step I of the adaptation nursing process, the nurse evaluates the adapting person's coping stance in relation to the triggering event and the effectiveness of his behavior in maintaining the level of adequacy. This evaluation is reflected in two nursing judgments. The *first judgment defines the person's coping stance and strategies*. In addition, it *identifies the congruence between coping behaviors and the environment* and summarizes the type of coping behavior the nurse sees in relation to a particular triggering event. The *second judgment defines the threat to the level of adequacy*. This judgment *identifies the effectiveness of the behavioral response* in maintaining the level of adequacy. In other words, the adaptation nurse summarizes her behavioral observations and identifies them as effective or ineffective in relation to the focal stimuli.

Before examining the judgment process in detail, it seems important to review the regulator/cognator process briefly. From Chapter 1 the reader will recall that the regulator has three functions: to stimulate the protective behaviors associated with physiological readiness; to activate the second stage of the body's defense system when the triggering event is physical, chemical, or infectious; and to alert the cognator of the need for action. The cognator then processes the triggering event and selects the most appropriate coping stance and strategies. The cognator does not, however, effect the physiological behavioral response. The cognator helps the adapting person to terminate the triggering event by preparing for or seeking outside help. This preparatory or help-seeking behavior is expressed in the role performance mode. For this reason, when examining the physiological mode, the cognator process is not considered but deferred to the role performance mode. Therefore, the adaptation nurse does not formulate two judgments, but formulates only the first judgment reflecting the relationship between the physiological behavioral response and adequacy. Assuredly there are physiological mechanisms that are equivalent to the cognator function, but a discussion of these is beyond the scope of this text. Therefore, in subsequent case studies the adaptation nurse will formulate one judgment in the physiological mode and two judgments in the role performance, self-concept, and interdependence modes. Analyzing the case study of Carol Mackie, we will use data collection to formulate a nursing judgment for each mode.

Case study

Physiological mode. In the physiological mode the data collection revealed that Carol's level of physiological adequacy has been disrupted. She has pain and decreased mobility and is losing sleep as a result of her recent surgery and the application of a full leg cast. Using the previously stated criteria, the *first judgment* would be as follows: *Carol's lack of sleep and hesitancy to move about will not effectively maintain physiological adequacy in the musculoskeletal category*. A second judgment is not formulated here. The reader is referred to the section on judgments in the role performance mode, where Carol's coping behaviors will be examined in the client role. The judgment for the physiological mode simply states whether the automatic physiological behavior instituted by the regulator is decreasing, maintaining, or increasing adequacy. Let us continue to examine the process in the self-concept mode.

Self-concept mode. Again the nurse examines meaningful clusters of behavior and stimuli and formulates two nursing judgments. The cluster reveals that there is a disruption in Carol's level of psychological adequacy: she has changed her activity pattern as a result of her surgery and the full leg cast. The *first judgment* would read as follows: *Carol is using compromise and self-enhancement to cope with the threat to her body image posed by her surgery and resultant disability*. The *second judgment* would be stated as follows: *Carol's verbalizations of areas of inadequacy do not maintain her positive body image*. The two judgments identify Carol's coping stance, the relationship to the triggering event, and the effectiveness of the behavioral response.

Role performance mode. In reviewing Carol's role behavior and influencing stimuli, the nurse sees a meaningful cluster of behaviors that indicate that Carol is having difficulty with her role as a client. The *first judgment* would read *Carol is using compromise to deal with the conflict between her positive body image and the expectation that she behave as an injured person*. The *second judgment* would read *Carol's impatience with discharge and her minimal compliance with ambulation restrictions will not maintain her client role performance*. Again the coping stance is examined; the relationship to the triggering event is identified; and the effectiveness of the behavioral response is stated.

Interdependence mode. The behavioral cluster and the influencing stimuli reflect that Carol is maintaining her affectional adequacy. The *first judgment* would state the following: *Carol is using compromise and self-enhancement to maintain and enhance her relationships with others*. The *second judgment* would be *Carol is successfully giving and receiving love and support in her spiritual, wife, and client roles*. Again the coping stance is identified, the relationship to the triggering event is stated, and the effectiveness of the behavioral response is defined.

In summary, nursing judgments are made by grouping collections of behaviors and stimuli in a meaningful way. These judgments serve two purposes. First, they clearly define the relationship among behavioral response, coping stance, and the environment. Secondly, they clearly prescribe the goal of nursing intervention. The pieces of the puzzle are beginning to fall into meaningful patterns.

Diagnostic categories

Three major diagnostic categories can exist when the judgments are examined. The categories of nursing diagnosis reflect the degree of disruption in the level of adequacy and the quantity and quality of nursing intervention required. Assignment to a diagnostic category is based on the congruence between the behavioral response and the triggering event. This congruence is determined in a slightly different way when examining the physiological mode. Therefore, the process of determining diagnostic categories will be discussed as it relates to the physiological mode and then as it relates to the psychological and sociological modes.

In the physiological mode the judgment indicates that the person is decreasing, maintaining, or increasing the level of adequacy. The adapting person is experiencing either adequacy or inadequacy. A judgment that reflects adequacy qualifies the adapting person to be classified in the first diagnostic category. A judgment that reflects inadequacy qualifies the adapting person to be classified in the third diagnostic category. The adapting person's physiological status is considered in absolute terms: his physiological behavior is either adequate or inadequate; there is no in-between status as represented by the second diagnostic category in the other modes. This classification has relevance for nursing action, because it clearly identifies whether the person requires physiological assistance. If the judgment reflects adequacy, the person is considered to be in the first diagnostic category and therefore requires no outside assistance from the health care system in this mode. If the judgment reflects inadequacy, the person is considered to be in the third diagnostic category and therefore requires outside assistance from the health care system in this mode.

In the psychological and sociological modes (self-concept, role performance, and interdependence), diagnostic categories are assigned based on the relationship between the two judgments. In particular, *clusters of behavior and stimuli* are said to *reflect the first diagnostic category when the two judgments are congruent*. The adapting person's behavioral response is successfully maintaining adequacy, and the coping stance and strategies are congruent with the triggering event. As is the case in the physiological mode, this diagnostic category indicates that the person is functioning adequately and therefore does not require assistance from the health care system.

The adapting person can be said to be in the *second diagnostic category* when the first judgment indicates congruence between the coping stance and strategies and the triggering event but the second judgment indicates that the person is experiencing a decline in the level of adequacy. Assessment reveals that the adapting person has made an accurate evaluation of the circumstances but has chosen a behavioral response that is quantitatively or qualitatively unable to maintain the level of adequacy. This diagnostic category indicates that the adapting person requires some assistance from the health care system. Additionally, it indicates that the person is capable of participating actively in his own care.

Finally, an adapting person can be considered to be in the *third diagnostic category* when there is *lack of congruence in both judgments*. This category indicates that the behavioral response is ineffective in maintaining adequacy and that the coping stance and strategies are incongruent with the triggering event. This assessment reveals that the person has interpreted the environment incorrectly, and as a result his behavioral response is ineffective. The adapting person in this category needs extensive assistance from the health care system.

To summarize, the three diagnostic categories include the following.

CATEGORY I

Physiological mode
   Judgment I—Behavioral response is effective in maintaining adequacy.
Self-concept, role performance, and interdependence modes
   Judgment I—Coping stance and strategies are congruent with the triggering event and
      influencing stimuli.
   Judgment II—Behavioral response is effective in maintaining the level of adequacy.

CATEGORY II

Physiological mode—There is no physiological judgment or diagnosis in this category.
Self-concept, role performance, and interdependence modes
   Judgment I—Coping stance and strategies are congruent with the triggering event and
      influencing stimuli.
   Judgment II—Behavioral response is ineffective in maintaining the level of adequacy.

CATEGORY III

Physiological mode
   Judgment I—Behavioral response is ineffective in maintaining the level of adequacy.
Self-concept, role performance, and interdependence modes
   Judgment I—Coping stance and strategies are incongruent with the triggering event
      and influencing stimuli.
   Judgment II—Behavioral response is ineffective in maintaining the level of adequacy.

Case study

Physiological mode. In the physiological mode Carol is having pain and difficulty sleeping and walking. Carol's behavior does not maintain her level of phsyiological adequacy. *In the physiological mode, then, Carol falls into the third diagnostic category. The behavioral output is misdirected and will not maintain Carol's sense of physiological adequacy.*

Self-concept mode. In the self-concept mode Carol is experiencing a threat to her body image. As she learns to walk on crutches, she thinks and talks about all the changes she must make in her usual life-style. She is using compromise as a coping stance, which is an appropriate response to the threat of a 6-week immobilization for an extremely active young woman. Carol's behavior is only partially effective in maintaining her level of physiological adequacy. *In the self-concept mode Carol falls into the second diagnostic category. Her regulator and cognator have appropriately processed the triggering event and have chosen an appropriate coping stance. Her behavioral output, however, is contributing to the disruption she is experiencing in this mode.*

Role performance mode. In the role performance mode Carol is having difficulty taking on the role of client. Her healthy body image is making it difficult for her to accept her immobilization; she is using suppression to cope with the threat to her healthy body image. Her difficulty assuming the client role is interfering with her ability to maintain adequacy in this role performance mode. *In the role performance* *mode Carol again falls into the second diagnostic category. Her regulator and cognator have correctly assessed the situation, but her behavioral response is not sufficient to maintain sociological adequacy.*

Interdependence mode. Finally, in the interdependence mode Carol's behavior is effectively maintaining her level of social adequacy. She has Jeff to provide nurturance and support, and she is able to nurture and support Jeff in return. In addition, Carol is receiving phone calls from significant others and is utilizing her religion as a source of support. Suppressing parts of her experience, she is also using manipulation to make her hospitalization a self-enhancing experience. As a result, she is coping very effectively with the threat hospitalization poses to her new marriage and her other significant relationships. *In the interdependence mode Carol's behavior is indicative of the first diagnostic category. Her regulator and cognator have appropriately assessed the triggering event and selected a very effective coping stance. Her behavioral response is highly effective in maintaining her level of social adequacy.*

In summary, then, the adaptation nurse implements step II of the adaptation nursing process by formulating one or two judgments regarding the data she has categorized in step I. In the physiological mode she uses the judgment regarding the adapting person's level of adequacy to determine whether the person is in diagnostic category I or III. In the self-concept, role performance, and interdependence modes the judgments reflect the relationship between the coping stance and the triggering event as well as the effectiveness of the behavioral response in maintaining or enhancing the level of adequacy. Based on these judgments the adaptation nurse identifies one of three diagnostic categories that represents the level of congruence between the judgments as well as the health care needs of the person. The process of making judgments and assigning judgments to diagnostic categories represents the internal thought processes of the adaptation nurse. Once she has completed these internal processes, she must be able to make a diagnostic statement that she can share with other caregivers. This statement is commonly called the nursing diagnosis.

Nursing diagnosis

In adaptation nursing the diagnosis is a statement showing the relationship between the adapting person's coping behavior and the level of adequacy. *The diagnosis clearly defines the level of adequacy, labeling it as maintained, enhanced, disrupted, or decreased, and identifies the major coping behavior affecting the level of adequacy.* The behavioral statement labels the area where intervention will be most helpful and becomes a focus for nursing action. The nursing diagnosis is a summary statement of all the internal work the nurse accomplishes in step II.

You will recall that Carol Mackie's behavior in the physiological mode was classified in the third diagnostic category; her behavior in the self-concept and role performance modes was classified in the second diagnostic category; and her behavior in the interdependence mode was classified in the first diagnostic category. In formulating the nursing diagnosis and transcribing these judgments, it is helpful to use significant words that reflect the diagnostic categories so that other caregivers can understand the diagnosis. The first diagnostic category represents *maintenance or enhancement* of adequacy; the second diagnostic category represents a *disruption* in the level of adequacy; and the third diagnostic category represents a *decrease* in the level of adequacy. Using Carol's diagnostic categories, let us write a nursing diagnosis for the four modes.

Case study

Physiological mode. In the physiological mode Carol's behaviors do not maintain her level of adequacy. She is therefore assigned to the third diagnostic category. A *nursing diagnosis for the physiological mode* that reflects the data collection and the judgments, and the diagnostic category would read as follows: [sleep activity, decreased physiological adequacy; pain]. *Carol is experiencing a decrease in her level of physiological adequacy and a deficit in the musculoskeletal category by limiting her activities and sleep periods in an attempt to cope with the pain and immobilization associated with the surgical repair of her ligament and the application of a full leg cast.* The diagnosis defines the effect of the behavioral response on the level of adequacy. It identifies the threat to the adapting person and the focus of nursing action.

Self-concept mode. In the self-concept mode Carol's regulator and cognator have correctly assessed the triggering event and have selected compromise and self-enhancement as coping strategies. The behavioral response, however, is not maintaining Carol's level of adequacy. Her self-concept behavior can therefore be classified in the second diagnostic category. A *nursing diagnosis for Carol's self-concept mode* that reflects the data collection, the judgments, and the diagnostic category is as follows: [body image, disrupted psychological adequacy: full leg cast for 6 weeks]. *Carol is experiencing a disruption in her level of psychological adequacy and a change in her body image; verbalizations about her level of inadequacy are not helping her cope with the threat posed by 6 weeks in a full leg cast.* The diagnosis defines the effect of the behavioral response on the adequacy and identifies the threat to the adapting person. In addition, the focus of nursing action is defined; in this case, the nurse will help Carol select behaviors compatible with her healthy body image and the restrictions imposed by her leg cast.

Role performance mode. In the role performance mode Carol's regulator and cognator have correctly assessed the triggering event and have selected compromise as an appropriate coping stance. Her behavior, however, is not successful in allowing her to assume the client role. Carol's role performance is appropriately classified in the second diagnostic category. A *nursing diagnosis for Carol's role performance mode* that reflects the data collection, the judgments, and the diagnostic category would read as follows: [instrumental client and athletic role conflict, disrupted social adequacy: previous positive body image and athletic success]. *Carol is experiencing a disruption in her level of social adequacy and a client role conflict by refusing to comply with the limitations on her activities as an attempt to maintain her healthy body image*. The diagnosis defines the effect of the behavioral response on the level of adequacy and identifies the threat the adapting person is experiencing. In addition, the focus of nursing action is defined. In the role performance mode the nurse needs to help Carol select behaviors that will help her comply with the medical regimen while maintaining her healthy body image.

Interdependence mode. The behavior Carol has selected is effectively maintaining and enhancinig her level of social adequacy. Carol's interdependence behaviors can then be appropriately categorized in the first diagnostic category. A *nursing diagnosis for Carol's interdependence mode* that reflects the data collection, the judgments, and the diagnostic category would read as follows: expressive wife role enhances social adequacy: husband shows receptive and contributive behavior. Expressive client role enhances social adequacy: caregiver is receptive and contributive. Expressive spiritual role enhances social adequacy: belief. *Carol is enhancing her level of social adequacy and is both receiving and giving love and support by engaging in emotional, self-gratifying behavior in her wife, spiritual, and client roles*. The diagnosis again defines the effect of the behavioral response on the level of adequacy and identifies the threat to the adapting person. In addition, the focus of nursing action is identified. As is usually the case in the first diagnostic category, the nurse will support Carol's self-enhancing behaviors.

In summary, then, the adaptation nurse formulates a nursing diagnosis that reflects the data collection, the nursing judgments, and the diagnostic category. When the nurse has formulated these diagnoses, she has defined the level of adequacy, the threat to the adapting person, and the focus of nursing action. Having identified several threats and multiple directions for nursing action, the adaptation nurse must rank these diagnoses in relation to their priority.

Priority setting

The adaptation nurse must be constantly vigilant, making critical decisions regarding the timing of her interactions with the adapting person. Priority setting is an ongoing process that the nurse engages in throughout the assessment. It helps the adaptation nurse decide which behavioral response to attend to, which influencing stimuli to pursue, and when to interact with the adapting person. Priority setting assumes the greatest significance following the nurse's formulation of the nursing diagnosis. Because there are four modes or channels for energy response, the nurse must formulate a minimum of four diagnoses. She must then rank these diagnoses according to the priority for action. Adaptation nurses base their priorities on the degree of threat to the level of adequacy in each mode and on the relationship between the diagnoses. The adaptation nurse wants to intervene quickly in situations posing a major threat to the adapting person's survival. In addition, she wants her interventions to be effective and expedient; therefore, she examines the relationship between all of the diagnoses.

Priority setting in an emergent situation is based on a review of the diagnostic categories. Any diagnosis that is included in the third diagnostic category is given priority. This category implies a severe threat to the peron's survival in at least one of the four modes. The behavioral response is not maintaining the level of adequacy because the regulator and the cognator have failed to process the environment and the triggering event effectively or because the regulator's automatic physiological response was ineffective. The adapting person almost totally depends on the adaptation nurse to maintain the level of adequacy. Usually second diagnostic category threats will be handled next, because they represent inadequate coping behavior. Should the adaptation nurse fail to interact with a client adapting at this level, the client may progress to the third category, where the threat increases. Finally, the adaptation nurse focuses on diagnoses that fall into the first category. These interactions involve support and teaching. The adaptation nurse's effectiveness in these categories is greatly decreased unless she first deals with the more disruptive areas.

In summary, a diagnosis in the third diagnostic category represents an emergent situation and requires immediate action. The second priority should be given to diagnoses that fall in the second category to prevent progression to a less functional level. Finally, the nurse deals with diagnoses in the first category.

In addition to the emergent needs of the adapting person, the nurse sets priorities based on the relationship between the modes. Frequently, a client will have several diagnoses that are in the second category. The adaptation nurse reviews the relationship between the behavioral response and the influencing stimuli, especially the focal stimuli, of each mode. Very often she will find that the coping strategy or the declining level of adequacy in one mode is the focal stimulus for another mode. Or she might discover that the person's physiological condition, which will remain unchanged for some time, is a contextual stimulus in several modes. By examining these relationships, the adaptation nurse and the client can identify which behavioral responses should be focused on and which sequence the intervention should follow. We will examine these criteria for priority setting by reviewing the nursing diagnosis formulated for Carol Mackie.

Case study. As you recall, Carol had one diagnosis in each mode. In the interdependence mode she is enhancing her level of affectional adequacy. She is coping effectively; the nursing diagnosis indicates she is in the first category. In the self-concept and role performance modes Carol's regulator and cognator have correctly processed her experience, but her behavioral response is not maintaining the level of adequacy. And finally, in the physiological mode Carol is in the third diagnostic category. Since the third diagnostic category calls for immediate action, the adaptation nurse would first identify that she must assist Carol to meet her physiological needs. If Carol could have an adequate amount of sleep and more consistent relief of pain, she would then be more prepared to deal with the disruptions in the other modes. Once Carol and the adaptation nurse are satisfied that more adequate physiological functioning is assured, they can then focus on the two diagnoses of the second diagnostic category. This examination reveals that her cast and the resultant limitations on her activity cannot be changed significantly for the next 6 weeks. In addition, it is obvious that these physical limitations are affecting Carol's body image, which in turn influences Carol's ability to take on the client role. Given these relationships, the adaptation nurse identifies that if she interacts with Carol regarding her body image, she will also have an impact on Carol's behavioral response in the role performance mode. The priority for Carol then becomes nursing action to be taken in the self-concept mode.

Simultaneously, the adaptation nurse reinforces Carol's recipient and contributive behaviors in her spiritual, client, and spouse roles and utilizes Carol and Jeff's relationship to facilitate maintenance of adaptation in the interdependence mode.

Summary

The adaptation nurse sets priorities by reviewing each diagnosis and evaluating it based on the diagnostic category and the relationship that exists between the diagnoses. Priorities allow the adaptation nurse to time her interactions so that they optimally maintain or enhance the client's level of adequacy.

Step II of the adaptation nursing process involves the formulation of judgments, diagnostic categorization, formulation of a nursing diagnosis, and priority setting. These activities complete the puzzle. In step II the adaptation nurse clearly expresses her understanding of the person's interaction with the environment. She has gathered the puzzle pieces into meaningful groups and assembled those groups; and she finally uses the nursing diagnosis to complete the puzzle, thus concluding step II.

Having defined much of the work that occurs in step II as an internal process engaged in by the adaptation nurse, it seems important to identify the significance of the adaptation nurse, especially in step II of the process. As each adapting person is unique, so is each adaptation nurse. The nurse's own internal state, especially her maturational level and perceptions, greatly influences how she classifies behavior and influencing factors in step I and is especially significant in the judgments and diagnoses formulated in step II. Although the adaptation nurse shares with her peers a common body of theoretical knowledge and nursing skills, she utilizes them in a manner that is uniquely her own. The nurse's own experience, beliefs, attitudes, ideas, developmental stage, and personal stress significantly influence the judgment and diagnostic process. As a result, the assessment reflects the uniqueness of the adapting person as well as the uniqueness of the adaptation nurse. As has been demonstrated in the preceding assessment, the adaptation nurse working with Carol Mackie is an experienced nurse. The following discussion of the goals, intervention, and evaluation will further demonstrate not only the nurse's adaptation skills but also the adaptation nurse's level of experience, clinical expertise, and maturation.

The adaptation nurse and the adapting person combine the efforts of their unique internal processes to solve the puzzle, thus clearly defining the person's adaptation needs. Having arrived at a solution, they are ready to begin step III of the adaptation nursing process. In step III we will examine goal setting, nursing intervention, and the formulation of evaluation criteria. One should first review the objectives and essential terms associated with this final step (see p. 43).

STEP III: INTERVENTION AND EVALUATION

In step III of the adaptation nursing process the nurse uses the diagnostic categories and the nursing diagnosis to interact with the person. Through this interaction goals are set; interventions are defined and implemented; and an evaluation is made of the change in the level of adequacy. To understand step III the components and their interrelationship will be reviewed.

Goal setting

The goal of the adaptation nurse is to interact with the adapting person so that he can maintain or enhance the level of adequacy—in a word, adapt. Utilizing this goal to guide her actions, the nurse helps the person formulate goals. The three diagnostic categories represent a progression from adequacy to a major decrease in the level of adequacy. Because adequacy is the goal the person constantly strives to attain, the overall goal of the adapting person is to have all category I diagnoses. Goals then can be stated progressively. A person whose behavior falls into the first diagnostic category would wish to maintain or enhance his current coping stance and behavioral response as these factors relate to triggering events and influencing stimuli. A person whose behavior is classified in the second diagnostic category would wish to increase the effectiveness of his behavioral response while maintaining or enhancing his coping stance. A person whose behavior is classified in the third category would wish to alter his perception of or input from the environment so that he might select a more appropriate coping stance and consequently engage in more effective behavior.

The goal of the adapting person, then, is to move in a stepwise fashion from inadequacy or disrupted adequacy to adequacy or a status of enhanced adequacy. The adaptation nurse acts with the person in their shared environment in a manner that will allow the person to make this step-by-step movement to the first diagnostic category as effectively as possible.

To accomplish this task, the nurse and the person must formulate a *goal statement that reflects the changes in coping stance and behaviors necessary for the adapting person to move toward a more adaptive diagnostic category. The goal statement should also reflect the triggering event or significant influencing stimuli.* It should be stated to reflect the step-by-step progression; it is unrealistic to suppose that a person whose behavior is indicative of a diagnostic category III would be able to move immediately to behavior indicative of a diagnostic category I. Therefore, the goal would be to assist the person to move toward a more adaptive diagnostic category.

To move from category III to category II would involve the person's reprocessing the triggering event with the result that the regulator and cognator select an alternative coping stance. A change in the quantity or quality of the behavioral response would be essential for movement from category II to category I. Finally, maintaining or enhancing the person's functioning in category I would involve maintenance of current coping and behavior as well as anticipation of future changes in influencing stimuli. As previously stated, changes in behavioral response and movement in a positive direction are direct results of changes in the adapting person's environment or internal state. The influencing stimuli must be manipulated during the interaction between the nurse and the client if the client is to move toward a more adaptive behavioral response. The goal of the adapting person is to maintain or enhance the level of adequacy in all four modes. The goal of the adaptation nurse, then, is to interact with the adapting person so that stimuli are altered or manipulated and adaptation occurs. Let us formulate a goal for each of the four modes.

Case study

Physiological goal. In the physiological mode Carol's behavior was classified in the third diagnostic category. The goal would then be for her to move in a positive direction toward category I behaviors. Carol's nursing diagnosis in the physiological mode stated that Carol's level of physiological adequacy has been disrupted and that she is deficient in her need for exercise and rest because she is limiting her activities and periods of sleep following the surgical repair and casting of a ligament in her right leg. Combining this diagnosis with an understanding of the meaning of diagnostic category III, the goal to assist Carol in increasing her level of adequacy would be stated in this way: *Carol will increase her level of physiological adequacy by engaging in the required ambulation and sleeping 7 hours per night during this immediate postoperative period*. The goal is a clear statement of the behaviors in which Carol must engage to increase her level of adequacy. In this instance, Carol's behavioral response is of insufficient quantity. The nurse must then interact with Carol to increase her behavioral response.

Self-concept goal. In the self-concept mode Carol's behavior was classified in the second diagnostic category. The goal she wishes to attain then is to move toward category I behaviors. The diagnosis in the self-concept mode reads as follows: "Carol is experiencing a disruption in her level of psychological adequacy and a change in her body image because she is verbalizing her areas of inadequacy in an attempt to cope with the threat posed by 6 weeks in a full leg cast." Combining this diagnosis with knowledge of the meaning of diagnostic category II, the goal to assist Carol in increasing her level of adequacy would be stated in this way: *Carol will increase her* *level of psychological adequacy and return to her positive body image by practicing those skills and activities in which she will be able to engage despite her leg cast.* In the self-concept mode Carol's cognator and regulator have made a correct assessment, and the coping stance is appropriate. Carol's behavioral response is having an opposite effect; therefore, the nurse must interact with Carol so that she can increase the quality of her response, both verbally and physically.

   Role performance goal. Again, as in the previous mode, Carol's behavior warrants classification in the second diagnostic category. She then wishes to alter her role behavior to move toward the first diagnostic category. Carol's diagnosis in the role performance mode stated that her level of social adequacy has been disrupted and that she is experiencing client role conflict by refusing to comply with the limitations to her activities in an attempt to maintain her positive body image. A combination of this diagnosis and knowledge of the second diagnostic category results in the following goal statement: *Carol will increase her level of social adequacy and perform the client role effectively by engaging in prescribed activities without further decreasing her body image.* Again, Carol's regulator and cognator have correctly assessed the threat and have selected an appropriate coping stance. The behavioral response is ineffective in maintaining Carol's sense of adequacy. The adaptation nurse needs to interact with her so that Carol can increase both the quantity and the quality of her behavioral response in this mode. Carol needs to select behaviors that will allow her body to perform optimally within the restrictions imposed by her physical condition.

   Interdependence goal. In the interdependence mode Carol's coping stance and behavioral responses were congruent with the triggering event. As a result, Carol was able to enhance her social adequacy, and her behavior was classified in the first diagnostic category. Her goal, then, is based on her desire to maintain this high level of functioning. Carol's diagnosis in the role performance mode stated that she is enhancing her level of social adequacy and is both giving and receiving love and support by engaging in spiritual, wife, and client expressive role behaviors. Utilizing this diagnosis and an understanding of the first diagnostic category, the goal for Carol's interdependence behavior would be stated as follows: *Carol will continue to enhance her level of social adequacy by continuing to spend time with Jeff, maintaining phone contact with her family, and expressing her religious beliefs.* The cognator and regulator have acted effectively, and Carol's behavior is enhancing her level of adequacy. The nurse needs to support Carol's efforts to engage in positive social behaviors.

   Summary. In conclusion, goal setting is accomplished by combining the nursing diagnosis with a knowledge of the diagnostic category. The goal is based on the assumption that the adapting person constantly strives for adequacy and therefore wishes to move in a positive direction toward the first diagnostic category. The adaptation goal is a statement of the desired change in level of adequacy and the necessary behavioral response to achieve this change. Once the goal is written, it is a prescriptive statement for the puzzle that will represent the adaptation nurse's interaction with the adapting person. The nurse assembles this puzzle via planned intervention.

Nursing intervention

As was suggested earlier, the type of nursing action required by the adapting person is influenced by the diagnostic category the person's behavior exemplifies. If a client is in the first diagnostic category, the role of the adaptation nurse is minimal. She is present in the adapting person's environment and can assist the person, if that is his desire. Often persons in the first diagnostic category want assistance in the realm of education or in anticipation of future triggering events. As a result, the client in this category may require the skills of an advanced practitioner. With a client in the second diagnostic category, the nurse and the adapting person form a partnership to facilitate adaptation. Finally, when the client is in the third diagnostic category, the nurse assumes major responsibility for the person's adaptation.

If the goal of the adapting person is to move in a positive direction toward the first diagnostic category, then when a person is in the third diagnostic category, the nurse assumes responsibility for moving the person to the second category. If the diagnosis indicates that the person is in the second category, both collaborate to move the person to the first diagnostic category. Finally, when the person has reached the first diagnostic category, he strives to maintain or enhance the level of adequacy with assistance from the adaptation nurse as he feels necessary.

Diagnostic category I

GOAL

Maintain or enhance current level of adequacy.

OUTCOME

Remain in category I diagnosis (adaptation).

Diagnostic category II

GOAL

Increase effectiveness of behavioral response. Maintain or enhance coping stance.

OUTCOME

Achieve category I diagnosis (adaptation).

Diagnostic category III

GOAL

Achieve awareness. Reprocess the triggering event and influencing stimuli. Select an appropriate coping stance and strategy.

OUTCOME

Achieve category II diagnosis.

The adaptation nurse and the adapting person interact within the shared environment to maintain or enhance the person's level of adequacy.

For the person to move from one diagnostic category to the next, the nurse must use certain methods of intervention that will increase the effectiveness of the action. These methods all serve one general purpose: to increase the person's level of adequacy by manipulating the stimuli that affect the person's behavior. In adaptation nursing there are four classifications of intervention that the adaptation nurse uses to interact with the adapting person: collaboration, support, teaching, and enabling. These terms are used widely in nursing literature and have a variety of meanings. In adaptation nursing each of these terms refers to a particular set of actions and skills the nurse must utilize when interacting with the adapting person. *Collaboration* refers to all the behaviors the adaptation nurse exhibits in cooperation with other caregivers for the purpose of *maintaining the person's physiological adequacy*. *Support* refers to behaviors in which the nurse engages to *approve, sanction or validate* the adaptive behavior of the person. The term *teach* refers to nursing actions and skills utilized to *impart knowledge, information and skill*. Finally, *enabling* refers to the complex set of behaviors in which the nurse engages to *strengthen, maintain, or give power* to the adapting person.

Collaboration. The first intervention utilized by the adaptation nurse is collaboration, which refers to all the activities the nurse engages in as prescribed by the person's medical regimen. These nursing activities include behaviors performed by order of a physician or in support of another discipline's treatment program. The nurse engages in collaborative activities in all diagnostic categories. These activities are extremely limited in the first diagnostic category but include all medical aspects of the physical examination or well client care. Collaborative nursing care in this category would include procedures considered to be routine in a general examination. In the second diagnostic category collaborative activities include all medical tasks in which the nurse engages to strengthen the person's behavioral response. This might include administering medication, monitoring intravenous infusions, changing dressings, and performing the other physiological procedures associated with medical management of the adapting person. In the third diagnostic category the nurse assumes her most active collaborative role. The person is responding least effectively to the triggering event and is experiencing a decrease in adequacy. Collaborative activities include emergency measures, surgical interventions, monitoring procedures, and the activities included in the first and second categories. The skills and knowledge essential for the adaptation nurse to fulfill this collaborative function include areas of content and practice associated with pathophysiology and medical procedures. Obviously, the examples of intervention in this section are not exhaustive but represent those types of collaborative activities associated with each diagnostic category.

Support. Support as a nursing intervention is used primarily with the first and second diagnostic categories. The nurse gives the adapting person feedback from the environment about the adequacy of his coping stance and strategies and the effectiveness of his behavioral response. The adaptation nurse acts as a source of information regarding the adapting person's level of adequacy. In a category I diagnosis the person has experienced a series of triggering events; the regulator and the cognator have selected a coping pattern; and the person has behaviorally implemented the internal recommendation. This behavioral response produces another triggering event, which the person processes as a source of feedback, thus resulting in a return to adequacy. As part of the person's environment, the adaptation nurse functions as a source of validation. She sanctions and approves behaviors that successfully maintain adequacy, using eye contact, touch, positive statements, and body posture to support the adapting person in diagnostic categories I and II. Support as defined here is seldom used with the person having a category III diagnosis. The level of adequacy in this category is so severely threatened that the nurse utilizes more aggressive interventions.

Teaching. Teaching, like support, is an intervention used in categories I and II diagnoses. The adaptation nurse provides the adapting person with knowledge, information, and skills. When interacting with the environment, the person often needs additional information or skills to cope effectively with a triggering event. The nurse uses teaching skills and learning principles to impart knowledge essential to the function of the cognator. The nurse does anticipatory teaching with the person in the first diagnostic category. Information and skills are provided in anticipation of a change in the level of adequacy or at the person's request. With the second diagnostic category the nurse does anticipatory teaching as well as provide information and skills necessary for the person to cope with an immediate triggering event. Teaching may serve to increase the effectiveness of a behavioral response or assist the cognator in selecting the most appropriate coping stance. Teaching provides the person with essential information necessary for effective manipulation of the environment and the internal stimuli. In teaching, the nurse must assess the person's readiness for learning, the areas of knowledge or skill deficit, and the best learning method for the person. Based on this assessment, she provides him with the information, knowledge, and skills esssential to the maintenance or enhancement of his level of adequacy. To provide this information the nurse uses a variety of skills including demonstration, positive reinforcement, modeling, and verbalization. The nurse would not use teaching as a method of intervention with a patient in the third diagnostic category, because the disruption in the level of adequacy and the degree of stress are so acute that the conditions for learning do not exist. In this case the nurse must use more active interventions or increase coping before introducing new information or skills.

Enabling. The last and perhaps most frequently utilized adaptive intervention is enabling, which refers to all the nursing activities engaged in for the purpose of increasing the adapting person's functioning. These nursing activities are designed to facilitate, strengthen, and empower. The adaptation nurse engages in enabling actions when assisting the person with behaviors in the second and third diagnostic categories. Enabling activities associated with a category II diagnosis include actions that increase the behavioral response of the person: environmental manipulation, problem-solving, and advocacy behaviors. In the third category the enabling activities are designed to allow the nurse to assume or assist the function of the person's regulator and cognator. She assists the person in responding to the triggering event, altering the coping stance, and implementing a more effective behavioral response. The knowledge and skills utilized by the nurse when performing enabling activities include the therapeutic relationship, counseling strategies, techniques of crisis intervention, and behavior management techniques. Enabling is not utilized with persons in the first diagnostic category because they are maintaining or enhancing their levels of adequacy independently and do not require facilitation, strengthening, or empowering.

When interacting with persons and their environments, adaptation nurses use four types of nursing interventions to manipulate the stimuli: collaboration, support, teaching, and enabling. A person in the first diagnostic category utilizes collaboration, support, and teaching to maintain or enhance the level of adequacy. A person in the second diagnostic category needs support, teaching, collaboration, and enabling to increase the effectiveness of his behavioral response and achieve a diagnosis in the first category. And finally, a person in the third category requires collaboration and enabling to increase awareness of the triggering event, alter the activities of the regulator and the cognator, and achieve a diagnosis in the second category. These relationships are shown diagramatically below.

Diagnostic category I

GOAL	INTERVENTION	OUTCOME
Maintain or enhance current level of adequacy.	1. *Support:* Eye contact, touch, body posture, positive verbal statements.	Maintain category I diagnosis (adaptation).
	2. *Teaching:* Assessment, demonstration, modeling, verbalization, positive reinforcement.	
	3. *Collaboration:* Medical activities, immunization, TPR, B.P.	

Diagnostic category II

GOAL	INTERVENTION	OUTCOME
Increase effectiveness of behavioral response. Maintain or enhance coping stance.	1. *Support:* See above. 2. *Teaching:* See above. 3. *Collaboration:* Administer medication, monitor IV's, dressing changes. 4. *Enabling:* Environmental manipulation, advocacy, and problem solving.	Category I diagnosis (adaptation).

Diagnostic category III

GOAL	INTERVENTION	OUTCOME
Achieve awareness; reprocess triggering event and influencing stimuli. Select a coping stance and strategies.	1. *Collaboration:* Emergency measures, surgical interventions, and monitoring procedures. 2. *Enabling:* Therapeutic relationship, counseling, strategies, crisis intervention, and behavior management.	Category II diagnosis.

Case study

Physiological intervention. Now let us examine the process of nursing intervention by identifying and planning the interventions necessary to assist Carol Mackie with increasing her level of adequacy in all four modes. You will recall that Carol's behavior in the physiological mode was classified in the third diagnostic category. The goal is to move Carol to the first category. The goal statement indicates that Carol needs to engage in the required ambulation and sleep at least 7 hours per night. In assisting Carol in this endeavor the adaptation nurse would use two types of nursing interventions to manipulate the environment and Carol's internal state. The nurse would use *collaboration* by administering desired medication promptly and suggesting that Carol take her pain medication before ambulation as well as 1 hour before bedtime; she also encourages her to use sleep medication at least for the first few nights. The adaptation nurse would also spend time with the physical therapist so that she can reinforce Carol's behavior during additional periods of ambulation. She would *support* Carol's efforts to crutch walk by praising her attempts, maintaining eye contact during these comments, and using touch when discussing the frustration of the inactivity, awkwardness, and exhaustion. Utilizing the two types of nursing intervention, the nurse works as a partner with Carol, allowing her to perform behaviors that maintain and enhance her level of physiological adequacy.

Self-concept intervention. In the self-concept mode Carol's behavior resulted in classification in the second diagnostic category. As a result, Carol's goal was to increase her level of psychological adequacy by moving in a positive direction toward the first diagnostic category. Her goal statement indicates that Carol could gain a more positive body image by discussing and practicing activities that she could engage in while wearing a cast. In assisting Carol in this endeavor, the adaptation nurse would use support, enabling, and teaching to facilitate Carol's adaptation. In this example there are no collaborative actions that would facilitate adaptation. The adaptation nurse would *support* Carol using positive verbal feedback regarding all her skills in the areas of swimming, jogging, and skiing and helping her to recognize that her optimal skill level would be easily regained at the end of the 6-week period. The adaptation nurse could then use *enabling,* utilizing the "therapeutic relationship" to solve problems with Carol and identifying the skills she would be able to engage in despite the cast. Carol would be able to conclude that she could drive her automatic car, attend class at the university with a friend, participate in sport activities as a spectator, and return to work 1 week after her discharge. The nurse could then utilize her *teaching* strategies to help Carol practice the skills necessary to accomplish these tasks. In addition, she might teach Carol to engage in some of her usual exercises without causing pain or damage to her repaired ligament. As Carol begins to assume a more positive attitude and engage in some normal activities, her body image will return to its usual positive state. Keeping in mind these positive changes, we will examine the role performance mode. Recall that Carol's behavior in this mode was predominantly influenced by her threatened body image.

Role performance intervention. As in the previous mode, Carol's behavior warranted classification in the second diagnostic category. Carol's goal, then, is to move to the first diagnostic category by increasing her level of social adequacy. The goal statement indicates that Carol could accomplish this positive outcome by engaging in prescribed client activities for her second postoperative day. To facilitate this activity the adaptation nurse will manipulate influencing stimuli by *teaching* and building on the *support and enabling activities* she initiated in the self-concept mode. Since Carol's major concern seems to be the threat to her body image, her increasing positive regard already facilitated by the nurse will make it easier to alter Carol's client behaviors. Because Carol values her independence and is already practicing new skills, the nurse can teach her to use crutches in the small space of the bathroom and to maneuver in and out of bed without assistance. In addition, the nurse can use *collaborative and teaching skills* to give Carol some control over her discharge. She can help Carol identify the activities that must be accomplished and the skills that must be learned prior to discharge; then she can help Carol problem solve as a means of speeding up this process. After she provides Carol with more information and helps her decrease the threat to her body image, the adaptation nurse will see a rise in the level of Carol's social adequacy. This is an excellent example of the ways in which the modes are interrelated and reminds us that the modes represent channels of energy for the "whole" person and are not easily or clearly segmented.

Interdependence intervention. In the interdependence mode Carol's behavior is enhancing her adequacy and is therefore classified in the first diagnostic category. Carol's goal, then, is to maintain the level of social adequacy at its current level. The goal statement in this case suggests that Carol could accomplish this by continuing to spend time with Jeff, maintaining phone contact with her family, and continuing her spiritual expression and behavior. As previously stated, nursing action activities with persons in the first diagnostic category are limited to support, teaching, and some collaboration. In this situation Carol can use support and some anticipatory teaching. These actions are engaged in to maintain influencing stimuli at the level necessary for optimal performance. The adaptation nurse can *support* Carol's wife role behavior by providing privacy, access to a phone, and optimal use of visiting privileges. In addition, by positive statements about Carol and Jeff's support of each other, the adaptation nurse would help maintain their behavior. Should Carol express an interest, the adaptation nurse might suggest that Carol share her concern about Jeff's job with him so that he can provide her with reassurance and a more realistic evaluation of the threat.

Carol's spiritual and client role behaviors can be facilitated by *support*. The adaptation nurse can provide contact and privacy for prayer, bible reading, and interactions with clergy or Jeff as Carol finds necessary. Additionally, the adaptation nurse can give Carol immediate feedback regarding her client role performance and acknowledge the praise and support Carol offers her. With a supportive environment Carol should have no difficulty in maintaining her level of social adequacy.

To assist the adapting person to move in a positive direction toward the first diagnostic category, the adaptation nurse uses the skills and actions associated with support, teaching, collaboration, and enabling. She interacts with the adapting person to provide an atmosphere for optimal functioning. When interacting with a client in the first category, the nurse utilizes support and teaching. In the second category she employs all four types of interventions with the client. Finally, when transacting with a client in the third diagnostic category, the nurse utilizes collaboration and enabling. Now let us examine the process the adaptation nurse uses to evaluate the outcome of interventions on the person's level of adequacy.

Evaluation

The goal of the adapting person is to strive constantly for an optimal level of adequacy. The goal of adaptation nursing is to interact with the person in a manner that facilitates this adaptation. Therefore, it seems reasonable to evaluate the effectiveness of nursing intervention based on the person's achievement of a higher level of adequacy. The nursing intervention should help the person to move up one diagnostic category. Evaluation criteria can therefore be developed based on the two judgments associated with each diagnostic category.

Evaluation involves a reassessment of the person's behavioral response and the relevant influencing stimuli. The adaptation nurse collects and categorizes this data following the interaction and begins to assemble still another part of the puzzle. When the nurse completes her assessment, a repeat of step I of the adaptation nursing process, she then initiates step II, formulating two judgments. The first identifies the effectiveness of the behavioral response in altering the level and adequacy, and the second reflects the coping stance in relation to the triggering event. These two judgments reflect one of the diagnostic categories. If the nursing intervention has had a positive effect, the reassessment will reveal that the level of adequacy increased, and the person's behavior will be classified according to a more positive diagnostic category.

The evaluation criteria for nursing interventions designed to facilitate adaptation of a person whose behavior is classified in the third diagnostic category would include all behavioral actions and statements that reflect the person's reassessment of the triggering event and the assumption of an appropriate coping stance. For a client whose behavior is classified in the second diagnostic category, the nurse looks for an outcome that indicates that the person has increased the quantity and/or quality of the behavioral response. Finally, a person whose interaction is classified in the first diagnostic category would demonstrate behavioral actions and statements that continue to reflect a congruence between the coping stance and the triggering event and the behavioral response and the level of adequacy.

Case study

Evaluation criteria in the physiological mode. The adaptation nurse interacted with Carol Mackie in the physiological mode to assist Carol to move from the second to the first diagnostic category. Based on the nursing diagnosis, the goal, and intervention, Carol should increase the quantity of her behavioral response in the musculoskeletal category. Therefore, the evaluation criteria would list the behavioral responses that would result in Carol moving to the first diagnostic category. She will need to walk for three 10-minute periods during the day and two 10-minute periods during the evening. For the next 2 days she will take pain medication prior to ambulation and sleep and take her prescribed sleep medicine at bedtime, sleeping at least 7 hours per day. If Carol achieves these behavioral responses, her coping behavior will remain congruent with the triggering event, and her behavioral responses will increase in quantity, thus resulting in the maintenance of her level of physiological adequacy. The evaluation criteria are based on the goal of moving in a positive direction toward the first diagnostic category. We will continue to examine the evaluative process by reviewing the self-concept mode.

Evaluation criteria in the self-concept mode. In the self-concept mode the adaptation nurse interacted with Carol to help her move from the second diagnostic category to the first. Based on the nursing diagnosis, goal, and intervention, Carol would improve the quality of her behavioral response in the area of physical self. Behavioral responses would reflect behavior congruent with psychological adequacy. These behaviors would include Carol's statements about resuming her sports activities at the end of the 6-week period and about the activities she can continue with despite her cast. Carol will request help practicing maneuvering in small places like the bathroom or a car and walking up and down stairs. Carol will also ask her employer about returning to work and discuss with the nurse how she plans to use the season basketball tickets she and Jeff ordered recently. If Carol achieves this level of behavioral response, she will have returned to her usual adaptive body image. The goal is based on moving in a positive direction toward the first diagnostic category. Carol has accomplished this by increasing the quality of her behavioral response.

Evaluation criteria in the role performance mode. Again the nurse has interacted with Carol to help her move from the second diagnostic category to the first. Based on the nursing diagnosis, goal, and intervention, Carol needs to improve the quality of her behavioral response in the client role. She would need to demonstrate client role behavior congruent with social adequacy. These behaviors would include using crutches to walk to the bathroom or chair with no weight bearing on her casted leg. In addition, Carol would verbalize that she will say in the hospital approximately 1 week and will be able to walk for ½ hour at a time, negotiate one flight of stairs, and position herself comfortably in bed and in a chair. Having engaged in these behaviors, Carol will have maintained the congruence between the coping stance and triggering events and increased the quality of her behavioral response so that it will be congruent with her usual level of social adequacy.

Evaluation criteria in the interdependence mode. In the interdependence mode the adaptation nurse has interacted with Carol to provide her with the support necessary for Carol to continue enhancing her level of social adequacy. Carol's goal was to continue to interact with the environment in a manner that would allow her to continue to give and receive support and nurturance. Carol's behavioral responses in this mode resulted in classification in the first diagnostic category. Carol wishes to maintain herself at this level of adequacy. To accomplish this goal Carol needs to continue to spend time with Jeff, maintain phone contact with her family, and pursue her spiritual needs by reading and visiting with the chaplain. In addition, Carol will verbalize her fears about Jeff's job and will receive feedback from Jeff that will give her reassurance. Maintaining this level of behavioral response will result in Carol continuing to enhance her level of social adequacy. She will maintain congruence between the coping stance and the triggering event, and her behavioral responses will be congruent with her desired level of adequacy.

In conclusion, evaluation criteria arise from the nursing diagnosis, goal, and intervention and are based on the person's desire to move in a positive direction toward the first diagnostic category. These criteria are stated in specific behavioral terms and reflect the category that represents adaptation.

Summary

Step III of the adaptation process involves three phases: goal setting, nursing intervention, and evaluation. Again, these components are not unique to adaptation nursing, but the method of implementation employed by the adaptation nurse contributes to the effectiveness and completeness of this process. Goals, interventions, and evaluations are based on the judgments and diagnostic categorization. The adapting person constantly strives for a desired level of adaptation. The adaptation nurse interacts with the adapting person to facilitate the person's attainment of that level of adequacy. The activities engaged in during step III are designed to meet the goal of the adapting person. The nursing care guides we have completed for Carol Mackie are shown below.

NURSING CARE GUIDE—Carol Mackie

PHYSIOLOGICAL MODE

Diagnostic category III

NURSING DIAGNOSIS: Sleep activity, decreased physiological adequacy: pain. Carol is experiencing a disruption in her level of physiological adequacy and is deficient in her need for exercise and rest because she is limiting her activities and periods of sleep following surgical repair and casting of her right leg.

GOAL: Carol will increase her level of physiological adequacy by engaging in the required ambulation and sleeping 7 hours per night during the immediate postoperative period.

INTERVENTION

1. *Collaboration:* Meperidine—50 mg intramuscularly every 4 hours and 1 hour before bedtime. Secobarbital 100 mg orally at bedtime for 3 days.
   Reinforce behaviors recommended by physical therapist whenever Carol walks.

2. *Support:* Praise for crutch walking and discuss the frustration experienced when learning a new skill. Maintain eye contact and use touch.

EVALUATION

1. Crutch walking for three 10-minute periods during the day and two 10-minute periods during the evening.

2. Carol takes meperidine at noon, 4 P.M., and 8 P.M. Carol takes secobarbital at bedtime for 2 days.

NURSING CARE GUIDE—Carol Mackie

SELF-CONCEPT MODE

Diagnostic category II

NURSING DIAGNOSIS: Body image, disrupted psychology adequacy: full leg cast for 6 weeks. Carol is experiencing a disruption in her level of psychological adequacy and a change in her body image by verbalizing her areas of inadequacy in an attempt to cope with the threat posed by 6 weeks in a full leg cast.

GOAL: Carol will increase her level of psychological adequacy and return to her positive body image by expressing the skills and activities she will be able to engage in despite her leg cast.

INTERVENTION

1. *Support:* Provide positive statements regarding Carol's athletic abilities and the fact that she can begin competing again at the end of the 6-week period.
2. *Enabling:* Use the "therapeutic relationship" to solve problems with Carol regarding activities she can continue to engage in and the new skills she will need.
3. *Teaching:* Provide Carol with the knowledge, skill, and opportunity to practice crutch walking on stairs and in small places. Also help her adapt her usual exercise regimen to her temporary limitation.

EVALUATION

1. Carol will continue to talk about her swimming, jogging, and skiing activities. She will also state how swimming can help her get her leg back in shape after the 6-week immobilization.
2. Carol will be able to list activities she can engage in (e.g., school, driving, work).
3. Carol will be able to get into a car, get out of bed, and maneuver a flight of stairs. Carol will be exercising 15 minutes per day prior to discharge.

NURSING CARE GUIDE—Carol Mackie

ROLE PERFORMANCE MODE

Diagnostic category II

NURSING DIAGNOSIS: Instrumental client and athletic role conflict, disrupted social adequacy: previous positive body image and athletic success. Carol is experiencing a disruption in her level of social adequacy and a client role conflict by refusing to comply with the limitations on her activities in an attempt to maintain her healthy body image despite her injury.

GOAL: Carol will increase her level of social adequacy and perform the client role effectively by engaging in prescribed activities without further decreasing her body image.

INTERVENTION

1. *Support:* Provide positive statements of Carol's increasing skills. Use eye contact and smiling.

2. *Collaboration and teaching:* Facilitate Carol's discussing her discharge plans with her physician. Provide Carol with the knowledge and skills to negotiate for a discharge date. Carol's request will be based on her progress as opposed to the desire to be home at any cost.

3. *Enabling:* Use therapeutic relationship with Carol, utilizing her competitive and athletic orientation, to motivate her to attempt the challenge of crutch walking.

4. *Teach:* Provide Carol with the knowledge and skill to practice crutch walking to the bathroom and reposition herself.

EVALUATION

1. Carol will continue to master new skills—repositioning and crutch walking.

2. Carol will accept her discharge date of 1 week and will work to learn the essential tasks (e.g., maneuvering stairs, ½-hour periods of ambulation, and positioning herself comfortably in bed and a chair.)

3. Carol states that she will "conquer these crutches." Asks questions of physical therapist and nurse.

4. Carol can reposition herself during the night and uses crutches to walk to the bathroom twice during the night.

NURSING CARE GUIDE—Carol Mackie

INTERDEPENDENCE MODE

Diagnostic category I

NURSING DIAGNOSIS: Expressive wife role, enhance social adequacy: husband shows receptive and contributive behavior. Expressive client role, enhance social adequacy: caregiver shows receptive and contributive behavior. Expressive spiritual role, enhance social adequacy: belief. Carol is enhancing her level of social adequacy and is receiving and giving love and support by engaging in wife, spiritual, and client role behavior, both as a recipient and a provider.

GOAL: Carol will continue to enhance her level of social adequacy by spending time with Jeff, maintaining phone contact with her family, and expressing her religious beliefs.

INTERVENTION

1. *Support:* Provide positive feedback to Carol regarding her nurturing, supportive behaviors with Jeff and her family. Reinforce Carol's ability to accept help from Jeff and her caregivers. Use touch and eye contact. Provide privacy for Carol (e.g., door shut, curtains drawn, a phone).

EVALUATION

1. Carol spends 10 hours per day with Jeff, and they share all meals. Carol continues to ask for help from Jeff and her caregivers.
   Carol calls her family daily and speaks for 15 minutes.
   Carol has seen the chaplain twice.

INTERVENTION

2. *Teaching:* Point out that Carol's stress can be reduced if she shares her concern about Jeff's job with him. Knowing the true ramifications of Jeff's extended stay will help her find an alternative if the threat is real.

EVALUATION

2. Carol asked Jeff about his job. Together they called his boss, who granted Jeff an additional leave.

CONCLUSION

In this chapter the adaptation nursing process has been described as process with three steps: data collection, judgment and diagnosis, and intervention and evaluation. Having completed this chapter, you should be able to describe and implement the phases of the nursing process inherent in each step of the adaptation nursing process.

When confronted with an adapting person interacting with the environment, you, as an adaptation nurse, should be able to solve and assemble the puzzle that represents the person's interactions with yourself and the environment. In step I you will be able to categorize behavioral responses and influencing stimuli according to the four modes. In step II you will be able to complete the internal process necessary to formulate judgments, assign these judgments to the appropriate diagnostic categories, formulate nursing diagnoses, and set priorities. Finally, in step III you will be able to interact with the adapting person by assisting in goal setting, intervention, and evaluation. As an adaptation nurse you can demonstrate your understanding and skills in the adaptation nursing process by completing the following exercises.

LEARNING EXPERIENCE

1 Describe your understanding of the following concepts.
  a Step I
    1. Adaptive mode
    2. Focal stimuli
  b Step II
    1. Nursing judgments
    2. Nursing diagnosis
    3. Priority setting
  c Step III
    1. Intervention
    2. Evaluation
2 List the four modes and describe the components of each.
3 List the three types of stimuli and describe their relationship to each other.

4 List and describe the three steps of the adaptation nursing process.
5 Read the following case study and complete the three steps of the adaptation nursing process for the mode that is demonstrating a disruption in the level of adequacy. In your answer assess the behaviors and stimuli of the mode, formulate two nursing judgments, select a diagnostic category, write a nursing diagnosis, set a goal, plan appropriate interventions, and identify evaluation criteria.

Case study

Dr. William Henderson, a 56-year-old plastic surgeon, was admitted to the hospital 7 days ago complaining of shortness of breath and radiating chest pain. He was taken to the cardiac care unit, and his condition was monitored for 5 days. During that time the symptoms did not recur. However, laboratory tests and an electrocardiogram indicated that Dr. Henderson had suffered an acute myocardial infarction. On the fifth day Dr. Henderson was transferred to the postcardiac unit, and continuous monitoring was discontinued. He was instructed to remain in bed and that he could complete some of his hygiene, such as shaving and brushing his teeth, while in bed. In addition, he was told that within the week he would receive commode privileges but that for now he would have to request a bedpan. He would continue to receive a low-sodium diet.

Following his transfer, Dr. Henderson was frequently found out of bed completing his hygiene in the bathroom or reading his paper in the chair. His primary nurse on the day shift reported that she had heard Dr. Henderson on the phone with a member of his office staff requesting that his surgery schedule begin the following week. On two occasions Dr. Henderson refused his evening tray stating, "My son is bringing me something special from home. Irish stew, I think. I can't tolerate this bland food."

When reminded that he should be in bed or should be maintaining the low-sodium diet, Dr. Henderson responds, "Oh, I haven't had any more pain. I'm practically fine." Dr. Henderson is a very active man—a regular tennis player and frequent jogger who has paid special attention to his physical health. "I've had regular checkups. I've been on a low-cholesterol diet for years. I'm not a candidate for an MI. Honey, would you get me the phone? I want to call my wife and remind her to bring in the bills. We're going to go over the household account this afternoon."

Dr. Henderson is the head of a large Catholic household and is visited daily by his wife and five children. Mrs. Henderson frequently reminds her husband about the limitations on his activities. She has remarked to nursing staff, "He's used to doing what he wants, you know, being in control. This is hard for him." Dr. Henderson responds, "I've lain around for a week now. I've got a busy practice, three teenagers still at home, private schools and colleges to pay for. My brother had a coronary 3 years ago—scared him to death. He did everything they told him and he still died within the year."

REFERENCES

Anthony, W.A., and Carkhoff, R.R.: The art of health care: a handbook of psychological first aid skills, Amherst, Mass., 1976, Human Resource Development Press.

Banton, M.M.: Roles: an introduction to the study of social relations, New York, 1965, Basic Books, Inc., Publishers.

Beauchamp, T.L., and Walter, L.: Contemporary issues in bioethics, Belmont, Calif., 1978, Wadsworth Publishing Co., Inc.

Bower, F.L.: The process of planning nursing care: a model for practice, ed. 2, St. Louis, 1977, The C.V. Mosby Co.

Bower, F.L., and Wheeler, R.T., editors: The nursing assessment (Wiley Nursing Concept Modules), New York, 1977, John Wiley & Sons, Inc.

Brammer, L.: The helping relationship: process and skills, Englewood Cliffs, N.J., 1973, Prentice-Hall, Inc.

Combs, A.W., Avila, D.L., and Purkey, W.W.: Helping relationships: basic concepts for the helping professions, Boston, 1971, Allyn & Bacon, Inc.

Combs, A.W., and Snygg, D.: Individual behavior: a perceptual approach to behavior, New York, 1959, Harper & Row, Publishers, Inc.

Dickelmann, N.: Primary health care of the well adult, New York, 1977, McGraw-Hill Book Co.

Driever, M.J.: Unpublished data, 1969 to 1970.

Erikson, E.H.: Childhood and society, ed. 2, New York, 1963, W.W. Norton & Co., Inc.

Ford, J.A.G., Trygstad-Durland, L.N., and Nelms, B.C.: Applied decision making for nurses, St. Louis, 1979, The C.V. Mosby Co.

Freedman, A.M., Kaplan, H.I., and Sadock, B.J.: Modern synopsis of comprehensive textbook of psychiatry, Baltimore, Md., 1972, The Williams & Wilkins Co.

Fromm, E.: The art of loving, New York, 1956, Harper & Row, Publishers, Inc.

Johnson, D.: Reaching out, Englewood Cliffs, N.J., 1972, Prentice-Hall, Inc.

Jourard, S.M.: To be or not to be, Gainesville, 1967, University of Florida Press.

Jourard, S.M.: Disclosing man to himself, New York, 1968, D. Van Nostrand Co.

Kalish, R.A.: The psychology of human behavior, Belmont, Calif., 1966, Wadsworth Publishing Co., Inc.

La Monica, E.L.: *The nursing process: a humanistic approach*, Menlo Park, Calif., 1979, Addison-Wesley Publishing Co.

Levine, M.E.: Holistic nursing, *Nursing Clinics of North America* 6:253, 1971.

Mahler, M.: Separation-individuation, New York, 1979, Jason Aronson, Inc.

Marram, G., Barrett, M.W., and Bevis, E.O.: *Primary nursing: a model for individualized care*, ed. 2, St. Louis, 1979, The C.V. Mosby Co.

Maslow, A.H.: Toward a psychology of being, New York, 1968, D. Van Nostrand Co.

Mayeroff, M.: On caring, New York, 1971, Harper & Row, Publishers, Inc.

Mayers, M.G.: A systematic approach to the nursing care plan, ed. 2, 1978, Appleton-Century-Crofts.

Nursing Theories Conference Group: Nursing theories: the base for professional nursing practice, Englewood Cliffs, N.J., 1980, Prentice-Hall, Inc.

Parsons, T., and Shils, E., editors: Toward a general theory of action, Cambridge, Mass., 1951, Harvard University Press.

Purtilo, R.: Health professional/patient inter-action, ed. 2, Philadelphia, 1978, W.B. Saunders Co.

Redman, B.K.: The process of patient teaching in nursing, ed. 3, St. Louis, 1976, The C.V. Mosby Co.

Reihl, J., and Roy, C.: Conceptual models for nursing practice, ed. 2, New York, 1980, Appleton-Century-Crofts.

Rodgers, C.: On becoming a person, Boston, 1961, Houghton Mifflin Co.

Roy, C.: Introduction to nursing: an adaptation model, Englewood Cliffs, N.J., 1976, Prentice-Hall, Inc.

Satir, V.: Peoplemaking, Palo Alto, Calif., 1972, Science & Behavior Books.

Selman, R., and Selman, A.: Children's ideas about friendship: a new theory, *Psychology Today*, 10:71-80, 1979.

Stuart, G.W., and Sundeen, S.J.: Principles and practice of psychiatric nursing, St. Louis, 1979, The C.V. Mosby Co.

Weiss, P.: Reality, Carbondale, 1967, Southern Illinois University Press.

Wu, R.: Behavior and illness (Scientific Foundations of Nursing Practice Series), Englewood Cliffs, N.J., 1973, Prentice-Hall, Inc.

Yura, H., and Walsh, M.B.: Human needs and the nursing process, New York, 1978, Appleton-Century-Crofts.

Taking it apart
looking at critical elements

CHAPTER 4

The health/illness continuum

List and define the essential terms associated with the health/illness continuum.
Describe the health care needs associated with wellness, disrupted wellness, and illness.
List three health care facilities and three medical conditions commonly associated with wellness, disrupted wellness, and illness.
Describe the relationship between the three major divisions of the continuum (wellness, disrupted wellness, and illness).
Explain the difficulties associated with relating common medical diagnoses with adaptation diagnoses. Give an example of a common medical condition, and describe the circumstances that might move it along the continuum through the three adaptive diagnoses.

In previous chapters concepts about the adapting person, the adaptation nurse, and the adaptation nursing process have been examined in detail. Before proceeding to the application of these concepts to the client population, the student should be oriented to the relationship between diagnostic categories and nursing action. Therefore, in this chapter the process of judgment making will be reviewed, and the significance of each diagnostic category will be explored. Then the health/illness continuum will be examined, with special attention given to the stages of wellness, disrupted wellness, and illness. Finally, the relationship between the stages of the health/illness continuum, the health care facilities, and common medical conditions will be presented (Figure 4-1).

Upon completion of this chapter, the student should be able to (1) define the categories of the adaptation health/illness continuum and describe the needs of the adaptation person in each of the categories; (2) describe the relationship among positions on the adaptation health/illness continuum, common medical conditions, and the associated health care facilities; and (3) explain how and why a person is classified in a particular category on the continuum.

Mastery of the following essential terms should precede study of this chapter.

ESSENTIAL TERMS

Health/illness continuum   A graphic representation of the possible range of levels of adequacy that the adapting person may experience. The levels of adequacy are arranged in a progression from growth and self-enhancement to an absence of adequate functioning.

95

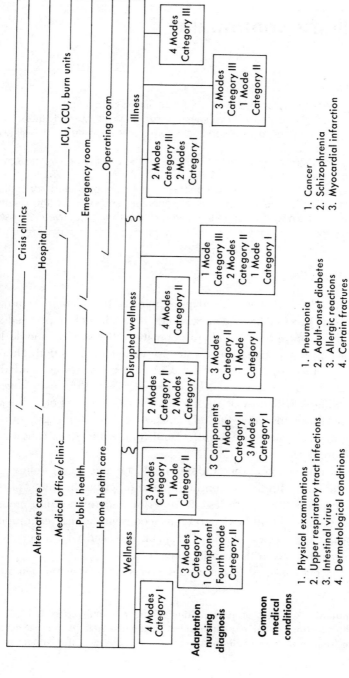

FIGURE 4-1

The complex set of relationships that exist between the adaptation nursing diagnosis, the health/illness continuum, health care facilities, and common medical conditions.

Nursing judgments   Two statements formulated during step II of the adaptation nursing process. The first statement defines the person's coping stance and strategies and identifies the congruence between coping behaviors and the environment. The second statement defines the threat to the level of adequacy and identifies the effectiveness of the behavioral response.

Diagnostic category I   Represents congruence between both nursing judgments. The coping stance and strategies are congruent with the triggering event, and the behavioral response is maintaining or enhancing the level of adequacy. In the physiological mode this diagnosis occurs when the behavioral response is maintaining adequacy.

Diagnostic category II   Is applied when the behavioral response is ineffective in maintaining adequacy. The coping stance and strategies and the triggering event are congruent. There is incongruence between the behavioral response and the level of adequacy.

Diagnostic category III   Represents a lack of congruence in both nursing judgments. The coping stance and strategies are incongruent with the influencing stimuli, and as a result, the behavioral response is ineffective for maintaining adequacy.

Wellness   Refers to adapting persons who demonstrate category I diagnoses in three of four modes or all but two components of a single mode. In addition, the mode or two components demonstrating incongruence between the judgments must be a category II level.

Disrupted wellness   Refers to adapting persons who demonstrate behavior in the second diagnostic category in at least two modes or in three or more components of a single mode.

Illness   Refers to adapting persons who demonstrate behavior in the third diagnostic category in two or more modes.

DIAGNOSTIC CATEGORY I: WELLNESS

How does one describe an adapting person in the state of wellness? The well person is in control of his internal state and feels competent in the face of triggering events (stimulating occurrences used by the well person to enhance his sense of adequacy) in the environment. The person in the first diagnostic category is able to take risks, make decisions, and continue to strive for adequacy and self-enhancement. He uses the environment to produce additional triggering events that are both satisfying and stimulating. The adapting person in the first diagnostic category looks and feels well and satisfied; he is perceived to be an effective, competent person.

Definition

According to this description, the well person's behavioral responses in all four modes should be congruent with the triggering events, and the person should be experiencing adequacy or growth. The definition of the first diagnostic category states that the two judgments are congruent, that the coping stance and strategies are

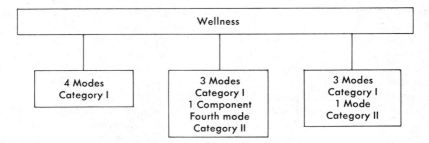

FIGURE 4-2
The wellness portion of the health/illness continuum and the three possible diagnostic combinations that are found in this range of the continuum.

congruent with the triggering event, and that the behavioral response is maintaining or enhancing the level of adequacy. Although this category can frequently be identified in several components of a mode or in two or three modes, the nurse seldom sees an adapting person who demonstrates the category I diagnoses in all four modes, because, as adapting persons in a constantly changing environment, we seldom succeed in maintaining such a high level of adaptation. What, then, is a realistic description of a category I client, a person experiencing wellness? In our discussions *wellness refers to adapting persons who demonstrate category I diagnoses in three of four modes or in all but two components of a single mode. In addition, the mode or two components demonstrating incongruence must be at the category II level* (Figure 4-2).

Example

Wellness is characterized by a person whose coping abilities are effective in three of the four modes. In the fourth mode the person may be experiencing a triggering event that has been effectively assessed and an appropriate coping stance that has been identified. The behavioral response, however, is ineffective. For example, a school nurse may observe a 5-year-old girl who is crying on her first day of school but who is apparently in good physical health and has a positive sense of self and an adequate attachment to significant adults. The child's diagnostic category would be I in the physiological, self-concept, and role performance modes. However, the nurse might diagnose the little girl as being in category II in the interdependence mode. The child has correctly identified and interpreted the triggering event—the first day of school—but she needs help in selecting a more effective coping behavior than crying. The child's response is a common one, and in view of her adaptive behavior in the other three modes, her coping resources are more than adequate. She is in the process of striving for adequacy.

In summary, the person classified in the first diagnostic category is considered well, adequate, and growing. This overall diagnosis is made when a person has a category I diagnosis in at least three of the four adaptive modes. In addition, the mode that does not represent a category I diagnosis must reflect that the person has made a correct assessment but has not as yet identified the most effective coping behavior; therefore, this represents a category II diagnosis.

DIAGNOSTIC CATEGORY II: DISRUPTED WELLNESS

How does one describe an adapting person in the stage of disrupted wellness? This person lacks optimal energy and feels harassed, concerned, and confused. Triggering events seem to require more energy than the person in this state seems to possess; he lacks a sense of equilibrium. The adaptation nurse would place him in the middle of the health/illness continuum. A person in the second diagnostic category is able to cope effectively but often feels bombarded by triggering events: they are either too numerous or too intense. All adaptive energy is channeled to maintain adequacy, and the person is unable to focus on growth or self-enhancement. The person in the stage of disrupted wellness makes essential decisions but takes few risks. The adapting person in the second diagnostic category often looks and feels tired and overwhelmed. He is perceived as willing or adequate in terms of capability but currently unable to function optimally.

Definition

From these descriptions of disrupted wellness one can assume that the person's behavioral responses are frequently ineffective in maintaining the level of adequacy. The definition of the second diagnostic category states that the first judgment represents congruence; the coping strategies and triggering event are congruent. The second judgment, however, reflects incongruence between the behavioral response and the level of adequacy. The person has correctly assessed the environment and assumed an appropriate coping stance. The behavioral response, although appropriate to the strategy, is not effective in maintaining the person's level of adequacy.

As might be expected, the adaptation nurse observes many persons in the second diagnostic category. In our discussion *disrupted wellness refers to an adapting person who demonstrates category II behavior in three or more components of a single mode*. This diagnostic category needs to be identified in at least three components of a single mode or in two or more modes for the person to be considered in the stage of disrupted wellness. Persons in this diagnostic category constitute a significant number of positions on the health/illness continuum. For example, a person with behavioral response in the first diagnostic category in three modes and in the second diagnostic category in three components of the fourth mode is experiencing significantly less disruption than is a person with behavioral responses in the second diagnostic category in all four modes.

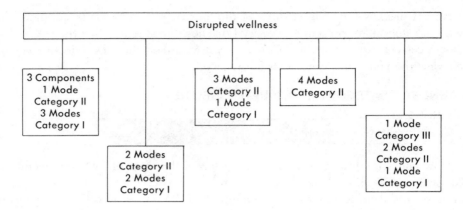

FIGURE 4-3
The disrupted wellness portion of the health/illness continuum and the five most common diagnostic combinations that are found in this range of the continuum.

Example

Disrupted wellness is represented by a person who may be coping and behaving effectively in some modes but having difficulties in others. The person in this category is effectively utilizing the regulator/cognator process, making an accurate assessment and selecting a correct coping stance. However, the behavioral responses in some components or modes are ineffective for maintaining the person's level of adequacy. For example, a nurse in an acute care setting may observe an elderly man with congestive heart failure who has many disruptions in the components of the physiological mode. He is demonstrating inadequate coping behavior in the categories of fluid and electrolytes, oxygen, circulation, and regulatory mechanisms. At the same time, however, he is experiencing adequacy in the other modes. Because he has had many previous episodes of this illness, he understands expected role behaviors and performs them effectively; he has a well-defined sense of self and has incorporated his chronic illness into his body image. In addition, he is surrounded by concerned significant persons and is actively receiving support. Therefore, this elderly man falls into the first diagnostic category in the self-concept, role performance, and interdependence modes. However, in the physiological mode his body needs assistance to achieve a behavioral response that will effectively maintain his level of adequacy. For this reason he is classified in the second diagnostic category as one who is in the disrupted wellness stage.

In summary, a person classified in the second diagnostic category is in the stage of disrupted wellness; he is coping somewhat effectively but not optimally. This diagnosis is made when the nurse's assessment reveals a person with a category II diagnosis in at least two modes or three components of a single mode. All other modes or components must be in the first diagnostic category (Figure 4-3). These categorizations indicate the areas in which the person's assessment is correct but the behavioral response is not sufficient for maintaining his level of adequacy.

DIAGNOSTIC CATEGORY III: ILLNESS

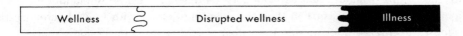

How does one describe an adapting person in the stage of illness? The ill person is exhausted and cannot assume responsibility for himself. He cannot process triggering events effectively, and he misinterprets reality; the disruption has reached crisis proportions. When the person exhibits these behaviors, he is moving toward the illness section of the health/illness continuum. He has an insufficient amount of adaptation energy available for coping effectively with the constantly changing environment. Furthermore, he has no growth or self-enhancing experiences, and his level of adequacy is declining. Unless he receives outside intervention, a person in the third diagnostic category may experience permanent impairment and an irreversible change in his level of adequacy. He looks anxious and feels exhausted and is perceived as incapable of providing for and maintaining his level of adequacy.

Definition

It is clear from this description that the person in category III is not processing the environment effectively and that his behavioral responses are ineffective in maintaining adequate functioning. Typical of the behavior of a person in the third diagnostic category, his coping stance and strategy are incongruent with the triggering event and influencing stimuli. His behavioral response is ineffective in maintaining the level of adequacy. Both judgments represent incongruence. The person's regulator and cognator processes have distorted or incorrectly perceived the triggering event; as a result, the internal problem-solving process that terminates in the selection of the coping stance and strategy is ineffective. The behavioral response, then, reflects these inaccurate perceptions and either has no impact on the environment or produces additional triggering events that are destructive to the person's declining level of adequacy.

The person in the third diagnostic category is greatly in need of and dependent on the services rendered by health care agencies and the adaptation nurse. In our discussions the term *illness describes the person who demonstrates a category III diagnosis in two or more modes*. This classification may seem somewhat inflexible, and yet the condition of a person with two category III diagnoses can worsen rapidly. The third diagnostic category pulls energy from all areas, leaving severe energy deficits in the other modes and frequent deterioration of the person's overall adaptive capacity. As a result, an adapting person in the third diagnostic category requires immediate assistance in all phases of the adaptation process.

Again, as in the second diagnostic category, there are a number of positions on the health/illness continuum occupied by the third category. These positions vary from mild to severe levels of illness. Undoubtedly, an adaptive person with category I diagnoses in two modes and two category III diagnoses in the remaining modes is experiencing far less disruption than the adapting person with several category III diagnoses in three of four modes and category II diagnoses in the fourth mode.

Example

A complex example of a category III diagnosis might be represented by a middle-aged man admitted to the emergency room with an acute myocardial infarction. In his physiological mode he has several components representing acute physiological inadequacies, although he has previously been healthy and athletic with no prior record of hospitalization. He is experiencing behaviors and stimuli that result in body image disturbances and role failure. Furthermore, his interdependence needs are compromised by his wife's recent suit for divorce. This man represents the third diagnostic category, because he has severe category III diagnoses in the physiological mode as well as additional category III diagnoses in the self-concept and role performance modes. The other modes and components represent category II diagnoses. This man is overcome with triggering events and has insufficient adaptation energy to cope effectively. He needs immediate assistance to maintain his level of adequacy.

The person classified in the third diagnostic category, then, is in the stage of illness, overwhelmed and unable to maintain the level of adequacy. This diagnosis is made when the assessment reveals a person with a category III diagnosis in two or more modes, indicating that his regulator and cognator have made an incorrect assessment and that the coping stance and behavioral response are not maintaining the level of adequacy (Figure 4-4).

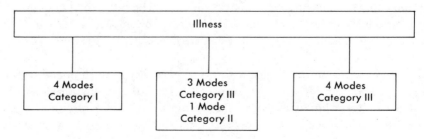

FIGURE 4-4
The illness portion of the health/illness continuum and three of the most common diagnostic combinations that are found in this range of the continuum.

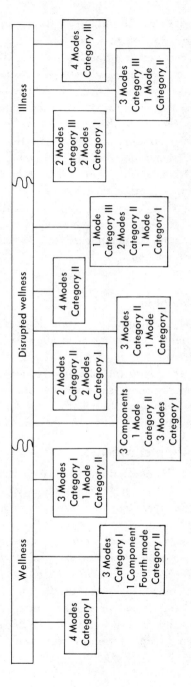

FIGURE 4-5
The complete health/illness continuum with eleven of the common diagnostic combinations.

SUMMARY

The adapting person may be classified in any of three categories on the health/ illness continuum. Each category has within it various positions indicative of the type and severity of adaptive problems confronting the person. Wellness is on one end of the continuum and includes any person whose assessment reveals judgments in the first category in three out of four modes or in all but two components of a single mode. The judgment in the fourth mode must be in the second diagnostic category. Disrupted wellness can be considered in the middle of the continuum and includes any person with two or more judgments in category II. Illness falls on the end of the continuum opposite wellness and includes any person with two or more category III diagnoses (Figure 4-5). Other combinations exist when the modes are further broken down into the respective components; however, Figure 4-5 illustrates the progressive nature of the adaptive person's movement from wellness to illness on the health/illness continuum. Having defined the concepts of wellness, disrupted wellness, and illness, let us examine the health care settings and the common medical conditions associated with each concept.

HEALTH CARE FACILITIES
Facilities associated with wellness

The well person is coping adequately and feels competent and in control of interactions with the environment. *This person generally seeks health care to validate the level of wellness, to acquire information for growth and stimulation, and to gain suppport and information to cope with the category II diagnosis.* The well person who is seeking any of these three services is likely to be seen by the adaptation nurse in an ambulatory care facility such as a physician's office, clinic, school, industrial setting, or alternative care facility (e.g., holistic health and birthing centers).

Facilities associated with disrupted wellness

The person in disrupted wellness often looks and feels tired and overwhelmed. He is perceived as willing or adequate in his coping ability but currently unable to function optimally. *This person seeks health care to gain information about and assistance with his category II diagnosis.* Aware that his behavioral response is not effectively maintaining the desired level of adequacy, *he seeks validation that his regulator/cognator process is operating effectively, and he desires information or actions that will increase the effectiveness of his behavioral response.* This person can be seen by the adaptation nurse in almost any health care facility. The range would include physicians' offices, clinics, emergency rooms, acute hospitals, crisis clinics, birthing centers, and public health and home health care agencies. The only facilities in which the person in disrupted wellness would not be seen are specialized intensive care units.

Health care facilities

Alternate care
Medical office/clinic
Public health
Home health care

Crisis clinics
Hospital
ICU, CCU, burn units
Emergency room
Operating room

Wellness ∿ Disrupted wellness // Illness ∿

FIGURE 4-6
The range of health care facilities and their relationship to the health/illness continuum.

Facilities associated with illness

The ill person looks anxious and feels exhausted. He is perceived as incapable of maintaining adequacy. *This person seeks health care or (more frequently) is brought to the health care facility for management of his third category diagnosis and prevention of further deterioration in the level of adequacy.* This person's regulator and cognator functioning are disrupted, and he needs help in processing triggering events, selecting coping stances and strategies, and achieving effective behavioral responses. The ill person is seen in acute care settings that include emergency rooms, operating rooms, and intensive care units (medical, surgical, and psychiatric).

In summary, then, health care facilities, like diagnostic categories, can be visualized on a continuum ranging from alternate care facilities to intensive treatment units (Figure 4-6). These facilities and the positions on the health/illness continuum are linked, depending on the amount and type of assistance the adapting person needs to maintain or regain the desired level of adequacy. There are many other possible variations, but based on current practice, the charts indicate a fair sampling of relationships that can exist between facilities and adaptive levels.

RELATIONSHIP BETWEEN DIAGNOSTIC CATEGORIES AND MEDICAL CONDITIONS

It is difficult to indicate precise relationships between the adaptive diagnostic categories and medical conditions, because medical diagnoses generally refer only to the person's physiological aspects and do not usually take into consideration the psychological and sociological components considered in the adaptation conceptualization. Equating the adaptation diagnostic categories of wellness, disrupted wellness, and illness with medical conditions is a challenge, given the difference between the way a person is commonly viewed in a medical setting and the way an adaptation nurse views the person in the same setting. However, because the medical model remains a powerful force in the practice of health care and the operation of health care facilities, the adaptation nurse must be able to recognize and express the relationship between her view of the adapting person and the views held by other disciplines. For this reason a brief description of the relationship between each category and the associated medical diagnosis follows.

Conditions associated with wellness

The well person who is coping adequately and feeling competent and in control of his interactions with the environment frequently has no medical diagnosis and experiences no physiological disruption. His contact with health care agencies usually occurs only once per year, if at all, when he has a physical examination. If there is a medical diagnosis, it might be an upper respiratory tract infection, an intestinal virus, or a dermatological condition. *Medical conditions associated with wellness are commonly occurring in a wide range of the population, require minimal or no medical intervention, and can be assessed and controlled in the person's natural environment.* These conditions can be included in the disrupted wellness category and occasionally in the illness category if they occur in combination with other medical conditions or if psychosocial factors further compromise the person's level of adequacy.

For example, a 27-year-old woman in excellent physical health is diagnosed as being in her eighth week of a normal pregnancy. This is a common medical condition associated with wellness. However, if she has poorly controlled diabetes, she may move rather rapidly toward the stage of disrupted wellness or illness. If she is physiologically healthy but emotionally stressed, identifying herself as unprepared for pregnancy, socially isolated, and economically incapable of providing for another person, she can be considered to be in the stage of disrupted wellness and has the potential of moving into the stage of illness.

The common medical conditions associated with wellness, then, result in the disruption of not more than two components of the physiological mode. These conditions are commonly occurring in the general population, require little or no medical intervention, and are easily managed within the person's natural environment.

Conditions associated with disrupted wellness

The person in disrupted wellness appears overstimulated; he responds to the environment appropriately but requires external support to achieve behavioral responses that will effectively maintain adequacy. He is typically part of a larger group of persons whose *medical conditions include acute medical illnesses treatable on an outpatient basis or with a short hospitalization, stable chronic conditions, and emergencies that do not require surgical intervention.* Conditions such as pneumonia, adult-onset diabetes, allergic reactions, and certain fractures, burns, and lacerations can be included in this category. *Persons in the stage of disrupted wellness require some intervention to maintain the level of physiological adequacy.* The conditions could move toward wellness or illness, depending on whether other physiological disruptions or psychosocial factors further influence the person's adaptive level.

For example, a young man in otherwise good health who exercises regularly and does not smoke is diagnosed as having bronchial pneumonia. In the absence of any other pathological condition, if he maintains a positive sense of self, exhibits adequate role performance, and has effective interdependent relationships, this man can be considered well. However, if he is observed in this physical condition shortly after being fired from his job, he would be considered in the stage of disrupted wellness. Despite the same physiological mode status, this person would demonstrate a category II diagnosis in role performance. When two or more modes demonstrate judgments that reflect the second diagnostic category, the person is said to be experiencing disrupted wellness.

If the young man is assessed as having another medical condition, such as chronic

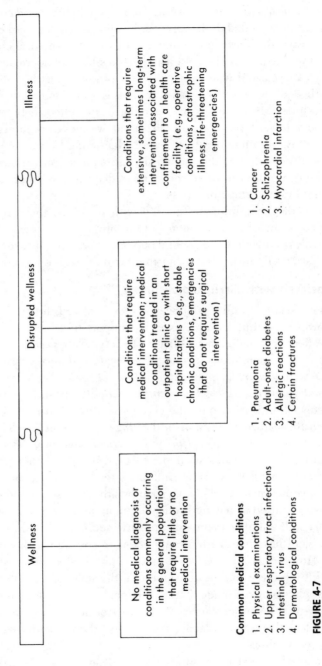

Wellness

No medical diagnosis or conditions commonly occurring in the general population that require little or no medical intervention

Disrupted wellness

Conditions that require medical intervention; medical conditions treated in an outpatient clinic or with short hospitalizations (e.g., stable chronic conditions, emergencies that do not require surgical intervention)

Illness

Conditions that require extensive, sometimes long-term intervention associated with confinement to a health care facility (e.g., operative conditions, catastrophic illness, life-threatening emergencies)

Common medical conditions

1. Physical examinations
2. Upper respiratory tract infections
3. Intestinal virus
4. Dermatological conditions

1. Pneumonia
2. Adult-onset diabetes
3. Allergic reactions
4. Certain fractures

1. Cancer
2. Schizophrenia
3. Myocardial infarction

FIGURE 4-7

The relationship that exists between common medical conditions and the health/illness continuum.

schizophrenia, in addition to the bronchial pneumonia, he can easily be considered to be in the stage of illness. This classification could be based on the assessment that the person is actively psychotic, is out of touch with reality, and shows a major disruption in the self-concept mode. Therefore, a person with a category III diagnosis in two modes, regardless of the physiological disruption, is said to be in the stage of illness.

Disrupted wellness, then, is associated with medical conditions that require external intervention. These conditions may be acute medical illnesses, stable chronic conditions, or emergencies that do not require surgical intervention.

A person with a medical condition that is considered disrupted wellness must demonstrate physiological disruption in the second diagnostic category of three or more components of the physiological mode. A person with one or two components involved in the physiological mode but with second category diagnoses in one or more of the other modes is also considered to be in the stage of disrupted wellness.

Conditions associated with illness

The ill person is overwhelmed and unable to maintain his level of adequacy. He is one of a large group of hospitalized persons with an operative condition, catastrophic illness, or life-threatening emergency. Medical conditions commonly associated with this category include eclampsia, metastatic cancer, rheumatoid arthritis, schizophrenia, and myocardial infarction. *The illness category relates to physiological conditions that require extensive, sometimes long-term medical intervention. The person must for a time be confined to a health care facility.* If the person has such a condition, he is automatically considered in the stage of illness. In addition, a person with a less threatening medical condition might be classified as ill if he has a third category diagnosis in another mode. For example, a woman with adult-onset diabetes whose physical condition has been stable for the past 3 years may be considered in the stage of illness if she is experiencing pathological grief following the loss of her spouse in an automobile accident.

The medical conditions commonly associated with illness are catastrophic illness, life-threatening emergencies, and conditions requiring surgical intervention. The person is automatically considered in the stage of illness if he has a category III diagnosis in two modes. Medical conditions associated with each adaptation concept have been added to the health/illness continuum in Figure 4-7.

CONCLUSION

Wellness, then, is a state characterized by feelings of competence and well-being in which a person is able to maintain the level of adequacy and experience growth and self-enhancement. In adaptation terminology wellness is evidenced by a category II diagnosis in the components of a single mode; all other diagnoses are classified in

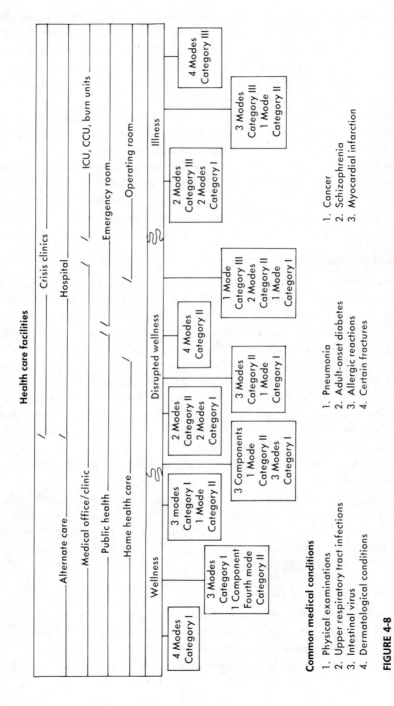

Health care facilities

Alternate care

Medical office/clinic

Public health

Home health care

Crisis clinics

Hospital

ICU, CCU, burn units

Emergency room

Operating room

Wellness

Disrupted wellness

Illness

4 Modes
Category I

3 modes
Category I
1 Mode
Category II

3 Modes
Category I
1 Component
Fourth mode
Category II

2 Modes
Category II
2 Modes
Category I

3 Components
1 Mode
Category II
3 Modes
Category I

4 Modes
Category II

3 Modes
Category II
1 Mode
Category I

1 Mode
Category III
2 Modes
Category II
1 Mode
Category I

2 Modes
Category III
2 Modes
Category I

3 Modes
Category III
1 Mode
Category II

4 Modes
Category III

Common medical conditions

1. Physical examinations
2. Upper respiratory tract infections
3. Intestinal virus
4. Dermatological conditions

1. Pneumonia
2. Adult-onset diabetes
3. Allergic reactions
4. Certain fractures

1. Cancer
2. Schizophrenia
3. Myocardial infarction

FIGURE 4-8

The complex set of relationships that exist between the adaptation nursing diagnosis, the health/illness continuum, health care facilities, and common medical conditions.

category I. Well persons are seen in alternative care facilities, physicians' offices, clinics, public health agencies, schools, and industrial settings. Wellness conditions treated in these facilities commonly occur in the general population; they require little or no medical intervention and can be treated in the person's natural environment.

Disrupted wellness is a state manifesting feelings of fatigue and pressure in which the person feels certain about his problems and needs but is unable to achieve adequacy without intervention. In adaptation theory disrupted wellness is evidenced by two or more modes with a category II diagnosis or three or more components of a single mode with a category II diagnosis. Persons in disrupted wellness are treated in the same health care facilities as well persons and in hospitals, emergency rooms, and crisis clinics. Disrupted wellness conditions seen in these facilities require some type of external intervention, such as outpatient treatment or a short hospitalization. These conditions include acute medical conditions, stable chronic conditions, or emergencies that do not require surgical intervention.

Finally, illness is a state manifested by anxiety in which the person is unable to process the environment or maintain adequacy. In adaptation terminology illness is manifested by a category III diagnosis in two or more modes. Ill persons can be observed in acute care facilities such as hospitals, intensive care units, emergency rooms, operating rooms, and crisis clinics. Included in this category are ill persons who need extensive and sometimes long-term interventions requiring confinement in a health care facility. Illness states comprise operative conditions, catastrophic illness, and life-threatening emergencies (Figure 4-8).

Complete the following exercises to demonstrate your understanding of the concepts presented in this chapter.

LEARNING EXPERIENCE

1 Describe your understanding of the following concepts.
   Wellness
   Nursing judgments
   Category II diagnoses
   Disrupted wellness
   Health/illness continuum
2 Define the relationship between the position of wellness on the health/illness continuum and its relationship to health care facilities and medical conditions.
3 Select an example of a person who reflects the category of disrupted wellness, and give your rationale for classifying the client in that position on the health-illness continuum.

REFERENCES

Dunn, H.: High-level wellness, Arlington, Va., 1961, R.W. Beatty, Ltd.

Engel, G.L.: Psychological development in health and disease, Philadelphia, 1962, W.B. Saunders Co.

Folta, J.R., and Deck, E.S., editors: A sociological framework for patient care, New York, 1979, John Wiley & Sons, Inc.

Freman, V.J.: Human aspects of health and illness: beyond the germ theory. In Folta, J.R., and Deck, E.S., editors: A sociological framework for patient care, New York, 1979, John Wiley & Sons, Inc.

Gordon, G.: Role theory and illness, New Haven, Conn., 1966, College & University Press.

Hall, J., and Weaver, B.: A systems approach to community health, Philadelphia, 1977, Lippincott Co.

Maslow, A.: Motivation and personality, New York, 1954, Harper & Row, Publishers, Inc.

Menninger, K., Mayman, M., and Pruyser, P.: The vital balance: the life process in mental health and illness, New York, 1963, Viking Press.

Parsons, T.: Definitions of health and illness in the light of American values and social structure. In Jaco, E., editor: Patients, physicians, and illness, New York, 1958, The Free Press.

Schneider, D.E.: Revolution in the body-minded, Easthampton, N.Y., 1977, Alexa Press.

Wilson, R.: The sociology of health: an introduction, New York, 1970, Random House, Inc.

CHAPTER 5

Developmental stages in the adaptation nurse's professional growth

---

OBJECTIVES

List and define the essential terms related to the development of the adaptation nurse.

Describe the relationship between influencing stimuli and the professional development of the adaptation nurse.

Explain the regulator/cognator process and its relationship to the selection of a nursing action.

Describe the relationship between the adaptation nurse's stage of development and the diagnostic categories.

List the three stages of development of the adaptation nurse and explain the progression from the adolescent to the generative stage.

The adaptation nursing process is a complex, organized approach to the practice of nursing. The educational process introduces the student to the complexity of the process and prepares the newly graduated adaptation nurse to utilize this process in her practice. The educational process, however, only begins the specialization of the adaptation nurse. Upon graduation, she has the tools and the knowledge to make complex judgments but lacks the experience and professional maturation to exhibit the optimal performance suggested by her education. This discrepancy between her theoretical knowledge and her ability to put that theory into practice is not unique to the nurse prepared as a practitioner of the Roy adaptation model.

In Chapter 5 the developmental framework of Erik Erikson (1963) will be used to demonstrate the course of professional maturation of the adaptation nurse. This development will be explored by examining her regulator/cognator process. Additionally, the reciprocal relationship between the adaptation nurse's developmental stage and the needs of the client with whom she interacts in varying diagnostic categories will be examined. This chapter will trace the development of the adaptation nurse from recent graduate to specialized practitioner. The regulator/cognator process at each stage will be described, showing the relationship between her coping stance and strategies, the nursing actions she takes, the diagnostic categories she selects, and the health care setting in which she works. The relationship between influencing stimuli and professional development will also be explored. This chapter will have significance for the student nearing graduation and should aid in the socialization process for entry into practice. In addition, the chapter can be utilized to add

113

perspective to the chapters discussing clinical practice that make up Section Three of this book. As the adaptation nurse moves through the stages of nursing practice, her facility with the adaptation nursing process increases. In addition, if the adaptation nurse interacts with a client whose adaptation needs are compatible with her developmental stage, both the client and the nurse will maintain or enhance their levels of adequacy. Optimal nursing care results when the relationship between the adapting person and the nurse is reciprocal. For this reason the significance of the adaptation nurse and her regulator/cognator will be explored as it affects the client's needs and level of adequacy.

The new terms introduced in this chapter should be mastered and terms from preceding chapters reviewed before continuing with Chapter 5.

ESSENTIAL TERMS

Development   The progressive changes in adaptive functioning. Development is a process that focuses on the dynamic, unidirectional elements of change, an integration of constitutional and learned changes that make up the person's ever-developing professional role performance.

Adolescent stage   The developmental stage of the adaptation nurse who has recently graduated from an adaptation curriculum. The tasks of this stage of development include selecting an appropriate model, separating from the influence of the educational institution, and establishing identity as an adaptation nurse.

Young adult stage   The developmental stage of the adaptation nurse who has accomplished the tasks of the adolescent stage. The tasks of this stage of development include increasing and solidifying role performance and acquiring professional intimacy.

Generative stage   The developmental stage of the adaptation nurse who has accomplished the tasks of the young adult stage and has acquired additional formal education. The tasks of this stage of development include increasing productivity and care, experiencing growth and enhancement, and educating and socializing future adaptation nurses.

Client   The adapting person who interacts with the adaptation nurse in a health care setting to gain support, assistance, or knowledge regarding the level of adequacy.

ERIKSON'S THEORY OF DEVELOPMENT AS IT RELATES TO THE ADAPTATION NURSE'S PROFESSIONAL DEVELOPMENT

Erikson (1963) identifies eight stages of psychosocial development. He postulates that from birth to death the person encounters certain life crises whose resolution determines future competency. He further states that certain life experiences may cause the person to reexperience previously completed stages. For example, when making a major life change (such as marrying or becoming pregnant), a person may psychologically repeat previous stages.

When taking on a new role, a person's behavior can also reflect the stages defined by Erikson. For example, it could be said that the adaptation student discussed in Chapter 2 experienced Erikson's first four stages of psychosocial development. A beginning nursing student has minimal skill and is largely dependent on faculty for support and nurturance. During the student experience she establishes a trusting relationship, begins to be autonomous, acquires a sense of initiative, and establishes a pattern of industry. On completion of her baccalaureate education, the adaptation graduate has a basic belief in herself and her ability to function. In addition, she is motivated and productive. Having completed the "childhood stage" of her career, the recently graduated adaptation nurse proceeds to the next stage of development.

The recent graduate

Newly graduated from an adaptation curriculum, the nurse then enters into the "adolescent" stage of her professional development. As described by Erikson, adolescence is the culmination of the stages of childhood, a time in which the task of the adolescent is to acquire a sense of identity. The individual utilizes experience and the environment to achieve a more permanent sense of self. This is also true when one begins to assume a new role. The graduate, then, uses her educational experiences and current nursing environment to establish her identity as an adaptation nurse. The process in which she engages is very similar to the process she used when coping with the original developmental crises of adolescence.

In this stage of her development the adaptation nurse strives to establish her professional identity by selecting an appropriate model, separating herself from the influence of the educational institution, and taking on the behaviors she believes to be essential to adaptation nursing.

The graduate often estranges herself from part or all of the beliefs of her educational experience. She seeks and selects a job, usually in an institution she believes will provide opportunities to develop the skills and characteristics she believed were lacking or underemphasized in her education and essential to her fulfillment of her role as an adaptation nurse. In addition, she quickly seeks another nurse (or group of nurses) who she believes embodies the skills and characteristics she strives to reinforce, and she seeks attachment to that person (or group). The energy of the graduate is directed toward the task of self-identity; she therefore is concerned with achieving recognition for her role competencies and association with the nurse she considers ideal.

The experienced nurse

The adaptation nurse who has accomplished the tasks of the adolescent stage progresses to the young adult stage. According to Erikson, this stage marks the person's entrance into society as a full-fledged member and is characterized not only by the enjoyment of adult liberty but also by the responsibility of full participation in the community. It is also a period of continual growth and a time devoted to a specified career. The themes of this stage are commitment and involvement. The adaptation nurse demonstrates commitment and involvement by striving for solidarity in her role performance and utilizing her newly acquired professional identity to achieve professional closeness in her interactions.

The "young adult" adaptation nurse is clear about her professional identity and therefore moves from the self-orientation of the adolescent to an orientation that allows her to focus more directly on the client. She seeks closeness by expanding her knowledge and the depth of her interactions with clients. She acquires solidarity by continuing to expand her adaptation practice, and her professional confidence allows her to take risks in an effort to stabilize her functioning.

The specialized practitioner

The adaptation nurse who has accomplished the tasks of the young adult stage and is acquiring or has acquired advanced formal education is ready to progress to the generative stage of development. According to Erikson, the tasks of this developmental stage are production and care. In the generative stage of development the adaptation nurse achieves these tasks by engaging in advanced role performance and production, fostering growth and enhancement, and assuming responsibility for the education and socialization of future adaptation nurses.

The adaptation nurse in the generative stage of development represents the autonomous, independent practitioner of adaptation nursing. Her efforts are directed toward the most complex and subtle problems of adaptation, and her greatest contribution is to the support and enhancement of students and beginning practitioners of adaptation nursing.

In summary, the new graduate moves through the stages of adolescence, young adulthood, and generativity by accomplishing the tasks of professional development associated with each stage. This development is a dynamic, unidirectional process that involves the integration of change into the nurse's evolving perception of her professional role.

STIMULI THAT INFLUENCE DEVELOPMENT
External stimuli

Let us examine some of the external stimuli that influence the adaptation nurse's growth from adolescent to young adult and, finally, to generative adult. First, and perhaps most significant, is the passage of time, which brings with it varying degrees of development to most of life's experiences. However, time alone will not account for the growth described in the developmental process of an adaptation nurse. Essential changes must occur. Because time is needed for the adaptation nurse to gain experience, be exposed to the health/illness continuum, and use her education to make comprehensive nursing judgments, you will not find a generative adaptation nurse stepping forward to receive her diploma from a baccalaureate school of nursing. Time is essential for the adaptation nurse to examine her environment and alter her internal state. If used properly, time will provide the proper framework in which development will occur.

In addition to time, the adaptation nurse must be nurtured in a stimulating environment that provides new learning experiences, challenges and appropriate rewards as she puts adaptation nursing theory effectively into practice. The environment should also offer role models and experiences that foster growth and development.

Adaptation nurses, even though they may share similar environments and time spans with other nurses, do not move through the developmental stages in the same way; in fact, some do not progress at all. To understand these discrepancies in the developmental process, we will examine the internal influencing stimuli.

Internal stimuli

The progress an adaptation nurse makes through the developmental stages is largely influenced by internal stimuli. Adaptation nursing is a rigorous, physically demanding career. Some graduates may discover they do not have the stamina to practice adaptation nursing and also participate in other growth-producing experiences. When this situation occurs, the adaptation nurse either moves more slowly through the stages or remains at the adolescent or young adult stage of development. She has the tools and the knowledge to achieve a more developed level of practice but lacks the ability to take advantage of the resources present in her environment.

The development of the adaptation nurse is also influenced by the nurse's maturational level. For example, the recent graduate who is in the adolescent stage of her personal development as well as her career development has more difficulties than does the nurse whose personal development is at the generative level. Often the nurse who is striving for personal and professional identity simultaneously demonstrates slowed or delayed professional growth; until her personal identity is established, career and other life choices are often in serious conflict. Hopefully, this group constitutes a minority. The majority of recently graduated adaptation nurses are in the young adult stage and can simultaneously assume their career responsibilities and strive for the closeness and commitment essential to their lives. The adaptation nurse's maturational level, like her physical state, can account for a major delay in or even the termination of her career. Although adaptation nurses possess the tools and the knowledge to practice as more fully developed adaptation nurses, because of their developmental needs they may lack the energy to accomplish the tasks of professional role development.

Finally, the evolution of the adaptation nurse is influenced by the nurse's unique perceptions, beliefs, values, and knowledge. Her personality, motivation, and beliefs about people, the health care system, and the profession of nursing combine to profoundly affect her practice and development as an adaptation nurse. For example, the nurse who wishes only to carry out orders, believes that the client has only physiological needs, and considers her professional development complete upon graduation from nursing school will be very dissatisfied with adaptation nursing and will probably not progress beyond the adolescent stage. However, the adaptation nurse who wishes to be an independent practitioner, believes in interacting with the client (whom she views as unified and complex), and realizes that she will have to strive continually to improve and expand her practice has the potential to move through the developmental stages of adaptation nursing.

In summary, the adaptation nurse's progress through the developmental stages is influenced by her nursing environment, physical state, maturational level, and internal state and the passage of time. These factors combine to support or delay the next developmental stage. A brief examination of this process and how it affects the nursing action taken by the adaptation nurse follows.

REVIEW OF THE REGULATOR/COGNATOR PROCESS

You will recall that the adapting person interacts with the environment by utilizing a five-phase internal process to transact with triggering events. The adaptation nurse utilizes the same process to interact with the environment.

In phase I the environment and the person come together, and a triggering event occurs. In phase II the regulator sends a physiological signal that alerts the cognator. During phase III the cognator assesses the triggering event and selects a coping stance. In phase IV the cognator translates this coping stance into a coping strategy. Finally, the person exhibits a behavioral response that reflects the coping stance and strategy.

The adaptation nurse processes many triggering events automatically. Other triggering events, because they are novel or complex, require energy and attention. The adaptation nurse at a more fully developed stage must devote energy and attention to different triggering events. The stimuli that influence her and her place in the development process determine the triggering events to which she will respond. The adaptation nurse in the adolescent stage responds to very few nursing triggering events automatically; therefore, she must devote a great deal of attention to many triggering events. As she moves toward the generative stage of development, she encounters fewer novel situations and can devote her energy to complex interactions.

Adaptation nurse graduates are able to apply the Roy model in all patient care situations with varying degrees of skill. They have been taught to think in an organized manner that allows them to process and respond to substantial amounts of complex information. They have the ability to conceptualize and formulate accurate judgments based on an organized perception of complex data. The most important factor that distinguishes adaptation nurses in the adolescent stage from nurses in the young adult or generative stage is the operation of the regulator/cognator process.

THE ADOLESCENT STAGE
Regulator/cognator process

As you will recall, the regulator/cognator process involves five phases. In phase I the adaptation nurse experiences a triggering event. In phase II she experiences neural and hormonal stimulation and demonstrates behavior that indicates that stress is occurring. She is in a state of readiness in which the regulator signals the cognator to label and define the stimulus. In the third, fourth, and fifth phases the cognator determines the different behavioral responses associated with each developmental level. In phase III the cognator selects one of three coping stances: approach/avoidance, compromise, or inaction. This selection is influenced by the person's internal state or the external environment. In phase IV the cognator selects the coping strategy, a plan for implementing the coping stance. Finally, in phase V the adaptation nurse engages in a behavioral response, usually a nursing action, that allows her to cope with the triggering event.

Coping stance

The cognator of the adaptation nurse in the adolescent stage processes the triggering event differently than does the nurse in the young adult or generative stage of development. In phase III the adaptation nurse in the adolescent stage is likely to choose approach/avoidance, compromise, or inaction as a coping stance. You will recall that the nurse in the adolescent stage of development is self-oriented, and her major concern is the establishment of her identity. For this reason she makes choices that, first, meet her need for professional identity and, second, meet the needs of the adapting person. She has the capability and potential for making the same judgments as the adaptation nurse in more advanced stages of development, but she seldom does so because most of her energy is devoted to self-development. Let us discuss the rationale for her selection of coping stances.

Ideally, the adaptation nurse in the adolescent developmental phase will choose the coping stance of compromise, which allows her to deal with her own anxiety and still meet the immediate needs of the adapting person. As she experiences stress, her cognator helps her sift the data and select a stance that will allow her to maintain her level of adequacy (in this instance her professional identity) while meeting the essential adaptation needs of the patient. This is optimal performance at the adolescent stage of development. A less desirable coping stance is approach/avoidance. If the nurse selects this coping stance, she has perceived the situation as dangerous, and she is experiencing a severe threat to her professional identity. The triggering event has produced a demand that is too great for her to respond as an adaptive person. Generally, she will respond automatically by removing herself from a threat that could destroy her perception of herself as a professional nurse. Finally, the adaptation nurse could choose a coping stance of inaction. In this situation the triggering event is so threatening to her sense of professional identity that she chooses not to acknowledge this threat. This is obviously the least effective stance to take. If it is adopted too regularly, the adaptation nurse will fail to assume her professional role. Few environments can tolerate a nurse at any stage of practice who repeatedly fails to identify the need for nursing action.

Coping strategies

Optimally, when the adaptation nurse labels a triggering event as stressful and selects a coping stance of compromise, she has decided that she is capable of coping with the triggering event if she engages in certain defensive maneuvers that will allow her to reduce tension. Essentially, she reevaluates the stress and uses suppression, projection, or substitution to diminish the threat to her professional identity. With suppression the newly graduated adaptation nurse attempts to keep hidden behaviors that are incompatible with her professional identity. For example, in a first job experience she knows that she should asseses the client in all four modes, make nursing judgments and formulate nursing diagnoses, set priorities, plan goals and interventions, and evaluate the person's behavioral response. However, when confronted with a new clinical environment, a new institution, and a demanding patient load, she is realistically unable to engage in an optimal nursing process. Therefore, she engages in behaviors that will help her provide adequate patient care and also establish and maintain her professional identity and sense of adequacy. The adaptation nurse in the adolescent stage of development then engages in obvious nursing activities and neglects or suppresses the existence of less urgent needs, formulates obvious judgments and diagnoses, has only one or two priorities, and seldom evaluates outcomes, except as they relate to her professional identity. In addition she uses projection to rid herself of any unpleasant, unprofessional aspects of her performance. She does this by ascribing her feelings of inadequacy and incompetence to her peers, the patient, or the environment. Her failure to assume the professional identity to which she aspires may be due to a shorthanded staff, ridiculous rules or unrealistic expectations of the institution, a "difficult" or "obnoxious" patient, demanding physicians, or her perhaps inadequate education. There are many available objects for projection, and because there are often problems within the institution or the nurse's experiences, this method of explaining one's professional deficit is quite effective in allaying fears of incompetence. The adaptation nurse in the adolescent stage of development can give less than optimal but safe nursing care without feeling inadequate, because she has projected these nonprofessional feelings onto appropriate objects in the environment.

Finally, substitution allows the newly graduated adaptation nurse to invest energy in objects that will allow her to experience adequacy and positive professional identity. She will quickly learn which settings and clients will allow her to function at an optimal level. She will therefore manipulate the environment to minimize stress-producing experiences. For example, she will avoid switching to other clinical units, decrease the number of times she is assigned to a "difficult" client, and diminish her contacts with a nonsupportive supervisor. The adaptation nurse focuses on situations and clients who reinforce her positive professional identity. She diminishes her energy investment in situations or clients who disrupt her level of adequacy.

Compromise represents the optimal coping stance assumed by the adaptation nurse in the adolescent stage. The strategies of suppression, projection, and substitution allow the adaptation nurse to provide adequate client interactions and establish a positive professional identity while not providing all the elements of the care she learned as a student. This is not the performance for which she was educated, and yet this is usual performance for the beginning adaptation nurse. Until she masters the environment and establishes her identity, she will not be able to expand her practice to include the more complex practices of adaptation nursing.

Approach/avoidance is a less than optimal coping stance choice. Flight is the most effective alternative in the nursing situation and is the alternative the new graduate should choose when she is overwhelmed. She recognizes the fact that the triggering event is overpowering and removes herself from the situation. In most cases she will transfer the responsibility of coping to a more competent nurse, usually an adaptation nurse at a higher level of professional development. This coping strategy allows for optimal care and safety for the client, but when it is chosen repeatedly, it results in diminished professional adequacy for the adaptation nurse. On the other hand, the nurse in this stage of development who chooses fight, striking out reflexively at fear-evoking triggering events, is likely to make ineffective clinical judgments that adversely affect the client's level of adequacy. In these situations medication errors may be made, material may be contaminated, procedures may be done incorrectly, and client anxiety may be increased. This strategy may result in a positive response if the nurse's intuitive responses are valid; however, the more frequently this strategy is used, the greater the possibility that outcomes will be ineffective. When this happens, the adapting person's level of adequacy is disrupted, and the adaptation nurse's professional identity is threatened.

Fight or flight, then, can be an effective coping strategy. When used infrequently, it generally results in a positive response for the client and allows the adaptation nurse in the adolescent stage to maintain her professional identity. However, when this strategy must be used repeatedly, the client may not receive adequate assistance with adaptive problems, and the nurse's sense of professional identity will be decreased or distorted. Hence, new graduates in overly stressful environments will have difficulty achieving the goal of a positive professional identity.

Finally, should the adaptation nurse in this stage of development select inaction as a coping stance, she must choose from several defensive maneuvers including denial, reaction formation, and dissociation. She must then deny the experience of a triggering event. If these strategies are utilized repeatedly, the new graduate's option to practice adaptation nursing is usually curtailed.

When the adaptation nurse chooses denial as a coping strategy, the cognator signals that it is overwhelmed and will not respond. The message of the regulator is blocked, and the triggering event is maintained outside of conscious awareness. When the graduate chooses this strategy, she experiences the physiological alert but fails to respond. She is in a constant state of physical readiness but cannot acknowledge the reason for her tension. If she resorts to denial, she will fail to meet the expectations of her supervisor, the client, and herself. The outward signs of denial include a heightened physiological response and behavior that resembles noncompliance, insubordination, negligence, or ignorance. In her attempt to maintain her professional identity, the nurse has produced the opposite effect. By denying an experience and failing to act, she has decreased her level of professional adequacy.

Reaction formation has a similar effect. The nurse in this instance is so overwhelmed by the triggering event that she replaces her pain with an inappropriate response such as laughing or joking when the situation calls for seriousness. This response may be evident when the new graduate has her initial experiences with some of the tragedies associated with caring for clients. If the adaptation nurse considers her emotional response nonprofessional, she may assume a stance perceived by observers as inappropriate. As a result, she may be labeled incompassionate and uncaring. If continued, this behavior will seriously affect the new graduate's ability to meet professional expectations.

Finally, dissociation is a mechanism that allows the nurse to separate herself totally from the triggering event. The nurse might deny a particular occurrence or when questioned about a particular incident have no awareness of the experience. The cognator allows the person to say, "This is not happening to me." This behavior is rarely observed in a hospital, because it represents overt disregard of reality. Should a nurse employ this strategy, she might be labeled as "ill" or insane or as a liar. A nurse who must resort to dissociation to maintain her professional identity should not be in any health care setting.

Inaction is the least effective coping strategy the adaptation nurse in the adolescent phase can choose. For example, when called on to assist during a cardiac arrest, a recent graduate may stand immobile, unable to respond. If the nursing environment is so disruptive for the adaptation nurse that she must block, deny, or remove herself from it to maintain her professional identity, she will not be effective in assisting the client in maintaining his level of adequacy.

Behavioral response: nursing action

We have alluded to the behavioral response that might occur when the adaptation nurse selects a particular coping stance and strategy. Now let us explore the specific nursing actions that this adaptation nurse might take.

In the fifth phase of the regulator/cognator process, the adaptation nurse demonstrates a variety of behaviors that represent her attempt to achieve or maintain biological, psychological, and social adequacy. These behaviors are expressed through energy channels that include the physiological, psychological, and sociological adapting modes. When a triggering event occurs and the regulator/cognator process terminates with a behavioral response, the behavior can be observed in all four modes. Usually one mode predominates, and this is true in the professional development of the adaptation nurse. When she experiences a triggering event, she has physiological, psychological, and sociological responses. For our discussion in this chapter we are primarily concerned with her sociological response—her professional adaptation nurse role behaviors. We will focus on the other modes only as they influence these role behaviors.

Let us consider some of the categories of nursing action and identify the relationship between these categories and the coping stance and strategies selected by the adaptation nurse in the adolescent stage. When engaging in the coping behavior of compromise, the adaptation nurse in this developmental stage suppresses or disregards portions of the triggering event and uses the nursing process to assist the client with overt and predictable problems of adaptation. To do this she utilizes the nursing interventions of support and collaboration.

Support (behavior that approves, sanctions, or validates) is rather easily learned, frequently used, and sanctioned by most caregivers and clients as an appropriate nursing action. Collaboration (cooperation with other caregivers intended to maintain the client's physiological adequacy) is a nursing intervention with great public sanction and a high degree of professional value as a result of its historical significance to nursing. Support and collaboration are usually mastered as nursing interventions during the adolescent stage of development. They continue to have value but are utilized less frequently by adaptation nurses at all levels of professional development.

The adaptation nurse in the adolescent stage uses the coping stance of compromise to deal with the stress produced when she interacts with a client. She employs support and collaboration to deal with obvious problems of adaptation. Although she is able to deal with complex problems of adaptation, her energy during this adolescent stage is primarily directed toward becoming an adaptation nurse. She therefore uses the easily learned and widely applicable support skills and the universally sanctioned, more complex collaborative skills to meet the adaptation needs of her clients and her own need for professional adequacy.

In the compromise coping stance as well as the flight component of approach/avoidance, the newly graduated adaptation nurse must be able to identify problems of adaptation that are beyond her current stage of development. When she makes this assessment, she should be able to realize that the client requires the assistance of an adaptation nurse in the young adult or generative stage of development. During the adolescent stage the nurse can usually identify the behavioral responses and some of the more obvious influencing stimuli. She may not be able to formulate the necessary judgments and diagnoses or determine whether the client requires teaching or enabling actions from the adaptation nurse. For the adolescent level of development, optimal functioning in both compromise and avoidance is evident when the adaptation nurse recognizes the client's need for additional assistance and makes that assistance available to him.

In approach/avoidance, during which the behavioral response is automatic, the adaptation nurse in this stage of development may use support, collaboration, teaching, or enabling. These nursing actions, however, are exercised impulsively. The adaptation nurse makes an intuitive response. She has not taken the time or been allowed to make a thoughtful decision or apply the adaptation process. As a result, the effect on the client's level of adequacy is not predictable. If the adaptation nurse's intuitive response is sound, both the person and the nurse will experience a positive impact on their respective levels of adequacy. However, if the intuitive action is invalid, the client and the nurse will experience further disruption in the level of adequacy. In approach/avoidance, then, the adolescent adaptation nurse may apply any one of or all four nursing actions, but she does so impulsively without the assistance of her usual organized and structured approach to the client. This type of intuitive functioning should be used infrequently during the adolescent stage of development.

Finally, if the adaptation nurse in the adolescent stage chooses the inaction coping stance, she will not engage in any of the four nursing actions. For this reason, her behavior will consistently fail to meet role expectations, and her attempt to establish her professional identity will be disrupted.

In summary, then, the adaptation nurse in the adolescent stage of development typically engages in the coping behaviors associated with compromise and approach/avoidance. These coping behaviors allow her to use the nursing actions of support and collaboration effectively. In addition, she must be able to identify the client's need for more advanced assistance and make certain that the assistance is made available. Finally, she may impulsively utilize any of the four nursing actions in emergent situations.

Health/illness continuum

Given the nature of support and collaboration and the developmental tasks of the adolescent stage of professional development, the newly graduated adaptation nurse functions optimally with patients in the second diagnostic category, patients who need support in their cognator/regulator process and who can use assistance with increasing the effectiveness of their behavioral response. These clients are found in the middle range of the health/illness continuum. Clients experiencing disrupted wellness are ideally matched with the adaptation nurse in the adolescent stage of development.

Clients who occupy the second diagnostic category, disrupted wellness, usually seek health care assistance in traditional settings, require support, and often need collaborative intervention with their behaviors in the second diagnostic category. As the client in disrupted wellness moves in either direction on the health/illness continuum, he may need to be referred to an adaptation nurse at a higher developmental level. For example, as the client moves toward wellness, the adaptation nurse may refer him to the nurse who plans discharges. On the other hand, should the client move toward illness, he might require the enabling skills of the adaptation nurse in the young adult stage of development. The client in disrupted wellness allows the adaptation nurse in the adolescent stage to develop her professional identity. She can identify with a role model usually found in an institution with well-defined expectations. She can practice and gain proficiency in the skills she associates with her professional ideal. Finally, she can delegate or disregard more complicated parts of her education until she has the energy to cope adequately with the full demands of her professional role.

In conclusion, the adaptation nurse in the adolescent stage of development is capable of taking on the full range of responsibilities and actions associated with adaptation nursing. However, until she establishes her professional identity, the scope of her practice is limited. During this adolescent stage, her regulator processes triggering events in the same manner as do those of more experienced adaptation nurses. Her cognator, however, responds in a more limited fashion. Because of the influence of a variety of stimuli, her coping abilities are limited to compromise and approach/avoidance. The behavioral responses are limited almost exclusively to support and collaboration. As a result, the adaptation nurse in this stage of development finds most satisfaction and is most effective interacting with clients in the stage of disrupted wellness. With the passage of time, increased knowledge, and support and nurturance, the adaptation nurse will move to the stage of the young adult.

THE YOUNG ADULT STAGE
Regulator/cognator process

The adaptation nurse in the young adult stage also experiences a five-phase regulator/cognator process. In phase I she experiences a triggering event, and in phase II her regulator signals a physiological alert and triggers the cognator. In phase III the difference between the young adult and the adolescent stages of development becomes apparent. The adaptation nurse in the young adult stage can select from the four coping stances: approach/avoidance, compromise, self-enhancement, and inaction. She then chooses a coping strategy and engages in a nursing action that will affect her level of adequacy as well as that of the client. As you will recall, the tasks of the young adult are directed toward solidarity and intimacy. The adaptation nurse in this stage of development has an established, clearly defined identity and therefore devotes her energy toward solidifying her role performance and expanding her skills. She expresses her needs for intimacy by moving from the self-orientation of adolescence to an orientation directed toward another person. The adaptation nurse in this stage of development takes more risks, using the adaptation nursing process and her knowledge of the client's regulator/cognator process to plan individualized care for clients in complex situations.

Coping stance

The cognator of the adaptation nurse in this developmental stage processes a similarly experienced triggering event differently from that of a nurse in the adolescent stage. In phase III of the transaction the young adult's cognator usually chooses a coping stance of compromise or self-enhancement. Occasionally, she may choose a coping stance of approach/avoidance, but in this stage she should never select inaction as a coping stance. Like the adaptation nurse in the adolescent stage, she uses compromise to reduce the stress in potentially overwhelming situations. This defensive maneuver allows her to meet the adaptation needs of the client while maintaining her level of professional adequacy. In addition, she begins to assume self-enhancing coping behaviors. She is looking for growth-producing situations and therefore exposes herself to more complex environments and to adaptation problems that require her to utilize a higher level of adaptation skills. Because of her clearly defined professional identity and proficiency in the adaptation nursing process, she seldom confronts a situation that is frightening enough to elicit an approach/avoidance stance. The nurse in this stage will rarely need to engage in impulsive or intuitive nursing action. Furthermore, the adaptation nurse who is striving for intimacy and solidarity should have no need to distort reality in the manner associated with the inaction coping stance.

Coping strategies

As she did in her adolescent stage, the "young adult" adaptation nurse uses the coping strategies of suppression, projection, and substitution when her cognator selects the coping stance of compromise. She uses these stances and strategies less frequently as she progresses through this developmental stage. Compromise, especially suppression, is used to solidify her perception of herself as an adaptation nurse and to strengthen her group identity. She uses suppression to block out portions of a triggering event with which she feels unable to cope. Because of her increased developmental skills, she needs to block out less of the triggering event than does the adolescent. She will seldom choose this strategy except when confronted with a new problem of adaptation. This adaptation nurse seldom needs to use projection or substitution; in fact, the frequency with which she uses these defensive maneuvers indicates the degree of solidarity she experiences in her professional identity. She can assume accountability for her interactions with the client and rarely needs to project her tension on the institution, her peers, or the client. She utilizes substitution less often because she gains satisfaction and solidifies her role with increasing numbers of adaptation problems and clients.

As she moves through this developmental stage she uses compromise and the associated coping strategies less frequently. She utilizes coping stances and strategies that help her to solidify her role as a professional adaptation nurse while increasing the quality of her interactions with the client.

With increasing frequency, the adaptation nurse in this stage of development chooses the self-enhancing coping strategies of confrontation, negotiation, and manipulation, which allow her to move toward both of her goals during this stage of development. The self-enhancing strategies serve primarily to increase the adaptation nurse's degree of closeness with the client, which improves the adaptation nurse's effectiveness and thereby increases her sense of solidarity. She utilizes all three strategies, using confrontation as an effective nursing skill most frequently. She is beginning to use manipulation, and she seldom attempts negotiation.

The adaptation nurse in the young adult stage of development utilizes confrontation when her cognator suggests that immediate, direct action will have the optimal effect. If she is willing to approach the triggering event directly, if she takes the risk, the nurse will experience growth and participate with the client in an interaction that will be extremely effective. For example, when the adaptation nurse at this stage of development is confronted with a new environment or a complex problem of adaptation, she may choose compromise to block out the new or complex portions of the interaction and focus on the familiar portions of the interactions. However, the nurse in this stage of development is more likely to utilize the full potential of her adaptation skills to increase her closeness and involvement with the client. The adaptation nurse usually chooses confrontation for one of two reasons: either a belief that the time is right and that hesitation will result in a less desirable response or when there exists a lack of knowledge, skill, or potential to further influence the environment or the internal state. In confrontation the adaptation nurse approaches the environment and her interactions directly, utilizing all of her adaptation abilities. She recognizes the risk but seeks the personal challenge as well as the potential for optimal effectiveness.

Like confrontation, manipulation allows the adaptation nurse in the young adult stage of development to increase both her intimacy and solidarity. Manipulation is more complex than confrontation and is therefore a greater challenge for the nurse. As she encounters a new or complex situation, she uses manipulation when she repeatedly engages in the adaptation process until she can facilitate an optimal interaction between herself and the client. Her primary effect is on the environment.

When the adaptation nurse in this stage of her development interacts with the client to increase the client's level of adequacy, she must repeatedly process data before establishing an optimal environment for the client's interactions. This process involves manipulation. The nurse uses manipulation when she brings together simultaneously several physicians who are sharing their observations and goals with the client. The adaptation nurse maintains and promotes the interaction until an optimal environment can be achieved. This strategy brings the adaptation nurse and the client into a more intimate relationship and increases the adaptation nurse's feelings of solidarity when it is completed effectively.

The adaptation nurse may occasionally use negotiation as a coping strategy. This strategy is the most complex of the self-enhancing strategies, because it involves changes or alterations in the adapting person's internal state. For this reason it is usually associated with the adaptation nurse in the generative stage of development and will therefore be considered when discussing that stage of development.

The adaptation nurse engages in the coping strategies of suppression, substitution, projection, confrontation, and manipulation to accomplish the tasks of this developmental stage and to increase her solidarity and intimacy.

Behavioral response—nursing action

In the fifth phase of the regulator/cognator process the adaptation nurse demonstrates a variety of behaviors that represent her attempt to achieve or maintain physiological, psychological, and sociological adequacy. Energy is expressed in the form of behavioral responses through the physiological, self-concept, role performance, and interdependence modes. As is true in the case of the adolescent nurse, the majority of the "young adult" nurse's professional behaviors are expressed sociologically, in the role performance and interdependence adaptive modes. The other modes will be considered only as influencing stimuli at this time.

The adaptation nurse in the young adult stage also engages in the nursing actions of support and collaboration when she selects the coping stance of compromise, utilizing these actions with more skill and in more complex and subtle situations. You will recall from previous discussions that the nurse blocks out or disregards smaller portions of the interaction and therefore is more likely to deal with the total client rather than with isolated elements. In addition, the adaptation nurse in the young adult stage of development is able to assess and formulate judgments in situations in which she may feel uncomfortable carrying out the nursing action. In such a compromise situation she brings these judgments to the attention of the nurse in the generative stage and is thus assured that the client will experience an optimal interaction. Through compromise the adaptation nurse is able to solidify her professional role while increasing her involvement with the client. When she achieves these personal goals, she has had an optimal impact on the client's level of adequacy.

Now we will examine the self-enhancing coping strategies and the associated nursing actions. Teaching (actions and skills utilized to impart knowledge, information, and skill) is used frequently. In addition, enabling behaviors, which strengthen, maintain, or give power to the adapting person, are also used.

When the adaptation nurse in this stage of development selects the coping stance of confrontation, she has made the decision to confront the triggering event directly. When engaging in this coping strategy, the nurse predominantly utilizes the nursing action of enabling. Based on her assessment, she is aware that the client is unable to maintain his level of adequacy. She therefore promotes an interaction with the client that will maintain, strengthen, or provide necessary power. This nursing action has a high degree of involvement and therefore requires closeness with the client. Such enabling actions include establishing the therapeutic relationship, using counseling strategies and self-awareness techniques, and engaging in patient advocacy. These actions support the adaptation nurse's need for increased intimacy and also provide the client with maintenance or with an increase in his level of adequacy.

When the adaptation nurse selects the coping strategy of manipulation, she engages primarily in the nursing action of enabling. You will recall that manipulation involves repeated processing of the interaction to arrive at an optimal solution. The nurse in the young adult stage uses these repeated interactions to collect data and to provide the client with the necessary resources to increase his level of adequacy. In these repeated interactions the adaptation nurse often provides the client with access to the environment that he did not previously possess. In addition, she may engage in enabling actions to prepare the client for the teaching/learning experience, or she may use enabling actions to facilitate the client's use of newly acquired skills or ideas. Manipulation represents a complex strategy utilized by the nurse in the later stages of the developmental process. It involves repeated assessment of a complex adaptation situation, and it requires attention to subtle behavior. Finally, it requires the adaptation nurse to engage in an intricate combination or sequence of nursing actions that provide the client with an optimal adaptation experience. In addition, this process involves risk and challenge for the nurse and solidifies her professional role and peer group identity. It also meets her need for intimacy because functioning successfully at this level involves a comprehensive experience and closeness with the client.

To summarize, then, the adaptation nurse in the young adult stage of development uses the nursing actions of support, collaboration, teaching, and enabling. As she progresses through this stage, she relies less often on the coping strategy of compromise and hence reduces her use of support and collaboration. As she matures and moves toward the generative stage of development, she increases her facility with the nursing actions of teaching and enabling. In the complex situations in which the nurse assumes the self-enhancing coping stance and utilizes confrontation and manipulation, she will continue to use some supportive and collaborative actions in support of the more complex actions of teaching and enabling.

Health/illness continuum

Given the tasks of the young adult stage of professional development and the fact that the adaptation nurse in this stage can utilize all four of the nursing actions, she is qualified to work with a client at any point on the health/illness continuum. Her personal goals of solidarity and intimacy and her skill level make her best suited for interaction with ill persons. The newly acquired self-enhancing coping stance, use of the strategies of confrontation and negotiation, and increasing skill in the nursing action of enabling make the adaptation nurse in this stage especially adept at interacting with persons experiencing the complex category II diagnoses and persons with two or more category III diagnoses. These clients require some support of functional behaviors, and complex collaborative activities, and many require the adaptation nurse to take control and engage in enabling activities. In addition, the adaptation nurse may participate in some teaching activities with the client in the second diagnostic category. The client in disrupted wellness and the client experiencing illness are ideally matched with the skills, performance level, and personal and professional goals of the adaptation nurse in the young adult stage of development.

Clients in the second and third diagnostic categories are usually found in traditional health care settings. In addition, they often need special services and therefore are seen in intensive care units, emergency rooms, operating rooms, and crisis centers. The adaptation nurse in the young adult stage of development may interact with these clients as the primary nursing caregiver, or she may see these clients on referral from a nurse in the adolescent stage. When confronted with a difficult problem of adaptation, she may consult with an adaptation nurse in the generative stage of professional development, and on rare occasions she may refer a client to this nurse. The ill client provides the adaptation nurse with the opportunity to achieve her professional goals. She experiences solidarity, because these more complex adapting interactions allow her to increase and perfect her nursing process. In addition, clients in illness categories require closeness. Therefore, the client's level of adequacy is improved, and the adaptation nurse's level of adequacy is maintained or enhanced.

In conclusion, the adaptation nurse in the young adult stage of development represents a large portion of practicing adaptation nurses. She is capable of providing for and interacting with clients in any position on the health/illness continuum. She is skilled in the nursing process and can implement all four nursing actions; however, because she is striving for solidarity and professional intimacy, she is optimally suited to interact with clients in the second and third diagnostic categories. She has a wide range of coping abilities, and her behavioral responses are applicable to a variety of situations. The adaptation nurse in this developmental stage is perhaps the most employable nurse. She is desired by agencies and individuals who seek to utilize adaptation nursing service. With the passage of time, increased knowledge, and support and nurturance, the adaptation nurse in the young adult stage of development will be able to move into the generative stage of development. Perhaps the most important aspects of this transition are education and knowledge. Time and experience alone are not sufficient to move the adaptation nurse into the generative stage of development.

THE GENERATIVE STAGE
Regulator/cognator process

The only difference between the nurse in the generative stage and those in other stages in the first step of the regulator/cognator process is in the number and kind of triggering events she experiences. The difference begins with phase III and the work of the cognator. The adaptation nurse in this stage of development can also select from the four coping stances of approach/avoidance, compromise, self-enhancement, and inaction. As you will recall, this choice is influenced by the task of this developmental stage. The adaptation nurse in the generative stage of development is concerned with production and care. She will accomplish these tasks by interacting with the client to fill his most subtle adaptation needs. She utilizes the adaptation process at the highest level and therefore has a comprehensive understanding of the client, which allows her to interact with him regarding his present and future adaptation needs. In addition, she assumes the responsibility for the education and preparation of future adaptation nurses. The energy of the generative adaptation nurse, then, is future oriented, directed toward preventive adaptation nursing and the preparation of other adaptation nurses.

Coping stance

The generative adaptation nurse responds to more complex triggering events and utilizes coping stances and strategies with different proficiency from those in the other stages of development. In the third phase of the regulator/cognator process the generative adaptation nurse usually chooses a coping stance of compromise or self-enhancement. She seldom chooses approach/avoidance and never chooses inaction. Her coping stances are similar to those of the nurse in the young adult stage of development. The difference arises in the kinds of triggering events she chooses to respond to. Although the generative nurse and the nurse in the young adult stage both engage primarily in compromise and self-enhancement, the generative adaptation nurse tends to use self-enhancement more frequently, and she does so with a more extensive knowledge base and a future- and growth-oriented perspective.

When the generative adaptation nurse chooses compromise, she uses it as a temporary defensive maneuver. When confronted with a complex, potentially overwhelming interaction, she may choose to block out portions of that interaction because they are distracting or because they cannot be dealt with at the time. Unlike the adaptation nurses in previous stages, she makes a point of returning to the blocked portion of the interaction and working it out. She has diminished need for this coping stance but will utilize it skillfully in emergent and complex situations.

The generative adaptation nurse chooses a self-enhancing coping stance most frequently because it is growth and future oriented, providing her with the opportunity of optimal interactions with the client. The effectiveness of this coping stance is based also on the degree of involvement and the knowledge the adaptation nurse has acquired about the client. Because she is so skilled in the adaptation process, the generative adaptation nurse is most likely to experience success when she copes in this manner. She has no need to act impulsively or distort professional reality; therefore, she does not engage in approach/avoidance or inaction.

Coping strategies

The adaptation nurse in the developmental stage of generativity utilizes the coping strategies of suppression, manipulation, negotiation, and occasionally confrontation. When she chooses the coping stance of compromise, she will use suppression as a defensive maneuver to protect herself or the client from being overwhelmed. She resorts to suppression only temporarily; when timing or circumstances improve, she deals with the suppressed portion of the interaction. Because of the comprehensive nature of the generative adaptation nurse's practice, she cannot ignore blocks of information or experience; to do so would diminish the effectiveness of her interaction with the client.

When the generative adaptation nurse assumes a self-enhancing coping stance, she utilizes negotiation and manipulation most frequently and uses confrontation only occasionally. If she does engage in confrontation, it is usually in an emergent, highly complex situation that requires immediate action. In this coping strategy, the adaptation nurse recognizes potential risk but makes the decision to take immediate, direct action to help the client stabilize his level of adequacy. Because of her orientation toward growth and future adaptation, the generative nurse seldom finds herself in a situation that requires confrontation. In addition, since she prefers to operate from a position of optimal information and understanding, confrontation is the least effective self-enhancing coping strategy for her needs.

The generative adaptation nurse is most likely to choose the coping strategies of negotiation and manipulation, which are most effective when the adaptation nurse has a close involvement with the client and comprehensive knowledge of that client, including the operation of the regulator/cognator process. In addition, she uses both of these strategies to enhance the client's level of adequacy. Therefore, the strategies are growth and future oriented. Based on the skill level of the generative adaptation nurse and her professional goals, these two strategies provide her with opportunities for optimal effectiveness.

Negotiation involves the generative nurse's repeated interactions with the client to produce an internal state of optimal adaptive functioning. Manipulation involves repeated interactions with the environment to create an optimal atmosphere for adaptive functioning. The generative nurse may engage in both strategies simultaneously to bring the client and the environment to a point of mutual compatibility. In either case, the nurse assumes the role of advocate for the client, assisting the client in achieving his adaptive potential. Simultaneously, she moves toward her professional goals of production and care and experiences an increase in her level of professional adequacy.

In summary, the adaptation nurse in the generative stage of development utilizes the coping strategies of suppression, confrontation, manipulation, and negotiation. She meets her needs for production and care by providing optimal circumstances for the client to increase the level of adequacy.

Behavioral response—nursing action

In the fifth phase of the regulator/cognator process the adaptation nurse in the generative stage of development again expresses behavior through the role performance mode. The behavioral response is expressed through nursing actions engaged in to facilitate the client's adaptation and to meet the adaptation nurse's goals of production and care.

The generative adaptation nurse uses support and collaboration, especially when engaging in the coping strategy of compromise. She utilizes support to acknowledge the client's appropriate regulator/cognator functions and to sustain adaptive behavioral responses. Collaborative skills are part of the adaptation nurse's actions at all stages of development, but these skills are used least frequently in the generative stage of development because the generative adaptation nurse has a firm, well-established identity and therefore has less need to utilize highly sanctioned, collaborative activities. Even more significantly, her growth orientation and ability to enhance adequacy seldom require collaborative actions. Instead, the goals of the generative adaptation nurse are aimed at autonomous functioning.

The nursing actions of enabling and teaching constitute the largest percentage of the generative adaptation nurse's behavior responses. When she adopts the strategy of manipulation, she engages primarily in enabling actions, utilizing these activities to mobilize the environment and provide the client with strength, power, or sustenance. The strategy of negotiation involves enabling as well as teaching. In this strategy the adaptation nurse employs the most complex adaptation nursing interaction. She attempts to influence the client's internal state—specifically his ideas, beliefs, and perceptions—in an effort to increase his level of adaptation. By using teaching/learning activities, she tries to add to the knowledge and enhance the beliefs of the client, thus bringing about an increase in his level of adequacy. In addition, she may select enabling actions, including a therapeutic relationship, to motivate the client to participate in the teaching/learning experience. These nursing actions usually result in an increase in the client's level of adaptation. In addition, they allow the adaptation nurse to move toward her professional goals of care and production. The generative adaptation nurse also serves as a role model for other adaptation nurses and provides consultation to nurses in the adolescent and young adult stages of development.

In summary, the behavior of the adaptation nurse in the generative stage of development results in nursing actions that include suppression, confrontation, negotiation, and manipulation. She is concerned with growth and enhancing experiences and therefore demonstrates the adaptive process at its highest level. She also assumes responsibility for the education and socialization of future adaptation nurses. Because of this responsibility, the generative adaptation nurse usually acquires advanced formal education. Experience and a stimulating environment alone do not provide the adaptation nurse with the ability to fulfill the tasks of this developmental stage. Formal advanced education makes it possible for the generative adaptation nurse to assume the task of educating adaptation nurses in various stages of development as well as engaging in the complex nursing strategy of negotiation.

Health/illness continuum

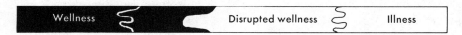

Wellness | Disrupted wellness | Illness

Given the tasks of the generative stage of professional development and the fact that she can skillfully utilize all four nursing actions, the generative adaptation nurse is qualified to work with the client in any position on the health/illness continuum. However, her personal goals of production and care, her commitment to growth and enhancement, and her responsibility for professional education makes this nurse best suited to interact with well clients and clients in disrupted wellness. These clients are identified as having diagnoses in the first and second categories. The client experiencing wellness seeks health care to validate the level of wellness, acquire information for growth and stimulation, and gain support and information to cope with a category II diagnosis. The client in disrupted wellness seeks health care to validate his regulator/cognator process and gain information about and assistance with his category II diagnosis. These diagnostic categories are generally found in outpatient clinics and alternate care facilities. Clients in wellness and the beginning stages of disrupted wellness enter these health care settings seeking knowledge and education. They are coping effectively in many aspects of their lives and are therefore open and receptive to self-enhancing experiences. Furthermore, the needs of these clients are compatible with the professional goals and needs of the generative adaptation nurse. As a result, the client experiences optimal interactions within the health care system, and the generative adaptation nurse experiences satisfaction and growth.

In her role as educator for future adaptation nurses, the adaptation nurse also functions as a consultant. In large institutions the generative nurse can supervise or consult with adaptation nurses in the adolescent and young adult stages of development. Her consultations involve clients at all positions on the health/illness continuum. In addition, she provides formal instruction in colleges and universities, where she assists adaptation nurses in varying stages of development to interact with adapting persons at any point on the continuum.

The generative adaptation nurse is capable of completing the adaptation nursing process in complex and subtle circumstances. She is competent in all four nursing actions but is especially skilled in the coping strategies of manipulation and negotiation. Because of her personal striving for care and production, her motivation toward growth and enhancement, and her commitment to the education of other adaptation nurses, she is especially suited to clients experiencing wellness and disrupted wellness. The adaptation nurse in this developmental stage usually has considerable professional experience, advanced formal education, and specialized knowledge in some area of nursing theory and practice. She may be employed by a larger service or educational institution or may be (more recently) self-employed, offering clinical and consultant services.

CONCLUSION

The graduate of an adaptation nursing curriculum has the skills and the knowledge to become an expert practitioner of adaptation nursing. The process by which she becomes that expert is developmental. In each developmental stage she must master certain tasks. The degree of ease or difficulty she experiences in achieving these tasks is dependent on the passage of time and the quality of her professional environment, as well as certain internal stimuli including her physical being, her maturational level, and her internal state. Additionally, her success is mediated by the internal transaction that processes and integrates her experiences.

In the adolescent stage of development the adaptation nurse responds to many triggering events and processes little of the environment automatically. In addition, the tasks of this stage require her to be self-centered and focused on the establishment of her identity. For these reasons she focuses attention on obvious, noncomplex interactions that enhance her professional identification. She utilizes the skills of support and collaboration and is most effective in traditional settings, interacting with clients who are experiencing disrupted wellness.

The adaptation nurse in the young adult stage of development processes many interactions automatically and devotes energy to novel or very complex interactions. The tasks of this stage are focused on solidifying her role and becoming other directed in her professional performance. For these reasons her energy is directed toward complex interactions. She utilizes all four nursing actions and is becoming proficient in enabling. She is most effective in specialized settings, interacting with clients who are experiencing disrupted wellness and illness.

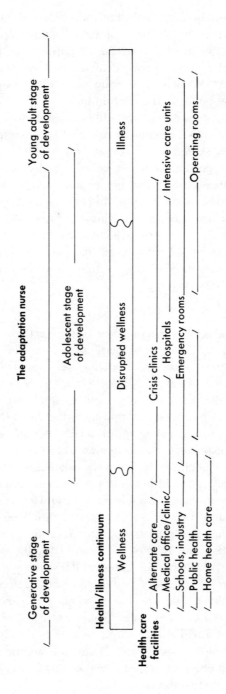

FIGURE 5-1
Reciprocal relationship between the client's diagnostic category and the nurse's developmental stage.

Finally, the adaptation nurse in the generative stage of development processes the majority of her nursing interactions automatically and expends additional energy in extremely complex or subtle interactions. The tasks of this stage are to provide optimal care and to assume the responsibility for the education and socialization of future adaptation nurses. As a result, she expends energy providing the highest level adaptation nursing performance. She is skilled in all four nursing actions and demonstrates excellent teaching and enabling skills. She assumes a consultative or educational role with clients in any position on the health/illness continuum but usually provides direct service to clients experiencing wellness or disrupted wellness.

This chapter has attempted to describe the adult development of the adaptation nurse. In addition, the reciprocal needs of the client and the developing adaptation nurse were identified. It is our belief that the client can receive optimal care and the adaptation nurse can experience enhancement when the diagnostic category and the developmental stage are paired appropriately (Figure 5-1). Please complete the following exercises to demonstrate mastery of the content.

LEARNING EXPERIENCE

1 Define the following terms.
   Development   Young adult stage
   Adolescent stage   Generative stage
2 Briefly review the five-phase regulator/cognator process.
3 List the coping stances and strategies commonly assumed by the adaptation nurse in the adolescent stage of development, and describe their relationship to the nursing action she utilizes.
4 Compare the nursing actions engaged in by the young adult and the generative adaptation nurse. Explain the differences by briefly examining the regulator/cognator process.
5 Observe a nurse practicing in your clinical setting. At what developmental level does she appear to be functioning? Request permission to interview her with regard to her experiences since graduation. Identify the stages and process she utilized to complete the tasks of each stage in her development.

REFERENCES

Ashley, J.A.: Hospitals, paternalism, and the role of nurse, New York, 1976, New York Teachers College Press.

Bliss, A., and Cohen, E.: The new health professionals: nurse practitioners and physicians' assistants, Germantown, Md., 1977, Aspen Systems Corp.

Bullough, B., and Bullough, V.: Expanding horizons for nurses, New York, 1977, Springer Publishing Co., Inc.

Carter, F.M.: Psychosocial nursing, ed. 2, New York, 1976, Macmillan Publishing Co., Inc.

Chaska, N.L.: The nursing professional: views through the mist, New York, 1978, McGraw-Hill Book Co.

Erikson, E.H.: Childhood and society, ed. 2, New York, 1963, Norton & Co., Inc.

Jacox, A.K., editor: Organizing for independent nursing practice, New York, 1977, Appleton-Century-Crofts.

Popiel, E.S., editor: Social issues and trends in nursing, New York, 1977, C.B. Black.

Schmalenberg, C., and Kramer, M.: Coping with reality shock: the voices of experience, *Nursing Research*, Wakefield, Mass.,1979, Contemporary Publications, Inc.

Stuart, G.W., and Sundeen, S.J.: Principles and practice of psychiatric nursing, St. Louis, 1979, The C.V. Mosby Co.

Putting it all together
adaptation nursing practice

CHAPTER 6

Disrupted wellness situations

THEORY OBJECTIVES

Describe the regulator/cognator transaction of the clients experiencing disrupted wellness in each of the diagnostic category II case studies.

Define the unique stimuli that influence the clients' transactions in the three case studies.

Characterize each adaptation nurse's regulator/cognator transaction.

Identify the unique stimuli that influence the adaptation nurse's transactions.

Explain how the adaptation nurse in each case study arrives at judgments, diagnoses, goals, and interventions based on the knowledge of the client's internal transaction.

Compare and contrast your present role performance with that engaged in by the adolescent or young adult adaptation nurse in each of the diagnostic category II case studies.

In this chapter three nurse/client interactions are used to demonstrate how an adaptation nurse in the adolescent or young adult stage of professional development uses the adaptation nursing process with clients who are experiencing disrupted wellness and who are therefore in diagnostic category II. The nurse will be practicing adaptation nursing with an adolescent undergoing surgery, an adult with an acute illness, and an adult with a chronic illness. The health care settings are in a hospital and an outpatient clinic.

The chapter reviews the complex thinking processes involved in adaptation nursing and the level of skill and knowledge of the adolescent or young adult adaptation nurse.

DISRUPTED WELLNESS: A REVIEW

The person experiencing disrupted wellness has been described as lacking a sense of equilibrium (Figure 6-1). A person in this second diagnostic category is able to cope effectively but often feels bombarded by triggering events: they are either too numerous or too intense. All adaptive energy is channeled to maintain adequacy, and the person is unable to focus on growth or self-enhancement. The person in the stage of disrupted wellness makes essential decisions but takes few risks. The adapting person in the second diagnostic category often looks and feels tired and overwhelmed. He is perceived as willing or adequate in terms of capability but currently unable to function optimally.

From these descriptions of disrupted wellness, it is clear that the person's behavioral responses are frequently ineffective in maintaining the level of adequacy.

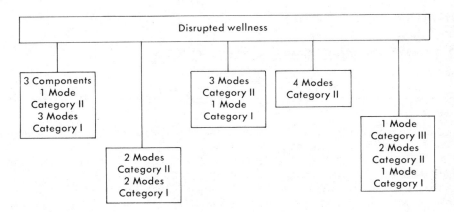

FIGURE 6-1
The disrupted wellness portion of the health/illness continuum and the five most common diagnostic combinations that are found in this range of the continuum.

The definition of the second diagnostic category states that the behavior in one, two, or three modes does not maintain the person's adequacy in that mode. The coping stance and strategy are congruent with the triggering event; thus, the intervention needed from the nurse may often be of a supportive or collaborative type. The adapting person with a category II diagnosis does indeed need support from a health care professional.

The person in disrupted wellness frequently seeks help from the health care system for two reasons: to gain information about and assistance with his category II diagnosis and to seek validation that his regulator/cognator process is operating effectively. Medical conditions commonly associated with disrupted wellness are acute medical illnesses that are to be treated on an outpatient basis or with a short hospitalization, stable chronic conditions, and injuries or illnesses that do not require surgical intervention. Medical diagnoses such as pneumonia, adult-onset diabetes, allergic reactions, and certain fractures can be included in this category. The adaptation nurse sees the client experiencing disrupted wellness in any health care facility except a specialized intensive care unit. Many clients who are using the health care system have category II diagnoses.

This chapter also focuses on the special skills of the adaptation nurse in both the adolescent and young adult stages of development. Before proceeding to the case studies, these special skills along with the developmental processes of these two stages of development, will be reviewed.

THE ADAPTATION NURSE IN THE ADOLESCENT STAGE: A REVIEW

The adaptation nurse in the adolescent stage of nursing practice is the nurse who is entering practice. She is prepared and capable of taking on the full range of responsibilities and actions associated with adaptation nursing; however, at this time she has fewer skills and less experience and knowledge than any other adaptation nurse. The adaptation nurse at the adolescent stage of development, while capable of taking on the full range of nursing actions, in actuality frequently refers many client needs or problems to a more advanced practitioner of nursing.

You will recall that the nurse in the adolescent phase of development is self-oriented, and her major concern is the establishment of her identity. For this reason she makes choices that, first, meet her need for professional identity and, second, meet the needs of the adapting person. She has the capability to make the same judgments as the adaptation nurse in more advanced stages of development, but she seldom does so, as most of her energy is devoted to self-development. Until she establishes her professional identity, she is limited in the scope of her practice. During this adolescent stage, her regulator processes triggering events in the same manner as all adaptation nurses. Her cognator responds in a more limited fashion. Because of the influence of a variety of previously described factors, her coping abilities are limited to compromise and fight or flight. The behavioral responses are also limited almost exclusively to support and collaboration. As a result, the adolescent adaptation nurse finds most satisfaction and is most effective interacting with adapting persons in the stage of disrupted wellness (the middle of the health/illness continuum). She is usually able to identify the adapting person's need for more advanced nursing intervention and see that the assistance is made available. With the passage of time, increased knowledge, and support and nurturance the adaptation nurse at the adolescent stage of development will move to the young adult stage.

THE ADAPTATION NURSE IN THE YOUNG ADULT STAGE: A REVIEW

The adaptation nurse in the young adult stage of development is very clear about her professional identity. She is other centered and balances her adult freedom with responsible participation. She is striving to achieve professional closeness and acquire intimacy in her nurse/client interactions. She responds to multiple triggering events and employs the coping stances of compromise and self-enhancement. When choosing the coping stance of compromise, the young adult nurse is able to both solidify her professional role and increase her holistic involvement with the adapting person. When using compromise, she engages in the nursing actions of support and collaboration.

Because the adaptation nurse in this stage of development looks for growth-producing situations and seeks more complex problems, she frequently selects the self-enhancement strategy of confrontation and the nursing actions of teaching and enabling. Although she is not yet at the high level of proficiency of the generative nurse, she is skilled in using the adaptation nursing process with persons located anywhere on the health/illness continuum. In her nurse/client interactions she focuses on immediate and potential problems. However, when she identifies future adaptation needs, she readily consults with an adaptation nurse in the generative stage.

Because of her personal striving for solidarity and professional intimacy and because of her skill in using all four nursing actions, the adaptation nurse in the young adult stage is ideally suited to interact with adapting persons in the second and third diagnostic categories (disrupted wellness and illness).

The person experiencing disrupted wellness is being bombarded with triggering events. The adaptive person's response to these triggering events is to maintain an appropriate coping stance and strategy and utilize *behaviors that are not effective in maintaining the level of adequacy*. Therefore, this person seeks health care for support to deal with these stimuli. The adaptation nurse at the young adult stage of development is able to interact with this client, using all four nursing intervention modalities, and seeks growth-producing clinical situations.

This chapter will focus on three clients interacting with three adaptation nurses in the adolescent or young adult stage of development. Before examining the case studies, it is recommended that the reader review the theoretical objectives, keeping in mind that written material can only teach theory. Only in the actual clinical environment can this theory be applied. Therefore, performance objectives have been included to help the reader, with or without supervision, examine his ability to utilize the complex thinking process essential to the practice of adaptation nursing.

PERFORMANCE OBJECTIVES

Given a specific nurse-client situation *use* the adaptation nursing process with clients experiencing a category II diagnosis:
    Identify the client's regulator/cognator transaction
    Identify the unique stimuli that influence the client's transaction
    Describe your regulator/cognator transaction
    Identify the unique stimuli that influence your internal transaction
    Formulate judgments, diagnoses, goals, and interventions based on the knowledge of your own and your client's internal transactions
Based on your use of the adaptation nursing process, *identify* your level of professional development.

CASE STUDY—PEDIATRIC EXPERIENCE: PLANNED SURGERY
The setting

This case study illustrates how Sally, an adaptation nurse in the adolescent phase of professional development, interacts with a 13-year old boy, Paul. Paul has been admitted to the hospital for knee surgery. Sally and Paul meet on the day after surgery. Paul's nursing diagnoses place him in disrupted wellness on the health/ illness continuum. (Again, disrupted wellness refers to an adaptive person who has nursing diagnoses that reflect a correct coping stance and strategy but *behaviors that are ineffective in maintaining adequacy*. Clients who are experiencing disrupted wellness are frequently hospitalized.) Paul is hospitalized in a 100-bed community hospital in a small midwestern city about 1 hour's drive from his home. The unit to which he has been admitted has 5 pediatric beds, and the remaining 25 beds are for adults with medical or surgical illnesses. Visiting hours are from 10:00 A.M. to 9:00 P.M. There is a television in each room; however, the unit does not contain a playroom or an adolescent recreation room. Sally is just beginning practice as an adaptation nurse. We will explore how Sally, the entry level practitioner, applies the nursing process and which coping stances and strategies she employs as she interacts with Paul.

The adaptation nurse

Sally is 22 years old, grew up on a farm in Iowa, and graduated 6 months ago from a nursing program at a local college. The nursing model she practices is the adaptation model of nursing. She has been on the evening shift for 5 months on the combined pediatric/surgical unit at the community hospital to which Paul has been admitted.

Sally is in the adolescent phase of her development of the professional nurse role, using only a small fraction of the knowledge she acquired in her nursing education. Ordinarily she uses the coping stance of compromise and applies the nursing process in situations in which she feels comfortable. Functioning as a team leader, she is relatively organized in terms of collaborative nursing tasks: she is able to administer intravenous infusions on time, dispense medications safely and on time, and assess and intervene safely in the physiological mode.

Because of her beginning stage of nursing role development, Sally is self-oriented. Her major concern is the establishment of her professional identity. Given a clinical situation in which she feels comfortable, Sally uses the coping stance of compromise and feels adequate and secure regarding her nursing judgments and actions. When she is dealing with a complex or new clinical situation, Sally may choose the coping stance of fight or flight. In this situation she also relies heavily on a professional colleague at a higher level of development.

External influencing stimuli. External stimuli are the people, places, and objects that make up the physical environment. Sally chose to begin practice in this hospital because she liked it as a student. She would like to move, in about 1 year, to a large medical center to increase her professional experiences. The hospital offers a continuing education class twice per year. The other educational programs are at the nearby college. A person that is important to Sally is Bertha, a nurse who has been in practice for 15 years and who has developed a caring approach with her clients. Bertha is in the young adult stage of professional development and frequently uses the nursing intervention modalities of collaboration and support. She has especially learned to intervene with the family unit and with neighbors and friends who visit during hospital stays. Sally often validates her nursing judgments and decisions with Bertha, who serves as her role model.

Internal influencing stimuli. Internal stimuli that influence Sally's cognator response include her physiological state, maturational level, knowledge, and beliefs. An examination of her phsyiological state indicates that she is healthy and has a sense of well-being; she enjoys sports and is especially fond of horseback riding. She was hospitalized once during her childhood when she had her tonsils removed and has only missed two evenings of work in her 5 months of employment.

Sally's maturational level affects the way she takes on her professional role as well as how she interacts with the staff and her clients. She is influenced by the developmental tasks of the young adult period. For example, she has rented an older home on the outskirts of the city and is trying to establish her independence. Several of her close college friends who work and live in the city often join her for water skiing, horseback riding, and attending movies. Sally has no special male friend but dates three different men and enjoys entertaining her family occasionally. Building a more adult relationship with her parents, she feels that it is easier now that she is not dependent on them for money. Acquiring her own set of values and establishing herself in a career are the other developmental tasks currently influencing Sally's behavior. She especially experiences conflict when her friends want to drive to the city for a concert on an evening when she is scheduled to work; she struggles with the value of having friends and the value of being responsible to her commitment.

Sally's values and beliefs arise from her family and the community in which she was raised, knows many people, and continues to live. Honesty and helping other people are community norms she has accepted as her own. Someday she hopes to save enough money to go to a large metropolitan area and work for a time to acquire further nursing experience, but she intends to return to her life in rural America, riding horses and refinishing antiques. By the age of 22 she has developed a clear identity of who she is, and she likes herself.

The adapting person

Paul, a 13-year-old boy who lives on a farm with his mother and father, has successfully completed the eighth grade. His most recent experience with an injury concerns his father, who had a total hip replacement 3 years ago. Paul played with his father's crutches then and has been "practicing" on them during the week prior to his own admission to the hospital. He is physically well and leads an active rural life, helping with the animals, training his dog, driving a tractor to plant and care for the crops, and riding horses and his minibike.

Paul injured his knee in a minibike accident 6 months ago when he was chasing cows. He continued to have pain and limited motion, but his parents and doctor decided to postpone surgery until summer vacation because Paul would be well before school starts in the fall, the planting season would be over and Paul would be well by the time the harvest season arrives, and there would be no snow or ice to make walking on crutches difficult.

Nurse/client interaction

Physiological mode. It is the evening of the first postoperative day. Sally has been off duty for 3 days; after making rounds at 3:00 P.M., she reviews the admitting data on Paul's chart. She notes the following information.

This is Paul's first hospital experience.
Paul's father had a total hip replacement 3 years ago and recovered without problems.
Paul has been practicing walking on his father's crutches.
Paul was able to state that his expectations of this surgery are that he will be asleep for
  the surgery and be in the hospital about 4 days.

Postoperative medical orders are as follows.

Meperidine, 50 mg, intramuscularly every 4 hours as needed for pain.
Diet and fluids as tolerated.
Discontinue when present intravenous infusion is absorbed.
Nerve/circulation check every 2 hours for the first 16 hours.
Ambulate in A.M. with no weight bearing on the left leg.
Begin crutch training tomorrow.

The nurse in phase I of the adaptation process is an open system, selectively responsive to influencing stimuli in the environment when she is in the nurse role. This means that her cognator directs her regulator to scan selectively for behaviors that represent the physiological, self-concept, role performance, and interdependence modes.

Because she is in the adolescent stage of nursing practice, Sally usually uses the coping stance of compromise. The clinical environment demands greater skills than she currently possesses, so she assesses the presenting behaviors. At this stage of her development, she usually does not assess all of her clients systematically in the four modes, although she learned the theory in her college nursing courses.

Her first contact with Paul occurs one afternoon as she is dispensing medications. The television is on in Paul's room; he is lying rigidly with his left knee elevated on a pillow and the head of his bed elevated 25 degrees. Sally begins her assessment of Paul in the physiological mode, because she knows that many life-threatening conditions occur in that mode. She also uses this mode to begin building a trusting relationship with her client.

Because this is Paul's first postoperative day, Sally focuses on the ingestive/eliminative, respiratory/circulatory, and musculoskeletal components of the physiological mode, noting the neurological component in terms of his affected extremity. Her judgments reflect the assessment in each component, and she compares Paul's behaviors with theory to ascertain whether he is maintaining physiological mode adequacy.

Ingestive   Paul is receiving a soft diet and is eating about half of the food served from all
  four food groups. He is not on intake and output but is drinking fluids freely.

Eliminative Paul's urine is clear and light amber. He is voiding four to five times per day. He has not had a bowel movement since the day of admission.

Respiratory Paul's pulse is 76 and regular, and his blood pressure is 114/76. His dressing is dry and intact. His skin is warm, dry, and pink. There is no evidence of postoperative bleeding or shock. Sally especially notes the circulation in the toes of the left foot. His nail beds blanch and refill in 1 second, and his toes are pink and warm. There is no swelling of the toes.

Neurological Paul demonstrates intact nerves in the toes of his left foot by wiggling his toes and reports sensation.

Musculoskeletal Sally notes on entering the room that Paul looks uncomfortable, and her assessment is illustrated below.

NURSING CARE GUIDE

PHYSIOLOGICAL MODE

MUSCULOSKELETAL BEHAVIORS

1. "I'm so tired."
2. "I couldn't sleep last night because my knee throbbed."
3. "I'm so tired, I'll never be able to run again."
4. "I'm getting so weak."
5. Conjunctiva of eyes are red.

INFLUENCING STIMULI

Focal: Incisional pain.

Contextual: Lack of knowledge regarding pain relief. An order for meperidine. Age 13 years, developmental cognition of formal operational thought. Usually takes aspirin for a headache.

Residual: Is afraid of shots. Boys should be strong.

JUDGMENT 1: Paul's lack of sleep will not effectively maintain his level of adequacy in the musculoskeletal component of the physiological mode.

NURSING DIAGNOSIS: Sleep pattern: decreased physiological adequacy: pain* (category III diagnosis). Paul is not getting enough sleep and rest because of pain caused by surgery yesterday.

GOAL: Paul will have pain-free periods and will get a good night's sleep tonight (category I diagnosis).

INTERVENTION

1. *Collaboration:* The stimulus to be manipulated is the order for meperidine. Sally talked with Paul about the need to take the meperidine shots to be comfortable and get a good night's sleep. She administered meperidine at 4:30 P.M. and 9:00 P.M.

EVALUATION CRITERIA

1. The night nurse will assess how much Paul slept during the night.
2. Paul will be asked to evaluate the quality and quantity of sleep the next morning.
3. At 9:30 P.M. Paul was asleep.

---

*National Conference on Nursing Diagnosis.

Sally believes that another stimulus affecting Paul is his lack of knowledge regarding the pattern of pain in the postoperative period. She will intervene in the role mode.

Sally assesses Paul's psychosocial mode throughout the evening. Because she is practicing at the adolescent phase of development, she spends less time with these modes. Sally does feel comfortable intervening by health teaching, so she will use this intervention modality in the role mode. Once again, recall that the beginning nurse is focused on herself and her attainment of professional identity. Sally's assessment of Paul is brief and focuses on presenting behaviors. Her behavior is consistent with her developmental stage and the demands made on her as a team leader.

Self-concept mode. Sally processes the data that she has collected and reflects that Paul stated that his scar wouldn't bother him. He laughingly said it was his "injury." He did say that he expected his leg to be as "good as new" in a few weeks. Sally's brief judgments and diagnosis follow.

> *Judgment 1*—Paul's self-concept behaviors will effectively maintain his level of adequacy in the self-concept mode
> *Judgment 2*—Paul is using self-enhancement and manipulation to deal with the stress of surgery.
> *Nursing diagnosis*—Self-concept body image: maintain: knee scar* (category I diagnosis). Paul has a moderate to high level of esteem and is incorporating the surgery and scar into his body image.

Sally chooses to end the nursing process at this point.

An adaptation nurse at the young adult or generative stage of development would use the nursing intervention modalities of support and enabling to explore with the adolescent the surgery and its meaning. Sally does not, but as she moves into the young adult stage of development, she will. If Sally had assessed that Paul was having difficulty incorporating his scar, she would have consulted with Bertha, her nurse colleague, and made decisions regarding how to intervene.

Interdependence mode. Sally's assessment of Paul's interdependence mode is brief. She looks at Paul's roles as son and grandson and reflects that Paul's mother and father were both at the hospital on the day of surgery and are visiting Paul today. They talk easily with each other and play cards with him and his grandmother, who is also visiting. Paul states, "I really miss Jeff—he's my best friend. I'm hoping he can come tomorrow." Sally makes the following judgments and diagnosis.

> *Judgment 1*—Paul's contributive and receptive nurturing behaviors will effectively maintain his level of affectional adequacy.
> *Judgment 2*—Paul is using self-enhancement and manipulation to deal with the five-day separation from his family and friends.
> *Nursing diagnosis*—Expressive role: maintenance: responsive family* (category I diagnosis). Paul's needs to be loved and supported are being met by his parents and grandmother.

---

*National Conference on Nursing Diagnosis.

Sally does not intervene at this time. She knows, because of the shared values and beliefs of the community, that the family unit is very supportive during times of illness. Once again, Sally has assessed presenting behaviors and made judgments on limited data. With the passage of time and exposure to role figures who assess and intervene at a higher level, Sally will increase her skills.

Role performance mode. You will recall that Sally feels especially comfortable in the area of health teaching. She does most of her health teaching in the client role. She systematically assesses Paul in his role of client and recalls, from her nursing knowledge, stimuli that are usually present in the postoperative period.

Sally has noted that Paul was very helpful and cooperative. She asked him questions, and he responded but did not initiate interaction. She concludes that he may need some information about his role as a sick person and his illness. The client role assessment is shown below.

NURSING CARE GUIDE

ROLE PERFORMANCE MODE

CLIENT ROLE BEHAVIORS	INFLUENCING STIMULI
1. Does not ask for pain medication.	*Focal:* Left arthrotomy yesterday.
2. Is cooperative with nurse.	*Contextual:* First hospitalization. Visited his father when he was hospitalized 3 years ago. Lack of knowledge regarding course of pain and healing process.
3. Lies in bed holding body rigid.	
4. Does deep-breathing exercises when requested.	
5. "I did not know surgery would feel like this."	*Residual:* Has not studied biology in high school. Thinks the nurse knows what is best for him.

JUDGMENT 1: The client role behaviors do not maintain Paul's level of social adequacy.

JUDGMENT 2: Paul is using compromise and suppression to deal with his hospitalization and arthrotomy.

NURSING DIAGNOSIS: Instrumental client role conflict, disrupted social adequacy: hospitalization* (category II diagnosis). Paul is demonstrating behaviors that reflect sick role conflict because of his lack of knowledge about pain and surgery.

GOAL: Paul will achieve instrumental client role mastery (category I diagnosis).

*National Conference on Nursing Diagnosis.

INTERVENTION

1. *Teaching:* The stimulus to be manipulated is the lack of knowledge regarding the course of pain and the healing process. Sally will talk with Paul about postoperative pain and how it decreases significantly after 24 to 48 hours. She will suggest that Paul ask the physician for an order for a pain pill in the morning. Sally will discuss the healing process and the need for eating high-protein and vitamin C foods for healing. She also explained why immobilizing the part aids healing.

EVALUATION

1. Paul will verbalize the course of postoperative pain.
2. Paul wilil ask the physician for pain medication.
3. Paul will eat high-protein foods as well as foods high in vitamin C. Paul will be able to state why immobilization of the part aids healing.

And thus we leave Sally and Paul. Paul is recovering from surgery, and Sally is using collaboration and health teaching to facilitate his recovery and her nurse role identity.

Summary

This case study illustrated a beginning adaptation nurse in a clinical setting interacting with an adolescent client experiencing disrupted wellness. Sally is focused on developing her own professional identity. She accomplished this by working with Paul as she chose a coping stance of compromise. She used a coping strategy of suppression as she dealt with the parts of the environment with which she could effectively deal. Because she did this, she increased her sense of adequacy in the nurse role. Sally provided safe, effective nursing care to Paul. A nurse in the young adult or generative stage of development would have assessed and intervened more in the psychosocial modes than did Sally. Sally has developed a colleague support system to facilitate both her sense of adequacy and her movement toward the young adult stage of development. She is clearly developing her sense of professional identity.

CASE STUDY—ANXIETY REACTION: AN EMERGENCY ROOM EXPERIENCE
The setting

Sister Janelle Washburn looks distraught, anxious, and drained of energy when she is brought into the emergency room with severe epistaxis. She is holding a blood-soaked towel to her nose, and her face is bloodstained. Sister Janelle is in disrupted wellness, experiencing a diagnostic category II in her physiological and self-concept modes and a diagnostic category I in her role and interdependence modes.

Trish Harbin, an adaptation nurse in the adolescent stage of development, meets Sister Janelle at the emergency room door and takes her into one of the examination cubicles. She quietly explains what she is doing as she positions Sister Janelle on the examination table and applies pressure on her nostrils. Her initial assessment is rapid. She wants to ascertain the patency of Sister Janelle's airways, her need for oxygen, and her blood pressure. Trish orders tests for hemoglobin level and hematocrit to better assess the client's circulatory status.

The section Nurse/Client Interaction suggests ways in which an adaptation nurse in Trish's stage of development might use her skills of support and collaboration to assist the adapting person with overt and predictable problems of adaptation. Because Trish's use of the adaptation nursing process is influenced by her internal transaction and unique stimuli, these factors are addressed first.

The adaptation nurse

Trish is a 21-year-old white woman who graduated 3 months ago from a university school of nursing in Portland, Oregon, whose curriculum is based on the Roy adaptation model. She is capable of using the adaptation concepts and process in her client interactions and nursing care plans.

External influencing stimuli. After graduation, Trish started working in the university's emergency treatment center, where she is striving to be an efficient and capable emergency room nurse. She is excited about the variety and number of emergencies she helps with each evening. Trish's enthusiasm is influenced by her unique stimuli. The external stimuli that affect her regulator/cognator process are the objects, places, and people in the emergency treatment center. The center is large and can accommodate 20 persons who have life-threatening conditions or need emergency surgery and 20 persons with minor emergencies who need temporary or minimal care. The unit is staffed by 10 professional nurses on the evening and night shifts, and 6 nurses on the morning shift. A triage nurse is present to keep the flow of traffic moving steadily and to direct persons to appropriate resources. Trish works closely with Peter and Dodie, who are also adaptation nurses in the adolescent stage of development. She shares an apartment with another emergency room nurse, Gail, who is an adaptation nurse in the young adult stage of development. Trish thinks Gail is an exceptional person; she is in awe of Gail's ability to assess, diagnose adaptation needs, and intervene with clients in emergency situations. Trish finds the fast pace and endless variety in emergency situations both stimulating and challenging. She is becoming adept in her physical assessment skills and is able to carry out physician's orders without delay or confusion.

Internal influencing stimuli. Trish's regulator/cognator transactions are also influenced by her internal stimuli: her physiological state, maturational level, knowledge, and beliefs. Trish is a tall, slender young woman who enjoys jogging and tennis. She is 5 feet 9 inches tall, weighs 128 pounds, and is capable of working with equipment and in emergency situations.

Striving to establish her professional identity, Trish considers Gail an excellent role model. She talks to her about the fact that she really believes in the adaptation conceptual model but is delighted that she is no longer in school, because writing nursing care guides was so difficult. She confides that it is good to be away from home and on her own; however, she also tells Gail how frustrated she feels at being inexperienced and trying to carry out physician's orders while trying to assess the psychosocial adequacy of the clients. "I am getting adept at physical assessments, and I am good at asking questions; but I keep getting called away to another emergency. I get excited, anxious, and nervous. Do you think I will ever master all this?" Gail assures her that this learning experience is part of becoming an adaptation nurse and tells her to keep in mind that it is the client, not she, who is experiencing the emergency.

The pertinent facts about Trish's internal state involve her overwhelming desire for excitement and making things happen. She believes that life is the way one makes it and that parents and friends are great to have around, but in the final analysis, a person has only herself to rely on. Trish's parents are both college instructors, and they encouraged Trish to be independent and make her own way. She worked to help pay for her college education and took a student tour through Europe in her junior year. As an only child, she believes she has had many advantages, for she was encouraged to read and articulate her own opinions long before attending grade school. Her parents attend an Episcopal church but were not upset when Trish stopped going to church last year. Trish feels that her liberal background has helped her to understand and interact with people from all walks of life.

Trish is an adaptation nurse in the adolescent stage of development who is enthusiastic about her entry into the nursing profession and who sees and values the direction that Gail, an adaptation nurse in the young adult stage, has taken. However, even though Trish is considered a "good" nurse, she is still concentrating only on mastering skills rather than on providing clients with adaptation nursing. Although she is capable of providing total care, Trish concentrates on helping adapting persons cope with their sudden threats to physiological adequacy, and she seeks an adaptation resource person to help clients whose levels of psychosocial adequacy have been threatened.

The adapting person

Sister Janelle Washburn is a 27-year-old black woman who teaches fifth grade at a parochial school and lives in a convent with five other members of her religious community. She works as a teaching team member with Sister Janet and Sister Virginia, who are fun to be with and turn everyday stresses into workable opportunities. Sister Janelle is the only daughter of a prosperous lawyer. She is very close to both parents even though they live in New York. They call regularly and plan vacations around visits to their daughter. Sister Janelle believes that she is not only a meaningful member of society but that she has special gifts as a religious person and as a professional to offer the children she teaches. She considers herself a spiritually rooted person and describes her faith and her parent's love as the force that helped her develop into a happy, loving, whole person. She states that it is an exciting time to be a black person in the Catholic church, because the black movement has helped the church look to the future and address the social, economic, and spiritual needs of the world. She is a competent fifth grade teacher and helps tutor eighth grade students who have difficulty with mathematics. Sister Janelle is a natural food fanatic and tells everyone this is why she is so healthy and can jog before Mass each morning. She is enthusiastic about all sports; in fact, the nosebleed that brought her to the emergency room began with an accident that occurred while she was teaching football to a group of fourth grade boys.

Nurse/client interaction

While Trish introduces herself to Sister Janelle and her two companions, she takes and records Sister Janelle's blood pressure. It is 90/60, and Trish asks her if she can recall what her last blood pressure recording may have been. Sister Janelle looks vague and doesn't respond, but Sister Janet interjects that she remembers it was 96/68 when she last accompanied her friend to her doctor. Trish checks Sister Janelle's conjunctiva, oral mucosa, and nail beds and can detect no apparent color change. She monitors her breathing and pulse, which register 18 and 96, respectively. The bleeding has begun to abate, and Trish rapidly assesses all the components of Sister Janelle's physiological mode. She determines that, except for the disrupted circulatory component, Sister Janelle's physiological mode is intact and maintaining adequacy.

Trish inspects the internal nares with a nasal speculum, noting the important landmarks of the vestibules and nasal septum. There is no inflammation of the vestibules, and there is no deviation present. At Kiesselbach's area she notes the rupture of the small fragile arteries and veins located in the left anterior superior portion of the septum. She confirms her suspicion of a superficial but momentarily profuse hemorrhage of the left anterior nostril. Before notifying the physician, Trish asks Sister Janelle to explain how and when the nosebleed began. Sister Virginia answers for her friend, describing how Sister Janelle was hit in the head with a football about 40 minutes ago. "However," she continues, "the injury itself is not what we are most concerned about." She explains that Sister Janelle panicked when Sister Janet tried to stem the flow of blood by applying ice and pressure with a folded towel and failed to do so. The bleeding continued to be profuse, so they rushed their friend to the emergency treatment center. Sister Virginia states she is very concerned, because she has never seen Sister Janelle so distraught. Sister Janelle could hardly talk after the accident, looked dazed, and kept repeating the query, "Oh, my, do you think it's hereditary? Do you think it's because I'm black? I meant to ask Dad if he had hypertension, but I keep forgetting. Do you think my blood pressure's been up all this time?" Nothing the two friends had said seemed to alter Sister Janelle's flustered and apprehensive reaction.

Trish tells the two friends that she will address Sister's response as soon as the physician checks her assessment and determines the treatment. Before she calls in the physician, she records the results of the blood tests. The hemoglobin level is 13.5 gm/100 ml, and the hematocrit is 38% (both are within normal limits). When the physician arrives, he examines the nose and reviews Trish's recordings. He confirms her assessment and orders a topical cocaine spray as a vasoconstricting agent and a 40-minute rest with an assessment of vital signs every 15 minutes. He states that if the vital signs remain stable, the client can be discharged.

As Trish applies the spray, the triage nurse comes in, tells her that they have just been informed of a major automobile accident, and asks Trish if she can help staff the casualty suite. Trish says, "Yes, of course," turns to Sister Janelle and her friends, and explains that Sister Janelle should rest in this examination cubicle for another 40 minutes or so and that she will send in another nurse to be with them.

On her way to the casualty suite Trish pages Gail. When Gail responds, Trish hurriedly tells her conclusion about Sister Janelle: that she has been experiencing a diagnostic category III in her physiological mode but that the bleeding has stopped and there are no indications of hypertension or shock. She also tells Gail that she is concerned about the diagnostic category II in the self-concept mode, for Sister Janelle is extremely anxious and fearful that she might be having a hypertensive episode. Gail says that she will be glad to interact with Sister Janelle but asks why Trish is not completing the intervention herself. Trish explains that she has been called away because of an automobile accident. Gail than asks Trish if she would like her to exchange places with her so she can complete the process with Sister Janelle. Trish says, "Oh, no, this is my first traffic accident this evening, and I may get to go to surgery." Gail smiles and says, "Okay, I'll go see Sister Janelle for you."

In order to get a clear picture of Trish's use of the adaptation nursing process with Sister Janelle, their cognator/regulator processes will be explored.

Regulator/cognator process

The nurse. Sister Janelle's arrival in the emergency room with a bleeding nose is a triggering event for Trish. Her regulator alerts her as she meets Sister Janelle at the emergency room entrance. Trish selects a coping stance of compromise and the strategy of repression/suppression to concentrate on Sister Janelle's bleeding and not on her apparent anxiety. Throughout the examination, Trish focuses on the physiological assessment and attends to Sister Janelle's psychological threat of anxiety only when her friends, Sisters Virginia and Janet, explain their concern about it. Trish uses support during the physical examination, however.

She completes her assessment, still using suppression, until the physiological disruption is reversed. Once the collaborative intervention has taken place, Trish is called to another triggering event, the arrival of accident victims in the emergency center. Using the same strategy of suppression, Trish calls on her friend Gail and asks her to help Sister Janelle cope with her psychological threat of anxiety, because her own energies are centered on becoming skilled in the assessment process and in her emergency room activities.

The client. Sister Janelle's triggering event is still her unexpected nosebleed. Her automatic response is appropriate to the threat of hemorrhage; however, her cognator misinterprets the triggering event and defines it as a precursor to hypertension, which has a high incidence in the black population. Her cognator selects the coping stance of avoidance and the strategy of flight. This stance and strategy are inappropriate to the primary triggering event of hemorrhage and the secondary triggering event of fear of hypertension; therefore, Sister Janelle's behavioral response of anxiety is ineffective in coping with the situation. Because her perceptions and beliefs are involved, Sister Janelle needs both teaching and enabling. Trish has provided for these interventions by asking Gail to interact with Sister Janelle. Sister Janelle's response is based on a misperception of the triggering event. With Gail's support, clarification, and review of options, Sister Janelle can select a more effective coping stance and strategy and therefore reestablish her level of adequacy.

To complete Trish's use of the nursing process with Sister Janelle, physiological and self-concept nursing care guides are presented below.

NURSING CARE GUIDE

PHYSIOLOGICAL MODE

CIRCULATORY BEHAVIORS

1. Profuse bleeding for approximately 20 to 30 minutes (towel is soaked).
2. Blood pressure is 90/60.
3. Conjunctiva are light pink. Oral mucosa is pink.
4. Hemoglobin level is 13.5 gm/100 ml (within normal limits); hematocrit is 38% (within normal limits).

INFLUENCING STIMULI

Focal: Nose hit by football. Rupture of small fragile arteries and veins in left anterior superior nostril.

Contextual: Was teaching fourth graders to play football and was in a vulnerable position. Is in sound physical health (all other components within normal limits). Jogs daily. Likes all sports. Teaches grade school.

Residual: Believes it is important to teach sports to fourth grade boys. Believes she is competent to teach football.

JUDGMENT 1: Sister Janelle's general alarm reaction and bleeding nose are congruent with her ruptured vessels; however, if this response continues, it will rapidly deplete her physiological reserves, result in hypovolemic shock, and markedly reduce her level of adequacy.

NURSING DIAGNOSIS: Fluid volume integrity, disrupted physiologic adequacy: ruptured, fragile, nasal arteries* (category II diagnosis). Sister Janelle is undergoing a temporary emergency and has a category II physiological mode diagnosis. Her fragile nasal vessels, ruptured when hit with a football, are susceptible to hemorrhage, which, if not terminated, will result in shock and a marked reduction in her level of physiological adequacy. The termination of the bleeding depends on pressure and is reinforced with the topical application of cocaine, a vasoconstricting agent.

GOAL: Sister Janelle will experience an increase in physiological adequacy (category I diagnosis). Sister Janelle will promote vascular and mucosal tissue repair by resting quietly for 6 to 8 hours, not engaging in strenuous activity for the next 2 or 3 days, and refraining from blowing or applying pressure to her nostrils for the next 48 hours.

INTERVENTION

1. *Collaboration:* Trish will provide external pressure, apply topical cocaine as a vasoconstrictor, and monitor hemorrhage and defense response by assessing vital signs every 15 minutes for first hour. She will obtain a blood sample for hemoglobin and hematocrit tests. Validate the patient's ongoing response by asking about the onset, duration, and amount of bleeding and the presence of pain, weakness, or faintness.

EVALUATION CRITERIA

1. Sister's nose will stop bleeding.
2. The ruptured vessels will reseal themselves.
3. Blood coagulation will be effected.
4. Sister Janelle will state she has no pain, discomfort, or sense of faintness or dizziness.
5. Hemoglobin and hematocrit will be within normal limits.

---

*National Conference on Nursing Diagnosis.

Trish accurately assesses that Sister Janelle's automatic and hemorrhagic responses place her in a diagnostic category II in her physiological mode. By employing collaborative nursing actions, Trish is able to terminate the regulator's alarm response and help her client to reestablish physiological adequacy. Sister Janelle's manner of coping, by using avoidance and flight, is threatening to her self-concept mode and her psychological adequacy. This coping strategy, if continued, could result in a lowered self-esteem, which would eventually affect her role performance and physiological modes. Therefore, the adaptation nurse will need to use support, teaching, and enabling to help Sister Janelle regain her level of psychological adequacy.

NURSING CARE GUIDE

SELF-CONCEPT MODE

PHYSICAL SELF BEHAVIORS

1. Perceives self as experiencing a hypertensive episode: "Oh, my, do you think it's hereditary?"
2. "Do you think my blood pressure has been up all this time?"
3. Can hardly talk.
4. Looks dazed, anxious, and apprehensive.
5. Keeps repeating herself.

SELF-CONSISTENCY BEHAVIORS

1. "Do you think my blood pressure has been up all this time?"

MORAL-ETHICAL SELF BEHAVIORS

1. "Do you think it's because I'm black?"
2. "I meant to ask Dad if he had hypertension, but I kept forgetting."

INFLUENCING STIMULI

Focal: Her unexpected hemorrhage after a football hit her nose. Her layman's knowledge about the incidence of hypertension among black population.

Contextual: Has been healthy and fit. Participates in sports. Has a high self-esteem. Previously had blood pressure of 96/68.

Residual: Believes that hemorrhage is a sure sign of hypertension. Believes because she is black, she will get hypertension. Fears that hypertension will alter her high self-esteem.

JUDGMENT 1: Sister Janelle's panic is not congruent with the triggering event of a traumatic, yet minor, nosebleed. Therefore, her level of psychological adequacy is reduced.

JUDGMENT 2: Sister Janelle, by using a coping stance of avoidance and the strategy of flight, is using inappropriate behaviors for coping with the triggering event of a nosebleed. If she continues responding this way, she will markedly reduce her psychological adequacy.

NURSING DIAGNOSIS: Self-esteem, disrupted psychological adequacy: misperception that nosebleeds denote hypertension* (category II diagnosis). Sister Janelle has a category II diagnosis in her self-concept mode. She is experiencing a threat to her self-esteem and feels incomplete because she believes her nosebleed is indicative of a hypertensive episode. Her coping stance and strategies are incongruent with the triggering event.

GOAL: Sister Janelle will alter her perception of the implication of her nosebleed. She will understand that hemorrhage from a blow on the nose does not constitute a hypertensive episode, and she will perceive herself as whole, thus reestablishing her high self-esteem. (Sister Janelle will increase her psychological adequacy [category I diagnosis]).

INTERVENTION

1. *Support:* Trish will contract with Gail to spend time with Sister Janelle to help her explore her perceptions and beliefs.

EVALUATION

1. Sister Janelle will relax and speak calmly and articulately. She will smile and respond to questions or conversations.

*National Conference on Nursing Diagnosis.

INTERVENTION

2. *Teaching:* Trish will ask Gail to help Sister Janelle focus on the realities of hypertension and nosebleeds from trauma and to clarify her perception of hypertension, its incidence, its hereditary basis, and its early signs and symptoms.

3. *Enabling:* Trish will contract with Gail to help Sister Janelle explore family involvement with hypertension, common treatment for hypertension, and preventive measures for hypertension (diet, exercise, rest, freedom from undue stress, and an overall feeling of wellness).

EVALUATION

2. Sister Janelle will state the factors involved in hypertension and measure them against her traumatic nosebleed. She will state that she understands she did not have a hypertensive episode.

3. Sister Janelle will call her parents and validate the presence or absence of a family tendency toward hypertension.

4. Sister Janelle will incorporate and schedule her present eating, exercise, and athletic activities into a program for prevention of hypertension.

Summary

In this adaptation nursing process special emphasis has been placed on both Trish's and Sister Janelle's regulator/cognator transactions. Sister Janelle's transaction reflects the holistic nature of the adapting person and the interrelationship of the four modes, even when only two modes are affected. Trish's transaction reflects her developmental strengths and limitations, demonstrating how she uses the adaptation nursing process systematically to assess, judge, and intervene effectively with the total person. Trish's regulator/cognator process is influenced by her knowledge, understanding, and ability to perceive her client's needs. Thus, an adaptation nurse forms a partnership with her client to achieve the principal goal of adaptation nursing, which is to help the adapting person to cope more effectively, thereby maintaining or increasing the level of adequacy to meet holistic needs.

CASE STUDY—CHRONIC ILLNESS: FAMILY-CENTERED EXPERIENCE
The setting

This case study illustrates an adaptation nurse at the young adult stage of development interacting with a client with chronic illness, cancer. The family unit will be included in the discussion.

The client, Susie, is receiving chemotherapy at an oncology clinic affiliated with a general hospital in a large city. Her nurse, Paula, functions independently in the clinic as a colleague of the physician: interacting with the clients, she orders the blood tests and assesses and intervenes with them as they deal with their illnesses. The lives of these two adaptive persons come together in the oncology clinic. Susie has been coming to the clinic every other week for 2 months. Paula has assessed her during these visits and worked with Susie as she undergoes some side effects of chemotherapy. Paula will work with her client in this situation as she experiences nursing diagnoses in categories I and II.

The adaptation nurse

At 43 years of age, Paula is a graduate of an adaptation nursing curriculum. She entered nursing school at age 32 years, obtained her bachelor's degree, and went to work on an oncology unit, where she practiced primary nursing care. During the past 5 years Paula has also attended many conferences and nursing workshops to increase her knowledge and skills about the person/family affected by cancer. She transferred to the oncology clinic 18 months ago.

Paula is a typical nurse in the young adult stage of development who has attained a solid professional identity and is confident of her knowledge and skills as a nurse. She chooses the coping stance of compromise less often than she did in the early stages of her nursing career and now uses self-enhancing coping strategies more often when intervening with clients. She feels comfortable with a variety of intervention modalities as she uses her skills of supporting, collaborating, teaching, and enabling to aid her clients. Paula has intentionally chosen a work environment that provides her with growth opportunities as well as a milieu in which she can utilize all of her nursing knowledge and skills. She is married and has two daughters, ages 13 and 18 years. Her father died 5 years ago after a 10-year illness with emphysema.

External influencing stimuli. The external stimuli that influence Paula are the people, places, and objects that compose the physical environment. In this situation the immediate physical environment is an outpatient clinic in a large medical center. The staff consists of two nurses and two oncologists. There are also the support departments usually associated with this type of clinic. The clinic staff does some research and presents findings at conferences. There are many small clinics of this type at the university. The goal of the small clinics is to increase personal contact for the client as well as the health professional within the larger university complex.

Internal influencing stimuli. Many stimuli influence Paula's internal state. Her physiological self is healthy. She has been hospitalized for the delivery of her daughters and had a hysterectomy at the age of 40 years. She is 5 feet 7 inches tall and weighs 145 pounds. Paula recognizes that she is at risk for the burnout phenomenon because she works with clients who are experiencing varying degrees of stress. Because of this, she maintains a physical exercise regimen by riding her bike twice a week and does aerobic dancing once a week. Paula's maturational level indicates that she is working on the developmental tasks of the generative adult period. Manifesting behaviors that are influenced by the task of assisting in the establishment and guidance of the next generation, she is a sponsor for a club to which her younger daughter belongs. She also chose the clinic environment because she wanted to work with families as well as the clients; furthermore, she is active in the state nurses' association.

Finally, Paula's unique internal self, values, and beliefs affect the kind of nursing she practices. She is a warm, approachable person who has experienced many struggles in her life, the most recent of which was her return to school as a mature learner.

In addition, the death of her father after a long illness has forced her to deal with her beliefs regarding life and death. She believes that each person has the ability to learn from struggles and crises in their lives and that people need other people to help them during times of trouble. Although she has lived in a city composed of many ethnic groups, Paula feels most comfortable working with people from a middle-class socioeconomic group. She believes in God but is not certain about the role God plays in individual lives.

In summary, Paula is a mature, supportive woman interested in working with clients and their families who are dealing with multiple problems; therefore, she has chosen to work in an oncology clinic to use her special skills and abilities.

The adapting person

Susie is 32 years old, and her left breast was removed (modified mastectomy) 3 months ago. She had two positive lymph nodes, recovered from surgery without infection, returned home to her family, and is on sick leave from work. Her family consists of a husband and two small children, a boy 5 years old and a girl 5 months old. Susie was born and grew up in the Midwest. She married her college sweetheart after they graduated from college, and they moved to the coast soon afterwards. Susie and her husband remain close to Susie's family. Susie has enjoyed bringing her son "home" to play with his grandparents every year. She and her husband are Catholic and are involved in their local community. Susie has friends who she values, and she works with most of them. She is concerned that she is her husband's best and only friend and believes that he needs to have some other good friends. She and her husband adore their children and family life together. Susie feels that she approaches problems straight on and makes good decisions and that her greatest stress is juggling the roles of wife, woman, professional, and mother. Susie does reflect with regret that "We had just gotten it all together, and then this cancer came along." Susie pursued graduate education in nursing. She has worked as a faculty member at a school of nursing that adopted the adaptation model as a curriculum framework. She is now pursuing an advanced degree in nursing. Her education is partially funded, so she is continuing her studies during this illness. She is a nurse in the generative stage of development and really values the contributions that nurses make to society.

Regulator/cognator process

The nurse. Paula, organizing her day, notes that Susie has an appointment for 1:00 P.M. She orders the blood tests to be done when Susie arrives. Before she and her client meet, Paula reviews the care plan that has evolved from her interaction with Susie over the past few months.

Because she is an adaptation nurse, Paula thinks in terms of the adapting person's needs and the four modes of behavioral response. Also, she is at the young adult stage of development as a nurse, so she is able to use a self-enhancing coping stance, thereby using a major portion of her nursing knowledge. She utilizes her cognator process in phase III of the adaptive process to focus on Susie's probable areas of concern. Because Susie is 32 years old and has young children, Paula especially assessed her client's role as mother; she has also assessed her role as a wife, knowing that it has been seriously affected by the cancer. Susie's student role and spiritual role are likewise important in Paula's assessment.

As she considers the interdependence mode, Paula is aware of ways in which a mastectomy, with its accompanying body image changes, can influence affectional needs and relationships. She is sensitive to the fact that Susie needs more love and support at this point in her life and that she may feel more vulnerable when asking for affectional expression. Furthermore, Paula knows that the self-concept mode of behavior will probably reflect such themes as fear of death, loss concerning body image, and possibly some moral/ethical questions implicit in the questions, "Why me? Why did I get cancer?"

In the physiological mode the focus is on the effect chemotherapy is having on Susie. The components most often affected are circulatory, with behaviors of decreased white blood cells and platelets. The ingestive components consist of lack of appetite, nausea, and possibly vomiting. The protective components are hair loss and stomatitis. These typical behaviors are processed by Paula's cognator as she begins her assessment of Susie. She has used the nursing process as a means of organizing her data and intervening with her client.

The following 2-month care plans completed for Susie demonstrate the regulator/cognator responses that Susie is probably using for each mode and illustrate the behavioral/stimuli assessments that Paula made, followed by a judgment and diagnoses from the data. The basic care plan includes goals, nursing interventions, and evaluation.

Physiological mode. Susie underwent her initial chemotherapy during her hospitalization; the instruction she received regarding drug and side effects of antimetabolite chemotherapy was good, which is helping her now as the problems of nausea and hair loss persist. The assessment of the physiological mode has remained relatively constant.

NURSING CARE GUIDE

PHYSIOLOGICAL MODE

CIRCULATORY BEHAVIORS

1. White blood cell count varies between 600 and 1000/cu mm (all other behaviors in the circulatory component indicate physiological adequacy).

INFLUENCING STIMULI

Focal: Chemotherapy, 5-fluorouracil.

Contextual: Mastectomy for cancer 3 months ago.

Residual: No cancer in family. Very stressed individual.

JUDGMENT 1: Susie's white blood cell count above 500 mm will maintain her adequacy in the circulatory component.

NURSING DIAGNOSIS: Circulatory, maintained physiological adequacy: chemotherapy* (category I diagnosis). Susie's white blood cell count varies between 600 and 1000/cu mm because she receives 5-fluorouracil [15 m/kg] every other week.

GOAL: Susie's white blood cell count will be maintained at 600 to 1000/cu mm during her chemotherapy regimen.

INTERVENTION	EVALUATION CRITERIA
1. *Collaboration:* Paula will monitor the white blood cell count every 2 weeks and administer the 5-fluorouracil in a dosage that is determined by the white blood cell count.	1. Susie will keep her appointments for blood tests. 2. Susie will maintain a white blood cell count of 500 to 1000/cu mm.

---

*National Conference on Nursing Diagnosis.

Susie's ingestive assessment looks like this:

NURSING CARE GUIDE

PHYSIOLOGICAL MODE

INGESTIVE BEHAVIORS

1. "I have a lot of nausea the third and fourth days after my shot" (all other behaviors in the ingestive component reflect physiological adequacy). "I eat primarily carbohydrate foods on those two days."

INFLUENCING STIMULI

Focal: Chemotherapy, 5-fluorouracil.

Contextual: Compazine, and suppositories to be used every 6 hours as needed. Eats two dry saltine crackers with sips of warm coke.

Residual: Family eating patterns.

JUDGMENT 1: Susie has learned behaviors that effectively maintain her level of adequacy in the ingestive component of the physiological mode.

NURSING DIAGNOSIS: Maintained physiological adequacy: chemotherapy* (category I diagnosis). Susie has learned to prevent vomiting on the third and fourth day after her chemotherapy.

---

*National Conference on Nursing Diagnosis.

Paula does not proceed to intervene because this is a category I diagnosis, and Susie does not need collaborative intervention. The other components of the physiological mode demonstrate a maintained level of adequacy.

Role performance mode. The role performance assessment begins with the primary role. Because Susie is a 32-year-old woman, Paula reviews the developmental tasks of the young adult period. Erikson states that the young adult is eager to fuse his identity with that of others; thus, the period of intimacy occurs. Other tasks defined for this period are to establish oneself as an independent individual; to nurture, support, and provide for spouse and offspring; and to continue in a line of work. Because of the developmental tasks involved with mastectomy and chemotherapy, Paula knows that the four roles at risk are sick role, wife role, mother role, and spiritual role.

The following example illustrates the adaptation nursing process used by Paula with each of the four roles. She began by assessing the chronic sick role, recalling that adaptive persons are truly integrated and their behaviors cannot be separated into four modes. Thus, she reflects that there is a direct relationship between the physiological mode and the sick role. Paula frequently finds that there are many areas of health teaching available to her after assessing the sick role.

NURSING CARE GUIDE

ROLE PERFORMANCE MODE

CHRONIC CLIENT ROLE BEHAVIORS

1. "I rest whenever I'm tired."
2. "I've learned that eating dry crackers decreases my nausea."
3. Keeps appointments for chemotherapy regimen.
4. "I avoid crowds during the flu season."
5. "I have a knight from the chess set on my dresser, and I visualize him killing my cancer cells."

INFLUENCING STIMULI

Focal: Knowledge of chronic client role tasks.

Contextual: Modified mastectomy 3 months ago, chemotherapy, 5-fluorouracil, adaptation nurse, physician. Client is a nurse and has knowledge of chemotherapy and visualization theory.

Residual: Culture.

JUDGMENT 1: Susie is using self-enhancement and negotiation to deal with the stress of cancer and chemotherapy.

JUDGMENT 2: Susie's behaviors are maintaining her level of social adequacy.

NURSING DIAGNOSIS: Instrumental client role: maintained social adequacy: knowledge of role tasks* (category I diagnosis). Susie is performing the tasks of the chronic sick role because of her knowledge of the role prescriptions.

GOAL: Susie will continue to keep her chemotherapy apppointments and actively participate in the healing process.

---

*National Conference on Nursing Diagnosis.

Paula has focused on teaching Susie about the chemotherapy and its effects on her body. She especially talked with Susie about her decreased resistance to infectious organisms while she is taking the 5-fluorouracil. Paula moved to supportive intervention as she also talked about avoiding large crowds during the "flu" season and avoiding people who are ill. Evaluation would be accomplished by assessing for behaviors that illustrate Susie's keeping her biweekly appointments at the clinic and continuing to "take care" of herself. Paula then interviewed Susie about her mother role to determine what her concerns are, how this illness is affecting her mother role, and what her knowledge base is regarding children's natural growth and development.

NURSING CARE GUIDE

ROLE PERFORMANCE MODE

MOTHER ROLE BEHAVIORS

1. "I have a babysitter/housekeeper 5 days a week, so I'm able to spend time playing with the children. I'm not always doing the laundry."
2. "I take John, age 5, swimming two times a week."
3. "I feed and play with the baby."
4. "John really enjoys kindergarten."

INFLUENCING STIMULI

Focal: John, 5 years old; Laura, 5 months old.

Contextual: Modified radical mastectomy for primary cancer of the breast. Knowledge of children's normal growth and development and readiness to learn. Young adult stage of development: to support and nurture offspring.

Residual: Family role prescriptions.

JUDGMENT 1: Susie is using self-enhancement and negotiation to maintain her mother role while being treated for cancer.

JUDGMENT 2: Susie's mother role behaviors are maintaining her level of social adequacy.

NURSING DIAGNOSIS: Instrumental mother role: maintained social adequacy: knowledge of children's needs* (category 1 diagnosis). Susie is meeting her children's normal growth and development needs while she is being treated for cancer.

---

*National Conference on Nursing Diagnosis.

Paula decided that Susie will probably continue to maintain her adequacy in her role of mother; thus, she does not intervene at this time. Paula then turns her attention to the secondary role of wife and makes the following assessment.

NURSING CARE GUIDE

ROLE PERFORMANCE MODE

WIFE ROLE BEHAVIORS

1. Meets Sam for lunch on days she has chemotherapy.
2. "We go out Monday evenings."
3. "I fix dinner one evening a week so Sam and I dine alone at home."
4. "I use a babysitter so I have some free time."
5. "Things are pretty much the same as before my surgery."

INFLUENCING STIMULI

Focal: Married 10 years; has worked out the division of work; husband is available, helpful.

Contextual: Money to hire child care. Feels it is important to do things together. Left mastectomy for cancer. Young adult stage of development: to nurture and support spouse.

Residual: Fears that this cancer may be too stressful for the marriage.

JUDGMENT 1: Susie is again using a coping stance of self-enhancement and manipulation and negotiation to maintain her role of wife while being treated for cancer.

JUDGMENT 2: Susie's behaviors in the role of wife are effective in maintaining her level of social adequacy.

NURSING DIAGNOSIS: Instrumental wife role: maintain social adequacy: values relationship* (category I diagnosis). Susie is performing the tasks of the wife role; she has reached an understanding of the needed tasks during the 10 years of her marriage.

---

*National Conference on Nursing Diagnosis.

Paula is also concerned about Susie's level of social adequacy in the emotional or interdependence component of wife role and will assess that in the Interdependence Mode. She intervenes by supporting Susie, i.e., she praises her for the priorities she is setting and the effort she is expending to maintain her wife role with Sam. In conclusion Paula examines Susie's spiritual role and makes the following assessment:

NURSING CARE GUIDE

ROLE PERFORMANCE MODE

SPIRITUAL ROLE BEHAVIORS

1. "I believe in God."
2. "I go to Mass once in awhile."
3. "I pray to God for healing."
4. "I'm glad my husband is Catholic."
5. Has not talked to or been counseled by her parish priest regarding her cancer.

INFLUENCING STIMULI

Focal: Raised a Catholic.

Contextual: Parish nearby; likes the priest at her parish. Believes church should help in times of need. Is being treated for cancer.

Residual: Feels she should go to church.

JUDGMENT 1: Susie is using self-enhancement and negotiation to maintain her spiritual role while being treated for cancer.

JUDGMENT 2: Susie is maintaining her level of social adequacy in the spiritual role.

NURSING DIAGNOSIS: Instrumental spiritual role, maintain social adequacy: practicing Catholic* (category I diagnosis). Susie assumes a spiritual role and performs the tasks associated with a Christian spiritual role.

---

*National Conference on Nursing Diagnosis.

Paula almost always chooses to intervene briefly with a diagnosis that represents adequacy. Again she uses the intervention modality of support, telling Susie, "I am glad you have faith in God and are a part of a caring, Christian community." She also notes that Susie might be able to use her religion more to meet some of her nurturing needs and will assess for that in the interdependence mode.

Paula concludes, after assessing the role mode, that Susie's behaviors indicate that she is using a self-enhancing coping stance. Susie is clearly maintaining her level of adequacy in all of the roles assessed. She has used the coping strategy of manipulation in her role as mother by arranging her environment to include a babysitter/housekeeper; thus, she can maintain the tasks she considers important in her role as mother. She is also using both negotiation and manipulation in her role as wife. Paula has written a nursing diagnosis that is in category I for each role in the role mode.

Interdependence mode. The interdependence mode is then assessed in relation to the role mode. Recall that, as Paula assessed the instrumental behaviors in the role, she had hunches that led her to assess the feelings associated with Susie's roles as mother, wife, and spiritual person. Paula assessed whether Susie's needs to love and be loved were being met.

NURSING CARE GUIDE

ROLE PERFORMANCE MODE

CHRONIC CLIENT ROLE BEHAVIORS	INFLUENCING STIMULI
Recipient	*Focal:* Mastectomy 3 months ago for cancer.
1. Accepts touch from nurse.	*Contextual:* Caring adaptation nurse with effective communication skills. Needs for nurturing are increased because of mastectomy 3 months ago. Young adult task to maintain career. Physician whom she trusts.
2. Cries with nurse.	
3. Is able to express feelings to nurse.	
Contributive	
1. "I really appreciate having someone I can finally talk to."	*Residual:* Is a nurse and values how nurses help people.

JUDGMENT 1: Susie is using self-enhancement and manipulation to deal with the stress of being treated for cancer.

JUDGMENT 2: Susie's behaviors in the sick role maintain her level of social adequacy in this relationship.

NURSING DIAGNOSIS: Expressive client role, maintain social adequacy: nurse who cares* (category I diagnosis). Susie has a relationship with the nurse that meets some of her nurturing needs.

---

*National Conference on Nursing Diagnosis. ₁

Paula knows that she is very effective in providing nurturing support to clients and will continue to do so for Susie. She looks at ways in which Susie's nurturing needs are being met in her role as a mother.

NURSING CARE GUIDE

INTERDEPENDENCE MODE

MOTHER ROLE BEHAVIORS

Recipient
1. John tells her, "I love you."
2. John cuddles with mommy.
3. John says, "You're pretty, mommy."
4. Baby smiles at her mother.

Contributive
1. Holds and touches children.
2. Reads stories to John.
3. "I love you."
4. "I'm afraid that I won't be alive to raise them."
5. "I'm so delighted with my baby daughter."

INFLUENCING STIMULI

Focal: John, age 5 years, Laura, age 5 months.

Contextual: Always wanted to be a mother. Developmental task of providing nurturing and support to offspring. Catholic and really values her children. Own experience of living in a large, loving family as a child. Cancer removed by mastectomy 3 months ago.

Residual: Believes it is her right to raise her children.

JUDGMENT 1: Susie is using self-enhancement and negotiation to deal with the stress of having cancer while being a mother of young children.

JUDGMENT 2: Susie's nurturing behaviors to and from her children are effectively maintaining her level of social adequacy.

NURSING DIAGNOSIS: Expressive mother role, maintain social adequacy: children* (category I diagnosis). Susie feels loved and nurtured by her children and is able to love and nurture them in return.

---

*National Conference on Nursing Diagnosis.

Paula supports Susie with the statement, "Your joy in mothering is reflected in your face as you talk about John and your baby." Paula believes Susie will maintain these behaviors without nursing intervention.

The next area Paula will assess is the nurturing and love portion of Susie's wife role. She chooses to use a supportive statement in summary. She says, "You two have really weathered this crisis of a mastectomy, and apparently you've deepened your relationship in the process. I'm delighted for you."

NURSING CARE GUIDE

INTERDEPENDENCE MODE

WIFE ROLE BEHAVIORS

Recipient
1. "Sam is very affectionate."
2. "He really loves the children."
3. "Our sex life is okay now that we've resumed it."
4. "I feel very loved."
5. "Sometimes I feel like Sam doesn't have any idea of what it's like to have cancer, but he tries to understand."

Contributive
1. Touches Sam often.
2. Talks to him about her feelings.
3. Meets his nurturing needs by some maintaining wife role behaviors.
4. "I really worry about Sam needing a good male friend."

INFLUENCING STIMULI

Focal: Sam loves Susie.

Contextual: Married 10 years learned how to meet each other's needs. "My best features are my face/hair." Both committed to lifetime relationships with each other and children. Susie's parents have a long and happy marriage. Young adult developmental task of nurturing spouse. Cancer removed from breast 3 months ago.

Residual: Both sets of parents have "good marriages."

JUDGMENT 1: Susie is using self-enhancement and negotiation to deal with ways in which cancer affects her nurturing relationship with Sam.

JUDGMENT 2: Susie's behaviors are maintaining her level of social adequacy in her relationship to Sam.

NURSING DIAGNOSIS: Expressive wife role, maintain social adequacy: husband* (category I diagnosis). Susie is receiving nurturing and love from her husband and is able to freely express nurturing and love to him.

*National Conference on Nursing Diagnosis.

The final area of assessment in the Interdependence Mode is the spiritual role. Paula is particularly concerned with the ways in which Susie is meeting her nurturing needs in the spiritual role.

NURSING CARE GUIDE

INTERDEPENDENCE MODE

SPIRITUAL ROLE BEHAVIORS

Recipient
1. "I believe God can help me heal my body."
2. "Sometimes I'm not sure God is there."
3. "I need to talk to someone about this cancer."

Contributive
1. "I thank God for each day that I have."
2. "Why did I have to get cancer?"
3. "I promised God that I would be an active Catholic if I could live."

INFLUENCING STIMULI

Focal: Raised a Catholic.

Contextual: Likes the priest at the nearby church. Parents have been active Catholics for years. Cancer removed 3 months ago. Receiving chemotherapy.

Residual: Lives in a Catholic community.

JUDGMENT 1: Susie is using compromise and substitution to deal with the stress of having cancer.

JUDGMENT 2: Susie's behaviors in the nurturing component of the spiritual role will not maintain her level of social adequacy.

NURSING DIAGNOSIS: Expressive spiritual role, disturbed social adequacy: cancer* (category II diagnosis). Susie is having some doubts about her faith and is not utilizing the church for support.

GOAL: Susie will approach the parish priest as a supportive counselor within the next month. She will also explore a women's support group in the church and will attend a meeting within the next month.

---

*National Conference on Nursing Diagnosis.

Nursing interventions would include supporting Susie's belief that the church should help in times of need. The nurse would intervene by verbally exploring this belief and the possible benefits to Susie and her family of using the parish priest and women's group as support systems. Many enabling intervention modalities are effected in this approach. Often, when clients discuss problems, they arrive at a positive conclusion with minimal assistance from the nurse.

Paula can complete the evaluation by assessing Susie's behavior after 1 month and evaluating if she had indeed contacted the parish priest to include him in her support system. Paula would also assess whether Susie has found a women's support group at the church and attended a meeting.

Susie's regulator/cognator process in the interdependence mode is reflected in a coping stance of self-enhancement, except for her utilization of the church for support. Her behaviors regarding the church show that she is using compromise and substitution and has not acknowledged her need for support as she experiences the triggering events of cancer and chemotherapy.

Self-concept mode. Paula recognizes that people experiencing loss have special needs in the self-concept mode. Susie's self-concept mode assessment is shown below.

NURSING CARE GUIDE

SELF-CONCEPT MODE

BODY IMAGE BEHAVIORS

1. "My scars are less red."
2. "My best features are my face and my hair."
3. "I never thought too much about my breasts."
4. "I'd rather be alive than have breasts."
5. "My prosthesis is about the same size as my breast was."
6. "My hair falling out has been more difficult than the breast being gone."
7. "My pubic hair is half gone." "I've hardly got any hair left on my arms."

INFLUENCING STIMULI

Focal: Chemotherapy, 5-fluorouracil.

Contextual: Left modified mastectomy 3 months ago for cancer. Mother of young children, wants to raise them. Prosthesis makes clothes fit well. Young adult task of intimacy.

Residual: Not a vain person. American youth/beauty culture.

JUDGMENT 1: Susie is using self-enhancement and negotiation to deal with the stress of chemotherapy.

JUDGMENT 2: Susie's behaviors are maintaining her level of psychological adequacy.

NURSING DIAGNOSIS: Body image, maintained psychological adequacy: loss of breast* (category I diagnosis). Susie has accepted into her body image the loss of her breast.

---

*National Conference on Nursing Diagnosis.

Paula supports Susie by briefly recognizing that Susie's statement that her life is more important than her breasts is "good."

Susie's regulator/cognator process in the self-concept mode continues to maintain her level of adequacy. She has chosen the coping stance of self-enhancement, dealing with her body image changes by using the coping strategy of negotiation. The remainder of the assessment of the self-concept mode shows that Susie has a moderately high level of self-esteem.

Nurse/client interaction

Paula has now worked with Susie for four visits and has established a trusting and open relationship. Her client has been receptive of Paula's skills and intervention. The preceding nursing care guides reflect Susie and Paula's relationship. The following anecdote will illustrate Susie's adaptation process as she interacts with Paula and will show how Paula uses the adaptation nursing process as a tool to solve problems with Susie. In this interaction Paula will exemplify an adaptation nurse at the young adult stage of professional development and will complete a nursing care guide that reflects today's interaction.

It is 1:00 P.M., and Susie is again at the clinic for chemotherapy. She has her blood drawn and tells Paula that she is "fine" but feels "a little more tired than usual." When the white blood cell count is reported as 1/cu mm, Susie bursts into tears. Paula supports her by touching her arm while she cries and encourages her to talk more about it. Susie states that the white blood count means "everything will be off schedule." She then explains, "Well, I feel so sick the week of chemotherapy, and then I have a good week. Now I'll have chemotherapy the week of Christmas." She begins to cry again and says, "I did want this to be a special Christmas for John. He's 5, and I don't know how I'll be feeling next Christmas." Paula responds with a supportive and accepting statement: "I know how very difficult it is for you right now." Susie nods and Paula continues to assess. Susie begins to cry again; Paula continues to touch her arm and sit quietly. She then asks, "What else is causing those tears?" Susie responds, "Oh, I just don't know how to deal with this cancer and John. He's only 5, and I love him so much. I'm afraid he'll see my scar. Oh, I just don't know how to handle all of this." Paula continues to assess Susie's mother role and refers to her earlier assessment of the mother role.

Role performance mode. Paula moves to phase III in her own adaptive process and begins processing the data from Susie. Paula, because she is mature and has experienced the successful resolution of several life struggles, chooses a self-enhancing and confronting approach with Susie, as can be noted in the following nursing care guide.

NURSING CARE GUIDE—revised assessment

ROLE PERFORMANCE MODE

MOTHER ROLE BEHAVIORS	INFLUENCING STIMULI
1. "I'm afraid John will see my scar."	*Focal:* Mastectomy for cancer.
2. "I just don't know how to deal with this cancer and John."	*Contextual:* Chemotherapy effects. Afraid John will be hurt. Afraid John will reject her love.
3. "I did want this to be a special Christmas for John."	
4. Bursts into tears.	*Residual:* Knowledge that children are afraid of differences.

NURSING CARE GUIDE—revised assessment

INTERDEPENDENCE MODE

MOTHER ROLE BEHAVIORS

Contributive
1. "I just don't know how to deal with this cancer and John."
2. "He's only 5, and I love him so much."
3. "What if I handle it all wrong and I 'scar' John for life?"

INFLUENCING STIMULI

Focal: Cancer and chemotherapy.

Contextual: John, age 5 years. Lack of knowledge about how children deal with major illness and loss. Afraid John will reject her love.

Residual: Feels like this shouldn't be happening to her.

JUDGMENT 1: Susie is using compromise and repression to deal with the stress of being a mother of small children and having cancer.

JUDGMENT 2: Susie's behaviors of not helping John deal with her illness is ineffective in maintaining her level of social adequacy.

NURSING DIAGNOSIS: Expressive mother role, disrupted social adequacy: cancer* (category II diagnosis). Paula postulates a crossmodal role and interdependence nursing diagnosis that states: Susie has not helped John understand and accept her illness and feels unable to do so because she is afraid that John will reject her and because she needs more education about how children deal with major illnesses and loss.

GOAL: Susie will decide how to share information about her illness with John and will have this talk with John within 2 weeks (category I diagnosis).

INTERVENTION

1. *Enabling:* The stimulus to be manipulated is the fear that John will be hurt and reject her love.
   Paula begins by deciding to use herself therapeutically. She knows teaching and making decisions will be more effective if feelings are explored first. Paula is striving to help Susie verbalize and become clear about her feelings about her cancer and how that affects John.
   Paula decides to relate to Susie her own experience of sharing with her daughters about how their grandfather was dying. She describes to Susie her ambivalence and insecurity in dealing with her daughters, how her husband helped, and how a good friend helped

EVALUATION

1. Susie will state how she thinks her cancer illness will affect John.
2. Susie will express her hopes regarding herself, her illness, and John.
3. Susie will implement the approach chosen.
4. Susie will express an understanding of the selected literature.
5. Susie will decide how to share information with John.
6. Susie will develop and implement a plan of action related to John and his understanding of the illness.

*National Conference on Nursing Diagnosis.

her. She also tells Susie that she recognizes the two situations are vastly different. Paula knows that after exploring their feelings, many people can then evaluate the choices open to them as well as the consequences of each choice.

2. *Teaching:* The stimulus to be manipulated is the lack of sufficient knowledge about how children deal with major illness and loss.

Paula is using a coping strategy of negotiation with the intervention modality of teaching. She chooses to apply a teaching process to explore common literature with Susie about children as they experience loss and major illness. She is using the following teaching process: determining that the client is ready for teaching (she and Susie agreed on this strategy in the diagnosis and goal-setting steps of the nursing process). The goal is to share information and resources regarding children's responses to illness. The plan is to discuss resources, nursing literature, and nursing experiences. The teaching/discussion of chosen literature will be done the following week during Susie's clinic appointment. (Paula chose to emphasize nursing literature because she and Susie share this common frame of reference. Paula will then implement the teaching plan.

Summary

Susie will continue to deal with the triggering event of her illness, which at this stage can be called disrupted wellness. Paula will continue to interact with Susie until the state of disrupted wellness is moved to wellness or again to illness, offering invaluable intervention modalities to Susie. Several alternatives are open to Paula. She may judge herself as limited in professional knowledge and skills, at which time she may choose to further her education in a graduate program and move to the generative stage of the professional nurse role. On the other hand, she may find satisfaction in her nurse role by remaining at the young adult stage of development.

In this case study Paula has demonstrated the nursing intervention modalities of collaboration, teaching, support, and enabling. She has chosen a self-enhancing coping stance and strategies of confrontation, manipulation, and negotiation as ways of processing triggering events that Susie provided, thus effectively facilitating her client's ability to maintain and increase her level of adequacy, the primary goal of adaptation nursing.

REFERENCES

Brunner, L.S.: The Lippincott manual of nursing practice, ed. 2, Philadelphia, 1978, J.B. Lippincott Co.

Carter, F.M.: Psychosocial nursing, theory, and practice in hospital and community mental health, New York, 1981, Macmillan Publishing Co., Inc.

Diekelmann, N.: Primary health care of the well adult, New York, 1977, McGraw-Hill Book Co.

Garfield, C.A., editor: Stress and survival: the emotional realities of life-threatening illness, St. Louis, 1979, The C.V. Mosby Co.

Hall, J.E., and Weaver, B.: Nursing of families in crisis, Philadelphia, 1974, J.B. Lippincott Co.

Havighurst, R.J.: Human development and education, New York, 1953, Longmans Green & Co.

Luckmann, J., and Sorensen, K.C.: Medical-surgical nursing: a psychophysiologic approach, ed. 2, Philadelphia, 1980, W.B. Saunders Co.

Maier, H.W.: Three theories of child development, New York, 1969, Harper & Row, Publishers, Inc.

Martinez, R.A., editor: Hispanic culture and health care: fact, fiction, folklore, St. Louis, 1978, The C.V. Mosby Co.

Meares, A.: The management of the anxious patient, Philadelphia, 1963, W.B. Saunders Co.

Mercer, R.T.: Perspectives in adolescent health care, Philadelphia, 1979, J.B. Lippincott Co.

Pasquali, E.A., Alesi, E.G., Arnold, H.M., and DeBasio, N.: Mental health nursing: a bio-psycho-cultural approach, St. Louis, 1981, The C.V. Mosby Co.

Roberts, S.L.: Behavioral concepts and the critically ill patient, Englewood Cliffs, N.J., 1976, Prentice-Hall, Inc.

Selye, H.: Stress without distress, New York, 1974, New American Library, Inc.

Sontag, S.: Illness as metaphor, New York, 1977, Farrar, Straus, & Giroux, Inc.

Stuart, G.W., and Sundeen, S.J.: Principles and practice of psychiatric nursing, St. Louis, 1979, The C.V. Mosby Co.

Sutterly, D.C., and Connelly, G.F.: Perspectives in human development, Philadelphia, 1973, J.B. Lippincott Co.

Werner, E.E.: Cross-cultural child development: a view from the planet earth, Monterey, Calif., 1979, Brooks/Cole Publishing Co.

Whaley, L.F., and Wong, D.L.: Nursing care of infants and children, St. Louis, 1979, The C.V. Mosby Co.

CHAPTER 7

Illness situations

THEORY OBJECTIVES

Describe the client's regulator/cognator transaction in each of the diagnostic category III case studies.

Define the unique stimuli that influence each of the client transactions in the three case studies.

Characterize each adaptation nurse's regulator/cognator transaction.

Describe each of the unique stimuli that influence the adaptation nurse's transactions.

Explain how the adaptation nurse in each case study arrives at judgments, diagnoses, goals, and interventions based on knowledge of the client's internal transaction.

Compare your present role performance with that of the adaptation nurse in each of the diagnostic category III case studies.

In this chapter three nurse/client interactions are used to demonstrate how an adaptation nurse in the young adult stage of professional development uses the adaptation nursing process with clients who are experiencing illness and who are therefore in diagnostic category III. The chapter is designed to help the reader understand how the adaptation nurse in the young adult stage (1) employs the complex thinking process involved in adaptation nursing, (2) demonstrates a specific level of knowledge and skill, and (3) judges and plans in complex illness situations. Before venturing into the case studies, the reader is advised to review the sections on diagnostic category III, illness (below), and the adaptation nurse in the young adult stage (pp. 125 to 129).

DIAGNOSTIC CATEGORY III—ILLNESS: A REVIEW

The ill person has been described as an adaptive person who is exhausted and cannot assume responsibility for himself. This person cannot process triggering events effectively, and he misinterprets reality. Therefore, he is in a state of crisis and does not have enough adaptive energy to cope effectively with the constantly changing environment. The ill person has no growth or self-enhancing experiences, and his level of adequacy is declining. Unless he receives outside intervention, this person may experience permanent impairment and an irreversible change in his level of adequacy. Therefore, he is perceived by others as incapable of maintaining his level of adequacy.

Because the ill person is not processing the environment effectively, his behavioral

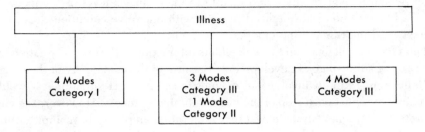

FIGURE 7-1
The illness portion of the health/illness continuum and three of the most common diagnostic combinations that are found in this range of the continuum.

responses are ineffective in maintaining adequate functioning. His coping stance and strategy are incongruent with the triggering event and influencing stimuli. This person's regulator and cognator processes have distorted or incorrectly interpreted the triggering event; as a result, the person's internal problem-solving process proves ineffective. The ill person's behavioral response reflects these inaccurate perceptions and either fails to impact on the environment or produces additional triggering events that prove destructive to the person's declining level of adequacy.

A realistic description of a category III classification would be as follows: illness refers to adapting persons who demonstrate a category III diagnosis in two or more modes. This description may seem inflexible, and yet the condition of a person with two category III diagnoses can deteriorate rapidly. The third diagnostic category draws energy from all areas, leaving severe energy deficits in the other modes; this leads to deterioration of the person's overall adaptive capacity.

There are several positions on the health/illness continuum occupied by the third category. They vary from mild to severe levels of illness. An adaptive person with a category I diagnosis in two modes and two category III diagnoses in the other two modes is experiencing far less disruption than the adapting person with several category III diagnoses in three of four modes and a category II diagnosis in the fourth mode.

The ill person looks anxious and feels exhausted. He is perceived as being incapable of maintaining his level of adequacy. This person seeks health care or, more frequently, is brought to the health care facility for management of his third category diagnoses and for prevention of further deterioration in his level of adequacy. This person's regulator and cognator functions are disrupted, and he needs help processing triggering events, selecting coping stances and strategies, and achieving effective behavioral responses. The medical conditions associated with illness are life-threatening states and those that prove highly disruptive of the person's level of adequacy. Therefore, the ill person is seen in acute care settings including emergency rooms, operating rooms, and medical, surgical, and psychiatric intensive care units. Because the ill person is overwhelmed and unable to maintain his level of adequacy, he is one of a large group of hospitalized persons with operative conditions, catastrophic illnesses, and life-threatening emergencies.

This chapter will focus on three ill clients interacting with three adaptation nurses in the young adult stage of development. Because of the complexity of the situations and influencing stimuli involved in diagnostic category III situations, it would be impossible to reflect each step of the nurse's thinking process. However, the chapter attempts to (1) demonstrate how the young adult employs the complex thinking process involved in such situations, (2) reflect a specific level of knowledge of skill performance, and (3) show how the young adult nurse exercises judgments and plans in complex illness situations.

Before proceeding to the case studies, it is recommended that the reader review the theoretical objectives and read the following performance objectives. Keep in mind the fact that written materials can only teach to the theoretical objectives of adaptation nursing. Only in the actual clinical milieu can adaptation theory be applied. Therefore, performance objectives have been included to help the reader, with or without supervision, to examine her or his ability to utilize the complex *thinking* process essential to the practice of adaptation nursing.

PERFORMANCE OBJECTIVES

Given a specific nurse-client situation, use the adaptation nursing process with clients experiencing a category III diagnosis:
    Identify the client's regulator/cognator transaction.
    Identify the unique stimuli that influence the client's transaction.
    Describe your regulator/cognator transaction.
    Identify the unique stimuli which influence your internal transaction.
    Formulate judgments, diagnoses, goals and interventions based on the knowledge of your
        own and your client's internal transactions.
Based on your use of the adaptation nursing process, identify your level of professional development.

CASE STUDY—CARDIAC DISTRESS: AN ACUTE AND UNPLANNED EXPERIENCE
The setting

Dr. Powell Baxter exemplifies the adaptive person who encounters illness and experiences a category III diagnosis. He is overwhelmed by stress, exhausted, and in a state of crisis when he is admitted to the hospital with an acute myocardial infarction. He exhibits a diagnostic category III in three of his adaptive modes and a diagnostic category II in his remaining mode. At present he is in the coronary intensive care unit, where he was transferred immediately after his emergency admission 2 evenings ago. Elena Sanchez, an adaptation nurse in the young adult stage of development, is assigned to care for Dr. Baxter. Returning from 3 days off duty, Elena arrives early to start planning for her newly assigned clients.

In planning for Dr. Baxter, Elena reviews his chart and discovers that he was admitted 32 hours ago and that since then he has appeared tense and preoccupied. He speaks infrequently; when he does respond verbally, it is in a tense, clipped manner. Whenever someone monitors his vital signs or oscilloscope readings, Dr. Baxter seems to become very impatient and irritable. Upon admission, he exhibited 8 to 10 premature ventricular contractions per minute, and an intravenous drip of 1 gm of lidocaine in 500 ml of 5% dextrose in water was started. Thereafter, he exhibited only an occasional premature beat. The previous evening Dr. Baxter had two episodes of nausea and diaphoresis. When asked if he had pain, he closed his eyes, frowned, and told the nurse in a controlled and rigid voice, "I'm fine, just completely exhausted. Will you please leave me alone so I can rest?"

Elena's planning for Dr. Baxter is influenced by her personal transaction process and unique stimuli; therefore, these will be addressed before exploring how Elena uses the adaptation nursing process to assess, formulate judgments, validate, generate diagnoses, establish priorities and goals, intervene, and evaluate Dr. Baxter's illness and adaptation needs.

The adaptation nurse

Elena is a charming, vivacious 22-year-old Mexican American who graduated with top honors from a university school of nursing whose curriculum is based on the Roy adaptation model. After graduation, Elena decided to work in a general hospital in Albuquerque. She chose a fast-paced general medical/surgical unit for her first job experience and focused on physiological mode integrity, maintenance, and recovery. Her nursing interventions of collaboration and support provided opportunities for her to enhance her physical assessment and medical assistant skills. Her interactional skills were also developed on a daily basis as she helped clients cope with triggering events of hospitalization, procedures, examinations, surgical interventions, pain, discomfort, loss, recovery, and rehabilitation.

Last year, after 2 years of general medical/surgical nursing, Elena decided to expand her adaptation nursing skills in another health care setting. She moved to Denver to accept a staff nurse position in the critical care unit of a general hospital.

External influencing stimuli. Like all adaptation nurses, Elena processes interactions with her environment by way of the regulator/cognator transaction. This transaction is influenced by Elena's external and internal stimuli. The unique external stimuli that influence her interactions with Dr. Baxter center around Elena's immediate environmental setting. Elena had an 8-week concentrated orientation to the coronary intensive care unit and has been a participating member of the nursing team for the past 10 months. She has expanded her assessment skills and her comprehension of the complex monitoring equipment and life-support and maintenance devices used in the unit. At present she is concentrating on her interactional skills to help clients cope more effectively with the overwhelming stress of coronary disruption.

Elena has excellent rapport with the attending cardiologists, residents, interns, and nursing personnel. She enjoys the independence and self-direction the unit affords and consistently takes advantages of the unit resource materials and hospital library. When the spring semester begins, Elena plans to enroll in a course on biochemical and psychosocial aspects of intensive care nursing.

A capable and effective adaptation nurse, Elena experiences a sense of challenge along with stress when treatment demands conflict with client-centered needs. At such times she is torn between the desire to spend time helping persons cope with client role demands and the necessity for offering and monitoring life-support measures essential for their recovery. Despite these areas of conflict, Elena enthusiastically seeks challenging situations. She laughingly tells her colleagues that if she gets in over her head, she can always call on her adaptation clinical specialist to come to her assistance.

Internal influencing stimuli. Physiologically, Elena is bursting with good health. Her childhood was normal except for an emergency appendectomy, which she recalls as a time when she was the star of the show and loved every minute of the experience. She rarely has a cold or "flu" and prides herself on the fact that during the past 10 months she has missed only 2 days of work. She is a petite 5 feet 2 inches tall and weighs 100 pounds. Although she appears fragile, she has proven herself more than capable and adept at working with patients and handling equipment.

Elena is involved with the tasks of young adulthood both personally and professionally. She is independent and assumes personal autonomy while striving for professional and personal intimacy. She is excited about the ways she has been able to satisfy her needs for professional growth and expand her nursing career in the intensive care setting. Both confident and competent, she is well respected by her medical and nursing colleagues and is known as an excellent adaptation nurse.

Elena's internal state is reflected in her unbounding enthusiasm and idealism. She considers life an exciting experience and believes that nursing has a role in changing the quality of health care delivery and that her personal and professional goals are mutually enriching. Her optimistic search for answers and alternatives has enhanced her delight in learning, thus expanding her knowledge of cause-and-effect relationships, which in turn influences her problem-solving approaches in all situations. When asked, Elena attributes much of this outlook to her family. A member of a Mexican American culture, Elena was surrounded with a loving, caring family who gently encouraged her to take risks because they believed in her. The youngest of the six children, she was encouraged to participate in sports and to become involved in civic and church affairs. These activities did not distract Elena from her course of studies (she ranked in the top fifth percentile of her classes throughout her elementary, secondary, and collegiate education).

Partly because of her exposure to an ethnic culture, civic activities, and a midwestern society, Elena trusts in the essential goodness of people, believing that they will approach situations and other people as she would if they were placed in her situation. Occasionally this has led Elena to make invalid assumptions about her client's needs and thus to manifest a stress-filled reaction.

In summary, as a young adult adaptation nurse Elena is developing personally and professionally in an environment that supports her enhanced autonomy and professional intimacy. She takes risks, provides life-support measures, searches for answers to complex questions, and effectively interacts with clients to help them cope with their life-threatening experiences. With her colleagues, she explores more effective ways of delivering nursing care and helping clients cope with their overwhelming experiences of illness. Elena also strives to resolve some of the ongoing conflicts between providing life-support measures and identifying the stimuli influencing the client's response to the crisis of a category III diagnosis. All of these factors are reflected in Elena's planning and her nurse/client interactions.

Although Elena has not met Dr. Baxter yet, she has begun his plan of care. She is slightly nervous about caring for a physician, especially one with his knowledge of cardiovascular disruption and prescribed medical therapy (Dr. Baxter is a skilled neurosurgeon). Elena has assembled pertinent data concerning Dr. Baxter's presence in the coronary intensive care unit. This initial information will now be reviewed.

The adapting person

Dr. Powell Baxter is a 43-year-old neurosurgeon who lives with his wife, Rebecca, on the outskirts of Denver. They have become involved in a closely knit athletic and cultural group consisting of 50 professional couples who enjoy the comradery and release from tension the group provides. Rebecca is a beautiful, poised, and charming 26-year-old woman who is terribly distressed about Dr. Baxter's heart condition. She is upset that Dr. Baxter's surgery schedule has tripled in the past year and that his consultation service has expanded to four hospitals. She indicated to the emergency room nurse that he had been more fatigued and irritable than she can remember in their 6 years of marriage. He has repeatedly canceled their sports activities and been too exhausted to take advantage of their season tickets at the music center. Lately he has demanded that she stop being so dependent on him and start doing more things on her own.

Dr. Baxter told the resident that his father died of a coronary at the age of 45 years. Powell had just turned 20 at the time. He and his two brothers were totally unprepared for their father's death; their mother had died of cancer only 1 year before their father died. As the oldest of the three children, Powell dropped out of school to help support his brothers until their graduation from high school. He reentered medical school at the age of 24 years and specialized in neurosurgery. Rebecca told the admitting nurse that Powell had an acute stress reaction during his last year at medical school but still managed to graduate first in a class of 300 students. Dr. Baxter had denied any previous episodes of chest pain or shortness of breath, even though Rebecca stated that he had become more "driven," did not sleep well, and had assumed erratic and poorly balanced eating habits. Dr. Baxter shared the fact that for the past 3 weeks he had experienced intermittent chest discomfort, shortness of breath, and a persistent need to eructate. He ignored the pain, proving to himself that it was nothing serious by climbing three flights of stairs rather than taking the hospital elevator to the surgical suite. Also, he increased his consultation appointments during this time. However, 2 evenings ago during dinner he experienced constricting anterior substernal chest pain accompanied by diaphoresis and nausea. Losing consciousness for a brief period of time, he was resuscitated by a terrified Rebecca. Once he regained consciousness, Rebecca called the paramedics, who rushed Dr. Baxter to the hospital. In the ambulance Dr. Baxter told Rebecca not to worry, that his condition was not serious, and that he would be back home and ready to work in no time. He squeezed her hand and told her he loved her very much. Rebecca kissed him, held his hand tightly, and shifted her position so that he would not see her crying.

Nurse/client interaction

Physiological mode. Upon admission to the coronary intensive care unit, Dr. Baxter was given oxygen and morphine and then was connected to an electrical monitoring device. His electrocardiogram registered 8 to 10 premature ventricular contractions per minute. An intravenous lidocaine drip was administered immediately. Once the premature contractions had begun to subside, the resident physician inserted an arterial line to monitor his arterial pressure and measure his blood gases.

Dr. Baxter's blood pressure was 70/40, his temperature 99.8° F, and his respirations rapid, irregular, and gaspy. His heart rate was 100 beats/minute. The report of his blood tests revealed the following values: hemoglobin, 15 gm/100 ml; hematocrit, 46.7%; and white blood cell count, 15,400/cu mm. His cardiac enzyme, creatinine phosphokinase (CPK), lactic dehydrogenase (LDH), and serum glutamic oxaloacetic transaminase (SGOT) levels were elevated. He still appeared ashen, but the diaphoresis had subsided somewhat. A catheter was inserted to better monitor his urine flow. When asked, he stated that he was 6 feet tall, weighed 180 pounds, and had never had a weight problem. His face was drawn and tense, and he admitted that he still had chest pain; however, the pain that had radiated to his shoulder, elbow, jaw, and back had begun to let up.

After reviewing his chart, Elena realizes that Dr. Baxter has adaptation problems in all four modes. She judges that he has a category III diagnosis in his physiological, role performance, and self-concept modes. She postulates that his interdependence mode may be threatened and therefore may be a category II diagnosis. Dr. Baxter is not processing his triggering event effectively. He has misinterpreted the regulator response and repressed its signal to the cognator. As a result, his adaptive energy is depleted, and his body is having difficulty coping with the overwhelming impact of cardiac muscle occlusion, necrosis, and consequent ischemia. He is anxious, feels exhausted, and is unable to maintain his physiological adequacy. Dr. Baxter's need to drive himself and perform as a neurosurgeon is adversely influencing his cardiac and respiratory adequacy.

Elena plans to continue the collaborative nursing actions initiated upon admission and wants to validate her initial assessment and nursing conclusions. With this in mind, she listens to report, notes that it is time for trays to arrive, and starts toward his room. She wants to introduce herself and begin her morning assessment before he eats breakfast. As she walks down the corridor his electrocardiogram alarm goes off, and she rushes into his room. Dr. Baxter has disconnected his electrocardiogram leads and is leaning against the bedside stand attempting to shave himself. He is ashen and has broken out in profuse diaphoresis. His legs are trembling, and his intravenous infusion flow has slowed to nonperfusion. Elena, dreading another infarction or arrhythmia or a possible heart block, rushes to his side and gently remonstrates with him about being out of bed. In a gasping voice he angrily demands to know who she is. Elena introduces herself as she firmly guides him back into bed. She then restarts his oxygen flow, reestablishes his leads, explains what she is doing and why, and reassesses his physical status. As she does this, she asks Dr. Baxter if he is aware of the risks involved in such early and strenuous activity. He growls, "Dammit, yes" but adds that he has to get his strength back as quickly as possible. "I have already been here 32 hours, and I have to get back to my practice. My patients need me, and they deserve my consideration. This blasted chest is hurting again." Elena readjusts his oxygen apparatus, reestablishes the infusion flow, and monitors the electrocardiogram readings, heart rate, and respirations. His blood pressure has dropped to 70/40, and the labored respirations and diaphoresis are still present. Elena calmly explains the importance of rest at this critical period of cardiac ischemia. She reiterates that stress and activity increase his heart rate and oxygen requirements and therefore increase the vulnerability for arrhythmias and heart block. After he closes his eyes and starts breathing easier, Elena exhorts him to stay in bed while she leaves to get his pain medication and tranquilizer to provide rest and better relaxation for his traumatized heart muscle. Dr. Baxter grumbles and attempts to relax his body even though he still looks exhausted. Elena rushes to the nurse's station, prepares the morphine injection and the oral valium, and returns to administer the medication. Pulling up a chair, she stays with him until the medication begins to take effect. In a quiet, gentle voice she tells Dr. Baxter that as soon as he has time to rest and restore his taxed heart, they will discuss his need to move more quickly than his body can tolerate. Dr. Baxter opens his eyes, and mutters, "Well, okay, if you really think it can help." Elena notices that his ashen color has diminished, his breathing is easier, and the electrocardiogram readings have returned to their previous rhythm. His face and extremities begin to relax. He tells Elena that he feels sleepy and that if she will leave him alone for a while, he believes that he can go to sleep. Elena readily agrees. She tells him that she will draw the curtain but keep the door ajar so that she can keep him in view outside the room. Elena explains that she will be in frequently to check his cardiac activity but will not disturb him unless it is absolutely necessary to do so.

Returning to the nurse's station, Elena reexamines her plan of care while keeping an eye on Dr. Baxter. His electrocardiogram reading displays an occasional premature beat but demonstrates a more normal cardiac rhythm.

The following nursing care guide reflects Elena's reassessment, judgment, diagnosis, goals, interventions, and evaluation of Dr. Baxter's physiological mode.

NURSING CARE GUIDE

PHYSIOLOGICAL MODE

MUSCULOSKELETAL BEHAVIOR

1. Stands at bedside leaning against bed-stand; legs trembling, weak. States he is "worn out, exhausted."

CIRCULATORY BEHAVIORS

1. Ashen color.
2. Skin is cold and clammy.
3. Heart rate is 100 beats/minute.
4. Pulse is weak and rapid.
5. Has two to three PVCs/minute for 10 minutes, which then subside.
6. Heart sounds normal but has muffled S_1, with the presence of diminished extrasystoles.
7. Blood pressure is 70/40.
8. White blood cell count is elevated (15,400/cumm).
9. Hemoglobin and hematocrit are within normal range (15 gm/100 ml and 46.7%, respectively).
10. Elevated serum enzyme, LDH, SGOT, and CPK levels.

ELIMINATIVE BEHAVIORS

1. Urine output is 40 ml/hour.
2. Sedimentation rate is elevated.

RESPIRATORY BEHAVIORS

1. Increased respirations (20 to 24/minute).
2. Respirations labored.

INFLUENCING STIMULI

Focal: Abrupt increase in Dr. Baxter's activity increases his heart rate and oxygen requirement because his heart is ischemic and damaged by an inferior wall myocardial infarction. (This sudden occlusion of a coronary artery with the abrupt cessation of blood and oxygen flow to heart muscles causes a necrotic area within the myocardium. Until scar tissue can form, the surrounding tissue is vulnerable to arrhythmias and heart block.)

Contextual: Attempts to get out of bed and shave even though experiencing severe cardiac disruption. Ectopic rhythms arise in or near borders of ischemic myocardium. Restlessness and anxiety increase heart rate and oxygen requirements. Destruction of myocardial tissue triggers inflammatory process. Pain can cause reduction in cardiac output, and inadequate tissue perfusion results in tissue hypoxia. Presence of metabolic acidosis, which results from anaerobic metabolism caused by poor tissue perfusion.

Residual: Pattern of stress over past years. Worry and pressure of growing practice. Disrupted sleep patterns. Cessation of athletic life-style and improper exercise patterns. Poor eating pattern. Age of 43 years (high-risk age).

INGESTIVE BEHAVIORS

1. Intravenous lidocaine drip.

ENDOCRINE BEHAVIORS

1. Is 6 feet tall, and weighs 180 pounds.
2. Is slim, well built.

NEUROLOGICAL BEHAVIORS

1. Temperature is 100° F.
2. Is awake, oriented to time and place.
3. States his "chest is hurting again."
4. Face appears drawn and tense.

JUDGMENT: Dr. Baxter's general alarm reaction is congruent with the heart's increased demands for oxygen; however, if this response continues, it will rapidly deplete his physiological reserves and be inadequate for maintaining his level of physiological adequacy.

NURSING DIAGNOSIS: Cardiac output integrity, decreased physiological adequacy, myocardial occlusion and ischemia* (category III diagnosis). (Dr. Baxter is experiencing a life-threatening category III physiological diagnosis. His heart muscle, damaged by necrosis and ischemia, is vulnerable to sudden increases in the demand for oxygen. Dr. Baxter's automatic regulator response is appropriate when he suddenly attempts to increase his activities; however, this response must be terminated or it may overwhelm his physiological adequacy. The termination of this alarm reaction is dependent on Dr. Baxter's assumption of the client role; therefore, this mode will be the next one Elena addresses.)

GOAL: Dr. Baxter will experience an increase in physiological adequacy (category II diagnosis). Dr. Baxter's myocardium is already damaged and very susceptible to episodes of ischemia and necrosis. Therefore, he will rest and use the prescribed medical regimen to (1) effect tissue repair and scar formation; (2) reduce the need for oxygen and increased cardiac output; (3) reduce his pain, irritability, and anxiety; (4) depress his cardiac conduction system; (5) decrease myocardial irritability; (6) increase arterial blood oxygenation; and (7) promote muscle relaxation.

INTERVENTION

1. *Collaboration:* Elena will monitor electrocardiogram readings with rhythm strips every 2 hours, make a periodic PVC count after 48 hours, and monitor blood pressure, pulse, and respirations by electronic means. She will take his temperature every 4 hours, and measure and record his intake and output, especially urine (Foley catheter). She will also measure specific gravity and analyze arterial blood gases. Elena will promote rest,

EVALUATION

1. Dr. Baxter's cardiac rhythm will return to normal by the fourth day.
2. Dr. Baxter will rest undisturbed at 2- to 4-hour intervals.
3. Pain will disappear by the third day.
4. Breathing will be relaxed, regular, and easy by the fourth day.
5. Skin will be warm and dry by the third day.
6. Expression will be calm and alert by third day.

*National Conference on Nursing Diagnosis.

INTERVENTION

myocardial tissue healing, increased oxygenation, and reduction of anxiety and tension by administering the following measures and agents: An intravenous drip of 1 g of lidocaine in 500 ml of 5% dextrose in water; 3 liters of oxygen per minute via nasal catheter; 1 to 4 mg of morphine sulfate intravenously as needed for pain; 10 mg of diazepam orally for restlessness and anxiety; docusate sodium (Colace) daily; clear liquid diet for 48 hours, then 1200-calorie, soft, 2-gm sodium diet in several (six) small feedings. She will position Dr. Baxter for comfort and complete bed rest in semi-Fowler's position and will validate his ongoing response by asking about the presence of pain, discomfort, tension, or anxiety. She will assess the need for oxygen or the presence of respiratory changes. She will provide an atmosphere of quiet and controlled activity by reducing the noise level, dimming the lights, limiting number of visits to Dr. Baxter's room, partially closing the door, drawing the curtains, planning for the maximum number of nursing actions to occur at the same time (thus allowing longer periods of undisturbed rest), staying within his view, and explaining the precise hospital and medical regimen schedules.

EVALUATION

7. Dr. Baxter will eat and eliminate in a normal pattern by the fourth day.
8. Oxygen support will be discontinued by the fourth day.

Role performance mode. Realizing that Dr. Baxter's physiological mode behaviors and influencing stimuli place him in a diagnostic category III, Elena is anxious for him to move in a more positive direction on the health/illness continuum. In order to do this effectively, Dr. Baxter must engage in client role behaviors that provide him with meaningful rest, relaxation, and cardiac healing time. Therefore, Elena directs her attention toward Dr. Baxter's role performance and interdependence modes. In these two modes Elena has identified that Dr. Baxter occupies the primary role of generative adult. He has been performing the tasks and striving to achieve the gratification and support needed in this developmental stage. He has been forcefully expanding his professional endeavors and has tripled his practice in the past year. Dr. Baxter has responsibly undertaken the secondary role of husband,

and from the beginning he and Rebecca have had a close, caring relationship. They have similar interests and enjoy the same recreational activities. However, Rebecca discloses that over the past few months he has been irritable and impatient, asking her to do more things on her own, to be more independent.

Throughout the first 24 hours of Dr. Baxter's hospitalization, Rebecca remained at the hospital and visited him for 5 minutes each hour. But last evening Dr. Baxter insisted that she go home to rest, because he was worried about her lack of sleep and ongoing experience of stress.

Since his admission to the coronary intensive care unit, Dr. Baxter has been called upon to assume the tertiary role of critical care client. At first he was too exhausted to resist performing the role; he remained in bed and allowed the medical and nursing staff to initiate lifesaving measures. Although he was reluctant to converse with the critical care staff, he acknowledged feeling fatigued and wanting to rest. Today he ignored his critical care needs, got out of bed, discontinued his oxygen support, stood at the side of the bed, and attempted to shave himself.

Based on this assessment Elena correctly assumes that Dr. Baxter is having difficulty in taking on the client role and that his adaptation problem may be a result of his overwhelming desire to continue his high level of professional performance. She judges that his client role behaviors are ineffective in coping with his damaged and vulnerable myocardium. His level of adequacy is severely threatened, and his client role performance reflects a category III diagnosis. His difficulties seem to be compounded by his drive to prematurely resume his physician role; consequently, Elena concludes that this role also evidences a category III diagnosis. In contrast, his husband role seems intact, and she assumes that this role is a category I diagnosis.

The goal Elena establishes for Dr. Baxter is to accomplish three tasks: achieve client role mastery, temporarily relinquish his physician role, and sustain his husband role interactions with Rebecca. Elena plans to use teaching and support to help him perform these adaptive roles more effectively. The following nursing care guide indicates Elena's assessment, judgments, diagnosis, goals, interventions, and evaluation for his role performance mode.

NURSING CARE GUIDE

ROLE PERFORMANCE MODE

CRITICAL CLIENT ROLE BEHAVIORS

Noncompliance
1. Out of bed, standing and shaving (against physician's orders).
2. "I am fine, if the nursing personnel will just leave me alone to rest."

INFLUENCING STIMULI

Focal: Presence of and demands of caregivers. Refusal to acknowledge cardiac disruption and need to perform as usual.

Contextual: Concern about his career responsibilities. Drive to be in control of his own activities. Lack of experience being ill.

CRITICAL CLIENT ROLE BEHAVIORS

3. Statement to Rebecca that his condition is not serious.
4. Disconnected electrocardiogram leads.

INFLUENCING STIMULI

Residual: Belief that he can control body despite disruption and that getting up right away and resuming activities of daily living will help him get his strength back more quickly. Suddenness of the illness. Positive body image as physically fit and adept. Belief that his physician role is most important aspect of his life.

Compliance

1. Returned to bed when Elena directed him to do so.
2. Closed his eyes (face relaxed and body appeared less tense).
3. Accepted pain medication without complaint.
4. Accepted tranquilizer and allowed Elena to help him swallow it.
5. Stated he would talk with Elena if she thought it would help.

Focal: Presence of caregiver, Elena, who insists that he perform critical client role.

Contextual: Coronary intensive care unit itself. Clarifications made by Elena on consequences of his actions and on his expected and needed response as a critical client. Presence in hospital 32 hours.

Residual: Belief that medical decisions do make a difference in crisis situations.

PHYSICIAN ROLE BEHAVIORS

1. "I have to get back to my practice."
2. "My patients need me. They deserve my consideration."

Focal: Presence of and demands of his patients. His belief that patients are important and must have first consideration.

Contextual: Rapid expansion of his practice. Repeatedly canceled sports and civic center activities to meet demands of growing practice. Resultant irritableness and impatience with husband role demands.

Residual: Beliefs that his physician role is most important aspect of his life. Drive to master medical school despite acute stress reaction. Inexperience with any previous demands to master the sick role.

JUDGMENT 1: Dr. Baxter's behaviors will not help him to take on the critical client role and will therefore pose a radical threat to his social and physical adequacy.

JUDGMENT 2: Dr. Baxter is using a coping stance of compromise and the strategies of repression and substitution to cope with his needs to rest and provide a healing environment for his damaged myocardium. He is repressing and suppressing his knowledge about the seriousness of his condition and attempting to use his professional success to maintain his social adequacy.

NURSING DIAGNOSIS: Instrumental client and professional roles conflict: decreased social adequacy; decreased physiological trauma and limitations* (category III diagnoses). (Dr. Baxter is expe-

*National Conference on Nursing Diagnosis.

riencing a category III diagnosis in his critical client and physician behaviors. He has refused to alter his neurosurgeon behaviors to meet his physiological need to rest and restore his damaged heart. The coping stance of compromise is appropriate, but his excessive use of repression, suppression, and substitution radically threaten his social and physiological adequacy.).

GOAL: Dr. Baxter will experience an increase in social adequacy (category II diagnosis). Dr. Baxter will engage in appropriate critical client role behaviors and temporarily relinquish his physician role behaviors to regain social adequacy and thus restore his physiological adequacy. To achieve this Dr. Baxter will spend time with his primary nurse, Elena, and discuss needs for client role change, clarify prescribed critical client role mastery behaviors, and explore the behaviors that effect compliance with his medical regimen.)

INTERVENTION

1. *Support and teaching:* Elena and Dr. Baxter will meet for 30 minutes after he has had 4 hours of effective rest. Elena will help him identify both positive and negative client role behaviors and help him explore the stimuli that have influenced his noncompliance during the past 32 hours of hospitalization. She will clarify for Dr. Baxter the consequences of overexertion and will listen to him as he expresses his feelings about illness, his loss of performing as a surgeon and consultant, and his drive to prove to himself that his body is not injured or vulnerable. For 15 minutes each day Elena will help Dr. Baxter identify how he will perform needed client role behaviors not only in the critical care setting but also when he returns home. Dr. Baxter will tell Elena how he plans to balance his physiological and social needs to retain biopsychosocial adequacy. Dr. Baxter will meet with Rebecca and Elena to plan for his eventual discharge and for maintenance of his adaptive response.

EVALUATION

1. Dr. Baxter will meet with Elena each day for 3 days to discuss his client role mastery, relinquishing (temporarily) his professional role mastery, and how to maintain his husband role performance and avoid potential conflict in this area.
2. With Elena's help Dr. Baxter will write out his client role activities for the next 4 days.
3. He will design a plan for balancing the demands of his physiological adequacy with his professional demands.
4. He will ask Elena or Rebecca to write down his plans for discharge.

Elena has not had the opportunity to implement these nursing actions but will do so before the end of the shift. She anticipates that Dr. Baxter will then be able to move into a category II diagnosis and eventually achieve a diagnostic category I in his role performance mode. She judges that he will do this by following his medical regimen, participating in prescribed activities, and using their shared planning to redefine his professional commitment. Elena realizes that she must use enabling if Dr. Baxter is to alter his life-style, so she plans to confer with her adaptation clinical specialist, Catherine, about further effective actions.

Interdependence mode. Regarding his interdependence mode Elena thinks that Dr. Baxter's behaviors are indicative of a category II diagnosis. He has Rebecca's support but seems to be having difficulty nurturing and supporting her. Just before his hospitalization Dr. Baxter was demanding that Rebecca become more independent, and during his critical care experience he has sent her home to rest. Elena has already noted that her client's stated religion is Lutheran; because of her own Catholic heritage, she is very concerned that his spiritual needs be met. She calculates the time Rebecca has had to rest at home and decides to call and ask her about Dr. Baxter's needs in this area. Rebecca informs her that Dr. Baxter is very active in the church, serving as usher each Sunday; he is very close to their pastor, Reverend Hammond. She also tells Elena that she herself is a recent convert to the Lutheran religion and that her husband was very influential in this decision. She states that he is a reverent person who feels strongly that he is here on earth to serve others. She then tells Elena that she tried to contact Reverend Hammond to inform him of her husband's condition but that he is out of town for a few days.

Rebecca also tells Elena that for several months before the heart attack Dr. Baxter seemed too tired to pay much attention to her and that this hurt her deeply. She explains that he used to be attentive and affectionate, always caressing and hugging her. Recently, however, his work has been taking all of his time and energy. Elena tells Rebecca that she is welcome to come to the coronary intensive care unit and that if he has been given medication and is resting she can at least look in on him.

After talking to Rebecca, Elena reviews her assessment of Dr. Baxter and judges that his ability to give and receive support is threatened at this time. For although his expressive behaviors seem adequate for helping him cope with his sudden illness, they seem potentially ineffective for helping him sustain affectional adequacy. In his spiritual role Dr. Baxter's past instrumental and expressive behaviors make him highly eligible for support and nurturance from his religious beliefs. However, his pastor is absent at this critical time. Based on these judgments, Elena concludes that Dr. Baxter has a category II diagnosis in his interdependence mode. His overwhelming physical stress has posed a threat to his relationship with Rebecca. This physical strain has prevented him from processing his affectional and spiritual needs clearly. Realizing this, Elena plans to explore these needs with him as soon as possible to help him establish ways of strengthening his affectional and spiritual bonds, especially during this crisis time. Elena will use support and teaching to accomplish this task, as outlined in the following nursing care guide.

NURSING CARE GUIDE

INTERDEPENDENCE MODE

PRIMARY ROLE (GENERATIVE ADULT) BEHAVIORS

INFLUENCING STIMULI

SECONDARY ROLE (HUSBAND) BEHAVIORS

Contributive
1. Tells Rebecca not to worry, that his condition is not serious, and that he will be back home in no time.
2. Squeezes Rebecca's hand.
3. Has demanded that Rebecca stop being so dependent on him and start doing more things on her own.
4. Has insisted that Rebecca go home and sleep.
5. Lately is too tired to pay attention to Rebecca.
6. Used to be attentive and affectionate.

Recipient
1. Accepted Rebecca's presence, kisses, and 5-minute visits each hour for first 24 hours.

Focal: Rebecca, his wife.

Contextual: Fatigue from work. Tripled surgery schedule in past few months. Expanded consultations to three other hospitals. Worried about Rebecca's lack of sleep and experience of stress. Lack of awareness and ability to cope with mushrooming medical practice while sustaining affectional support behavior.

Residual: Belief that he is a responsible, caring person. Conflict about serving others and having no energy to devote to his wife.

TERTIARY ROLE (SPIRITUAL) BEHAVIORS

Contributive
1. Very active in Lutheran church.
2. Very close to pastor.
3. Influenced Rebecca's conversion to church.

Recipient
1. Very deep and reverent person.
2. Feels strongly that he is here on earth to serve others.
3. Has not asked about his pastor.
4. Has not referred to spiritual needs.

Focal: Active participation in Lutheran church.

Contextual: Strong commitment to church beliefs. Strong sense of spiritual purpose and direction. Stong sense of giving and serving. Lack of time and privacy to share needs.

Residual: Lutheran religious views he holds. Beliefs that God speaks and directs him through the church and that church and God are important in his life.

TERTIARY ROLE (CLIENT) BEHAVIORS

Recipient
1. Accepts medications and oxygen.
2. Accepts Elena's helping him back to bed and sitting beside him until medications take effect.
3. Becomes impatient and irritable when caregivers monitor his vital signs.
4. Responds in tense, terse, preoccupied manner.

Focal: Presence of health care providers and Elena.

Contextual: Critical care environment (rushed, tense, crisis oriented). Lack of experience in client role and in being dependent and told what to do. Elena's positive response. Lack of privacy and time for sharing feelings.

TERTIARY ROLE (CLIENT) BEHAVIORS

5. When asked about pain, closes his eyes, frowns, and denies its presence in controlled and rigid voice.
6. States he is fine, just completely exhausted and would they please leave him alone so he can rest.
7. Grumbles when Elena tells him she is going to get pain medication and tranquilizers.

Contributive
1. When Elena tells him that they will discuss his needs after he has rested he states "Well, okay, if you really think it will help."

INFLUENCING STIMULI

Residual: Fear of dependency and of being out of control. Beliefs that he is not seriously ill and that he must return to take care of his patients immediately. Lack of expertise sharing his feelings and fears with strangers.

JUDGMENT 1: Dr. Baxter is engaging in ineffective receptive behaviors in his husband, spiritual, and client roles. He is demonstrating sporadic contributive and recipient behaviors in all three roles. Therefore, he is not effectively maintaining his level of social adequacy.

JUDGMENT 2: Dr. Baxter has chosen the coping stance of compromise and is using suppression to block out his stress-producing hospitalization. Because this strategy is only successful for a brief period of time, he will need to select a more effective strategy to cope meaningfully with the demands for giving and receiving nurturance.

NURSING DIAGNOSIS: Expressive client, husband, and spiritual role insufficiency, disrupted social adequacy; exhausted from work and illness* (category II diagnosis). Dr. Baxter is experiencing a category II diagnosis in the interdependence mode in his roles as husband, church member, and client. Therefore, his ability to give and receive nurturance and support is markedly threatened. The inconsistent behaviors engaged in by this client will eventually decrease his level of social adequacy.)

GOAL: Dr. Baxter will experience an increase in social adequacy (category I diagnosis). Dr. Baxter will nurture and support his wife, receiving nurturance and support from her, Reverend Hammond, and his caregivers, expecially Elena. In order to achieve this balanced giving and receiving, Dr. Baxter will exhibit contributive and receptive behaviors that will enhance the response of others who are significant in his achieving social adequacy.

INTERVENTION

1. *Support:* Elena will provide nurturance and support, encouraging Dr. Baxter to discuss his feelings about hospitalization and the need to be dependent. Elena will use touch, eye contact, positive facial expressions, and verbal encouragement

EVALUATION

1. Dr. Baxter will utilize the nursing staff as a source of support and nurturance during his hospital stay.
2. He will ask for help and discuss specific ways that others can help him during this stress time.

*National Conference on Nursing Diagnosis.

INTERVENTION

when interacting with him. Rebecca will be with her husband, hold his hand, and visit even when he is asleep.

2. *Teaching:* Elena will clarify with Dr. Baxter his preferences in relation to significant others and help him plan which dependent behaviors he would be comfortable using to receive needed support and nurturance during his hospitalization. She will also help Dr. Baxter design a plan for when significant persons would be present so that he can have time for maximum rest. Elena will also help Dr. Baxter plan for ways of providing support and nurturance to Rebecca.

EVALUATION

3. Dr. Baxter will identify the two persons who can provide support and nurturance during his stay in critical care.
4. He will list behaviors he would like others to use when they are indicating care and concern.
5. He will describe how he will support and nurture Rebecca during this time.
6. He will describe when and how often he would like to visit his pastor.
7. Dr. Baxter will state when he wishes to pray the kinds of prayer he wishes to engage in.

Elena knows that without meaningful support and nurturance during this time of stress, Dr. Baxter will have difficulty moving in a more positive direction on the health/illness continuum. Therefore, she is eager to carry out her plan with Dr. Baxter but is aware that her interaction with him will have to wait until his rest period is ended. She realizes that enabling nursing actions are also needed and plans to consult with her clinical specialist, Catherine, about which actions would be most appropriate and how they can be implemented.

Self concept mode. In Dr. Baxter's self-concept mode Elena judges that his behavior reflects a category III diagnosis. His moral/ethical self demands a selfless giving of his medical skills and gifts. He represses and suppresses the importance of physical warnings and consequent disruption to increase the power to give. His body image is also reflected in his drive to expand his medical practice; he perceives that he is healthy, fit, and able to give limitless energy to his professional activities. Dr. Baxter's self-consistency and self-ideal are operative here as well. He has always been able to give in this selfless, boundless way and plans to do so for years to come.

Elena's own beliefs help her to identify with Dr. Baxter's perception of self-worth and life's purpose and direction. She can sympathize with his demanding pattern but knows that if it is not curtailed, Dr. Baxter will have a recurrent myocardial infarction or even succumb to cardiac arrest. Therefore, she concludes that his self-concept mode indicates a category III diagnosis. The following nursing care guide represents her assessment, judgments, diagnoses, goals, interventions, and evaluation of Dr. Baxter's self-concept mode.

NURSING CARE GUIDE

SELF-CONCEPT MODE

PHYSICAL SELF BEHAVIORS

1. Decided to stand up and shave despite fatigue, pain, and weakness.
2. Gives orders to leave him alone so he can rest.
3. Climbing stairs to prove to himself that chest discomfort and pain are nothing.
4. Telling Rebecca not to worry, that his condition is not serious, and that he will soon be back home ready to work.

SELF-CONSISTENCY BEHAVIORS

1. Statement that he has to get back his strength so he can return to his practice.
2. Shaving.

MORAL/ETHICAL SELF BEHAVIORS

1. Statement that he has to get back to his practice because patients need him and deserve his consideration.

SELF-IDEAL BEHAVIORS

1. Able to support two brothers, go back to medical school, and establish an excellent practice against great odds.

INFLUENCING STIMULI

Focal: Perception that he is healthy, fit, and able to control his own body. Belief that he must give to others in a selfless, boundless manner.

Contextual: Physiological disruption and experience of warning signs and eventual cardiac crisis. Was rushed to hospital and forced to rest and let others take care of him. Expansion of his medical practice and consultative services. Relinquished his athletic and cultural activities, which had previously relaxed him.

Residual: Belief that he is on this earth to serve others and that he can achieve what he sets out to do. Apparent support from Rebecca. Belief he is essential to his patients.

JUDGMENT 1: Dr. Baxter's drive to maintain former behaviors despite structural damage can meet his self-consistency needs but will result in cardiac impairment or cardiac arrest and will overwhelm his total biopsychosocial adequacy.

JUDGMENT 2: Dr. Baxter's coping stance of compromise and strategies of repression and substitution stem from his denial of physical weakness and belief that he can always control his own body. His responses however are inappropriate to his triggering event of sudden overwhelming cardiac disruption.

NURSING DIAGNOSIS: Diminished self-esteem, decreased physiological adequacy: belief he must work despite cardiac trauma* (category III diagnosis). (Dr. Baxter has a category III diagnosis in his self-concept mode. He is refusing to acknowledge his physiological trauma and is attempting to perform as if nothing had occurred to reduce his physiological adequacy. His coping stance and strategies of compromise and repression are dramatically incongruent with his myocardial tissue damage and ischemia, which will eventually result in decreased psychological adequacy, just as his physiological adequacy has already been reduced.)

*National Conference on Nursing Diagnosis.

GOAL: Dr. Baxter will experience an increase in physiological adequacy (category II diagnosis). Dr. Baxter will alter his perception of his physical, moral/ethical, ideal, and consistent self to better match the overwhelming alterations in his physiological adequacy. He will comply with the imposed cardiac regimen and redesign his personal goals and beliefs in light of his physiological disruption. With the help of supportive persons like Rebecca, Reverend Hammond, Elena, and Catherine, he will also explore alternative life-styles, which will be reflected in better managed and constrained professional endeavors.

INTERVENTION	EVALUATION
1. *Support:* Elena will provide time for Dr. Baxter to discuss his concerns and needs and to explore the consequences of returning to his former pattern of living and working.	1. Dr. Baxter will stop activities that prevent maximum rest and relaxation.
2. *Teaching:* Elena will acknowledge Dr. Baxter's feelings while helping him to focus on realistic goals now that he has cardiac structural damage as well as myocardial ischemia, which can disrupt cardiac functioning at any time. She will explore alternatives of performance that will be compatible with Dr. Baxter's physiological changes and yet maintain his self-concept energy channel. She will discuss with him the idea of consulting, on a long-term basis, with enabling professionals.	2. Dr. Baxter will express enthusiasm for other options and alternatives in his lifestyle and professional activities.
3. *Enabling:* She will provide for consultation with one or more of the following persons: generative adult adaptation nurse, pastor, psychiatric social worker, and psychologist.	

Dr. Baxter's manner of coping, by using compromise and repression, suppression, and substitution, is threatening to overwhelm his total biopsychosocial adequacy. Elena uses the adaptation nursing process to help her client meet his holistic need for adequacy.

Summary

In this adaptation nursing process special emphasis has been placed on Dr. Baxter's and Elena's regulator/cognator transactions. Dr. Baxter's transactions reflect the holistic nature of the adaptive person. His modes or energy channels are so interrelated that it is impossible to address only one. However, as would any adaptation nurse, Elena needs a clear framework to systematically assess, judge, and intervene effectively with such a complex person. Elena's transaction reflects her development level and her concern that Dr. Baxter's total adequacy needs be met, even if she is unable to effect this on her own. Elena's influencing stimuli are clearly evident and represent her ability to reach out to Dr. Baxter and Rebecca, plan for his nurturance and spiritual needs, plan for his ongoing support and teaching needs in the critical care setting, and provide him with enabling nursing actions to help him to reestablish his total biopsychosocial adequacy.

Elena's regulator/cognator process is strongly influenced by her knowledge, comprehension of total needs, internal state, and level of professional development. Based on her own coping style, Elena was able to establish a partnership with Dr. Baxter to help him increase his threatened level of adequacy.

CASE STUDY—DEPRESSION AND LOSS
The setting

In this situation we will meet Mrs. Levy; she is experiencing category III diagnoses in three out of four modes and also has several category II diagnoses. She is currently an inpatient on a locked psychiatric unit. She was hospitalized 5 days ago when her mood had deteriorated, and she had begun discussing suicide as an alternative to her circumstances. Mrs. Levy's primary nurse is David Weston, an adaptation nurse in the young adult stage of development.

As we encounter Mrs. Levy, she is in acute distress. The process David uses to assess, formulate judgments, diagnose, establish priorities and goals, intervene, and evaluate the situation will be explored in detail. David has worked with Mrs. Levy since her admission and has therefore completed the major part of his nursing care plan. However, he will be expanding his assessment of her self-concept and formulating a plan for the weekend staff because he will be off for 2 days and because Mrs. Levy's condition seems to be deteriorating.

The adaptation nurse

David is a 23-year-old man who graduated 2 years ago from a midwestern university school of nursing whose curriculum is based on the Roy adaptation model. David's nursing process guides and client interactions demonstrate an excellent grasp and utilization of adaptation concepts.

Since graduation David has had two jobs. His first employment experience was on a stroke rehabilitation unit, where most of the clients had acute medical problems that were interfering with their rehabilitative process. David describes his nursing performance in this setting as primarily providing collaborative actions designed to assist clients with their acute physiological problems. In that setting he became increasingly adept at providing clients with support in coping with their disabilities.

David acquired his second job when he moved to California 6 months ago. Upon his arrival he was hired at the university medical center as a beginning psychiatric nurse. He had decided that he had enjoyed the interaction process and would like to further develop his interviewing and communication skills. He was also impressed with the educational opportunities available to staff as well as the independence and autonomy offered by the unit's philosophy of primary nursing.

External influencing stimuli. As you will recall, the adaptation nurse interacts with the environment by way of the regulator/cognator process, which is influenced by external and internal stimuli. The external stimuli that affect the regulator/cognator process are the people, places, and objects that compose the physical environment. In this situation the physical environment is an 18-bed, locked, inpatient psychiatric unit staffed by six to seven professional nursing staff members per shift. The unit is small and institutional looking despite attempts to make the dayroom and dining room "homey." There are currently 16 adults hospitalized here. Their medical diagnoses include depression, schizophrenia, paranoid reactions, and borderline personality. The unit does not provide long-term treatment: the average length of stay is 14 to 21 days. The clients participate in a program that includes group therapy, occupational and recreational therapy, and individual therapeutic meetings. As this is a university teaching facility, there are many students and projects that interact with and provide input for the patients and the milieu.

Internal influencing stimuli. You will recall that internal stimuli include the physiological state, maturational level, knowledge, and beliefs. Regarding the physiological state, David is a healthy, 23-year-old man who has never had surgery or been hospitalized. He is 6 feet tall, weighs 165 pounds, and is physically capable of working and expanding his practice as an adaptation nurse.

David's personal and professional maturational levels affect his interaction with Mrs. Levy. He is coping with the tasks of young adulthood, establishing himself as an autonomous person who is striving for intimacy, both personally and professionally. He is also striving to solidify and expand his career. Since graduation David has gained confidence in his skills and is identified with a peer group of psychiatric nurses. He has formed a professional identity and is improving his skills by continuing his education and working in the atmosphere of a university teaching hospital. David appears to be developing positively as an individual and as a professional adaptation nurse.

Finally, we must consider David's unique internal state. Obviously, we cannot explore this aspect of the person in great depth, but we can look at some obvious stimuli that will influence David's interactions with Mrs. Levy. First, he is generally a positive person with an optimistic outlook about personal potential. He believes that adapting persons frequently triumph over incredible odds and that perseverence is a positive attribute. David has never experienced anything he felt was really difficult or traumatic. He readily admits that his life has been effortless and that he has always achieved what he has set out to accomplish. David attributes much of his positive attitude and the ease of his life to his nurturing, supportive family.

The second of five children in a middle-class Protestant family, he was raised in a small farming community in northeastern Kansas. David has not been exposed to many ethnic groups or cultural differences. Since coming to southern California, he has expanded his contacts considerably, but he still finds himself overwhelmed when dealing with persons from vastly different backgrounds than his own. Despite his education, which has exposed him to theoretical knowledge about other cultures and values, David still tends to believe that most people think and feel as he does.

In summary, David is an adaptation nurse in the young adult stage of development who is a positive, optimistic young man with values rooted in the Midwest as opposed to his current southern California environment. Practicing adaptation nursing in a setting that is professionally supportive and nurturing, he is successfully interacting with a wide variety of adapting persons and is expanding his skill to solidify his role performance.

The adapting person

Mrs. Levy is a 54-year-old Jewish woman who was born in New York but who has lived in Los Angeles since she was 8 years old. She was widowed 6 months ago when Max, her husband of 30 years, died suddenly of coronary thrombosis. Mrs. Levy lives alone in a large house about 10 minutes away from the hospital. She has lived in her home in this affluent suburb for about 25 years. Although she no longer needs the space, she cannot bring herself to move to a condominium. Mrs. Levy has two children: a son, Matt, who is 22 years of age and is in his first year of medical school at an eastern university; and Shelly, a freshman at a local university.

Mrs. Levy started exhibiting symptoms of depression about 2 weeks after her husband's death. She seemed to be coping adequately until 3 months ago, when Shelly moved into an apartment with friends. Since that time, Mrs. Levy has had weight loss and insomnia and has become increasingly withdrawn and preoccupied with negative aspects of her life. Despite repeated urging, Mrs. Levy has refused to seek psychiatric help.

Mrs. Levy was brought to the emergency room by a friend. The friend related that she had stopped to visit Mrs. Levy and found her still in bed at 2:00 P.M. The friend stated she was shocked at the change in Mrs. Levy's weight and appearance and was extremely concerned when Mrs. Levy could not seem to stop an uncontrolled crying episode as she made repeated statements about "ending it all" and wishing she were dead. The friend notified Shelly and reported that Mrs. Levy's daughter plans to meet them at the emergency room. After evaluation by the psychiatric resident on duty, Mrs. Levy was admitted to the inpatient psychiatric ward.

David meets Mrs. Levy the following morning when he reports to work on the day shift. She is wearing a pair of pants and a sweater that hangs loosely because of her recent weight loss. Her hair needs washing, and she is wearing no makeup. When approached, Mrs. Levy is tearful and repeatedly asks staff members when Shelly will arrive with her suitcase.

Upon completion of the initial assessment, David determines that Mrs. Levy has adaptation problems and category III diagnoses in all four modes.

Physiological mode. In the physiological mode David finds that Mrs. Levy is basically a healthy woman. She has experienced colds and flu but has never had surgery or been hospitalized except for the birth of her children. She had had regular physicals and until her husband's death had engaged in regular physical activity that included swimming and tennis. Mrs. Levy is 5 feet 5 inches tall, and her usual weight fluctuated between 120 to 125 pounds; she now weighs 100 pounds; her vital signs are normal: blood pressure 124/78, pulse 90, respirations 18, temperature 99° F. She has had insomnia, especially during the last 3 months, and has stated that her pattern at home was much like that of her first nights in the hospital: typically, Mrs. Levy would fall asleep watching television and then go to bed about 11 P.M., sleeping soundly until about 3 A.M., when she would awaken and be unable to return to sleep. In addition, Mrs. Levy complains of a lack of appetite, stating that at home she couldn't get used to cooking for one person. During her hospitalization she has only coffee for breakfast and seldom eats more than one-half serving of one or two items at other meals. She is overheard to remark, "I never did care much about eating; it was always a social ritual. Now I can't seem to get interested." Mrs. Levy also complains of constipation, stating that her bowel habits had always been regular but that now she always seems "blocked up": "I guess I don't go for days at a time."

Except for her recent weight loss, some gastrointestinal symptoms, and insomnia, Mrs. Levy's physiological assessment remains within normal limits. Based on these data, as well as his knowledge of Mrs. Levy's previous habits and the recent changes in her life-style, David attributes Mrs. Levy's problems in physiological adaptation to the slowing usually associated with the medical diagnosis of depression. David formulates judgments and a diagnosis, arriving at the opinion that his client is experiencing a category III disruption. Mrs. Levy's behavior is not maintaining her physiological adequacy. David and Mrs. Levy establish goals that will allow her to diminish symptoms of insomnia, weight and appetite loss, and constipation. David then engages in collaborative nursing action. The following nursing care guide represents David's assessment and the resultant plan of action.

NURSING CARE GUIDE

PHYSIOLOGICAL MODE

MUSCULOSKELETAL BEHAVIORS

1. Sleeps from 11 A.M. to 3 A.M.; has difficulty getting to sleep; once awake cannot return to sleep.
2. Currently engages in no regular form of exercise.
3. Sits in a chair or stays in bed for most of her waking time.
4. Occasionally walks from room to room.

INGESTIVE BEHAVIORS

1. Drinks four to five cups of black coffee per day.
2. Eats small portions of one or two food items at lunch and dinner.
3. "I've never been much interested in food; eating is a social ritual."
4. Is 5 feet 5 inches tall and weighs 100 pounds.

ELIMINATIVE BEHAVIORS

1. Small, hard, formed stool on third day of hospitalization.
2. "I feel blocked up."

INFLUENCING STIMULI

Focal: Neurochemical changes, accompanying stress of living alone.

Contextual: Living and eating alone for the first time in 30 years. Prior to depression had regular eating habits (never ate breakfast but did eat light lunch and complete dinner), regular sleep pattern, and regular activity pattern (played tennis two to three times per week, often rode bike to market, swam twice per week, walked a great deal, and did shopping and housework). Usual bowel pattern (well-formed soft stool daily without use of a laxative, occasionally drank prune juice). Since third day of hospitalization is receiving amitriptyline, flurazepam (30 mg at bedtime), and prune juice (every morning with coffee). Hospital environment, communal dining room, meals served cafeteria style to patient's order, must share bedroom and bath with others. History of health and current physical examination that reveals no other disruptions. Blood pressure 124/78, respirations 18, pulse 90, temperature 99° F.

Residual: Jewish cultural beliefs about food and eating. Adherence and involvement in cultural and religious activities. Age of 54 years.

JUDGMENT: Mrs. Levy's physiological response is congruent with the neurochemical changes associated with the medical diagnosis of depression, but this prolonged response is resulting in a decrease in Mrs. Levy's level of physiological adequacy.

NURSING DIAGNOSIS: Nutrition, sleep activity, bowel integrity, decreased physiological adequacy: neurochemical changes.* (Mrs. Levy is experiencing a category III physiological diagnosis. She has a decrease in appetite, lack of sleep, and constipation as a result of neurochemical changes.)

GOAL: Mrs. Levy desires 7 to 8 hours of uninterrupted sleep per night, regular daily bowel movements, and a stabilization of her current weight with an eventual gain of at least 10 pounds. To achieve this she will participate in a structured environment and follow the medical regimen designed to combat the physiological slowing associated with depression.

*National Conference on Nursing Diagnosis.

INTERVENTION	EVALUATION
1. *Collaboration:* Amitriptyline, 30 mg orally 3 times/day, flurazepam, 30 mg orally at bedtime, and prune juice, 6 oz with breakfast. David will provide an atmosphere that is conducive to ingestive behavior, encourage Mrs. Levy to come to dining room for meals and help select companions to share meals, allow her to select her diet, and suggest she might like family or friends to bring in special favorites. David will also provide an atmosphere conducive to sleep, explore previously effective sleep inducing activities (e.g., soft music and reading in bed), and help Mrs. Levy to structure the environment to provide these measures.	1. Mrs. Levy will have an increased appetite within 1 to 2 weeks.
	2. She will have 6 hours undisturbed sleep per night.
	3. She will have a normal bowel pattern daily (A.M.) by the second day of treatment plan.
	4. Mrs. Levy will come to the dining room at mealtimes. She has chosen to sit with Mrs. Adams and Connie. A staff member will also sit at that table once per week. Mrs. Levy will keep fruit and cheese in the patients' refrigerator. She will request at least one item from that refrigerator each evening.

Role performance mode. In the physiological mode Mrs. Levy is demonstrating behaviors and experiencing influencing stimuli indicative of the third diagnostic category (illness). In order to move in a more positive direction on the health/illness continuum, Mrs. Levy needs to engage in behaviors that will increase her appetite and periods of sleep as well as establish a regular bowel pattern. David will facilitate this adaptation process by using collaboration.

In the role performance and interdependence modes David has identified that Mrs. Levy occupies the primary role of generative adult. She must therefore accomplish the tasks and achieve the gratification and nurturance associated with this developmental stage. Generally these tasks include developing one's occupational choice and maintaining one's marital relationship, including the nurturance of the next generation. David observes that Mrs. Levy has rapidly moved toward the next developmental stage without sufficient anticipation or preparation. The sudden death of her husband resulted in the loss of a reciprocal role for Mrs. Levy's secondary role spouse behaviors. The maturation of her children and Shelly's recent move to her own apartment have also brought about recent changes in Mrs. Levy's expected mother role behaviors. Mrs. Levy has not worked out of the home in an occupational role since the first year of her marriage; she has occupied tertiary roles of volunteer, friend, and amateur athlete. Since her hospitalization, Mrs. Levy is also expected to assume the tertiary role of psychiatric client.

David has learned that during the last 25 years Mrs. Levy has devoted most of her energy to her roles of wife and mother. Her achievements and her satisfaction have been gained from these roles. Following her husband's death, she seemed to have diverted her energy to her relationship with Shelly.

Since her hospitalization, Mrs. Levy has demonstrated instrumental behaviors in the roles of mother and psychiatric client. She makes frequent calls to Shelly and talks of the tasks she performed for her daughter when she was living at home: "I tried to cook her diet menus. She was always worried about her weight. I was always taking things to the dry cleaner for her. Now, what can I do? She says I visit too often. I took over a sweater or T-shirt or something I saw that I thought she'd like. She was always so busy; I thought I could help." When Shelly visits, Mrs. Levy sits and talks with her, questioning her about her studies, her roommates, and her strict dieting.

In her role as psychiatric client Mrs. Levy demonstrates many instrumental role behaviors. She attends group therapy, participates in occupational and recreational therapy, and keeps daily appointments with her therapist and David. In addition, she requests her sleep medication and comes to the dining room for each meal as she and David have agreed she should. She continues to express concern about her need for hospitalization: "I can go home soon. I don't belong here."

Mrs. Levy is also attempting to assume the role of widow. She frequently verbalizes her inability to structure her time without her husband. "What am I going to do? A single woman isn't necessary at all those couple places. Now I have no one to cook for, no one to get to work on time, no one to travel with; I don't know what to do by myself."

Based on this assessment, David recognizes that Mrs. Levy is taking on the psychiatric client role but that she is having difficulty taking on the roles of widow and mother of a college-aged daughter. Her adaptation problems appear to be a result of her recent losses of significant others in reciprocal roles. The difficulties seemed to be compounded by Mrs. Levy's lack of preparation for these changes and the resultant lack of alternatives. David discerns that Mrs. Levy's client role performance is a category I and that her mother and widow roles evidence a category II disruption. David and Mrs. Levy establish goals that will allow her to maintain her client role performance while increasing her mother and widow adaptive behavior. David uses teaching and support to assist Mrs. Levy toward a more adaptive role function.

NURSING CARE GUIDE

ROLE PERFORMANCE MODE

MOTHER ROLE BEHAVIORS

1. "Shelly, when are you coming? Do you want me to order a tray so you can have dinner?"
2. "I tried to cook her diet menus; she is always worried about her weight."

INFLUENCING STIMULI

Focal: Shelly's move to her own apartment 3 months ago.

Contextual: Husband's death 6 months ago. Son Matt's move to east coast for school 5 months ago. Lack of experience and knowl-

MOTHER ROLE BEHAVIORS

3. "I was always taking things to the dry cleaner for her."
4. "Now she says I visit too often. I'd take over a sweater or a T-shirt or something I thought she'd like. She was always so busy. I thought I could help."

PSYCHIATRIC CLIENT ROLE BEHAVIORS

1. "Is it time for me to go to occupational therapy now?"
2. "I can't speak up in that group. There are too many people."
3. "What time is lunch? I'm going to try to eat today."
4. "I took the medicine, but it doesn't seem to make any difference."
5. "I don't belong in a place like this. I can go home soon."

INFLUENCING STIMULI

edge about appropriate role behaviors as mother of independent children. Lack of other fulfilling, time-consuming roles. Shelly's age and her desire to be independent.

Residual: Jewish woman 54 years of age. Relationship with own mother. Beliefs about independence and autonomy.

Focal: Presence of caregivers (nurse, physician, and social worker).

Contextual: Hospital milieu, hospital facilities (including dining room), occupational therapy and recreational therapy, and medications. Minimal knowledge regarding psychiatric illness and hospitalization. Never been hospitalized before.

Residual: Beliefs about psychiatric hospitalization. Desire to be a good client. Beliefs that health care professionals know best and that medical advice should be followed.

MOTHER ROLE

JUDGMENT 1: Mrs. Levy's behaviors will not maintain her relationship with Shelly, nor will they help her to take on her new role as widow.

JUDGMENT 2: Mrs. Levy is using a coping stance of compromise and the strategies of repression and substitution to cope with the loss of her husband and Matt's and Shelly's maturation. She is repressing her losses and her knowledge about aging while using her relationship with Shelly to maintain her social adequacy.

NURSING DIAGNOSIS: Instrumental mother role insufficiency, disruption of social adequacy: daughter's increased independence.* (Mrs. Levy is experiencing a category II diagnosis in mother role performance. She has not altered her mother role behaviors to meet the needs of her maturing children. The coping stance of compromise is appropriate, but the degree of repression and substitution of Shelly as her only reciprocal role are excessive.)

GOAL: In order to engage in appropriate mother role behaviors with Shelly, Mrs. Levy wishes to spend time with her primary nurse to discuss role changes and then with Shelly to plan alternative behaviors.

MOTHER ROLE INTERVENTION

1. *Support and teaching:* David and Mrs. Levy will meet three times per week. David will help her identify both positive and negative mother role behaviors, will provide her with reading materials, and then

EVALUATION

1. Mrs. Levy will meet with David three times per week to discuss mother role behaviors. She will read relevant material and discuss the significance of her readings to her behavior with Shelly.

*National Conference on Nursing Diagnosis.

MOTHER ROLE INTERVENTION

will discuss the materials regarding Shelly's increasing independence. David and Mrs. Levy will role play alternate interactions. Mrs. Levy will request Shelly meet with herself and David. She will solicit information regarding Shelly's needs and will share information about her own needs. Mrs. Levy and Shelly will identify mutually acceptable role behaviors. Mrs. Levy and Shelly will practice role behaviors and offer positive feedback. She and Shelly will complete at least two role-playing situations.

EVALUATION

2. Mrs. Levy will offer suggestions and engage in at least two role-playing experiences.
3. Mrs. Levy will schedule and keep appointments with Shelly.
4. Mrs. Levy will list her role expectations of Shelly and describe her desired mother role performance.
5. She will listen and write down Shelly's desires and expectations.

CLIENT ROLE

JUDGMENT 1: Mrs. Levy's behavioral responses are maintaining her level of social adequacy.

JUDGMENT 2: Mrs. Levy is using self-enhancement as a coping stance and confrontation and manipulation to cope with the new role of psychiatric client.

NURSING DIAGNOSIS: Instrumental client role, enhanced social adequacy: presence of caregiver.* (Mrs. Levy is experiencing a category I diagnosis in her client role performance. She is successfully taking on the role of hospitalized psychiatric client. Her coping stance and strategies are compatible with the triggering event and are maintaining adequacy.

GOAL: Mrs. Levy wishes to continue to assume the role of hospitalized psychiatric client as well as begin movement toward the role of client outside the hospital. To achieve this goal she will continue to participate in activities, follow her medical regimen, and begin collecting data regarding discharge and community resources.

INTERVENTION

1. *Support:* David will provide positive feedback regarding group session attendance, meal participation, and taking of medications. He will encourage her continued involvement as indicative of her readiness for discharge.

2. *Teaching:* David will provide input regarding Mrs. Levy's psychiatric needs following discharge. He will recommend appropriate treatment and support facilities and suggest that Mrs. Levy explore these resources. David will indicate to Mrs. Levy that her ability to pursue appropriate alternative care will indicate her preparedness for discharge. David will explain and discuss the rationale for drug

EVALUATION

1. Mrs. Levy will continue to attend all assigned group sessions and meals and take prescribed medication as necessary.
2. Mrs. Levy will contact and make an appointment to see a therapist 1 week prior to discharge.
3. Mrs. Levy will attend an appropriate group session 1 week prior to her discharge.
4. Mrs. Levy will state the names and effects of her medication by end of the first week of hospitalization.
5. Mrs. Levy will be able to identify physiological symptoms of depression and suggest activities to alleviate symptoms.

*National Conference on Nursing Diagnosis.

therapy (e.g., amitriptyline mood-eleva-
tor effects not noted immediately.
Changes in physiological symptoms noted first, sometimes as early as 1 week).
He will discuss the physiological effects
of depression and the active role the person must play in fighting these symptoms.

Interdependence mode. David feels that Mrs. Levy's behavior in the interdependence mode is indicative of a category III diagnosis. She is not experiencing
nurturance or support, and although she reaches out to others, she is unable adequately to nurture or support.

In the interdependence mode Mrs. Levy is apparently having difficulty with both
recipient and contributive behaviors. She is often whiney, tearful, and demanding
with Shelly. She negates any positive verbal feedback with a "Yes, but" response or
with an example of why she doesn't deserve the praise. She expresses her ambivalence
about her hospitalization by accusing her friend and daughter of not caring about
her and putting her away. Then almost immediately she becomes contrite and self-
condemning, suggesting that she deserves whatever she gets. Mrs. Levy is beginning
to realize that she is not used to needing or asking for help or support. "It's always
been my job to take care of everybody, not the other way around. Nobody needs
me anymore."

When David suggests that Mrs. Levy might want to talk with her rabbi or that
there might be a support group at her temple, Mrs. Levy again becomes tearful.
She states that she has not been involved with the temple except to buy a ticket for
the high holidays each year and that she believes it is dishonest and hypocritical to
turn to one's religion only when one is in trouble.

Based on his assessment David notes that Mrs. Levy is not giving or receiving
nurturance or support. Her expressive behaviors are ineffective in helping her to
cope with her many life changes. In her role as mother she reaches out, but when
Shelly visits, Mrs. Levy's behavior drives her away. In her role as widow she lacks
knowledge and complementary role figures. Her expressive behaviors indicate her
inability to achieve gratification. In her spiritual role Mrs. Levy believes that her
past instrumental behaviors or the lack of these behaviors make her ineligible for
support and nurturance from her religion. Having formulated judgments and a diagnosis, David concludes that Mrs. Levy is in diagnostic category III. He and Mrs.
Levy begin discussing her needs and establish goals that would allow Mrs. Levy to

begin taking on the widow role, change her interactions with Shelly, and explore her options to fulfill her spiritual needs. David will utilize support and teaching to help her achieve more adaptive interdependent behaviors.

NURSING CARE GUIDE

INTERDEPENDENCE MODE

PRIMARY ROLE (GENERATIVE ADULT) BEHAVIORS	INFLUENCING STIMULI

SECONDARY ROLE (WIDOW) BEHAVIORS

Recipient
1. "Who wants a single lady to tag along?"
2. "We did everything as couples."
3. "My friends are 'our' friends; I don't have any friends of my own."
4. "What am I supposed to do—go on little old lady tours?"
5. "I don't feel any different; why do people treat me differently?"

Focal: Lack of complementary role opposite.

Contextual: Loss of usual nurturing relationships (e.g., husband's death, Matt's move, and Shelly's living away from home). Lack of information about how to meet emotional needs as a widowed woman with grown children.

Residual: Jewish woman 54 years of age. Beliefs about aging and the meaning of widowhood.

SECONDARY ROLE (MOTHER) BEHAVIORS

Recipient
1. "Why don't you stay longer? I feel better when you're here."
2. "You put me here; the least you can do is visit regularly."
3. "Has Shelly called yet? I hope she comes this afternoon. She never stays very long. I think she's avoiding me."
4. "After Max died, Shelly was all I had."
5. "Did your brother call you? He's only called once since I've been here. Bet the 'young doctor' doesn't like having a nut for a mother."

Focal: Shelly's move from home to an apartment 3 months ago.

Contextual: Matt lives on the east coast and has only called once. Shelly visits daily. (Shelly is 19 years old and has never lived away from home.) Past role as the family nurturer; does not see herself as a recipient. Husband's death 6 months ago. Hospital environment. Knowledge about needs of grown children.

Residual: Past relationships with Matt and Shelly. Anger and difficulty expressing need for support.

TERTIARY ROLE (CLIENT) BEHAVIORS

Recipient
1. "What do you care about an old lady nobody wants?"
2. "What's so good about taking your medication and going to group?"
3. "I can't talk about how I feel in front of all those people."
4. "Thank you for calling Shelly."
5. "Can I take my sleeping pill now?"

Focal: Presence of health care givers.

Contextual: Hospital environment. Lack of experience in role. Lack of experience assuming a dependent position. Positive feedback and support from caregivers.

Residual: Beliefs about psychiatric hospitalization. Fears of dependency. Lack of experience with self expression.

TERTIARY ROLE (SPIRITUAL) BEHAVIORS

Recipient
1. "I've never been active in the temple. I can't ask for help now. I'd feel like a hypocrite."
2. "I wish I'd kept up my religion—maybe it would help."
3. "When my mother died, my father went to temple every day."
4. "I didn't even feel good when we sat schiva for Max."

INFLUENCING STIMULI

Focal: Lack of participation in temple since marriage.

Contextual: Raised in a family that actively practices Judaism. Feels unworthy of nurturance because of lack of recent participation. Not accustomed to asking for help.

Residual: Jewish religion's view of returning members. Mrs. Levy's knowledge of these views.

JUDGMENT 1: Mrs. Levy is engaging in inappropriate receptive behaviors in her roles as mother, widow, and temple member. Because she is demonstrating no contributive behaviors in any of these roles, these behaviors will not maintain her level of social adequacy.

JUDGMENT 2: Mrs. Levy has chosen the coping stance of inaction and is using denial to cope with her need to change to receive the nurturance and support to which she is accustomed.

NURSING DIAGNOSIS: Expressive widow role insufficiency, disrupted social adequacy: lack of complementary role opposite. Expressive mother role insufficiency, disrupted social adequacy: change in behavior of complementary role opposites. Expressive spiritual role insufficiency, disrupted social adequacy: lack of recent role performance.* (Mrs. Levy is experiencing a category II diagnosis in the interdependence mode in her roles as mother, widow, and temple member. Because of the recent losses or changes in complementary role opposites, Mrs. Levy is not experiencing nurturance and support. The receptive behaviors in which Mrs. Levy is engaging will decrease her level of social adequacy.)

GOAL: Mrs. Levy desires nurturance and support. In order to attain this goal she will need to exhibit some contributive behaviors as well as alter the types of receptive behaviors in which she is engaging.

INTERVENTION

1. *Support:* The nurses will provide nurturance and support in the form of praise for independent actions and non–self-deprecating statements. Additionally, the staff will use touch, eye contact, and positive facial expressions when communicating with her.

2. *Teaching:* David will spend time with Mrs. Levy to identify what she would like from significant others as well as to help her identify persons other than Shelly who can offer support and nurturance. David will help Mrs. Levy identify and expand her contributive behaviors with Shelly. He and Mrs. Levy will practice recipient behaviors that are not alienating.

EVALUATION

1. Mrs. Levy will identify nursing staff as a source of support and nurturance.
2. Mrs. Levy will manifest an increase in independent behavior and positive self-statements.
3. Mrs. Levy will be able to identify at least one other person who can provide support and nurturance.
4. Mrs. Levy will be able to list behaviors she would like others to exhibit to indicate care and concern and will describe behaviors that will alienate her from others.
5. Mrs. Levy will begin to demonstrate contributive behaviors in her relationship with Shelly.
6. She will begin to engage in alternate behaviors at mealtimes and during group meetings.

*National Conference on Nursing Diagnosis.

Nurse/client interaction

At 9:30 A.M. David returns from his coffee break to find Mrs. Levy sitting in the dayroom, crying and wringing her hands. He approaches Mrs. Levy and sits next to her on the couch. Mrs. Levy continues to rock back and forth, her arms crossed tightly across her chest. She repeatedly states, "Nobody wants me, nobody cares, I want to die." David tries to get her to tell him what happened during the morning to change her mood so drastically. She doesn't respond but continues to rock and cry. Connie, a young woman patient, walks by and says, "Hey, leave her alone. Can't you see she's upset? She got a phone call, see, something about a ski trip." Mrs. Levy turns to David. "I want to die, and I know how to do it." Mrs. Levy rises from the couch and walks slowly out of the room.

David's immediate assumption is that the phone call Connie mentioned was from Shelly. Perhaps she is planning a ski trip during spring break (some weeks away), which Mrs. Levy perceives as another desertion. He decided it must be difficult for Shelly to have a life of her own with her mother so dependent. David watches Mrs. Levy walk down the hall toward her room. He stops by the nurse's station and asks, "What happened to Mrs. Levy? Did she get a phone call?"

One of the nurses answers, "Yes, she's been crying ever since. Her daughter is going skiing for four days; she's leaving in the morning." David responds, "You're kidding! Her mother has only been here 4 days. She's suicidal. Her only resource is Shelly, and she's leaving. I figured the vacation was a couple of weeks from now. No wonder Mrs. Levy's so depressed; with family support like that, who needs enemies?"

Regulator/cognator process

The client. Mrs. Levy received the phone call from Shelly and learned of her plan to go out of town. This was a triggering event for Mrs. Levy. Her regulator signaled a general alarm, the cognator was signaled, and no other observable physiological response was stimulated. Mrs. Levy's cognator then processed the experience, assuming a coping stance of inaction and a strategy of denial. Her behavioral response is indicative of a decrease in her level of psychological adequacy. Mrs. Levy has experienced a threat to her already diminished self-image. Her crying behavior and statements of worthlessness and suicide are not maintaining her level of psychological adequacy.

Influencing stimuli. Mrs. Levy's cognator process was influenced by her physiological state, the external environment, her maturational level, and her internal state. Her body is not responding in its usual manner; although it is structurally sound, regulatory functions are causing her to feel slow, without energy, and generally less physically competent. The hospital environment, although essential to her safety, adds to her feelings of incapacity. Mrs. Levy frequently comments, "I can't believe I've sunk so low as to have to be locked up with these crazy people." The hospital setting is a constant reminder of her inability to cope effectively. In addition, her age is somewhat incompatible with the task of widowhood, and she is moving more rapidly than she had planned toward the development stage she associates with elderly, incompetent, or useless people. Finally, Mrs. Levy is influenced by her attitudes, beliefs, and knowledge. In her current state she believes Shelly is her only support and source of meaning. If she allows her daughter to leave, she will have nothing and therefore be nothing. She has used denial to block out her experiences and previous positive sense of self. She also refuses to acknowledge the information she has about the needs of maturing children and the tasks of a recently widowed woman. Mrs. Levy has chosen to focus exclusively on the negative aspects of herself and as a result feels worthless.

The nurse. David recognizes Mrs. Levy's behavioral response as a triggering event. His regulator stimulates the general alarm; he demonstrates no other observable physiological responses, and the cognator is signaled. His cognator processes the experience, and he assumes a coping stance of compromise and a strategy of substitution. His behavioral response of seeking information from alternate sources allows him to maintain his professional identity and therefore his social adequacy. When he receives validation from his peers that Mrs. Levy did indeed receive a disturbing call from Shelly, he experiences another triggering event. Again his regulator sounds the alarm; no other physiological behaviors are readily apparent, and the cognator is stimulated. This time David assumes a coping stance of approach and a coping strategy of fight. He strikes out verbally at the environment in a symbolic attempt to terminate this negative experience for Mrs. Levy.

Influencing stimuli. David's first response was influenced primarily by the physical environment and his maturational level. He was initially affected by Mrs. Levy's unresponsive, repetitive behavior, which acted as a somewhat noxious stimulus. It is often difficult to interact with someone who will not respond and who makes repeated self-deprecating comments. Connie was also part of the environment and added to David's knowledge and understanding of Mrs. Levy's behavior. He also identifies with Shelly; they share a similar level of development. Although David sees himself as more advanced in the process, he can still remember his experiences when first living away from home. These two groups of stimuli, the environment and his maturational level, lead David to believe that Mrs. Levy was overreacting and that Shelly is probably again the victim of her mother's demands. Before acting, however, David attempts to validate the environmental information he has received from Connie and therefore engages in verbal interaction with the other staff members.

David's second transaction was influenced by the environment, his maturational level, and his attitudes and beliefs. In this interaction the environment provided the triggering event in the form of the nurse's response regarding Mrs. Levy's phone call. In addition, David's presence in the nursing station, an enclosed nonclient area, allowed him the safety and freedom to make a verbally aggressive response. David's beliefs about families and supportive behavior had a significant effect on his cognator process. Although David's life experience has not included such a "needy" family member, he feels strongly that he or any of his brothers or sisters would be consistently available to one or both of his parents. David cannot identify with Shelly's behavior, and he labels her response as unfeeling. Finally, his level of maturation allows him to identify with Mrs. Levy despite his initial sympathy for her daughter. He has sufficiently accomplished autonomous functioning so that Shelly's needs are not threatening to him.

Nurse/client interaction

Following David's negative response to Shelly's behavior, several members of the staff suggest that David terminate such verbalizations and focus on helping Mrs. Levy to cope with her feelings of worthlessness. He acknowledges their suggestions and walks down the hall to Mrs. Levy's room. As he enters the room David sees Mrs. Levy sitting on the bed, using the sharp, curved end of a hanger to scratch her wrist. He moves quickly across the room to restrain Mrs. Levy and remove the hanger from her hand. He calls down the hall for assistance and escorts Mrs. Levy to the treatment room, asking someone to call her physician to report the incident. Simultaneously, he speaks to Mrs. Levy in a soft, even voice, reassuring her that he understands her feelings but cannot let her hurt herself. Mrs. Levy continues to cry, repeating, "Let me die, let me die," in a singsong voice.

Again we will examine the regulator/cognator process for Mrs. Levy and David. Mrs. Levy experienced a triggering event when she found herself alone in her room with a sharp object. The regulator stimulated the alarm reaction; there was no other observable physiological response, and the cognator was alerted. Mrs. Levy assumed a coping stance of inaction, using a combination of the strategies of denial and dissociation. She continued to block out knowledge, beliefs, and past positive associations and emotionally removed herself from the experience of inflicting physical harm on herself. Because she felt worthless, her self-destructive behavior became acceptable. The emotional blocking eliminated conflict and prompted the behavioral response of scratching her wrist.

Mrs. Levy's behavior was influenced by the presence of a sharp object in an isolated environment, her low self-esteem, and her recently perceived rejection precipitated by Shelly's announcement of her ski trip. Mrs. Levy's coping abilities were so limited at this time that the only option she could consider to decrease her discomfort was to cease to exist. The behavioral response was congruent with her perception of her situation, but this response would have the obvious result of decreasing her level of adequacy.

Mrs. Levy's self-destructive behavior was a triggering event for David. His regulator stimulated the general alarm reaction, and it instituted the automatic motor behavior that moved David across the room, helping him to restrain Mrs. Levy;

finally, the cognator was alerted. He assumed the coping stance of confrontation. Perhaps more optimal conclusions might have been attained, but David knew he would have a positive effect on Mrs. Levy's level of adequacy if he gave her reassurance, used touch to calm her, and moved her to a safe environment.

David's regulator and cognator were influenced by his physiological state as well as the hospital environment, but his behavior was primarily a response to his knowledge and beliefs about the suicidal person. He has a basic belief in the goodness of people and the worth of an individual life. His religious education taught him that suicide is a behavioral option that he cannot sanction. In addition, David's nursing education has given him insight into the dynamics of suicide. He recalls an instructor explaining ambivalence and the concept of tunnel vision. He knows that the suicidal person often does not want to die but is so limited in his coping choices that he selects only one alternative, death. Based on his beliefs, his knowledge, and his relationship with Mrs. Levy, David makes the choice immediately to terminate Mrs. Levy's behavior, protect her, and acknowledge her feelings while sharing his perception of her worth.

Following this incident, Mrs. Levy's physician examines her wrist, determines that the laceration requires suturing, and sends Mrs. Levy to the emergency room for treatment. David accompanies her, continuing his supportive approach. Upon their return to the unit, David orders one-to-one nursing support for Mrs. Levy, requests another nurse to spend time with her in the dayroom, and then joins other staff members in an afternoon staff meeting. The meeting is run by the unit nurse clinical specialist utilizing a consultation format to assist nursing staff to resolve clinical issues. When David joins the group, he immediately requests the opportunity to present Mrs. Levy's case and discuss his concerns about her behavior.

David presents his nursing care plan for Mrs. Levy, focusing specifically on his nursing diagnosis and his client's apparent regulator/cognator process. He concludes by stating his immediate concern and the problems for which he seeks assistance from the group.

> Mrs. Levy has experienced several significant losses in the last 6 months, and as a result she feels worthless and unwanted. Her hospital course was positive until today. She has been responding to the milieu and has had no recurrence of the suicidal ideation or behavior since her hospitalization. Now with the weekend coming, I'm scheduled off (the first time in a month, I might add), and her daughter decides to go skiing. I'm concerned that we provide a safe environment for Mrs. Levy this weekend, but I also think that Dr. Sheridan needs to talk to Shelly. She has to postpone this trip until her mother is better.

David received many responses to his summary. Many staff members agree with his recommendations, and others think he needs to alter his assessment. After a 45-minute discussion, the group has helped David form an effective plan for the weekend and has made some suggestions about ways David should proceed in his long-term interactions with Mrs. Levy.

The staff members agree with David that Mrs. Levy needs a safe, protective environment for the weekend. They believe the one-to-one nursing support can be maintained, and, although David's presence and his relationship with Mrs. Levy would facilitate this one-to-one coverage, there are other staff members who can help while he is away. Mrs. Levy's associate nurse on the evening shift will be on duty for the weekend, and it is recommended that David call her at home to discuss the day's events and the details of the care plan they agree to follow.

The staff also supports David's assessment of Mrs. Levy's needs in the physiological, role performance, and interdependence modes. They indicate that there seems to be a great deal of pressure on Shelly and that perhaps David needs to explore some community resources that Mrs. Levy might utilize and thereby decrease demands on her daughter. One of the staff nurses is aware of a widows' support group at a nearby temple. She suggests that David mention this to Mrs. Levy and recommends that the two of them might want to call the rabbi to obtain additional information.

Finally, the staff recognizes that David is expressing anger toward Shelly, and they suggest that perhaps he needs to see the situation from her perspective. The staff uses personal experience and theoretical knowledge about the depressive patient's tendency to deplete personal resources to help David identify this perspective. They point out David's obvious need for a weekend off as a parallel to Shelly's need for time off from Mom after the last 6 months of an intense relationship. As the interaction progresses, David begins to see the other point of view and can identify some positive outcomes as well. He notes that Shelly waited until her mother was safely in the hospital before meeting her own needs. Besides, her weekend away might be a growth-producing experience for Mrs. Levy. She would be safe in the hospital, and David and her therapist could help her look for more positive alternatives to her overdependence on her daughter. Shelly might be more open to working with the staff and her mother on her return, and David adds, especially "if I'm not out to get her. I guess I overreacted this morning. I think I felt the self destructiveness coming through, and I've never seen anyone actually try to hurt herself like that. I had to be angry with someone; it couldn't be poor Mrs. Levy, so I guess Shelly was a good target. I'm kind of angry at myself, too; if I'd gone down to the room with her, she wouldn't have done that."

The group finishes the discussion with some specific recommendations and support for David and his ability to accept and utilize feedback. He indicates that he will complete a detailed plan of care, asking the nurse clinical specialist if he can review it with her before he leaves for the day. He says, "I'll call Shelly, too. I think it's important that she feel supported. I'm sure she felt guilty when Dr. Sheridan called about the suicide attempt."

The following nursing care guide represents David's assessment, judgments, diagnosis, goals, interventions, and evaluation for the self-concept mode.

NURSING CARE GUIDE

SELF CONCEPT MODE

SELF-IDEAL BEHAVIORS

1. "Let me die, let me die."
2. Sitting with arms folded across chest, rocking back and forth.
3. "Nobody wants me, nobody cares."
4. "I want to die, and I know how to do it."
5. Scratching and gouging at wrist with sharp, curved end of hanger.

INFLUENCING STIMULI

Focal: Phone call from Shelly and knowledge of Shelly's plan to leave for the weekend.

Contextual: Husband's death 6 months ago. Matt's move to medical school and limited phone contact. Shelly's move to own apartment 3 months ago. Beliefs that she is a giver not a receiver, that she will not be able to maintain social relationships without her husband, and that she is unworthy of support from her temple. Alone in room with a sharp hanger.

Residual: Belief about self-destructive behavior. Hospital environment.

JUDGMENT 1: Mrs. Levy's self-destructive behavior could potentially decrease her pain but will result in a significant decrease in her psychological as well as physiological adequacy.

JUDGMENT 2: Mrs. Levy's coping stance of inaction and the strategies of denial and dissociation are inappropriate responses to the triggering events of isolation with a potentially harmful object.

NURSING DIAGNOSIS: Low self-esteem and worthlessness, decreased psychological adequacy: temporary loss of love relationship.* (Mrs. Levy is experiencing a category III diagnosis in the self-concept mode. She is expressing her feelings of low self-esteem and worthlessness by attempting to hurt herself with the hanger. Her coping stance and strategies are incongruent with the triggering event and will result in a decrease in her level of psychological adequacy.

GOAL: Mrs. Levy is not correctly responding to the environment because of her distorted self-perception. Until her perceptions become more reality oriented, she needs to be maintained in a safe environment and to receive reassurance regarding coping alternatives other than self-destructive behavior.

INTERVENTION

1. *Support:* Mrs. Levy will receive one-to-one nursing support. She will be within eyesight of a nursing staff member 24 hours per day. Mrs. Levy's status will be reevaluated at the Monday morning staff meeting. Staff will acknowledge Mrs. Levy's feelings but reassure her that the staff and her therapist will help her find other alternatives to cope with these feelings.

EVALUATION

1. Mrs. Levy will be safe from her own impulsive behavior.
2. Mrs. Levy will experience some hope and a feeling that she can be helped to again experience positive feelings.

*National Conference on Nursing Diagnosis.

Summary

The adaptation nursing process has been examined in detail. Special emphasis has been placed on the regulator/cognator process of both the client and the adaptation nurse. This emphasis is designed to focus on the uniqueness of the client's experience and the uniqueness of the adaptation nurse's use of the nursing process. Optimal adaptation nursing occurs when the uniqueness of the person and the nurse is utilized.

In this situation Mrs. Levy was responding to the loss of her husband and the changing relationships with her children. Her internal state and developmental level had a significant impact on the coping stance and strategies she assumed in response to these triggering events. Knowledge of these coping behaviors and the purpose they served for Mrs. Levy allowed David to assume the perspective of the patient. His regulator/cognator process was primarily influenced by his knowledge, his internal state, and his level of professional development. His internal transactions affected his assessment as well as his response to Mrs. Levy. Based on his understanding of Mrs. Levy's coping pattern and an awareness of his own coping style, David was able to form a partnership with Mrs. Levy to help her increase her declining level of adequacy.

CASE STUDY—DEVELOPMENTAL DELAY: A HOSPITAL EXPERIENCE
The setting

In illness situations the adaptive person demonstrates a diagnostic category III in at least two of his adaptive modes and a category II in his other modes. Therefore, he is faced with overwhelming stress, becomes exhausted, and experiences a state of crisis.

Jimmy Pendergast is a young boy who exemplifies this state when he is rushed to Cresthill Medical Center with a "hot" apendix. His pediatrician, Dr. Elizabeth Thomas, orders him to the hospital after examining him and confirming her suspicion about an inflammed appendix. Jimmy's father is tense and anxious as he drives through early morning traffic to reach the hospital. In the back seat Jimmy is crying and clutching his side as he lies curled up in his mother's arms. He tells her that it "just hurts all over." Both parents are worried about a possible ruptured appendix and its effect on Jimmy's cerebral palsy.

Jimmy and his parents are met in the pediatric unit by Kim Yamada, an adaptation nurse in the young adult stage who will be caring for Jimmy during his hospitalization. The process Kim uses to assess, validate, formulate judgments, diagnose, establish priorities and goals, intervene, and evaluate as she interacts with Jimmy will be examined below. The section Nurse/Client Interaction suggests ways in which an adaptation nurse in Kim's stage of development might use her skills of support and teaching to help a young client cope with a medical emergency. Because Kim's internal transaction and unique stimuli influence her use of the adaptation nursing process, these factors will be addressed first.

The adaptation nurse

Kim is a 24-year-old nisei who has been practicing nursing for 3 years. She graduated from a university school of nursing in New York whose curriculum is based on the Roy adaptation model. She demonstrates an excellent grasp and use of adaptation concepts and process in both her client interactions and nursing care planning. After graduation she worked in the pediatric unit at a university medical center where the child population was extensive and where she was able to interact with children with acute and chronic illnesses.

External influencing stimuli. Last year Kim moved to Alexandria, Virginia, and became a primary nurse in the surgical pediatric unit. She enjoys her work with young people and is striving to develop her interactional skills with them and their families, finding the increased independence in this setting challenging and exciting. This excitement is influenced by Kim's unique stimuli. The external stimuli that affect Kim's regulator/cognator process are the objects, places, and people in her physical environment, in this case, the surgical pediatric unit, located on the second floor of a central nursing tower. The pediatric area consists of 14 nursing units, each of which includes 4 private rooms leading from a controlled area equipped with individual charts, medications, toys, supplies, and linen. Each controlled section has a documentation room, business and interhouse phones, and a small resource library. A unit coordinator and secretary manage the organizational complex situated in the center of the tower. This area houses several conference rooms, two play centers, and a media center for child and family teaching.

The unit is staffed by 14 professional nurses who work 12-hour schedules to limit the number of interactions a child or his family experience during a given hospital stay.

The surgical area is busy and generally filled to capacity; despite its heavy schedule, the carpeted unit is quiet and well organized. The average hospital stay is 3 to 5 days. The youngsters and their families are involved in teaching programs when the surgical procedures are planned and prescheduled; however, in emergency situations such programs are bypassed until teaching can be more effective. Kim works closely with three other adaptation nurses who are in the young adult stage of development: Beverly, Dean, and Carla. They compare assessment data, share nursing plans, and join forces in carrying out many of their nursing activities.

Internal influencing stimuli. Kim's regulator/cognator transactions are also influenced by her internal stimuli: her physiological state, maturational level, knowledge, and beliefs. She is a slender, active, healthy young woman who has had the normal childhood illnesses without having surgery or being hospitalized. She is 5 feet 4 inches tall, weighs 115 pounds, and is physically adept in handling equipment and nursing situations.

Establishing herself personally and professionally, Kim has a wide circle of friends. Professionally, she helped initiate a "primary care" forum for the purpose of expanding professional competence and solidarity. She, Carla, Beverly, and Dean frequently consult with their adaptation clinical specialist, Marsha, to explore ways of upgrading and expanding their adaptation nursing practice.

Kim's internal state is also an important influence in her nursing practice. However, it would be impossible to examine it in depth. Therefore, only the factors that influence her interaction with Jimmy and his parents will be explored.

An incurable optimist, Kim is convinced that adapting persons can triumph over incredible odds and that personal knowledge, faith, and determination help them to achieve success. Her conviction stems from her parents' response to adversity. At the age of 17 years, her parents migrated to the United States, worked in many unskilled occupations, and yet were able to help their two sons and two daughters complete their college educations. They taught their children that the mind is the greatest treasure they own, for it brings enlightenment, which alone controls and balances the needs and desires of the body. They encouraged their children to remain calm and meditate in times of stress or alarm.

Kim experienced cultural tension during her formative years. Her father encouraged her to be independent, self-directed, and assertive, whereas her mother persuaded her to be polite, grateful, and obedient to authority. Although she has not completely resolved this conflict, Kim is able to collaborate with, confront, and negotiate with physicians at the medical center.

Kim's intellectual curiosity has led her into extensive reading, which she feels has helped her to understand people from different cultures and backgrounds; however, she prefers to socialize with Japanese men and women, believing that they have a better sense of direction and purpose in their lives.

In summary, Kim is an adaptation nurse in the young adult stage of development who is an optimistic, yet selective young woman with values rooted in two cultures, Japanese and American. She is practicing adaptation nursing in a setting that is professionally supportive and nurturing, interacting with a variety of adapting persons as she enhances her skills and solidifies her professional role performance. She enjoys working with Dr. Elizabeth Thomas, respecting her clinical judgment and sensitivity to children, parents, and nursing staff alike. Kim calls her "Dr. Elizabeth" and appreciates the fact that she personally notifies the staff when an emergency situation arises.

The adapting person

Jimmy, a 7-year-old boy, was delivered breech at Cresthill Medical Center. He appeared to progress normally until he was 18 months old, at which age his mother noticed his legs buckling when he tried to stand. Concerned, his parents took him to Dr. Thomas, Jimmy's pediatrician, who examined Jimmy and diagnosed his condition as atonic diplegia cerebral palsy, probably resulting from his breech delivery. She told them that his type of cerebral palsy represented diminished muscle tone of the lower extremities, that he would have mild developmental motor delay (especially with running and rapid climbing), but that it would normalize around the time he reaches 10 or 11 years of age. The Pendergasts were overwhelmed: Jimmy is their only child, and they feared he might also be mentally retarded. Although both are attorneys, they did not know how they would cope with such a disability. Dr. Thomas assured them that Jimmy had no impairment other than his muscle weakness and recommended that they treat him as a normal child.

Jimmy developed into a happy, sweet-tempered child. He was affectionate and enjoyed being with people. Just before his fifth birthday, however, he noticed he couldn't run and jump as well as his friends. He became irritable and demanding. The Pendergasts felt guilty about Jimmy's handicap and tended to cater to his demands; at the same time they found themselves becoming more and more impatient and often sent Jimmy to his room. They called Dr. Thomas, and she told them that this happens frequently in families of children with developmental delays. She then set up an appointment with Dr. Delaney, a psychologist who works with families experiencing this type of stress. With the psychologist's help, the Pendergasts were able to recognize the classic cycle of a demanding child, frustrated and rejective parents, and an even more demanding child as a result. They sat down with Jimmy and discussed what was happening and the consequences of inappropriate performance. Jimmy and his parents relaxed and began to enjoy each other again, and Jimmy returned to his bouncy, outgoing self. He did well in preschool and first grade, where he was surrounded by neighbor children who liked and played well with him. Proud of his accomplishment, Jimmy at times boasted that he was the "best." His parents would hug him and agree.

Now eager to learn how mechanical or electrical appliances work, Jimmy has had to be talked out of taking everything apart, including the microwave oven; however, his parents have enjoyed his intellectual curiosity and delight in learning. Jimmy still has some difficulty in maintaining his balance when he runs and plays too hard. He falls and tires easily if he runs or climbs for long periods. Even with these limitations he considers himself a good baseball and football player, telling his parents that he is going to be like Vince Ferragamo when he grows up. They have never tried to discourage him from such a goal, for they believe that handicaps greater than his have been overcome.

The Pendergasts have recently moved into a different section of Alexandria, making it necessary for Jimmy to transfer to a new grade school; he has attended the second grade there for 2 weeks. Mrs. Pendergast confided in Dr. Thomas that she has been worried about Jimmy's reaction to his new environment. In fact, that is why she didn't recognize how sick Jimmy really was. Since his second day at school he had been coming home quiet and subdued; when his parents asked him how school was he would only say, "Okay, I guess." He would change the subject and talk about his former best friends: Scott, Lauren, and Stacy. They encouraged Jimmy to call his friends, but he would say, "No, they wouldn't even remember me." He would come home from school, go to his room, and pretend to read. He complained that his legs hurt and that he thought his cerebral palsy was getting worse. Both parents spent time trying to identify what was wrong, but Jimmy would refuse to talk, saying he couldn't run anymore and "Who cares about playing sports anyway?" Mrs. Pendergast called his teacher at school and was told that Jimmy was a quiet, docile child who did well in his school work but seemed to prefer being by himself. His teacher did notice some older children teasing him about falling in the play yard; however, Jimmy wouldn't talk about it. Jimmy's increased quietness and whiney behavior impelled Mr. and Mrs. Pendergast to seek the advice of Dr. Delaney. They did not make a follow-up appointment, but with Jimmy's impending surgery, they realize it is still needed, because they are both feeling guilty about Jimmy's sudden illness.

At the time of his admittance to the hospital, Jimmy is slightly behind in his developmental milestone. He is 4 feet tall, weighs 46 pounds, and is able to participate in activities normal for a 7-year-old child despite a tendency toward muscular fatigue and imbalance.

Nurse/client interaction

Physiological mode. When Kim greets the Pendergast family, Jimmy is curled up in his father's arms, clinging to his neck and crying with apparent pain. Kim notices that Jimmy is a normally developed child but that his lower limbs are thin and seem to have less muscle tone than his upper arms.

She introduces herself to Jimmy and his parents and asks Jimmy if he and his father would please come with her to the room she has prepared especially for him. Jimmy closes his eyes but nods his head. The family and Kim proceed to a room that is colorfully decorated and tastefully arranged; the bed is turned back, and several books and puzzles have been placed on the bedstand.

Kim talks to Jimmy while they approach the bed and asks him if he can tell her where he hurts and how long he had the pain. He clings to his father and does not answer. Mrs. Pendergast explains that Jimmy started having pain last night. She gave him a child's laxative; however, when he finally had a bowel movement, the pain became worse. He began to perspire, and his temperature shot up to 100° F (rectal temperature). She gave him aspirin, and at 3:00 A.M. Jimmy began to vomit and cry almost constantly. He fell asleep around 4:00 A.M. and awakened again at 7:00 A.M., crying that his side was hurting again. Mr. Pendergast called Dr. Thomas to schedule an early morning appointment. Mrs. Pendergast told Kim that Jimmy had screamed and carried on in Dr. Thomas's office and that she had felt so embarrassed because Jimmy just never acted this way.

Kim approaches Jimmy and explains that she will be removing his clothes and helping him to put on his pajamas. She explains that the clothes he is wearing make it uncomfortable for him and prevent her from finding out what it making his tummy hurt. He starts to cry again but asks if his father can help him. Kim says, "Of course," and Mr. Pendergast proceeds to undress Jimmy. Kim explains that she will be taking Jimmy's temperature with an electrical thermometer and shows him how it works. She asks him if he knows how to keep a thermometer in his mouth; he answers yes tearfully. Kim suggests that he hold the electrical device and watch it register his temperature. He takes the thermometer and lets Kim place it in his mouth. It registers 101° F and Jimmy shows it to Kim. She explains about taking his blood pressure and asks if he would like to try placing the cuff on his arm. He fumbles with it and Kim helps him apply the apparatus. His blood pressure registers 102/60, his pulse is 115, and his respirations are 22. Kim explains about the need to examine his chest and tummy and requests his help with this procedure. He complies until she reaches his right lower quadrant, when he begins to cry and turn away. Kim explains that she knows it must hurt and perhaps Jimmy will place her hand over the part that hurts most and tell her what it feels like. Jimmy complies but still cries when Kim's hand touches McBurney's point. She gently hugs him and tells him how super he has been. He quiets down, and Kim asks him to urinate in the urinal, after which she prepares the specimen for the laboratory. Taking Jimmy's hand, Kim tells him that she will need to take a blood sample so they can really determine what is going on inside his tummy. She asks him if he knows what his appendix looks like; he nods and tells her that Dr. Elizabeth had drawn a picture of it for him. Kim asks him what he thinks it looks like. He reaches for his father's hand and says he thinks it looks a little like a football, only smaller. Kim then tells him how she will get his blood to check on his "football."

Jimmy watches every move Kim makes as she prepares the phlebotomy syringe. She asks Jimmy if he would help her with the tourniquet and if he would like to practice on her so he can see how it works. He shakes his head no but holds out his arm for the tourniquet. Before she applies the tourniquet to his arm, Kim asks him if he would like his mother and father to hold his hands while she pricks him, because it will hurt for just a moment. She tells him he can yell out "ouches" anytime he wishes. With tears in his eyes, Jimmy reaches for his parents' hands and closes his eyes. She applies the tourniquet, uses a povidone-iodine swab, and explains what she is doing. After the blood is drawn, Jimmy opens his eyes and tells her he only shouted two "ouches." Kim hugs him and praises him for doing so well, asking him if he knows what she is going to do with his blood. He says, "No," so she explains how it is viewed under a microscope where the white cells are counted to determine if there is any infection in his small "football." Kim asks, "Jimmy, did Dr. Elizabeth tell you about going to surgery?" Jimmy nods to say yes, that he guesses he has to go right away. Kim agrees and asks him to tell her what he thinks will go on in surgery. He turns toward her and says, "Well, don't you know nothing? I'll have to go to sleep, and Dr. Elizabeth will get someone to help her cut my football out, and I'll bleed a lot inside my tummy." Kim asks him if he knows what is going on inside his tummy. Jimmy nods and says, "Yes, it's my other sickness taking over my tummy like it did my legs." Kim asks him to tell her about his cerebral palsy. He explains that he was a "bad" baby and therefore his legs didn't develop right. Mrs. Pendergast looks aghast and begins to correct him. Kim gently asks Jimmy to explain what he means about being a "bad" baby. He says he must have done something really awful because his mom hurt him when he was born "breeched." Kim asks him how this made him feel. Tears well up in his eyes, and he turns away from his mother saying, "I can't do anything with my legs lately; they don't work right like they did before I went to that new school. At school, this kid Mike says I'm weird, and why don't I run and play ball like everyone else? Now, I'll never walk right, my stomach is making my legs worse. I haven't been bad for a long time. How come I'm getting cerebral palsy again?" He starts to cry. Kim explains what is really going on inside his tummy and what is happening with his legs. Jimmy nods, but the tears keep falling.

Kim explains that an appendix is a small attachment at the right side of his large intestine; that this small "football" can collect hair, gum, nails, and all sorts of things and become inflammed and swollen; and that it has nothing to do with his legs or doing "bad" things. She tells him that many children get a "hot" appendix just like they get the flu. She then asks Jimmy if he would like her to explain about his legs. He nods and she explains that sometimes babies try to come into the world feet first and their little heads receive pressure, which weakens a tiny part of the brain. Therefore, the messages that travel to his legs get slowed down, just like a poor television connection. This makes his legs weak when he gets tired, but they will develop, and this poor connection will eventually go away if he continues to work on his walking, running, and climbing.

"Does that make sense, Jimmy?" Kim asks. He stops crying and says yes. He pauses and adds, "You mean my mother didn't hurt me?" Kim smiles and says, "No, it was just the way some little guys try to rush out into the world; unfortunately, they can get hurt in their eagerness." Jimmy looks at his mother and says, "Gosh, Mom, I'm sorry." She hugs her son and gets tears in her eyes but tells him that she and his father love him very much and are so sorry he is sick right now. He holds her hand, looks at Kim, and asks, "Well, how come those kids at that second grade don't let me practice with my legs? My friends Scott and Lauren let me play ball. I used to be good."

Kim explains that this discussion will take time, and she promises to discuss it with him after his surgery if he would like. He nods and says, "Yes, I want to. You won't forget?" Kim assures him that she will not forget but that right now she needs to get him ready for surgery. Kim asks Jimmy if he is frightened or nervous. He holds his parents' hands and says no, that he can do lots of things he doesn't like to do. He asks, "Will you be with me?" Kim tells him that she will be giving him his medication and taking him to surgery, that she will be here when he gets back, but that she won't actually be in surgery with him. She adds that Dr. Thomas will tell her all about it. He nods and says, "Well, that's okay, then." Kim explains that she will be bringing his medications for surgery fairly soon and asks him about the pain. He tells her his tummy still hurts but that the pain is not as bad when he lies curled up and his mother and father are there. "My legs get tired, though." Kim shows him how to move slowly and change positions without starting a spasm. She asks Jimmy if he knows what a spasm is. He says yes, that he gets them in his legs sometimes.

Kim invites Mr. and Mrs. Pendergast to pull their chairs up close to the bed and explains that she will be back in 15 to 20 minutes. She tells them if they need her, she will be right outside in their unit's control area and that they should not hesitate to put on the call light or step out to get her. She calls for a floor relay person, sends Jimmy's blood and urine samples to the satellite laboratory, uses the computer to order Jimmy's laboratory tests, and is informed that Dr. Thomas has not yet arrived at the hospital. She calls the pediatric surgery suite and verifies that Jimmy's surgery is scheduled for 10:00 A.M., only $1\frac{1}{2}$ hours away. The anesthesiologist, Dr. Jeffrey, tells Kim that he will be there in 15 minutes to meet Jimmy and the Pendergasts and will order Jimmy's preoperative medication at this time.

Kim is notified that Jimmy's laboratory work-up is completed, and she reviews the computer readout, which indicates that his blood analysis is as follows: hemoglobin, 11 gm/100 ml; hematocrit, 34.2%; white blood cells, 15,000/cu mm. His urine shows an elevated specific gravity of 1.040, and there are traces of acetone. Dr. Thomas arrives on the unit and after consulting with Kim orders an immediate intravenous infusion of 500 ml of 5% dextrose in water. His preoperative medications are meperidine (15 mg), promethazine (8 mg), and atropine sulfate (0.15 mg), which are given immediately.

Jimmy's crying has decreased, but he says his tummy still hurts and "Please, don't touch it." Kim assures him that she will not do so and that in a few minutes he will become drowsy. She explains that she will be taking him to surgery right in his own hospital bed and that his parents and she will be in the room when he returns. Then she asks if there is anything he wishes to take to surgery with him. He says, yes, his teddy bear, which his mother has in her purse. Mrs. Pendergast seems embarrassed as she takes the scruffy toy out of her bag. Kim smiles and says she is so glad that Jimmy has a special friend going with him to surgery. Jimmy smiles and cuddles the little one-eyed bear as Kim and his parents accompany him to the surgical suite.

Because the surgery will take 1 to 2 hours, Kim encourages the Pendergasts to go for coffee and a brief walk. She promises to spend time with them when they return to the parent's waiting room or to Jimmy's room.

Kim sits down to organize her thinking and plans for Jimmy's biopsychosocial needs. Because of the immediacy of Jimmy's surgery and vulnerable physical condition, Kim has concentrated on his physiological adequacy. However, based on her total assessment, Kim is concerned about the threat to Jimmy's psychosocial adequacy as well. She judges that he exhibits category III diagnoses in his physiological and role performance modes and category II diagnoses in his other two modes. She begins her planning by organizing the data she has collected concerning Jimmy's physiological mode.

The following nursing care guide represents Kim's assessment, judgment, diagnosis, interventions, and evaluations of Jimmy's physiological mode.

NURSING CARE GUIDE

PHYSIOLOGICAL MODE

NEUROLOGICAL BEHAVIORS

1. Cries
2. "It hurts all over"
3. "Don't touch my tummy"
4. Turns away and cries when area is touched.
5. Temperature is 101° F.
6. Skin is warm to touch.
7. Right lower quadrant area very warm to touch.

MUSCULOSKELETAL BEHAVIORS

1. Curls up with knees drawn up close to chest.
2. Moves slowly.
3. Protects abdomen.
4. Abdomen rigid near McBurney's point.

CIRCULATORY BEHAVIORS

1. Pulse is 115.
2. Blood pressure is 102/60.
3. Hemoglobin level is 11 gm/100 ml (within normal limits).
4. Hematocrit is 34.2% (within normal limits).
5. White blood cell count is 15,000/cu mm.

PROTECTIVE BEHAVIORS

1. Skin is damp.
2. Mild diaphoresis.
3. Cheeks and forehead flushed.

INFLUENCING STIMULI

Focal: Inflamed and engorged appendix. Presence of infectious exudate and vulnerability to rupture.

Contextual: Presence of somatic nerves. Increased peristalsis from laxative taken previous evening. Potential perforation of appendix with spread of infection and peritonitis. Peritoneal tissue stretched and tense. Abdominal assessment by Kim, Dr. Thomas, and Dr. Jeffrey. Having to be carried to physician's office and hospital. Not able to receive pain medication until his surgical preoperative preparation. Dehydrated. Has elevated temperature. No previous emergency hospital experience.

Residual: Stress he has been experiencing at new school. School-age child is vulnerable to viral infections. Eating patterns may have changed in past year. Presence of cerebral palsy may have limited his activities and therefore his gastrointestinal motility. Change of activities because of school conditions.

INGESTIVE BEHAVIORS

1. Nauseated for 6-hour period.
2. Vomited (approximately 80 to 100 ml).
3. Food unappetizing.

ELIMINATIVE BEHAVIORS

1. Urine, 50-ml specimen collection.
2. Specific gravity, 1.040.
3. Traces of acetone.

ENDOCRINE BEHAVIORS

1. Is 4 feet and weighs 46 pounds.
2. Is well formed but has thin legs.

JUDGMENT: Jimmy's general alarm reaction is congruent with his inflamed and engorged appendix. However, if this response continues, it will rapidly deplete his physiological reserves and thereby drastically reduce his level of physiological adequacy.

NURSING DIAGNOSIS: Bowel integrity, decreased physiological adequacy: inflamed, engorged appendix* (category III diagnosis). (Jimmy is experiencing a life-threatening emergency. Therefore, he has a category III physiological mode diagnosis. His appendix, damaged by inflammation, infection, and edema, is vulnerable to rupture, peritonitis, and systemic infection. His automatic regulator response is appropriate for the abrupt inflammatory process but must be terminated, or it may overwhelm his physiological adequacy. The termination of this response is dependent on Jimmy's assuming the sick role.)

GOAL: Jimmy will experience an increase in physiological adequacy (category II diagnosis). Jimmy will promote scar formation and wound repair by (1) cooperating with Dr. Thomas and Dr. Jeffrey as they surgically intervene with Jimmy's appendectomy and (2) engaging in the post-operative activities that are essential for his healing process, especially eating, drinking fluids, exercising, deep breathing, resting, and meaningful playing.

INTERVENTION

1. *Collaboration:* Kim will monitor inflammatory and defense response by assessing his vital signs immediately upon admission, assessing his vital signs just before administration of medications and transfer to surgery, and obtaining blood and urine specimens to send to the laboratory. Kim will validate Jimmy's ongoing response by asking about the presence of pain and tenderness and the exact location of painful area. She will prepare him for surgery by starting an intravenous infusion of 500 ml of 5%

EVALUATION

1. Jimmy will stop crying.
2. He will relax his arms and legs.
3. He will say good-bye to his parents as he goes to surgery.
4. He will sleep within 20 minutes after receiving preoperative medications.
5. Jimmy will experience an uneventful surgery.
6. Jimmy will have a dry wound and reduced temperature and white blood cell count by first postoperative day.

*National Conference on Nursing Diagnosis.

INTERVENTION   EVALUATION

dextrose in water, administering preoperative medications (meperidine [Demerol], 15 mg; promethazine [Phenergan], 8 mg; and atropine sulfate, 0.15 mg), providing an emesis basin and intravenous infusion standard and transporting Jimmy to surgery suite. She will provide an atmosphere of calm and quiet by reducing the noise level, speaking in a calm, unhurried voice, staying with Jimmy and his parents during admission and surgery preparation, and explaining plans, schedules, and activities he will be experiencing.

Role performance mode. Kim identifies that Jimmy's autonomic response and influencing stimuli place him in a diagnostic category III in his physiological mode. Therefore, he needs to move in a more positive direction on the health/illness continuum. To do this effectively Jimmy must engage in emergency and postoperative client behaviors that will enable him to terminate his regulator alarm response and reestablish his physiological adequacy. As a growing, developing child, Jimmy is vulnerable to abrupt change. In addition, in the space of 2 weeks he has been confronted with the need to assume the role of a second grade student in a new shool, and before he can comply with this demand, he is confronted with the urgency of assuming the emergency client role. In order for Jimmy to master either of these roles, he needs extra nurturance and support. Unfortunately, his most meaningful support (his parents and former playmates) have been affected by his reaction to his new environment. As a consequence, Jimmy's view of his capabilities and self-worth is shaken. Kim concludes, then, that Jimmy is experiencing a diagnostic category III in his role performance mode and a diagnostic category II in his interdependence and self-concept modes. The goal Kim establishes for Jimmy is to (1) master his surgical client role, (2) strengthen his nurturing relationship with his parents and nurses, (3) plan how to reestablish his companionship with Lauren, Scott, and Stacy, and (4) plan how to establish his second grade athletic role. Kim plans to use teaching and support to help Jimmy perform his client role more effectively and strengthen his nurturing relationships with his parents and nurses. She also plans to consult with Marsha, her adaptation clinical specialist. She will ask Marsha to use enabling nursing action with Jimmy and his parents to help Jimmy reestablish his ability to receive and give love and support as well as help him increase his self-esteem. The following nursing care guide indicates Kim's assessment, judgments, diagnoses, goals, interventions, and evaluation of Jimmy's role performance.

NURSING CARE GUIDE

ROLE PERFORMANCE MODE

EMERGENCY AND SURGICAL CLIENT ROLE BEHAVIORS

Noncompliance
1. Clings to his father.
2. Closes his eyes when asked to perform client role behaviors.
3. Cries almost constantly.
4. Screamed and carried on in Dr. Thomas's office.

Compliance
1. Asked if his father could put on his hospital pajamas.
2. Held the thermometer in his mouth and showed it to Kim.
3. Fumbled with the blood pressure cuff.
4. Complies with chest and abdominal examination.
5. Urinates for specimen.
6. Cooperates with phlebotomy procedure with only two "ouches."
7. "I guess I have to go to surgery right away."
8. Nods when Kim explains about his appendictis and cerebral palsy.
9. Says he is not nervous or scared about surgery.
10. Accepts intravenous and preoperative medications.
11. Gets sleepy on the way to surgery.

STUDENT AND ATHLETE ROLE BEHAVIORS

1. Comes home in a quiet, subdued, and whiney mood, and when asked about school says, "Okay, I guess." Changes subject, talks about former best friends but won't call them.
2. Goes to his room, sits, pretends to read, complains that his legs hurt (thinks cerebral palsy is getting worse).
3. "Can't run anymore."
4. "Who cares about playing sports anyway?"
5. Refuses to talk about new school experiences.

INFLUENCING STIMULI

Focal: Presence of and demands of caregivers (especially Kim and Dr. Thomas). Jimmy's lack of experience with this kind of pain and emergency surgery.

Contextual: Abruptness of onset of appendicitis. Fears that his stomach is making his cerebral palsy worse and that his being "bad" has caused his appendicitis. Presence of pain from pressure on somatic nerve endings. Presence and security of his mother and father. Presence of his teddy bear. Concern about his athletic activities as a second grader.

Residual: Fear and anxiety about new and unhappy school experience. Sense of losing his previous playmates. Belief that his mother was punishing him. Belief that adults know best.

Focal: Presence and demands of teacher and classmates.

Contextual: Bigger children tease him about falling in the playground. Mike says he's weird and asks why Jimmy doesn't run and play ball like everyone else. Beliefs that his stomach is making his legs worse and that being "bad" has caused his cerebral palsy in the form of an appendicitis.

Residual: Beliefs that former playmates won't know him, that he can't play ball anymore, that his mother made him have cerebral palsy, and that he will never be accepted by new school mates. Fear that he is "different."

STUDENT AND ATHLETE ROLE BEHAVIORS   INFLUENCING STIMULI

6. Teacher states that he seems to prefer being by himself; that he is a quiet, docile child; that he does well in school work; and that he wouldn't talk about classmates teasing him.

JUDGMENT 1: Jimmy's behaviors are inadequate for mastering the critical client role, and they pose a threat to his social and physical adequacy.

JUDGMENT 2: Jimmy is using a coping stance of approach/avoidance and the strategy of flight/fight. He manifests approach and fight by soliciting help from his parents and letting Kim and Dr. Thomas prepare him for surgery and manifests avoidance/flight by crying, moving away, and refusing to do things for himself. These behaviors, although appropriate for the immediate emergency, are inadequate for reestablishing his ability to give and receive love and support; therefore, they will eventually threaten Jimmy's already vulnerable physiological and role mode adequacy.

NURSING DIAGNOSIS: Instrumental emergency client role insufficiency, decreased social adequacy; fear of unknown and experience of pain* (category III diagnosis). (Jimmy is experiencing a category III diagnosis in his critical client and student and athlete roles. He has not had the energy to assume either role. His coping stance of approach/avoidance is appropriate; however, his excessive use of flight radically threatens his social and hence his physiological adequacy.)

GOAL: Jimmy will experience an increase in social adequacy (category II diagnosis). Jimmy will engage in emergency client role behavior, especially the postsurgical activities that will help him resolve the infectious process, promote healing, and resume former activities of daily living. This will help him regain social adequacy, which in turn will help him to reestablish his physiological adequacy.

INTERVENTION

1. *Teaching:* Kim will spend time with Jimmy and explain each action she performs and why it is needed. She will tell him how to help in his surgical preparation and outline each step of his postoperative activities for relief of pain, sitting up, going to the bathroom, eating, walking, playing, and sleeping.

2. *Support:* Kim will have Jimmy state what he thinks is expected of him and how he would like to carry out these activities. Kim will encourage Jimmy to talk about his surgery, appendicitis, and cerebral palsy to clarify any misconceptions. She will ask him to role play about his operation and how he thinks he could best help himself get well.

EVALUATION

1. Jimmy's pain will lessen within 12 hours after surgery.
2. Jimmy's wound will be clean and dry.
3. Jimmy will be up running in carpeted halls the first day postoperatively.
4. Jimmy will play in play room for 2 to 4 hours during the day.
5. Jimmy will sleep and rest 8 hours at night and 2 to 4 hours during the day.
6. Jimmy will draw his perception of his needs and plans for getting well.

---

*National Conference on Nursing Diagnosis.

Interdependence mode. Kim continues her plan for care for Jimmy's psychosocial needs, and her planning is reflected in the next nursing care guide.

NURSING CARE GUIDE

INTERDEPENDENCE MODE

PRIMARY ROLE
(YOUNG SCHOOL-AGE CHILD) BEHAVIORS

INFLUENCING STIMULI

SECONDARY ROLE (SON) BEHAVIORS

Contributive
1. Clings to mother and father.
2. Reaches for his parents' hand.
3. Turns slightly away from his mother.
4. Thinks that he did something awful and that his mother hurt him when he was born breeched.
5. "You mean my mother didn't hurt me?" Looks at his mother and says, "Gosh Mom, I'm sorry." Holds his mother's hand.
6. Tells his parents good-bye when he goes to surgery.

Focal: Mr. and Mrs. Pendergast, his parents.

Contextual: Fear, pain, and distress of his appendicitis. Fear and anxiety about going to surgery. Fear of being abandoned and of unknowns (pain, hospital, and surgery).

Residual: Believes that his parents love him, that his mother had "hurt" him, and that he had been bad and therefore had been punished. Outgoing, loving disposition with parents before disruption in school and appendicitis.

Recipient
1. Accepts hugs, kisses, and hand holding.
2. Father and mother hold him curled up in their arms.
3. Mother stays up with him all night and holds him until he goes to sleep. She tells him "We love you."

TERTIARY ROLE (CLIENT) BEHAVIORS

Recipient
1. Accepts Kim's monitoring of his vital signs and administering phlebotomy, intravenous drip, and preoperative medications.
2. Accepts Kim's assessment of his chest and abdomen but cries when McBurney's point is touched.
3. Accepts Kim's hugs and presence when she explains about his appendix, surgery, and need for laboratory samples.
4. Allows Kim to transport him to surgery.

Focal: Presence of health care providers, especially Kim.

Contextual: Surgical pediatric environment. Private room, quiet, and time. Lack of experience as a client. Lack of experiencing being independent and supporting others. Positive caring expressed by Kim. Lack of time to prolong interaction and establish the growing bond between Kim and Jimmy.

Residual: Fear of being left alone. Ignorance of what is expected. Belief that he is worth love and support. Lack of experience in sharing feelings with strangers.

TERTIARY ROLE (CLIENT) BEHAVIORS

INFLUENCING STIMULI

Contributive
1. Responds to Kim's asking for clarification about his "tummy."
2. Cerebral palsy and "being a bad baby."
3. Tells Kim what Dr. Thomas said about his appendix and surgery.
4. Tells Kim he wants to talk about why kids at school tease him.
5. Holds Kim's hand.

TERTIARY ROLE (PLAYMATE) BEHAVIORS

Recipient
1. Friends sought out and played with Jimmy, enjoyed playing with him, and thought he was a good ball player.

Contributive
1. Sought out and played with Scott, Lauren, and Stacy. Missed them and wanted to talk about them. Refused to call them. "They will forget who I am."

Focal: Stacy, Scott, and Lauren.

Contextual: Neighborhood environment. Friends went to same preschool and first grade and did not perceive Jimmy as different.

Residual: Beliefs that they are his best friends, that they used to love him, and that they have forgotten him ("out of sight, out of mind"). Fear that he is different and that therefore they won't accept him as before.

JUDGMENT 1: Although Jimmy is engaging in some effective son and client role behaviors, he is demonstrating too many ineffective behaviors in the roles of son, client, and playmate to maintain his level of social adequacy effectively.

JUDGMENT 2: Jimmy has chosen the coping stance of fight/flight and is using approach/avoidance sporadically, which only temporarily reduces the stress of change and role demands. Therefore, he will need to select a more effective strategy to cope with the demands for giving and receiving nurturance.

NURSING DIAGNOSIS: Expressive client, son, and playmate role insufficiency, disrupted social adequacy: sudden changes, fear, and pain* (category II diagnosis). (Jimmy is experiencing a category II diagnosis in the interdependent mode in his roles as son, client, and playmate. Consequently, his ability to receive and give love and support is threatened, and if his behavior continues it will further decrease his level of social adequacy.)

GOAL: Jimmy will experience an increase in social adequacy (category I diagnosis). Jimmy will accept and give nurturance and support in his relationships with his parents, nurses, and playmates. In order to achieve this balance, he will exhibit contributive and receptive behaviors that will enhance the response of others who are significant in his achieving social adequacy.

*National Conference on Nursing Diagnosis.

INTERVENTION

1. *Support:* Kim will spend time talking with Jimmy and his parents concerning their feelings about the emergency surgery and hospitalization. She will use touch, hugs, and hand holding when she interacts with Jimmy. Kim will support Jimmy's parents so that they can spend time supporting and nurturing Jimmy.

2. *Teaching:* Kim will clarify for Jimmy the meaning of his illness, surgery, and cerebral palsy.

3. *Enabling:* Kim will plan for a clinical specialist to provide enabling nursing actions that will help Jimmy to (a) reestablish contact with his playmates, (b) role play how to interact with his new classmates to clarify his wishes to be friends and part of their athletic activities, and (c) role play and plan strategies for interacting with someone who teases about other limitations.

EVALUATION

1. Jimmy will utilize the nursing staff, especially Kim, as a source of support and nurturance during his hospital stay.

2. Jimmy will state, write, and paint a plan for giving and receiving love and support from his parents and his nurses.

3. Jimmy will demonstrate (through role playing) how he will cope with his new classmates.

Self-concept mode. Kim knows that Jimmy will have a very difficult time reestablishing his physiological and social adequacy if he does not have meaningful support, love, and nurturance. She also knows that the disruption in Jimmy's physiological and social modes threaten his psychological adequacy. In Jimmy's self-concept mode Kim judges that his behavior reflects a category II diagnosis. His moral-ethical self is saying that he has been bad and that therefore he is sick. His body image and self-consistency are altered in the sense that he is not sure if he is different and is upset that he is not performing in athletics as he had only a few weeks before his hospital stay. His ideal of being another Vince Ferragamo is being shaken, as is his perception that he is the "best" and therefore worthy of love, affection, and support.

Kim's own convictions help her to see it is imperative to reestablish Jimmy's faith in himself. She realizes she does not have sufficient knowledge and skills to effect this goal with Jimmy by herself, so she has planned for the nurse clinical specialist to provide enabling nursing actions for Jimmy and his family to help him reestablish his psychological adequacy. The following nursing care guide represents Kim's assessment, judgment, diagnosis, goals, interventions, and evaluations of Jimmy's self-concept mode.

NURSING CARE GUIDE

SELF-CONCEPT MODE

PHYSICAL SELF BEHAVIORS

1. Perceives himself as good baseball and football player.
2. Complains his legs hurt.
3. Thinks his cerebral palsy getting worse.
4. "I can't run anymore."
5. Falls when he runs or plays too hard.
6. Thinks the appendix looks a little like a football.
7. "I'll bleed a lot inside my tummy."
8. "The cerebral palsy is taking over my tummy."
9. "My legs didn't develop right."
10. "I can't do anything with my legs."
11. "I'll never walk right."
12. "My stomach is making my legs worse."

SELF/CONSISTENCY BEHAVIORS

1. "I can't run anymore."
2. "How come I'm getting cerebral palsy again?"
3. Even with limitations, considered himself the "best."
4. Thinks his best friends won't remember him.

MORAL/ETHICAL SELF BEHAVIORS

1. "I am the best"
2. "I haven't been bad for a long time"
3. "I was a bad baby" and therefore "my legs didn't develop right."
4. "Must have done something really awful because my mom hurt me."

SELF/IDEAL BEHAVIORS

1. "I am going to grow up like Vince Ferragamo."
2. "I am the best."

INFLUENCING STIMULI

Focal: Perception that his body has suddenly changed. Perception of being able to fit to engage in athletic activities before went to new school.

Contextual: Change to new school. Older children tease him about falling. Mike says he is weird and asks him why he doesn't play like everyone else. Abrupt onset of appendicitis. Pain and need to relieve pressure on somatic nerves by curling knees up. Legs feel tired and weak. Previous friends like him and enjoyed playing with him.

Residual: Beliefs that he is getting worse and therefore he is "different," that he is no longer a "good" person, that others no longer like him or want to be friends, and that his mother hurt him at birth. Former belief that he was good, loved, and the "best."

JUDGMENT 1: Jimmy's behaviors are inadequate for sustaining his self-esteem, and they pose a decided threat to his already vulnerable physiological and social adequacy.

JUDGMENT 2: By using a coping strategy of flight, Jimmy is manifesting inappropriate behaviors for coping with his emergency needs and will further threaten his already vulnerable physiological and social adequacy.

NURSING DIAGNOSIS: Altered body image, disrupted psychological adequacy; believes he has been bad: pain and fear* (category II diagnosis). (Jimmy is experiencing a category II diagnosis in his self-concept mode. He is using avoidance to cope with his emergency and with his recent role changes, and therefore his behavior will result in delayed healing and will further threaten his client and school athletic roles. His total biopsychosocial adequacy will be reduced.)

GOAL: Jimmy will experience an increase in psychological adequacy (a category I diagnosis) Jimmy will alter his perception of his physical, moral-ethical, ideal, and consistent self to match his changed roles and demands for getting well. He will see himself as physically sound, with some limitations but with no permanent damage. He will realize that he can again perform second grade athletics. Furthermore, he will believe that he can interact with his new classmates to master the second grade student role. He will therefore renew his self-perception and high self-esteem.

INTERVENTION	EVALUATION
1. *Support:* Kim will contract with Marsha to spend time with Jimmy to help him explore his perceptions and beliefs.	1. Jimmy will rest, state he feels good, play in the playroom, and state how he is going to act with his parents and his classmates. Jimmy will recognize and state how he will use new coping stances and strategies with his parents, nursing staff, his former friends, and with his new classmates.
2. *Teaching:* Kim will contract with Marsha to help Jimmy focus on realistic goals in his client and second grade roles and explore alternate ways of performing that will be compatible with his fatigue and imbalance, especially at school.	
3. *Enabling:* Kim will contract with Marsha and Dr. Delaney to explore family and peer group interaction and to offer new coping stances and strategies that will better effect psychological adequacy.	

*National Conference on Nursing Diagnosis.

Summary

Jimmy's manner of coping, by using approach and fight as well as avoidance and flight is threatening each of his adaptive modes. Kim uses the adaptation nursing process to help Jimmy meet his need for total biopsychosocial adequacy.

In this adaptation nursing process special empahsis has been placed on Jimmy's and Kim's regulator/cognator transactions. Jimmy's transactions reflect the holistic nature of the adaptive person and the interrelationship of his four modes, whereas Kim's transactions reflect her developmental strengths and limitations, demonstrating how she uses the adaptation nursing process systematically to assess, judge, and effectively intervene with the total person. Her regulator/cognator process is influenced by her knowledge, understanding, and ability to perceive her client's needs. Thus, an adaptation nurse forms a partnership with her client to achieve the primary goal of adaptation nursing, which is to help the person cope more effectively, thereby maintaining or increasing his level of adequacy to meet his biopsychosocial needs.

REFERENCES

Aguilera, D.: Crisis intervention: Theory and methodology, ed. 3, St. Louis, 1978, The C.V. Mosby Co.

Brown, I.W., and Hackett, T.P.: Emotional reaction to the threat of impending death: a study of patients on the monitor cardiac pacemaker, Jr. J. Medical Sci. 496:177-187, 1967.

Erickson, M.L.: Assessment and management of developmental changes in children, St. Louis, 1976, The C.V. Mosby Co.

Garfield, C.A., editor: Stress and Survival: the emotional realities of life-threatening illness, St. Louis, 1979, The C.V. Mosby Co.

Heckitt, T.P., Cassem, N.H. and Wishnie, H.A.: The Coronary Care Unit: An Appraisal of Its Psychological Hazards, New England Journal of Medicine 279:1365-1370, 1968.

Luckman, J. and Sorenson, K.C.: Medical-surgical nursing: a psychophysiologic approach. Philadelphia, 1974, W.B. Saunders. Co.

Parsons, T.: Definitions of health and illness in the light of American values and social structure. In Jaco, E., editor: Patients, physicians, and illness, New York, 1958, The Free Press.

Roberts, S.L.: Behavioral concepts and the critically ill patient, Englewood Cliffs, N.J., 1976, Prentice-Hall, Inc.

Stephenson, C.A.: Stress in critically ill patients, American Journal of Nursing 77:1806-1809, 1977.

Storlie, F.: Patient teaching in critical care, New York, Appleton-Century-Crofts, 1975.

Stuart, G.W., and Sundeen, S.J.: Principles and Practice of Psychiatric Nursing, St. Louis, 1979, The C.V. Mosby Co.

Werner, E.E.: Cross-Cultural Child Development: A View from the Planet Earth, Monterey, Calif., 1979, Brooks/Cole Publishing Co.

Werner, E., and Beland, J.: Grief response for the critically ill, Reston, Va., 1980.

Wellness situations

In this chapter three nurse/client interactions are used to demonstrate how an adaptation nurse in the generative stage of professional development uses the adaptation nursing process with clients who are experiencing wellness and who are therefore in diagnostic category I. This chapter is designed to expose the reader to the complex thinking processes involved in adaptation nursing, the generative adaptation nurse's level of skill and knowledge, and the shortcuts the generative nurse's skill and knowledge allow her to make in the outpatient setting. Before examining the three case studies, we will review the category of wellness and the practice of the adaptation nurse in the generative stage of development.

DIAGNOSTIC CATEGORY—WELLNESS: A REVIEW

The well person has been described as a person who is in control of his internal state and feels competent in the face of triggering events present in the environment. This person is able to take risks, make decisions, and continue to strive for adequacy and self-enhancement. He uses the environment to produce additional triggering events that are satisfying and stimulating. The adapting person in the first diagnostic category looks and feels well and satisfied; he is perceived to be an effective, competent person. According to this description, the well person's behavioral responses in all four modes should be congruent with the triggering events, and the person should be experiencing adequacy or growth. However, the adaptation nurse seldom sees an adapting person who demonstrates this level of functioning in all four modes. A realistic description is as follows: wellness refers to adapting persons who demonstrate category I diagnoses in three of four modes or in all but two components of a single mode. In addition, the mode or two components demonstrating incongruence must be at the category II level.

You will also recall that the well person who is coping adequately usually seeks health care for three reasons. He interacts with the health care system to validate the level of wellness, to acquire information for growth and stimulation, and to gain support and information to cope with the category II diagnosis. Medical conditions commonly associated with wellness are those that result in the disruption of not more than two components of the physiological mode. The conditions associated with wellness commonly occur in the general population, require little or no medical intervention, and are easily managed within the person's natural environment. The adaptation nurse ordinarily sees the client experiencing wellness in an ambulatory care facility such as a physician's office, clinic, school, industrial setting, or alternative care facility such as holistic health or birthing center.

THE ADAPTATION NURSE IN THE GENERATIVE STAGE: A REVIEW

As you will recall, the adaptation nurse in the generative stage of development has accomplished the tasks of adolescence and young adulthood and is acquiring or has acquired advanced formal education. She represents the autonomous, independent practitioner of adaptation nursing. Her efforts are directed toward the most complex and subtle problems of adaptation. She utilizes the adaptation process at the highest level and therefore has a comprehensive understanding of the adapting person, which allows her to interact with him regarding his current and future adaptation needs.

The generative adaptation nurse responds to complex triggering events and utilizes coping stances and strategies more effectively and with greater proficiency than do nurses in the other stages of development. She usually assumes a coping stance of compromise or self-enhancement. Of the two strategies, the generative nurse uses self-enhancement more frequently and from a more extensive knowledge base than a nurse in a less mature stage of development. Her perspective is future and growth oriented.

When the adaptation nurse assumes the coping stance of compromise, she generally utilizes the coping strategy of suppression. She uses suppression only temporarily as a defensive maneuver to protect herself or the adapting person from being overwhelmed. Because of the comprehensive nature of the generative adaptation nurse's practice, she cannot ignore blocks of information or experience, because to do so would diminish the effectiveness of her interaction with the adapting person. Suppressed material is dealt with as soon as possible.

When the generative adaptation nurse assumes a self-enhancing coping stance, she utilizes negotiation and manipulation most frequently and uses confrontation only in an emergent, highly complex situation that requires immediate action. Manipulation and negotiation are most effectively used when the adaptation nurse has

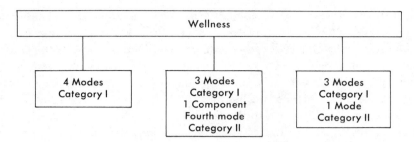

FIGURE 8-1
The wellness portion of the health/illness continuum and the three possible diagnostic combinations that are found in this range of the continuum.

a close involvement with and comprehensive knowledge of the adapting person, including the operation of the regulator/cognator process. These strategies provide the adaptation nurse with opportunities for optimal effectiveness and the client with the potential for enhancing his level of adequacy.

The adaptation nurse in the generative stage of development is skilled in the use of all four nursing actions. However, because her goals are oriented toward self-enhancement and growth for the client as well as independent, autonomous functioning for herself, most of her behavioral responses are from the enabling and teaching categories of nursing actions. Given her knowledge and skills, the generative adaptation nurse is qualified to work with the adapting person at any position on the health/illness continuum. However, her personal goals of production and care and her commitment to growth and enhancement make this nurse best suited to interact with the adapting person on the first half of the health/illness continuum, the person experiencing wellness and disrupted wellness.

In summary, the well person is in control of his internal state and able to cope with the ever-changing but somewhat predictable environment. He is capable of and striving for growth and self-enhancement. The adaptation nurse in the generative stage interacting with him is skilled in all levels of nursing action and is capable of completing the adaptation nursing process in complex and subtle circumstances. Because of these skills and knowledge and her motivation toward growth and enhancement, she is ideally suited to interact with the well person.

This chapter will focus on three clients interacting with three adaptation nurses in the generative stage of development. Although focusing totally on the well client who is interacting with a generative adaptation nurse tends to offer a limited view of the scope of the adaptation nurse's practice, the reader is reminded that the more complex aspects of the generative nurse's clinical and educational performance have been illustrated in previous chapters where reference is made to the clinical specialist. This presentation is designed primarily to demonstrate the adaptation nursing process as applied to the well client. In addition, the reader is exposed to (1) examples of the complex thinking process involved in adaptation nursing, (2) the generative adaptation nurse's level of skill and knowledge, and (3) the shortcuts the generative nurse's skill and knowledge allow her to make in the outpatient setting. Before examining the case studies, it is recommended that the reader review the theoretical objectives and read the following performance objectives, keeping in mind that written material can only teach to the theoretical objectives of adaptation nursing. Only in the actual clinical setting can this theory be applied. Therefore, performance objectives have been included to help the reader, with or without supervision, to examine her or his ability to utilize the complex thinking process essential to the practice of adaptation nursing.

PERFORMANCE OBJECTIVES

Given a specific nurse-client situation, use the adaptation nursing process with clients experiencing a category I diagnosis:

  Identify the client's regulator/cognator transaction.
  Identify the unique stimuli that influence the client's transaction.
  Describe your regulator/cognator transaction.
  Identify the unique stimuli which influence your internal transaction.
  Formulate judgments, diagnoses, goals and interventions based on the knowledge of your own and your client's internal transactions.

Based on your use of the adaptation nursing process, identify your level of professional development.

CASE STUDY—A POSTNATAL EXPERIENCE
The setting

Wellness is experienced when the adapting person demonstrates a category I diagnosis in three of four modes or in all but two components of a single mode. The mode or two components demonstrating incongruence must be at the category II level. In this situation you will meet Lisa Abbott, who is experiencing a category I diagnosis in four modes but a category II diagnosis in one component of one mode. Lisa is returning to the alternate birth center with a problem involving infant care. She will see Gretchen, an adaptation nurse and family nurse practitioner in the generative stage of development who specializes in working with families and infants. Lisa has been a client at the birth center since the eighth week of her pregnancy. She came for routine prenatal checks, attended natural childbirth classes, and participated in a parenting seminar. Her 8-pound 6-ounce son, Phillip, was born at the birth center only 7 days ago. After the birth of her child, Lisa was discharged with Phillip and told to schedule a postpartum check with Gretchen in about 2 weeks. She was also reminded of all the services available at the birth center and encouraged to call or come in sooner than her scheduled appointment if she felt the need.

    When we encounter Lisa, she is tearful and distressed and has made an appointment to see Gretchen, telling the clinic receptionist that she has somewhat of an emergency. We will examine the process Gretchen uses to establish the validity of her previous assessments, set priorities, make assessments, formulate judgments, diagnose, intervene, and evaluate Lisa's current acute situation. Gretchen has worked with Lisa for almost 8 months; as a result, she has previously made a detailed assessment of Lisa's self-concept and interdependence relationships. Also, when present at Phillip's delivery 7 days ago, Gretchen made a thorough physiological and mother role assessment; therefore, Gretchen has made a rather complete long-range care plan for Lisa. She will validate the current reliability of this assessment and then assess Lisa's present disruption in adequacy.

The adaptation nurse

Gretchen is a 36-year-old woman who has been practicing nursing for 15 years. She graduated from a baccalaureate program at the age of 21 years, began working in general medicine, and then began specializing in labor and delivery. After 2 years, she wanted to expand her practice, but then she met and married Elliot, a graduate student in economics. Because they needed her salary, Gretchen continued to work in a variety of hospital positions in maternal/child health. When Elliot completed his doctorate, they began job and graduate school hunting. They finally moved to the Chicago area, because it offered many job opportunities for Elliot and a graduate nursing program that was attractive to Gretchen. During their first year in Illinois, Gretchen became pregnant. She took a quarter off and was still able to complete her studies satisfactorily.

In graduate school Gretchen became acquainted with the Roy adaptation model of nursing. Typically, she found its concepts difficult to learn at first, but once they were incorporated into her pattern of thinking, they became an invaluable asset to her nursing practice.

If I'd have known that I was going to have to make major alterations in the way in which I thought about nursing and patients, I don't think I'd have gone to graduate school. It was really difficult in the beginning weeks and months. Now this kind of conceptualization is second nature to me. I even classify behavior and stimuli when I'm reading a journal article. I'm really an adaptation nurse, and I think it's improved my practice; I definitely feel more confident about my clinical judgments.

Since graduation Gretchen has had a second child, taught nursing at both undergraduate and in-service levels, and worked with physicians in setting up maternal/child health programs for lower-income families. About 3 years ago, Gretchen went back to school to complete a family nurse practitioner certification program. Since that time, she has worked in a family practice dealing with women's health and offering seminars and groups in parenting. Gretchen has been in her present position at the birth center for about 16 months. She is very enthusiastic about her work and loves the autonomy it offers.

External influencing stimuli. The external stimuli that affect the regulator/cognator process are the people, places, and objects that compose the physical environment. In this situation the physical environment is an alternate birth center in a middle-class neighborhood. The atmosphere can generally be described as expensive but "homey." The entire facility is carpeted in warm, durable colors; wallpaper is used extensively; plants are plentiful; and the sturdy furnishings are frequently complemented with an antique decorative item. There are many photographs and pictures depicting children in family settings. Toys and books are abundant and give evidence of the concern directed toward the younger clients. The general atmosphere is not that of a busy medical facility; rather, a quiet, efficient calm prevails.

The center has expanded recently, and although it retains the name alternate birth center, its services have been expanded to meet the needs of the childbearing family. The center has two family practice physicians, a part-time obstetrician, and a pediatrician, all of whom provide consultative services. The staff also includes four family nurse practitioners, two with expertise in pediatrics and two with expertise in women's health. In addition, there are several other registered nurses, a social worker, and a variety of clerical staff. The clients are predominately middle- or upper-income families from the immediate community. The center opened its doors 2 years ago but reached its present size and scope about 9 months ago. Lisa, her husband, and Phillip are three of the center's earliest clients.

Internal influencing stimuli. You will recall that internal stimuli include the person's physiological state, maturational level, knowledge, and beliefs. Gretchen's physiological state includes that she is a slightly overweight middle-aged woman who had normal childhood illnesses but otherwise has been in extremely good health. She has never had surgery and has only been hospitalized twice for the birth of her children. She has no physical limitations that will influence her performance as an adapation nurse.

Gretchen's personal and professional maturation levels affect her interactions with Lisa. Personally and professionally, Gretchen is coping with the tasks of the generative adult; i.e., she has established herself as a productive member of society and is providing for the development of future nurses. She has accomplished the task of young adulthood and has acquired advanced preparation in the form of a Master's degree and certification as a family nurse practitioner in women's health. In her personal development Gretchen has established a working marriage and has maintained that marriage for approximately 12 years. In addition, she has assumed the task of rearing two children. Gretchen's positive development as a person and as a professional will have a significant influence on her interaction with Lisa; she has the knowledge and professional skills required to meet the needs of the childbearing family.

Finally, we must consider Gretchen's unique internal state. We cannot have an indepth understanding of Gretchen, but we can isolate particular elements that influence her interaction with the client. First, we can say that Gretchen places high regard on the significance of the family and its relationship to childbearing. She also has strong beliefs regarding the needs and rights of women in the health care system. Gretchen is independent and self-sufficient; she admires these traits in others and gravitates toward persons who possess them. However, she is inclined to present herself as less competent than others perceive her to be. Her friends and colleagues all admire her ability to manage a home, family, and career with apparent ease. Gretchen, on the other hand, believes she often overextends herself and never quite completes anything at the level she would like. She might be described as a perfectionist, tending to attribute her success to luck or external sources as opposed to her own strength and initiative. She often comments,

> I've been very lucky in life. I always knew I wanted to be a nurse, but the rest sort of fell into place for me. I guess I've been at the right place at the right time. I have an excellent education and have had terrific work experiences and employment opportunities. I'm doing exactly what I want in a clinic that's less than a mile from my home; my kids can even walk to school from here. It's a good thing, because with our schedules if we weren't all close by, we'd never see each other. It gets very complex maintaining a career, a marriage, and the lives of two children, 8 and 10 years old.

Gretchen is the youngest of three girls from an upper middle-class New England family, coming from a rather sheltered existence as the daughter of a small-town physician. Since she is the youngest, she acknowledges that she was spoiled as a child; at the same time, she was always made to feel slightly incompetent: "Once the baby, always the baby." "We're all high achievers; academic success was a must as far as my parents were concerned. My father was disappointed when I chose nursing, not medicine, but even he agrees I've achieved some success for myself." Gretchen acknowledges that moving to Chicago and being the wife of a university professor has broadened her outlook. "I don't think I've retained too much of the Puritan background from which I came. I'm the family radical in a lot of ways."

Gretchen's education and specialized experience in maternal/child health are also of significance in her interactions with Lisa. She has the knowledge to provide expert assistance with adaptation problems. In addition, her ability to utilize the adaptation process at a high level enables her to provide optimal interactions in a highly specialized unique setting. A strong, motivated woman who practices adaptation nursing with special conviction to the needs of women, Gretchen is very competent but occasionally tends to make light of her own abilities. Now let us examine the data Gretchen has collected about Lisa and observe her use of the adaptation process as she interacts with her client.

The adapting person

Lisa is a 30-year-old woman who gave birth to an 8 pound 6 ounce boy 7 days ago. Her pregnancy and delivery were normal, and Phillip is a normal, healthy infant. She made her first visit to the alternate birth center in the eighth week of her pregnancy. She found the center after careful research into the options for nonhospital deliveries and decided that the center provided the delivery atmosphere she wanted and also had a comprehensive approach to children and families that appealed to herself and her husband, George. After several meetings with her physician and Gretchen, the nurse practitioner assigned to her, Lisa and George became clients of the alternate birth center. Their own positive experience as children who had family doctors was one of their reasons for choosing the center, and of course they were influenced by the opportunity of having a nonhospital delivery.

Lisa and George have been married for 3 years. George is an attorney involved in a family practice with his father, uncle, and brothers. Lisa was an elementary school teacher until about 14 months ago. When she and George began discussing having a baby, Lisa decided that she wanted to become more involved as a homemaker before actually becoming a mother. They sold their condominium and purchased a home in a residential area noted for good educational and recreational facilities for children. Since her retirement from teaching, Lisa has spent time working on their house, cultivating new non–work-related relationships, and doing some private tutoring. Once she became pregnant, she began concentrating on her diet and exercise and seeking relationships with other childbearing women. Lisa found that the birth center gave her the opportunity of interacting with other pregnant women and also offered classes and information essential to her preparation for motherhood.

On one occasion after she started coming to the center Lisa told Gretchen, "I'm rather compulsive about everything I do. I know most women just have babies; that's not the way I am. I approach everything as a big project, and I feel I have to be adequately prepared if I'm going to function like I think I should. I want us to be economically, physically, and socially ready for this baby. I know some of my friends think I'm nuts, but I don't think having a baby is something you do impulsively."

During the course of Lisa's prenatal visits Gretchen talked frequently with George and met Lisa's mother and her mother-in-law. Lisa frequently talked about how spoiled her child would be. "You know, this is the first grandchild on either side of the family; they've been waiting for a long time. Then, we have so many friends here; both George and I are third generation in the Chicago area. We know everybody. I mean, if George or I didn't go to school with someone, then someone in the family did. It's nice, though, you feel real safe and stable. When I went away to college I was terrified. Oh, I got used to it, but it was great to come home."

In the interaction we are going to examine, Lisa arrived at the birth center having scheduled an urgent appointment with Gretchen. Gretchen notes Lisa's stress and immediately asks some critical questions designed to isolate the area in which adequacy is threatened. She does this by reviewing and validating her previous assessment; any area that indicates a change is then followed up. As a result of this process Gretchen determined that Lisa was experiencing a category I diagnosis in the physiological, self-concept, and interdependence modes but a category II diagnosis in her mother role performance mode. We will now discuss the specific interaction and how Gretchen set priorities and arrived at her category I diagnosis.

Nurse/client interaction

Gretchen checks her appointment book upon her arrival and is surprised to see Lisa Abbot scheduled for an appointment. She consults the secretary, who says, "I didn't talk to her. I think Linda booked the appointment last night just before we left." Gretchen comments, "Well, I didn't expect to see her so soon. I guess my curiosity will be satisfied soon enough—she just walked in. I'll see her in my office first."

Lisa walks into Gretchen's office carrying Phillip in a woven basket bedecked with ribbons, lace, and ruffles. Her hair has been recently styled, and her clothes indicate the latest designer fashion; however, her face is drawn, there are circles under her eyes, and she looks as if she has been crying. After a brief greeting, Gretchen suggests that Lisa sit down. She pulls her chair up beside her and says, "You look lovely but exhausted. How can I help you?" Lisa bursts into tears. "Oh, I don't know, but you're the first person who has asked about me since Phillip was born. Nothing I do seems to be right; he never sleeps, and I'm exhausted. George keeps saying 'you're the one with the degree in child development—take care of him.' I was so excited about being a mother. I did all the right things: diet, exercise, everything. I loved shopping for baby clothes, furniture, and now it's awful. Nobody told me how helpless I'd feel."

Gretchen listens, resting her hand gently on Lisa's arm. She thinks,

> I've heard this often enough before, but I guess I'm kind of surprised to hear it coming from Lisa. This was truly a planned baby. Lisa quit her teaching job over a year ago, firmly committed to being a housewife and mother. She researched obstetricians and various methods of delivery, finally selecting this birth center because of our multiple services and family-centered approach. She's known us for months and she's an 'ideal' patient. Her life-style was developed for this baby; she has friends with babies. I really thought she was prepared for this experience. I can't believe this is a 'typical' role change problem. I've got to really listen. Maybe my first clue is her statement about feeling helpless—that's certainly something Lisa isn't used to feeling.

Gretchen says to Lisa, "This doesn't sound like the Lisa I'm used to. You're feeling overwhelmed."

Regulator/cognator process

The client. Gretchen's inquiry about Lisa's apparent exhaustion and upset functioned as a triggering event for Lisa. Her regulator signaled a general alarm, no other observable physiological behavior was stimulated, and the cognator was signaled. Lisa assumed a coping stance of self-enhancement and the strategy of confrontation. Based on her assessment of the situation, Lisa decided that if she took the risk of self-disclosure she might gain support from Gretchen. Her behavioral response was designed to gain her immediate access to resources in her environment.

Lisa's regulator/cognator process was influenced by her physical environment and her internal state. The alternate birth center and Gretchen had many positive associations for Lisa. The physical set-up and the people were familiar to her. She knew that she had been a "good" client and was perceived by the personnel, especially Gretchen, as a competent person. In addition, Lisa was influenced by her physiological status. Although she was extremely healthy and well nourished, her body was not fully readjusted following pregnancy and birth. This disequilibrium, coupled with lack of sleep, made Lisa look and feel less able to cope with the demands of her infant and therefore more in need of support. Lisa's maturational level was also an influencing stimulus. She had just added the task of caring for a member of the next generation to her role as a generative adult. Although Lisa was more than adequately prepared developmentally, she was dealing with a new role. Finally, her transaction was influenced by her unique set of beliefs and perceptions. She is an organized person who copes with the demands of her environment by being prepared. It has been her experience that she can cope with anything she has anticipated and planned for. In this situation Lisa's beliefs about her ability, knowledge, and planning are not maintaining her feelings of competence or adequacy. Thus, Lisa's tearful response comes because she is in a safe, supportive environment, is physically exhausted, and finds her own perceptions of herself incompatible with her performance in her role as mother.

The nurse. In turn, Lisa's behavioral response functions as a triggering event for Gretchen. Her regulator is triggered, a general alarm is sounded, no other physiological response is noted, and the cognator is stimulated. Gretchen assumes a coping stance of self-enhancement and a coping strategy of manipulation. Her behavioral response, which is reflected in her thinking process and her verbal statement, represents an attempt to organize the information that will explain Lisa's normal but somewhat unexpected behaviors.

Gretchen's transaction is influenced by the environment and her internal state. She has worked at the birth center for two years and has assumed major responsibility for the coordination of care delivered to more than 100 mothers and infants. Her environment is familiar and supportive. In addition, she has known Lisa for about 7 months. Their relationship is positive and well established. Furthermore, Gretchen has specialized training and education as a family nurse practitioner in maternal/child health. This knowledge has prepared her for reactions similar to Lisa's, and she has the skills to assess and intervene in this set of circumstances. Her knowledge and skills are further influenced by her beliefs and attitudes about Lisa and the demands of parenting. Gretchen sees her client as an extremely organized, competent person. She has sometimes envied Lisa's ability to create the "perfect" life. She once remarked to Lisa, "You're amazing. You have an incredible ability to orchestrate the events of your life. I was in graduate school when I got pregnant. Elliot had just started a new job; we lived in a one-bedroom apartment and had no money. I have an uncanny ability to create and live with chaos." Gretchen admired the purposeful qualities she observed in Lisa and saw missing in her own life. Finally, Gretchen's developmental level helped her to identify with Lisa. Although she was more advanced in accomplishing the tasks of the generative adult, she still remembered the experience and the feelings when her first baby arrived. Therefore, Gretchen's response to Lisa reflected her education, knowledge, and developmental level as well as her knowledge and beliefs about Lisa and her usual pattern of coping.

Nurse/client interaction

Lisa responds to Gretchen's statement by saying, "That's just it. I'm so competent I can't even get this baby to sleep. I'm used to getting things done. How can one little tiny person whom I love so much be such a problem to me?" Gretchen believes that the tears and verbalizations are helping Lisa but that she needs to ask some more specific questions to focus the discussion. She says, "You know, Lisa, what you're feeling is a very typical response. No matter how prepared we are, babies are unpredictable and don't always respond as we think they should. I'm sure knowing that others may have experienced what you're experiencing isn't enough. Let's see if we can discover exactly what would help you to feel more in control. What's the one thing you could change right now in this situation that would relieve some of the discomfort you're feeling?" Lisa responds immediately, "I don't have to think about that! If he'd sleep for 2 to 3 hours once or twice a day, I think I could cope. He sleeps for 15 or 20 minutes, then he's screaming. The only time he's quiet is when he's nursing. I really want to breast feed, but I can't sit around nursing 24 hours a day. Do you think he's getting enough to eat? He doesn't seem like he's grown to me, but judging from the amount of time he spends nursing, he should weigh 25 pounds." At that moment Phillip begins to cry. Lisa responds by reaching into the basket to pick him up, saying, "Well, now you can see for yourself. He always falls asleep in the car, but it doesn't last long. We're seriously thinking about getting a mobile home."

Gretchen listens to her client and notices that as Lisa talks more specifically she becomes calmer. She even tries to joke about the mobile home solution. Gretchen identifies two issues in Lisa's description of the problem: sleep and nursing. Although sleep is her initial concern, Lisa appears to equate a more adequate sleep cycle with a decrease in nursing time. This is a correct correlation that Gretchen believes warrants further exploration. Babies who are hungry often want to nurse constantly, experience little satisfaction, and are awakened frequently by the need to eat again. Based on these thoughts and her knowledge of breast-feeding problems, Gretchen suspects that Lisa may have what is called a "latch on" problem: the baby is not on the breast correctly and therefore is not getting sufficient quantities of milk despite almost constant sucking. In order to validate this perception, Gretchen needs to assess Lisa's nursing behaviors and Phillip's nutritional status.

Gretchen responds to Lisa by saying, "It seems like both sleeping and nursing are concerns to you, and you feel that if Phillip were getting enough to eat he would nurse less and sleep more?" Lisa comments, "Exactly. I have a friend who said her baby was just like Phillip, and her pediatrician suggested she just give up and give him bottles. Well, she did, and the baby slept 4 hours at a time from that day on. I've been tempted. I'm so exhausted, but I want to nurse him—I think it's better." Gretchen responds by saying, "There are lots of possible reasons for Phillip's behavior. I'd like to ask you some specific questions about his nursing, and then we'll weigh him and see if we can't satisfy his hunger without a bottle. You can nurse Phillip while we talk, if you like; that will give us an idea of how he's doing."

Lisa and Gretchen continue to choose self-enhancing stances, and their behavior continues to be influenced by their unique perceptions, especially their knowledge. Gretchen's restatement of Lisa's feelings of being out of control, coupled with the request for more specific information, acts as a triggering event for Lisa. The regulator is activated, a general alarm response is experienced, no other noticeable physiological behavior occurs, and the cognator is alerted. Lisa's cognator selects a coping stance of self-enhancement and the strategy of manipulation. Her behavioral response is designed to give information but also to gain information for herself. She engages in a coping pattern that will allow her to begin manipulating the environment and enhancing her level of social adequacy.

Lisa's transaction is influenced by many of the same stimuli that influenced her initial response. Now, because of the tension release she experienced through verbalization and tears, she is able to begin utilizing her cognitive abilities instead of responding emotionally because she is not in control of the situation. Lisa's beliefs about herself can now be used in a constructive way. Instead of feeling anxious about not meeting her personal expectations, she can use her belief in herself as a competent, organized person to develop her knowledge and skill regarding breast feeding. For this reason, she has chosen to interact in a positive environment that provides resources like Gretchen. Therefore, Lisa's behavioral response in this interaction is greatly influenced by her knowledge about child care and breast feeding, her belief in herself as a competent problem solver, and her presence in the supportive environment with Gretchen.

Lisa's verbalizations about sleep and breast feeding act as a triggering event for Gretchen. Her regulator is activated, the general alarm is sounded, there are no other observable physiological behaviors, and the cognator is signaled. In her transaction Gretchen adopts a coping stance of self-enhancement and the strategy of manipulation. She realizes that she must collect more data but believes with these data she will be able to provide Lisa with the knowledge and time to practice the skills essential to a successful breast-feeding experience. Gretchen's behavioral response is designed to acquire the additional assessment data she requires to help Lisa manipulate her environment and thereby achieve an increase in her level of social adequacy. As Gretchen successfully transacts, she also experiences mastery of her environment. Her successful interaction with Lisa will result in an increase in Gretchen's level of social adequacy.

Gretchen's transaction is influenced by many of the same stimuli that affected her previous behavior. However, she is now less responsive to her perception that Lisa should be coping without assistance because of Lisa's previous behavior pattern of competence. Gretchen is now responding to her knowledge of the nursing process and the problems associated with breast feeding. She also recognizes that her client's search for assistance as a problem-solving strategy is designed to put her in contact with necessary resources. Therefore, Gretchen's beliefs about Lisa's competence make her confident that a solution will be easily identified. Gretchen's behavior is greatly influenced by her professional knowledge and skills as well as her belief in Lisa's ability to solve problems and utilize information.

Role performance mode. Following this interaction, Gretchen engages in an interview designed to elicit information from Lisa regarding breast feeding while she observes her client nursing her son. Gretchen notes that Lisa moves from the chair to the couch and positions herself comfortably with a cushion under her left arm. Lisa then supports Phillip with her left arm, rests his head on the cushion, and moves him toward her left breast. Lisa then moves her body toward Phillip and directs her breast toward him with her right hand. As the nipple touches Phillip's mouth, he begins an open and closing motion. Lisa continues to push her breast toward Phillip, who begins sucking vigorously. As soon as Phillip begins to suck, Gretchen notices that Lisa jumps slightly and grimaces. Otherwise, Lisa appears relaxed; she holds Phillip firmly, and she seems confident in her approach.

In response to Gretchen's questions Lisa says that lately nursing has become painful; her nipples are raw and chapped. Despite the use of nipple creams, Phillip's constant sucking has caused a local irritation. Gretchen observes that Lisa's nipples are extremely red, and there are small blisters noticeable on close inspection. When questioned about the shape of her nipples after nursing, Lisa comments that they look funny, "kind of flattened and misshapen, and sometimes there is a white ridge noticeable, slightly to one side."

After listening and watching, Gretchen suggests that Lisa remove Phillip from her breast and attempt another position on the opposite breast. Gretchen observes that Lisa's nipple is indeed flattened and that there is a noticeable white ridge. Gretchen explains that Phillip's weight is down to 8 pounds but that this is not terribly significant for his age. Despite Lisa's discomfort, Phillip has been getting some milk but will need to show a weight gain. This gain is unlikely to occur unless they are able to get Phillip on the breast more effectively. Gretchen explains that Phillip is sucking primarily on the nipple, not the breast. Therefore, he must suck much harder and longer to get the milk. The fact that he has not been properly on the breast accounts for the misshapen nipple and the soreness. The white ridge becomes apparent when Phillip's jaw compresses the nipple repeatedly during sucking.

"That all makes sense, but how do I get him on right? I've tried every position except standing on my head," Lisa replies. Gretchen brings in two bed pillows and positions them at Lisa's right side. Then she asked Lisa to hold Phillip "like a football," with his feet over her right hip, her right arm supporting his trunk against her body, and her right hand supporting his head and neck. Gretchen demonstrates the position then asks Lisa to try. Lisa remarks, "This seems backward, but his head seems in a better position for my breast. Now what?" With Phillip positioned football style on the pillows, Gretchen says, "Now you need to put Phillip on the breast; he can't do that himself. I'll open his mouth (it has to be opened wide); you hold your breast with your left hand and push his head firmly into the breast." Lisa makes two attempts, and then Phillip begins sucking. She remarks, "It's not quite so painful, and I can feel the difference; he seems to have more leverage."

While Lisa is nursing Phillip, Gretchen attempts to validate her perceptions that Lisa is not getting enough support. Lisa's response indicates that her statements about her husband and other people in the environment not supporting her are not entirely correct.

> I guess I was in kind of a state when I got here. No sleeping makes me crazy. Just your saying there is a solution and doing something concrete with Phillip is a great relief. George has been up a lot, too, and then he has to go to work. My mother took the baby so I could get my hair cut, and George's parents took him so we could go out to dinner, just the two of us, on Saturday night. We've had lots of company, and of course they came to see me as well as the baby. I guess I had a fantasy about having a beautiful baby who did what he was supposed to do in his beautiful nursery. Babies just aren't like that, I'm learning. Phillip is sweet, and I love the way he cuddles; we'll manage this breast feeding thing. Look, he's asleep already.

Gretchen spends a few minutes with Lisa reinforcing the new breast-feeding position and suggesting that she practice on the opposite side before leaving. She encourages Lisa to call if she has any questions. "If I'm not here, I'll write this information in your chart, and someone else can go over the process with you. You might be interested in checking out the LaLeche League. They have an active program in this area and can be very supportive. I'll get a brochure for you."

Following this appointment, Gretchen completed the following nursing care guide to be utilized by all the staff members in their interactions with Lisa during the next week.

NURSING CARE GUIDE

ROLE PERFORMANCE MODE

MOTHER ROLE BEHAVIORS

1. Picks up Phillip when he cries.
2. Calls baby by name.
3. Makes eye contact with Phillip when speaking to him in a soothing voice.
4. Checks and changes diaper when Phillip awakes crying.
5. When breast feeding, supports arm with cushion, supports Phillip, guides nipple to baby, allows him to take nipple after stimulating his lips. Jumps slightly and grimaces when Phillip begins to suck.
6. Supports baby over shoulder and rubs his back after removing him from her breast.
7. "Nothing I do seems to be right; he never sleeps, and I'm exhausted."
8. "I was so excited about being a mother. I did all the right things: diet, exercise, everything."
9. "I loved shopping for baby clothes and furniture. Now it's awful."

INFLUENCING STIMULI

Focal: Ten-day-old infant who sleeps for short periods, cries frequently, and needs to nurse almost constantly.

Contextual: Lisa is a healthy, 30-year-old woman 10 days postpartum. Positive self-image, sees self as organized and competent. Prior to delivery had many support systems (e.g., husband, mother, in-laws, and friends). Now husband is tired and stressed by Phillip but continues to support (e.g., brings her flowers, takes her out to dinner, helps with infant care). Lisa's mother and George's parents have helped with child care. Has friends who have breast fed successfully but have not been able to offer help. Has a friend who had a similar breast feeding problem who changed to bottle feeding for successful outcome. Has knowledge of breast feeding and infant care and development. Sees alternate birth center and Gretchen as resources to help solve problems. Nipples tender.

JUDGMENT 1: Lisa's behavioral responses are maintaining her level of social adequacy at this time, but to prevent a decrease in her level of adequacy she needs to alter the quality of her responses.

JUDGMENT 2: Lisa is using self-enhancement as a coping stance and confrontation and manipulation to deal with the demands of her new mother role.

NURSING DIAGNOSIS: Instrumental mother role, maintained social adequacy: 10-day-old infant.* (Category I diagnosis). (Lisa is successfully taking on the new role of mother. Her coping stance and strategies are compatible with the triggering event and are maintaining adequacy.)

GOAL: Lisa wishes to have a successful breastfeeding experience. To achieve this goal she will utilize a new position, weigh Philip daily, and maintain daily contact with the center.

*National Conference on Nursing Diagnosis.

INTERVENTION

1. *Support:* Gretchen will provide Lisa with positive feedback that indicates what Lisa is experiencing is normal. She will also assure her that help is available and that she has done the right thing to ask for help. She will use touch and eye contact to reinforce statements.

2. *Teaching:* Gretchen will explain and demonstrate the alternate nursing position: use two pillows at side; hold Phillip like a football, feet extending backward over hip, use arm to support head and neck; open Phillip's mouth wide by manipulating jaw; use hand to firmly push Phillip into the breast, use other hand to hold breast while Phillip nurses; and be sure he is sucking breast, not just nipple. She will suggest that Lisa call if she has any questions and that she bring Phillip back in 1 week to be weighed (sooner if she has any concerns). Gretchen will ask Lisa to keep a record of frequency and duration of nursing and sleep behaviors and to call that information in for the next week. Gretchen will give Lisa the name and number of the local LaLeche League leader and encourage her to participate.

EVALUATION

1. Lisa will be noticeably relaxed (self-derogatory behavior will continue to decrease; she will be able to focus on her specific concerns and to follow instructions and experiment with alternate behavioral responses to Phillip).

2. Lisa will observe the demonstration of breast feeding and then repeat the behaviors while observed. Verbal statements regarding increased comfort and feeling that Phillip has a better grasp of the breast.

3. Lisa will call if she has any additional concerns.

4. Phillip will show a weight gain of at least 6 ounces by the end of the first week.

5. Lisa will call daily and report data. Staff members will record the information; Gretchen will check daily.

6. Lisa will call the LaLeche League and decide on participation based on her interest and need.

As was previously stated, Gretchen did some priority setting utilizing her past assessments of this client, her clinical knowledge, and the critical elements of the current interaction. As a result, Gretchen focused her efforts on Lisa's mother role but also arrived at a category I diagnosis for each of the other modes. The priority-setting process and the "mini-assessment" of each mode will be examined next. This examination will demonstrate how the nursing process can be telescoped by an experienced adaptation nurse working with a long-term client with whom a previous relationship exists.

Physiological mode. Gretchen recalls that Lisa was discharged with Phillip from the birth center in good physiological condition. She had been in labor for 14 hours, 6 of which were spent in the center. Phillip was delivered at 4:30 P.M., breathed spontaneously, and had an Apgar score of 9. Lisa had no medication and expelled the intact placenta without difficulty. Her vital signs were stable: blood pressure,

130/84; pulse, 84; temperature, 100° F; and respirations, 14. Her fundus was firm, about the size of a grapefruit, and palpable approximately 2 cm below the umbilicus. Her lochia was dark red, and she had saturated two pads since delivery. At discharge Lisa's diagnosis read: Circulatory and reproductive integrity, maintain physiological adequacy: vaginal delivery, normal healthy infant.* (Lisa is experiencing a category I diagnosis. Her physiological behaviors indicate that she is coping effectively with the physiological changes that initiated when she delivered an 8-pound 6-ounce infant at 4:30 this afternoon. Lisa is experiencing an increase in physiological adequacy.)

Based on this behavioral assessment, her knowledge of Lisa's prenatal health history, and this diagnosis for the physiological mode, Gretchen was certain that Lisa's concern was not physiological. However, she did need to validate this assumption, and she did so by first asking a general question to pinpoint Lisa's problem. Lisa's verbal response focused on mothering behavior and concerns, confirming Gretchen's suspicion. Gretchen would need to further validate her assumption by palpating Lisa's fundus and asking her to describe the amount and quality of her lochia. Additionally, Gretchen may explore appetite and energy levels.

Gretchen discovered that Lisa's uterus was descending appropriately and was palpable about midway between the symphysis pubis and the umbilicus. Lisa stated that she was using about four pads per day and described a thin serous discharge that was brownish and had no unusual odor. She described her appetite as too good and stated that her energy level was good despite the sleepless nights she was having. Gretchen completed this brief physiological assessment after she assisted Lisa with her immediate concerns. Gretchen made the judgment that the threat to Lisa's mother role performance took precedence over the physiological mode.

Self-concept mode. Gretchen had considerable knowledge regarding Lisa's perception of herself. She knew that Lisa had had a positive body image and was looking forward to the return of her slim figure. Her client's dress and grooming on the particular day confirmed that she continued to hold herself in high regard and was once again wearing what she called her "thin" clothes. Lisa commented that she still expected to succeed at whatever she tried and indicated that she continued to have high expectations of herself. Lisa's statements indicated to Gretchen that if Lisa were not able to establish the expected level of mother role performance, she might experience a decrease in her level of adequacy in self-consistency and self-ideal behaviors. Lisa seemed to be saying, "I know I'm competent and I'm not ready to give up yet, but if I don't get some relief soon, I'll be more anxious and even less effective."

Based on these observations, Gretchen believed her previous assessment of Lisa's self-concept mode was valid. She noted the potential threat, however, and made a note to herself to encourage Lisa at her regular postnatal check to participate in the

---

*National Conference on Nursing Diagnosis.

mother/infant group. Gretchen thought Lisa needed help setting realistic expectations for herself and Phillip. Perhaps the support of other mothers could help her to see that although planning and organization may help, they will not guarantee the "perfect baby." Gretchen felt she would need to help Lisa examine the possibility of loosening up her self-ideals regarding her mothering behavior. Therefore, Gretchen made the following diagnosis with the recommendation for some anticipatory guidance: self-esteem, maintain psychological adequacy: support and information.* (Lisa has a category I diagnosis in the self-concept mode. Her help-seeking and self-disclosing behaviors are allowing her to cope effectively with the stress produced by not meeting her expectations of herself as a mother. The coping stance of confrontation is very effective.)

Again Gretchen established priorities: Lisa's major concern seemed to be her inability to feed her baby. Gretchen focused her efforts in this area, believing that an increase in Lisa's level of mother role adequacy would decrease or eliminate the current threat to her self-concept adequacy. She further identified Lisa's need for assuming the coping stance of negotiation in an effort to alter her self-perceptions and therefore decrease her vulnerability to threats in this area.

Interdependence mode. Gretchen had considerable knowledge about Lisa's recipient and contributive behaviors in her roles as wife, daughter, and daughter-in-law. She was fairly certain that these well-established relationships were not disrupted but needed to validate this assumption. Initially, Lisa's comments about George indicated that there might be a disruption in this area. However, as Lisa's anxious behavior decreased she presented a more nurturing and supportive picture. Gretchen imagined that there was a decline in Lisa's contributive behaviors in all her roles except that of mother. But Lisa's significant others had been prepared that most of her energy would initially be focused on the baby.

Again Gretchen established priorities. Lisa needed to deal with her mother role behaviors; if she felt confident performing these tasks, she would be able to participate more fully in interdependent behaviors. Gretchen again made a mental note that the parenting group would help Lisa when she was ready to become a more active contributor, especially with George. Gretchen thought that should this become a problem and the marital relationship become stressed, the couples' group is always an alternative. Gretchen observed that this is probably an unnecessary option for the Abbots, but the relationship should be explored in about 1 month. Perhaps George could participate in the discussion if a late appointment was scheduled to accommodate his working hours.

Gretchen considered her previous assessment sound and added the nursing diagnosis to the chart: Expressive wife and daughter role, maintain social adequacy: complementary role opposites, contributive behavior.* (Lisa is experiencing a cat-

---

*National Conference on Nursing Diagnosis.

egory I diagnosis in the interdependence mode. Other requests for and positive response to nurturance from significant others and her contributive behaviors toward Phillip are appropriate and effective in response to the new role of mother. The coping strategies of confrontation and manipulation seem to be maintaining Lisa's level of social adequacy.)

Summary

Gretchen added her nursing care guide, the three category I diagnoses, and her plans for future interactions with Lisa to the chart. These plans reflected her areas of concern in each of the four modes and were especially designed to help Lisa continue to assume the coping stance of self-enhancement as she deals with the many triggering events that occur when an adapting person takes on a new role.

After Lisa left, Gretchen reflected on the interaction and felt very good about the change in Lisa's level of distress. Gretchen thought, "The very qualities that made me surprised to see Lisa here in distress are the qualities that allowed her to seek assistance and use that assistance to enhance her level of adequacy in the mother role. It makes me feel more adequate in my professional role, too, when I have a successful interaction with a client."

One week after this appointment, Gretchen saw Lisa in the clinic having Phillip weighed. Gretchen greeted Lisa and asked how Phillip was progressing. "From your daily reports I'd guess he's gained weight and is much easier for you to manage." Lisa smiled broadly, saying,

"He's a joy: sleeps 3 hours at a stretch, sometimes longer, nurses for ½ hour to 40 minutes, plays for a while, and goes back to sleep. I'm so grateful for that football hold. You know, I went to one of those LaLeche meetings, and there was a woman there having the same problem. I showed her what you'd taught me with Phillip. She seemed skeptical, but she tried. I'm not sure she'll follow through: she seemed pretty down, but I gave her your card and told her to call. I think I'll go to the group for a while. They were supportive, and it was fun talking with people who really know how tired and overwhelmed I'd been feeling. Wow! He weighs 8 pounds 10 ounces; he's going to be a big boy like his daddy."

Gretchen smiled and encouraged Lisa, saying she could discontinue her daily calls and suggesting that she schedule an appointment for herself and Phillip in about 2 weeks. "Don't hesitate to call if you need us sooner." Gretchen laughed to herself, thinking it was just like Lisa to take what she had gained and share it with others. She'd probably be a LaLeche League leader herself some day soon.

CASE STUDY—WELL CHILD
The setting

Wellness is experienced when the adapting person demonstrates a category I diagnosis in all four modes or demonstrates a category I diagnosis in three modes and a category II diagnosis in the fourth mode. In this wellness situation are Luis

Martinez, who is 4 years old, his mother, Lethie, and Gloria, the adaptation nurse.

The setting is a well-child clinic staffed by volunteers in a church. The clinic serves children from birth to age 12 years and has a dental clinic and a laboratory to do basic blood or urine examinations. Ill children are referred to a nearby medical clinic. Most of the children who are clients of the well-child clinic are very poor; many are illegal aliens, and the ethnic make-up is about half Mexican/American and half black. The only salaried person on the staff is the clinic's director, who is responsible for fund raising in addition to administrative duties. Other staff members donate their time and services.

The adaptation nurse

Gloria James is one of the volunteer nurses at the clinic. She is in the generative adult stage of development, having acquired an advanced degree in nursing. She is autonomous in her practice, has a comprehensive understanding of the adapting person, and is very proficient in applying the adaptation nursing process. This mature practitioner has many intervention modalities available to her but is especially adept at intervening by enabling the client. Practicing at this level, Gloria is oriented to the future and to growth. She also has a professional commitment to facilitating the growth of adaptation nurses who are in the adolescent and young adult stages of development; thus, she is helping to maintain and enhance the nursing profession.

External influencing stimuli. Gloria is black and grew up in a New York ghetto. Counseled into a licensed practical nursing program at age 18 years, she proceeded through the program at a general hospital, realizing late in her training that she was participating in a program far below her ability. Having to support herself and the first of her four children, Gloria became a registered nurse by going back to the same hospital and getting her diploma. At this point Gloria was 30 years old and identified with the matriarchal pattern. She maintained a home for her four children, working as a registered nurse to support them and a cousin who was living with her. Gloria experienced the denial of job opportunities because she lacked a baccalaureate degree. She applied for a federal nurse traineeship, and it was granted. Gloria completed her course work for a degree in nursing. She had the good fortune to attend a nursing program that has implemented an adaptation nursing curriculum. Gloria was ecstatic to learn about the nursing process and the adapting person. It was an experience that helped her make sense out of the client's behaviors and gave her some intervention skills to assist her clients.

That year Gloria's daughter graduated from high school, Gloria completed her Bachelor of Science degree, and her mother died. Gloria moved into a night supervisor position to increase her salary and to be home evenings with her children. About this time she also became aware that she was a very good nurse and saw relationships and consequences that many of her peers did not. Gloria also felt a need to share some of her nursing wisdom with nurses who were entering the profession and to work more with minorities and poor people, so she explored her choices and entered a Master's program for nursing. She persevered and graduated five years later with a Master's degree in nursing and certification as a pediatric nurse practitioner. She has continued to work in the pediatric office, where she did her preceptorship. She does volunteer work one Saturday a month at the well-child clinic. She serves as a clinical advisor for graduate students at the well-child clinic. Gloria is actively involved in the organization Black Nurses as well as the American Nurses Association.

Internal influencing stimuli. Gloria's internal environment consists of her physiological state, her maturational level, and her values and beliefs. First, let us look at Gloria's physiological state. She is 52 years old, is 5 feet 8 inches tall, weighs 185 pounds, has undergone menopause, and has hypertension. She acknowledges that life has not been easy; she knows stress plays a role in her hypertension. She has two children still at home (10 and 12 years of age) and continues to raise them as a single parent. Gloria has more energy now that she has completed graduate school. Her blood pressure is 140/98, the lowest it has been for several years; she knows she should lose 40 pounds and "may get around to that."

Gloria's level of personal maturity parallels that of her professional maturity. Working through the tasks of the generative adult, she has a high level of self-esteem and feels very capable about managing her own life. She is nurturing members of the next generation by caring for her own children as well as by being a surrogate "mom" to several of her children's friends. She is a spiritual woman who has sung in the choir at the Baptist Church for years. She believes that part of her responsibility as a Christian is to value all human life as sacred and to "help my neighbor along the way." She is an open, caring person who acts on the belief that humans can deal with a lot of trouble, most of which is brought on by themselves. People who know her feel drawn to Gloria and frequently discuss their problems with her.

In summary, Gloria has arrived. She feels good about where she is professionally and sees enough options to last her through retirement. She states that 13 years of nursing school were enough training for anyone to experience but that she would do it all again, if necessary. She likes herself and who she has become. Equally important, she feels good about her relationship with all of her children. Gloria says the favorite part of her career right now is "teaching the students." They appreciate the way she treats them as colleagues rather than as subordinates. She is well liked by her family, friends, and associates at the clinic.

The adapting person

Luis Martinez is a 4-year-old boy whose parents are illegal aliens from Mexico. Alonzo, his father, is 22 years old and works in a sheet metal factory. He earns a minimum wage and has hospitalization insurance for himself and the family. His 21-year-old wife, Lethie, has had five interrupted pregnancies and only one full-term pregnancy. Following a spontaneous abortion 1 year ago, she underwent a hysterectomy.

The Martinez family lives in a rented house with Alonzo's brother, his wife, and their four children. Spanish is the only language spoken in the home. The Martinez families are Catholic and participate regularly in parish activities.

Nurse/client interaction

Lethie has brought her son to the well-child clinic for "his shots." Gloria greets Lethie and Luis in a comfortable examining room. She introduces them to Sally Smith, a beginning graduate student who is observing Gloria as she practices her nursing skills. Sally will formulate some of the assessment, but Gloria chooses to take the health history because she is fluent in Spanish. She then leaves Sally to administer the Denver Developmental Screening Tool to assess developmental age. The two then share their initial data. Sally states that according to the screening tool, Luis is at the 3-year-old level in gross motor development. Gloria shares that Lethie said she felt guilty because Luis has not had his shots, because he is her only son and the only child she will ever have. Gloria notes that she said this with great sadness in her voice and in her body. Gloria discusses the usual identity of Mexican women as being closely tied to the behaviors of bearing and rearing children. They discuss the Catholic church and its emphasis on the sanctity of children and on the value of having many children. Gloria has a hunch that Lethie has not resolved the loss of her reproductive self, that the nieces and nephews who live with her are constant reminders of her own pain, and that Lethie is probably being overprotective of Luis because she is so afraid that something might happen to him. They discuss how this might be the triggering event for the delay in Luis's gross motor movement. Sally, the student, is learning about the adapting person, so she proceeds with the physiological mode assessment. Gloria then completes the physical assessment of the head, abdomen, chest, and external genitalia. Gloria interviews Lethie for data regarding play activities for Luis, outdoor play space at home, how he separates from his parents, and if he is in nursery school.

Physiological mode. Gloria and Sally organize the data they have gathered, using the adaptive modes and nursing process and postulating which stimuli they will manipulate and how they will intervene. Sally assesses the following data: the mother expresses no concerns about how Luis is doing; he seems healthy to her. His diet usually consists of beans, corn, cheese, tortillas, eggs, milk, and fresh fruit. Luis weighs 40 pounds and is 3 feet 4 inches tall. His hematocrit is 42%; his blood pressure is 100/64; his temperature is 98.8° F; and his respirations are easy. He had three ear infections last year and had medication for each of them. His bowel movements are normal, and he urinates four to five times per day. A gross analysis of the urine is negative. He sleeps well and plays energetically. His auditory screening and Snellen testing reveal no problems. The data, organized in the adaptation nursing process, might be summarized as in the following assessment.

NURSING CARE GUIDE

PHYSIOLOGICAL MODE

INGESTIVE BEHAVIORS

1. Eats three meals per day plus snacks from the basic four food groups.
2. Is 3 feet 4 inches tall and weighs 40 pounds.
3. Teeth are free of cavities.

RESPIRATORY BEHAVIORS

1. Respirations easy (24/minute). Chest sounds clear.
2. No mucus; no productive cough.
3. Ears clear, no redness.

ELIMINATIVE BEHAVIORS

1. Bowel movements normal. Voids four to five times per day. Urinalysis negative for sugar, protein, and acetone.

CIRCULATORY BEHAVIORS

1. Pulse, 96; apical rate, 96; regular blood pressure 100/64.

NEUROLOGICAL BEHAVIORS

1. Temperature, 98.8° F.

PROTECTIVE BEHAVIORS

1. Skin clear, bruises on anterior lower extremities.

MUSCULOSKELETAL BEHAVIORS

1. Sleeps 10 hours per night.
2. Plays hard and is very active.

INFLUENCING STIMULI

Focal: Adequately functioning body systems.

Contextual: Nutritious meals served. Several children in the home. Plays inside all the time. Small house (three bedrooms for four adults and five children). Mexican culture.

Residual: Poverty.

JUDGMENT 1: Luis's behaviors in all components of the physiological mode reflect adequacy.

NURSING DIAGNOSIS: Physiological wellness, maintained physiological adequacy: functional body and environment,* (cateogry I diagnosis). (Luis is demonstrating wellness in all components of the physiological mode because of adequately functioning body systems, good nutrition, and adequate exercise and rest.)

*National Conference on Nursing Diagnosis.

The nursing process is terminated at this point. Lethie clearly has adequate knowledge about how to care for a 4-year-old child in daily living situations.

Self-concept mode. Gloria confers with Sally and explains that with a child of this age, she is looking for behaviors that would indicate a clearly developing self-identity and that would demonstrate pride in himself as well as his accomplishments. She then interacts with Luis and his mother to gather the data needed. She hands Luis a book with pictures and words in Spanish. His mother shares that he enjoys books and likes them to be read to him. Luis tells the nurse that he is Luis, a chico, and that he is going to be a cowboy. He then proceeds to pull his imaginary guns and shoot Gloria. His mother reprimands him and says, "He knows right from wrong and is really a good boy." Sally formulates the following nursing care guide from these data.

NURSING CARE GUIDE

SELF-CONCEPT MODE

BODY IMAGE BEHAVIOR

1. Toilet-trained and feeds self.
2. Speaks in sentences in Spanish.
3. Enjoys playing with cars and looking at books.
4. Is clear that he is a boy "Chico."

SELF-IDEAL BEHAVIORS

"I'm going to be a cowboy when I grow up."

MORAL/ETHICAL BEHAVIORS;

1. Mother states, "He knows when he's been a bad boy."

INFLUENCING STIMULI

Focal: Healthy 4-year-old boy with adequately functioning neuromuscular system.

Contextual: Developmental tasks of distinguishing right from wrong, learning sex differences, and learning language. Lives in extended Spanish speaking family with cousins aged 9 months and 6, 3, and 2 years. Lives in English-speaking culture. Is still working on the developmental task of autonomy.

JUDGMENT 1: Luis's self-concept behaviors are maintaining his moderate level of self-esteem.

JUDGEMENT 2: Luis is using compromise and suppression to master the developmental tasks of a 4-year-old boy in a Mexican culture.

NURSING DIAGNOSIS: Self-concept, maintained psychological adequacy: English as a second language* (category I diagnosis). (Luis has only a moderate level of self-esteem because of his need to master 4-year-old–level developmental tasks and because he speaks only Spanish in an English-speaking culture.)

*National Conference on Nursing Diagnosis.

GOAL: Luis will continue to manifest behaviors congruent with his developmental tasks and begin to learn English.

INTERVENTION	EVALUATION
1. *Teaching:* The stimulus to be manipulated is that Luis speaks Spanish in an English-speaking culture. Gloria knows that Luis is at risk for a decreasing level of self-esteem as he enters kindergarten next year if he is not bilingual. She will utilize the principles of anticipatory guidance as she explores how the 6-year-old cousin learned English and how it is easier to learn English at age 4 years without the pressure of learning to read at the same time. She will emphasize the many benefits of a preschool experience for Luis. Gloria will encourage Lethie to buy or use the library for bilingual books that Luis and his father can read in English.	1. Luis will begin to learn English on a regular, planned basis.

Role performance mode. Luis shows a primary role of a 4-year-old boy and secondary roles of client, son, and friend with children; his physical motor skills are assessed as primary role behaviors. The behaviors assessed represent the kind of skills a child should be performing according to age. The Denver Developmental Screening Tool was used, and Luis's behaviors were normal in three of the four areas. Luis did not complete the gross motor activities at the 4-year-old level (he performs at the 3-year-old level). The specific behaviors are listed in the nursing guide.

As identified by Erik Erikson (1963), the developmental tasks influencing the role mode of a 4-year-old child include the state of initiative or guilt. The cognitive stage is called preoperational or preconceptual by Jean Piaget (1954). Havighurst (1953) defines the following developmental tasks for this period: (1) learning sex differences, (2) forming concepts and learning language, (3) getting ready to read, and (4) learning to distinguish between right and wrong. The role assessment and nursing process are illustrated in the following nursing care guide.

NURSING CARE GUIDE

ROLE PERFORMANCE MODE

BEHAVIORS

1. Is a 4-year-old boy.
2. Dresses with supervision.
3. Copies square.
4. Draws a person with 3 parts.
5. Recognizes colors.
6. Defines words.
7. Comprehends the terms *cold, tired,* and *hungry.*
8. Rides tricycle.
9. Is very awkward with ball.
10. Does not broad jump.

INFLUENCING STIMULI

Focal: Mother is overprotective.

Contextual: Plays inside the house all the time. Plays with cousins (ages 9 months and 6, 3, and 2 years). Yard of home is not fenced and opens onto a busy street. Has access to books in Spanish. Developmental tasks of preoperational thinking and initiative. Mother's knowledge regarding Luis's need for gross motor activities.

Residual: Mexican culture.

JUDGMENT 1: Luis's behaviors in the primary role are maintaining his level of adequacy in relation to his developmental tasks.

JUDGMENT 2: Luis is using a self-enhancing coping strategy to master his developmental tasks in a very limited environment.

NURSING DIAGNOSIS: Instrumental primary role, enhanced social adequacy; limited environment* (category I diagnosis). (Luis is in primary role mastery because of mastery of his developmental tasks in a very limited environment.)

GOALS: Luis will have opportunities to develop gross motor behaviors by having a larger play area.

INTERVENTION

1. *Teaching:* The stimulus to be manipulated is Lethie's knowledge regarding Luis's need for gross motor activities. Gloria will use a self-enhancing/confrontation approach to discuss the needs 4-year-old children have regarding active motor play. She will also explain to Lethie how difficult it will be for Luis when he begins school if he does not learn outdoor play skills now. Gloria will listen to Lethie's concerns, and then suggest that Luis and the 3-year-old cousin attend a local funded preschool 3 mornings a week. The preschool has a large outdoor playground area.

EVALUATION

1. Lethie will arrange some ways for Luis to have large muscle play on a regular basis (i.e., supervised play, preschool, or going to the park).
2. Luis will be able to ride a tricycle, jump, skip, and throw a ball at the 4-year-old level at the next visit.

---

*National Conference on Nursing Diagnosis.

Gloria quickly assesses Luis's performance in the client role. The nursing care guide follows.

NURSING CARE GUIDE

ROLE PERFORMANCE MODE

CLIENT BEHAVIORS

1. Has not received any immunizations against childhood communicable diseases.

INFLUENCING STIMULI

Focal: Parents are illegal aliens and are afraid to use county public health department.

Contextual: Parents did not know about free clinic, have limited income, and knew Luis could not start school without "shots."

JUDGMENT 1: Lethie has brought Luis to the clinic to begin his immunization series. This will maintain his level of adequacy in the immune system.

JUDGMENT 2: Lethie is using self-enhancing and confrontation as she brings Luis for immunizations prior to going to school.

NURSING DIAGNOSIS: Client role, maintained social adequacy: need for immunizations* (category I diagnosis). (Luis is beginning his immunizations late because of family financial concerns but will have completed the series before entering kindergarten.)

GOAL: Luis will be given immunizations until he is adequately protected.

INTERVENTION

1. *Collaboration:* Gloria will administer the diphtheria, pertussis and tetanus inoculation, the oral polio vaccine, and tuberculin test.
2. *Teaching:* Gloria will advise Lethie to return in 1 month for Luis's measles, mumps, and rubella immunizations. She will explain how to read the tuberculin test and give Lethie stamped addressed postcards to mail to the clinic.

EVALUATION

1. Luis will return at designated date to complete his immunization schedule.

*National Conference on Nursing Diagnosis.

Crossmodal diagnosis. Gloria talked with Sally about her hunches that the relationship between Luis and Lethie is intense and that Luis probably will not separate easily from her when he must leave for school. She said it indicates that the son role should be assessed in the role and interdependence modes. Assessment data reveal that Luis, when asked to go play in the clinic playroom where he had been playing earlier, protested, cried, and clung to his mother.

The information was organized into the role and interdependence modes, and a crossmodal nursing diagnosis was written. The organized data are illustrated in the nursing care guide below.

This is one of the places in which Gloria, because she is a nurse at the generative stage of development, can take shortcuts. The stimuli causing the behaviors in the role and interdependence modes are the same; thus, intervening with these stimuli will probably change Luis's son role behaviors in the role performance mode and the interdependence mode. Gloria also talks with Sally about the complexity of pediatric nursing and the maintenance of child health. This complexity arises from intervening with the client, the environment (to foster the mastery of developmental tasks), and one or both parents.

NURSING CARE GUIDE

ROLE PERFORMANCE MODE

SON ROLE BEHAVIORS

1. Follows mother's rules except for separating to go to the clinic playroom.
2. Clearly bonded to mother as mother.
3. Likes to go out with father to work on the car.
4. Likes to look at books with mother.

INFLUENCING STIMULI

Focal: Mother is overprotective.

Contextual: Mother is sterile. Family culture values a very large family. Only child, is working on the development task of autonomy, learning rules of society.

Residual: Parents do not see the need for Luis to separate at this age.

INTERDEPENDENCE MODE

SON BEHAVIORS

Contributive
1. Reaches out for mother's hand.
2. Sits on mother's lap.
3. Sleeps with mother and father.

Receptive
1. Mother says, "I love you" in Spanish.
2. Sits very close to mother and holds her hand. Cries loudly when asked to go to playroom so mother can stay and talk.

INFLUENCING STIMULI

Focal: Mother is overprotective.

Contextual: Mother is sterile. Only child, 4 years old, has not mastered earlier developmental talk of separating from mother. Is still working on developmental task of autonomy.

Residual: Parents may not value independence in Luis.

JUDGMENT 1: Luis's behaviors in his son role and in his interdependence mode, although effective in his protected environment, will not maintain his level of adequacy in a larger environment.

JUDGMENT 2: Luis is using approach and fight to deal with his conflict between the developmental tasks of autonomy and the overprotectiveness he experiences with his mother and father.

NURSING DIAGNOSIS: Expressive son role, disrupted social adequacy: overprotective mother* (category II diagnosis). (Luis is not able to separate from his mother easily in a safe environment because of his mother's overprotectiveness.)

GOAL: Luis will separate easily from his mother, continuing to know that his mother loves him (diagnosis I).

INTERVENTION

1. *Enabling:* Gloria will focus on Lethie's overprotectiveness, concentrating on Lethie's self-concept mode. Gloria will use the approach to get at Lethie's values, beliefs, losses, inability to have more children, and five miscarriages and how all this affects her self-ideal and her moral/ethical self. Gloria will confide how she shared similar feelings about her cousin who came to live with her because the rest of the family had been killed in an automobile accident. Gloria will focus on the mother role and Lethie's desire to be a good mother. She will discuss with Lethie Luis's need to go to nursery school and Lethie's own need for some new interests.

EVALUATION

1. At the next visit Luis will separate from his mother and go to the playroom.
2. Lethie will enroll Luis in a preschool program. Lethie will help Luis become a separate, secure, loved four-year-old boy.

---

*National Conference on Nursing Diagnosis.

The coping stance used by Luis in the social mode is approach. He is choosing the coping strategy of flight. Gloria points out to Sally that young children are evolving coping stances and strategies—that most coping mechanisms are learned in the home and are role modeled by the parents and older siblings.

Gloria demonstrates the coping stance of self-enhancement and the coping strategy of confrontation as she deals directly with Lethie regarding the consequences if she continues to overprotect Luis.

Summary

In summary, this case study demonstrates a nurse in the generative stage of professional development working in a free clinic that provides health care for well children. Because of her extensive knowledge base and her years of clinical practice, Gloria assessed Luis far beyond the need for immunizations, which was his presenting problem. Gloria clearly identified potential growth and development problems and used confrontation to help Lethie prevent problems from developing. Gloria did use all intervention modalities—collaboration, support, teaching, and enabling—but the focus was on enabling.

CASE STUDY—ELDERLY GRANDFATHER
The setting

In the state of wellness the adapting person demonstrates a diagnostic category I in three of four modes or in all but two components of a single mode. He also manifests a category II diagnosis in the other modes or components of a mode. Therefore, he is in control of his internal state and feels competent in coping with the environment.

Mr. Sotashi Komiko is in this state. He has a category I diagnosis in all four modes and a category II diagnosis in one component of his interdependence mode. At the insistence of his son he has gone to the San Francisco Health Clinic for his annual physical examination. Mr. Komiko is hurt and angry, because it has been more than 1 month since his son and grandchildren have traveled the 500 miles from Los Angeles to pay him a visit. Several times during the past week he has called his son, Taro, and chided him for abandoning his parents in their old age. Since his father has never acted this way before, Taro is concerned and calls a colleague and friend, Marge Hayes, who is an adaptation nurse practitioner at the clinic. She is delighted with the opportunity to work with Mr. Komiko, a longstanding family friend. While she is waiting for the completion of Mr. Komiko's physical examination, Marge reviews his health records and begins her plan of care. The process Marge uses to assess, validate, formulate diagnoses, intervene, and evaluate as she interacts with Mr. Komiko will be examined in the case study.

The section Nurse/Client Interaction suggests ways in which an adaptation nurse in Marge's stage of development might use her skills of support, teaching, and enabling to help an older client cope with threats to his social adequacy. Because Marge's internal transaction and unique stimuli influence her use of the adaptation nursing process, these factors will be addressed first.

The adaptation nurse

Marge is 34 years old and has been practicing nursing for 12 years. At the age of 22 years she graduated from a university school of nursing in Seattle, Washington. Marge is an only child. Her parents still live in Seattle, and she keeps in close contact with them. They both tease her about hurrying up to have a family of six children so they will have grandchildren, but because Marge never had grandparents of her own, she cannot really empathize with them. However, because she knows the importance of relationships and continuity, she can appreciate the need expressed by her parents.

External influencing stimuli. After graduation Marge worked on a surgical unit for 4 years. She met and married a surgical resident, Ken Hayes. When Ken joined a group practice in San Francisco, Marge took a position as discharge planning coordinator. Before 6 months had passed, Marge was frustrated. She felt that her teaching addressed the medical therapy rather than the needs of the person going home. After a lengthy discussion with Ken, she enrolled in a Master's program in nursing, where she was introduced to the Roy adaptation model.

Although she had wanted a better method of helping clients handle their discharge, Marge had not realized how such a method of organized thinking would permeate her daily living. She shared her excitement with Ken and their physician friend, Taro Komiko. All three enjoyed the intellectual stimulation and insight gained from their discussions. These discussions influenced and were influenced by Marge's unique stimuli. The external stimuli that affect Marge's regulator/cognator process are the objects, places, and people in her environment. After graduation from the Master's program, Marge accepted the nurse practitioner position at a San Francisco health clinic, where Dr. Komiko served as coordinator of physician services. He and Marge soon developed a program with a holistic approach to health care. After Taro moved to Los Angeles 2 years ago, his replacement, Dr. Stewart, continued the holistic-centered program and the colleague relationship with Marge and the other adaptation nurses. The clinic is busy and is open from 7:00 A.M. to 9:00 P.M. 5 days per week, servicing a large professional clientele in surrounding areas.

Internal influencing stimuli. The internal stimuli that influence Marge's regulator/cognator transactions are her physiological state, maturational level, knowledge, and beliefs. Marge is a tall (5 feet 10 inches), well-built woman weighing 150 pounds. She and her husband, Ken, enjoy water skiing, bowling, and indoor ice skating. She feels well and has unbounding energy and enthusiasm. She reads extensively and looks forward to the intellectual stimulation of discussing ideas with her husband, friends, and colleagues. She believes that nursing has endless potential if nurses would use a theoretical framework to organize and focus their thinking and judgments to help clients cope with health or illness rather than concentrating their energies on the disease or curative process. Therefore, she believes that the nurse needs even greater exposure to those bodies of knowledge that pertain to the whole person—anatomy, physiology, chemistry, physics, pathophysiology, economics, politics, cultural differences, philosophy, and religious and artistic thought—in order to discern those factors that either help the person maintain and increase adequacy or threaten and reduce the person's level of adequacy. Marge also believes that this broad knowledge base is needed to nurse in wellness situations, because the adaptation nurse who helps the client in wellness must be alert and knowledgeable about the total person's response to influencing stimuli, which she sees as more complex than the predictable way the body responds to trauma, infection, or disease. Marge would like to become involved in nursing education, because she believes that the most effective way of implementing adaptation nursing is by educating others to its effectiveness.

Ken and Marge are Methodists who are involved in a congregation governed by a minister and lay council who attend to the spiritual, social, and economic needs of their members. Marge edits the weekly church newsletter, which the council uses to clarify, discuss, and update church and world issues. Ken and Marge both believe that in addition to being responsible for their own well-being, they have a duty toward the next generation; therefore, they are involved with various youth groups in the city.

Marge enjoys working in the health clinic and has developed a fine skill in quickly sifting and sorting important presenting client behaviors and influencing stimuli to determine whether the person is coping effectively and whether the person's level of adequacy is threatened. She uses this skill when she reviews Mr. Komiko's health record and formulates some quick questions for validating her conclusions. Marge acquires the information from the following sources: Mr. Komiko's records; her knowledge of him as a personal friend; her knowledge of his developmental stage, tasks, and needs; and her ready skill in recognizing pertinent behavior and influencing stimuli from records and from nurse/client interactions.

The adapting person

Mr. Komiko was born in Japan 70 years ago and only recently retired from a position as a bank president. He and three other retired bank presidents have been asked to serve as executive consultants to the bank's management staff; he performs these duties 1 day each week and reads extensively to keep abreast of the financial world.

In social situations Mr. Komiko has a natural courtesy that is relaxing and easy to relate to. He speaks impeccable English but still enjoys speaking Japanese with his wife, Miko, who is also bilingual. They have warmly accepted Marge and Ken into their circle of close friends. Mr. Komiko is a stimulating conversationalist and enjoys intellectual discussion concerning philosophy and religion. The Komikos live in a new condominium complex located near the northern coast of California; they have become involved with the residents and have helped them to establish an art and music center.

Mr. Komiko walks 6 miles each day, swims in the ocean, and bicycles all over San Francisco. He enjoys fish and Japanese dishes. He believes this life-style is the reason he and his wife are so healthy. Neither of them has had a cold, flu, or illness for the past 8 years. Mr. Komiko says that retirement agrees with him. He enjoys the stimulation and continued contact with his bank and states, "It makes me feel honored that they still value my expertise. I can't help but believe they will be better managers for having benefited from my insight and skills."

Mr. and Mrs. Komiko are very close to their son, Taro, and love their daughter-in-law, Debbie. When the two grandchildren were born, Mr. and Mrs. Komiko centered their attention on the twins, Michael and Mioko. The children were in their grandparents' home constantly, and the Komikos would keep them every other weekend, telling Taro and Debbie that they needed time to delve into all the joys of being grandparents of Michael and Mioko "because they will be enriched by our presence; therefore, we need them near us."

When Taro moved to Los Angeles, he was concerned about this close relationship with the grandchildren, but his parents seemed to accept the separation and infrequent visits. They would come to visit four or five times during the year.

Mr. Komiko's past and present physical examination records demonstrate that he is within normal limits with every component of the physiological mode. At the bottom of the examination report the attending physician wrote, "a clean bill of health."

With the information she has gained so far, Marge concludes that physically Mr. Komiko is in excellent health, that in his self-concept mode he is demonstrating high self-esteem, and that in the role performance mode he is engaged in the tasks of the mature adult (he is retired but is still a participating member of the bank). He is actively engaged, along with his neighbors, in developing an art center. In the interdependence mode she concludes that Mr. Komiko has a nurturing, supportive relationship with significant people in his life: his wife, his son and daughter-in-law, and especially his grandchildren.

However, based on the brief information she has received from Taro, she is concerned that Mr. Komiko is experiencing a threat to his relationship with his son.

The following interaction will demonstrate how Marge validates her prejudgment and how she will clarify her final conclusion regarding Mr. Komiko's level of adequacy and state of wellness.

Nurse/client interaction

Marge enters the examination area and waits for Mr. Komiko to exit from the dressing room. When Mr. Komiko comes out of the dressing area, he shakes Marge's hand and bows slightly. They go into a carpeted meeting room, where the bustle of the department is muted. As they sit down, Marge begins the series of questions she has formulated to validate her judgment concerning Mr. Komiko's overall adequacy. She asks how he has been feeling lately, what he has been doing, and how Mrs. Komiko is feeling. To these questions he replies, "I couldn't be better; both Miko and I radiate with good health. When I do yoga, she swims, and then we exchange places. She is great fun to be with. We enjoy so many of the same things. I think arranged marriages have much to be said for them. The other day, she said I was getting old. I certainly don't feel old; in fact, it is great to be retired so we can concentrate on ourselves. You and Taro still have to think of everyone else." He continues, "You know that I still work at the bank. No pay, of course, but as a consultant. It is great. More companies ought to use such services. Besides, it keeps me abreast of the economic situation; I read volumes each week in order to follow the financial world."

Marge smiles and comments that he not only sounds great, but also looks that way. "But Taro called me and said you have been distressed with him. Would it help to talk about it?"

"Perhaps I will, Marge. You have influence over Taro and Debbie. Would you talk some sense into them?"

"Help me understand what you mean, Mr. Komiko."

"Well, they have stopped bringing my grandchildren to see me. It has been 2 months since their last visit. Michael and Mioko won't even know me when they see me next time. They will be starting grade school soon, and they won't want to play with their grandfather."

Marge leans forward in her chair and says, "I know that can be difficult, especially with that affectionate pair." Mr. Komiko responds, "That is the point. My friend, Mr. Yamabe, has six grandchildren, and they are over at the complex every weekend, sometimes during the week as well. His sons are professional people like Taro, but they make time to visit." Marge sits back in her chair and asks, "Is Mr. Yamabe a new neighbor? I don't remember meeting him when Ken and I had dinner with you last month." Mr. Komiko smiles and says, "Yes, he is. He and his wife have recently moved in next door. They are warm and friendly and seem to share our interests; they are helping us with the cataloging of the music collections. Their children honor them, and their grandchildren are a delight to have around. I just can't understand Taro; he used to be so thoughtful and caring. Miko says it is because I am jealous, but I have never been jealous in my life! I wish to enjoy being a grandfather; I have only two grandchildren and they will be grown soon."

Marge nods and says, "I can appreciate how difficult it must be when you miss the grandchildren so much. Have you thought of any plans or ways of sending for the children or having them stay over for longer periods of time?" Mr. Komiko straightens in his chair and asks, "Plans? I don't have any plans; that is Taro's responsibility." Marge smiles and says, "I can understand that, but would you agree with me that being grandparents is your and Mrs. Komiko's responsibility?" He laughs and replies, "Yes, I agree with you. What do you suggest?"

Marge continues with, "Well, I didn't have anything in mind but wondered if you would like to discuss some methods for bringing the children to visit oftener and staying longer." Mr. Komiko nods his head and says,

Yes, I would. Well, I suppose we could travel to Los Angeles more frequently, but, even better, we could send for them every other weekend. It's only an hour's flight, and we could meet them at the airport. Debbie is such a dear; I know she would let us have them. We could also plan to visit Los Angeles every third month or so. In fact, we could make it a party and invite the Yamabes to go with us. They would enjoy being at Taro's. I wonder what those television phones cost to install. I think I will investigate that possibility; the children would love it. We could also have Taro and Debbie videotape the children once in awhile. Then we could show them off to our neighbors. You know,

Marge, I like your suggestion; in fact, I think I will call Taro this evening and get this into motion. Marge, thank you, you have really helped. I was so angry with Taro, but now I can do something myself.

Marge accompanies Mr. Komiko to the door and returns to complete her nursing process.

Regulator/cognator process

The client. It is clear that Marge's questions and comments about Taro's concerns stimulated Mr. Komiko's alert response. His cognator was signaled and began to process the triggering event. Mr. Komiko assumed a self-enhancing coping stance and the strategy of confrontation. Because he was with a friend, he took a risk and verbalized his experience. He received support and enabling from Marge and was able to solve problems and select his own solutions for resolving the disturbance in his social adequacy.

Mr. Komiko was influenced by the facts that the center is familiar to him and that Marge is a family friend. He is aware that Marge considers him capable and in control of his own well-being. He is also influenced by his physical well-being and his sense of being valued and needed as a bank consultant. His maturational level is such that he could put all these factors into perspective. He believes in his own capabilities and expertise as a problem solver; therefore, when Marge asked him to explore options for resolving his conflict about his grandchildren, he was able to do so quickly and effectively. He believed he could control his interactions and environment, and he set out to do so at once.

The nurse. Mr. Komiko was a triggering event for Marge; so was the telephone call from her former colleague, Taro. She was alerted, and her cognator began to gather data—to categorize Mr. Komiko's behavioral response and influencing stimuli and present adaptive state. She made preliminary judgments and planned ways of validating them with Mr. Komiko. She planned (1) to validate her initial assessment and conclusions and (2) to structure the conversation in such a way that Mr. Komiko would be helped to clarify his own perceptions and to plan for better coping strategies to resolve the threat to his social adequacy. Ultimately, he selected the strategies of manipulation and negotiation; therefore, Marge did not have to offer him suggestions or alternate plans.

Marge chose the coping stance of self-enhancement and the strategy of negotiation to facilitate Mr. Komiko's movement to a category I diagnosis in his interdependence mode. Her enabling nursing actions helped Mr. Komiko to reestablish his social adequacy.

Marge was influenced by the facts that Mr. Komiko and Taro are her friends, that she perceives herself as competent, and that she believes adaptive persons are capable and effective in coping with their environment and achieving adequacy. She believes that the extended family is important, that all relationships are reciprocal, and that the responsibility for relationships is mutually shared. Each of these factors influenced Marge's interaction with Mr. Komiko, and they are reflected in the following nursing care guide, which she prepared for the client care conference scheduled for that afternoon.

NURSING CARE GUIDE

INTERDEPENDENCE MODE

PRIMARY ROLE (MATURE ADULT) BEHAVIORS	INFLUENCING STIMULI
SECONDARY ROLE (GRANDFATHER) BEHAVIORS	*Focal:* Absence of grandchildren. His perception that his son Taro and wife Debbie have stopped bringing his grandchildren to see him.
Recipient	
1. "Michael and Mioko won't even know me when they see me next time. They won't want to play with their grandfather."	
2. "Affectionate pair."	*Contextual:* Presence of Mr. Yamabe's six grandchildren. Taro lives 500 miles away and visits four to five times per year. Grandchildren have been away from area for 2 years.
Contributive	
1. "I just want to enjoy being a grandfather. I only have two, and they will be grown soon."	*Residual:* Belief that Taro has responsibility for bringing children to visit. Sense of competition. Jealousy. Wife commented about his age.
2. Calls his son and chides him for not bringing the children to visit.	

JUDGMENT 1: Despite his correct assessment, Mr. Komiko's behavioral response is not sufficient to change the circumstances and bring the children into closer physical contact. Therefore, his level of social adequacy is being threatened.

JUDGMENT 2: Mr. Komiko has chosen the coping stance of self-enhancement and the strategy of confrontation in response to his triggering event, which is the prolonged absence of his grandchildren. This coping stance is congruent with the environmental event.

NURSING DIAGNOSIS: Expressive grandfather role strain; disrupted social adequacy; grandchildren absent* (category II diagnosis). (Mr. Komiko is experiencing a category II diagnosis in his grandfather role component in the interdependence mode. He is experiencing stress because he is unable to engage in nurturing and affectional behaviors with his grandchildren. Mr. Komiko is experiencing disrupted wellness in the grandfather component of his interdependence mode.)

GOAL: Mr. Komiko will experience an increase in social adequacy (category I diagnosis). Mr. Komiko will interact with Taro and Debbie to plan to have the grandchildren visit more frequently. Mr. Komiko will take responsibility for alternate plans for his affectional interactions with his grandchildren.

*National Conference on Nursing Diagnosis.

INTERVENTION

1. *Support:* Marge will provide Mr. Komiko with feedback to help him clarify his perceptions and responsibilities in relationship to his grandchildren. She will help him understand that his reaction is normal.
2. *Enabling:* Marge will spend time with Mr. Komiko and help him to look at the situation from several perspectives. She will have him explore possible options for being with his grandchildren more frequently and will allow him to share the course of action he will pursue to reestablish his threatened level of social adequacy.

EVALUATION

1. Mr. Komiko will discuss the concern he has about Taro and will focus on specific plans for interacting more frequently with Michael and Mioko.
2. Mr. Komiko will state his exact plans when Marge goes to dinner with the Komikos next week.

By using support and enabling, Marge helped Mr. Komiko to select coping strategies of manipulation and negotiation; therefore, he left the interaction feeling competent and in control of the situation. Mr. Komiko is consequently moving toward a diagnostic category I in his threatened grandfather component of the interdependence mode.

Summary

In this adaptation nursing process special emphasis has been placed on Marge's and Mr. Komiko's regulator/cognator transactions. Mr. Komiko's transaction reflects the holistic nature of the adaptive person and the interrelationship of his four modes. Marge's transaction reflects the ability of the adaptation nurse in the generative stage of development to sift and sort pertinent client data and to use the nursing actions of enabling and support to help Mr. Komiko resolve his threatened social adequacy. Marge's regulator/cognator process is influenced by her knowledge, understanding, and ability to perceive her client's needs; therefore, as an adaptation nurse she forms a partnership with the client to achieve the goal of adaptation nursing, which is to help the person cope more effectively and thereby maintain or increase his level of biopsychosocial adequacy.

REFERENCES

Anthony, E.J., and Benedek, T.: Parenthood: its psychology and psychopathology, Boston, 1970, Little, Brown & Co.

Atchley, R.C.: The social forces in later life, Belmont, Calif., 1977, Wadsworth Publishing Co., Inc.

Branch, M.F., and Paxton, P.P.: Providing safe nursing care for ethnic people of color, New York, 1976, Appleton-Century-Crofts.

Burnside, I.M.: Working with the elderly: group practice and techniques, North Scituate, Mass., 1978, Duxbury Press.

Dunn, H.L.: What high-level wellness means. In high-level wellness, Arlington, Va., 1961, R.W. Beatty, Ltd.

Erickson, E.H.: Childhood and society, ed. 2, New York, 1963, W.W. Norton & Co., Inc.

Grossley, J., and Dores, K.: Common concerns of mothers who breast feed, Maternal-Child Nursing Journal 3:347, 1978.

Havighurst, R.J.: Human development and education, New York, 1953, Longmans Green & Co., Inc.

Jensen, M.D., Benson, R.C., and Bobak, I.M.: Maternity care: the nurse and the family, ed. 2, St. Louis, 1981, The C.V. Mosby Co.

Johnson, S.H.: High risk parenting, Philadelphia, 1979, J.B. Lippincott Co.

Klaus, M.H., and Kennell, J.H.: Maternal-infant bonding: the impact of early separation or loss on family development, St. Louis, 1976, The C.V. Mosby Co.

Klaus, M.H., Jerauld, R., Kreger, N.C., et al.: Maternal attachment: importance of the first post-partum days, New England Journal of Medicine 286:460-463, 1972.

Lewis, M., and Rosenblum, C.A.: The effect of the infant on its caregiver, New York, 1974, John Wiley & Sons, Inc.

MacKinnon, R.A., and Michels, R.: The psychiatric interview in clinical practice, Philadelphia, 1971, W.B. Saunders Co.

Maier, H.W.: Three theories of child development, New York, 1967, Harper & Row, Publishers, Inc.

Piaget, J.: The construction of reality and the child, New York, 1954, Basic Books, Inc., Publishers.

Sutterley, D.C., Donnelly, G.F.: Perspectives in human development, Philadelphia, 1973, J.B. Lippincott Co.

Whaley, L.F., and Wong, D.L.: Nursing care of infants and children, St. Louis, 1971, The C.V. Mosby Co.

The big picture revisited

an adaptation perspective

CHAPTER 9

Adaptation nursing and nursing practice

OBJECTIVES

List and describe the three processes that are essential in the practice of adaptation nursing.
Explain the implications for the practice of adaptation nursing and the areas of professional growth associated with each of the three processes.
Describe the adaptation nurse of the decade, and explain how her practice will differ from other nursing practices.

In the preface to this text the adaptation nurse is identified as the nurse of the 1980s: a thinker, a facilitator, and an independent practitioner. In the chapters that follow the emphasis is on process: the adaptive coping process, the process of becoming an adaptation nurse, and the adaptation nursing process. Because process can be described as a natural progression of changes that lead toward a particular result (in this case, growth), the reader's experience with this textbook should be growth producing. Therefore, Chapter 9 focuses once more on the stages of development, or growth, that are essential in the practice of adaptation nursing. The elements of practice—the internal transaction, the development of the adaptation nurse, and the three-step adaptation nursing process—are reviewed, and the implications for practice and the professional growth associated with each process are then explored. The chapter concludes with a prediction about the future of the adaptation nurse.

ADAPTIVE COPING PROCESS
The adaptive person

The person is described as an open, living system in constant interaction with an ever-changing but frequently predictable environment. In these interactions with the environment the person constantly experiences triggering events, which occur whenever the person and the environment make contact. This contact always produces stress, in this context defined as a change in the person's level of adequacy. This change is something with which the person must cope; in turn, this coping process becomes the concern of adaptation nursing. The adapting person's unique internal transaction, the regulator/cognator process, allows him to cope with triggering events by processing the experience physiologically and cognitively. The coping transaction has five phases, which warrant reiteration, because this transaction defines the unique responses that characterize the interaction between the person and the nurse.

Regulator/cognator transaction

The unique internal transaction, the adaptive coping process, is composed of the regulator and the cognator. The regulator functions as the alarm system. It initiates the automatic response essential to the maintenance of life; stimulates defensive responses to physical, chemical or infectious triggering events; and finally alerts the cognator that a triggering event has occurred. The cognator (the conscious or unconscious thinking process) evaluates the physiological experience to label, clarify, define, and initiate a behavioral response to stress. The regulator calls the person's attention to the contact with the environment and continues signaling as a constant source of feedback for the duration of the experience. The cognator is the mechanism by which the person interprets or makes sense of his environmental experience.

Five-phase transaction. The first phase of the adaptive coping process is represented by the adapting person's state of constant vigilance as well as his initial contact with the triggering event. In the second phase the regulator and cognator are activated. In response to the change in the level of adequacy, the regulator stimulates the general alarm reaction; initiates a physiological behavioral response to physical, chemical, or infectious triggering events; and alerts the cognator. In the third phase the cognator labels and defines the triggering event and selects one of four coping stances. In the fourth phase it chooses an appropriate coping strategy. The fifth and final phase represents the person's behavioral coping responses, which are the culmination of the work of the regulator and the cognator. These responses operate on the cognator's instructions to facilitate adaptation. All physiological behaviors are automatically stimulated by the regulator and represent the person's striving for physiological adequacy. Psychological and sociological behaviors are mediated by the cognator and manifest the person's striving for psychological and social adequacy.

Influencing stimuli. The person's coping process, the internal transaction, is influenced by stimuli that include the person's internal state and external environment. The internal stimuli that influence the adapting person's transactional process and behavioral responses consist of his physiological structure, maturational level, and unique perceptions. The environment refers to the adapting person's surroundings: the people, places, and objects that exist outside the person and influence how he transacts and behaves. Therefore, the triggering events and influencing stimuli arise from the person's internal state, which is a unique personal experience, and the external environment, which is a physical space shared by others.

The regulator/cognator process makes the person unique. Many people experience similar interactions between themselves and the environment, but the regulator and the cognator make the experience and the behavioral response uniquely personal. When the environment is combined with his internal state, the adapting person's

physiological response, coping stance, and coping strategy reflect his unique interpretation and response to the environment.

IMPLICATIONS FOR NURSING PRACTICE AND GROWTH

This unique internal transaction is the cornerstone for the practice of adaptation
nursing. It is the basis for a philosophical belief in the person as an individual, placing
the responsibility for adequacy and coping with the adapting person, not with some
external source. The adapting person, because of this internal transaction, is seen
as unique and responsible for his own adaptation. What impact do these beliefs then
have on the practice of the nurse who utilizes the Roy adaptation model?

First, this belief that the person is unique and competent is in many ways a new
concept in the application of nursing models. The person has always been considered
an individual in theory, but frequently lip service is given to this belief in practice.
A process that accounts for the uniqueness of the person or individualization of client
care has not been previously addressed and organized into a practical plan for nursing
care. Therefore, the nurse had to be content to say, "I believe in the uniqueness of
the individual, but I don't have a systematic way of looking at or measuring that
uniqueness; so I'll do the best I can." The description of the regulator and cognator
identifies a process that allows the adaptation nurse to put into practice the basic
belief that the adapting person is, in truth, a singular human being who responds
to the environment in a manner uniquely his own.

Second, the belief in the person as capable of accepting responsibility for his own
well-being is also a relatively new concept. Nursing practice has developed historically from the medical model. In the past nurses have typically offered parallel
services, defining their nursing practice based on the practice of medicine. The need
for nursing models grew in part out of the beliefs that nursing and medicine had
different goals and purposes and therefore could not operate from the same framework. Despite such attempts, nursing has remained influenced by a milieu long
dominated by the medical model. As a result, the nursing profession has for the
most part maintained an orientation to disease. According to this view, although the
client is recognized as a unique individual, he is primarily regarded as a sick, incompetent person who needs to be taken care of. Frequently, only lip service is
given to the idea that the patient is an essential resource in his recovery process.
Although nursing students are taught to write goals and interventions from the
perspective of the client, in practice nurses tend to write goals and interventions for
themselves. This seems to occur largely because the practicing nurse has not been
taught how to take the perspective of the adapting person. Defining and using the
regulator/cognator process allows the nurse to examine the person's perspective and
thus to formulate appropriate goals and interventions. If the nurse understands the
purpose of the person's coping behavior, she can facilitate his adaptive process,
intervening "with" the person as opposed to "for" the person.

Third, this internal transaction offers the nurse a mechanism for self-examination and growth, for the adaptation nurse is of course an adapting person herself who responds to triggering events in her own unique manner.

Historically nurses have been taught to be objective, to conceal their emotions, and to believe that they must meet everyone's needs in the health care system but their own. By incorporating the regulator/cognator process into her practice, the adaptation nurse can use her unique personal attributes to enhance her interactions with the adapting person. In addition, she can use this new awareness to identify and minimize the coping responses that are nonfunctional or potentially destructive to her interactions with the adapting person. This increased awareness of herself will result in an understanding of her own personal coping responses and make it easier for her to take the perspective of the adapting person. If she understands her own unique perspective and how it is similar and dissimilar from that of the person with whom she is interacting, she can truly be an adaptation nurse: a thinker, a facilitator, and an independent practitioner.

Summary

The adaptive coping response (the unique internal transaction) has a significant impact on the practice of the adaptation nurse. It allows her to describe and assign meaning to coping responses, thereby utilizing her belief in the client as a unique, competent, and responsible adapting person. In addition, the adaptive coping response allows her to increase her awareness of herself and to use this awareness to enhance her interactions with the adapting person. The regulator/cognator transaction provides the adaptation nurse and the adapting person with knowledge about themselves and about each other, which is essential to their mutual experience of adequacy.

THE PROCESS OF BECOMING AN ADAPTATION NURSE

The adaptation nurse is described as a person who uses specialized knowledge and intervention strategies to help the client maintain or enhance his sense of adequacy and security as he strives for survival, growth, reproduction, mastery, and autonomy. The adapting person who, by choice of profession, becomes an adaptation nurse experiences the process of role change in which she integrates society's role prescription of the nurse with her own specific environmental influencing stimuli and unique internal state. This role is characterized by a give-and-take relationship between herself and her environment, which includes classroom and clinical settings, persons who direct her learning experiences, and persons who require her professional service.

The transition from adaptation student nurse to adaptation nurse is influenced by many stimuli, both external and internal. Her environment includes such external stimuli as the adaptation nursing curriculum, the nursing profession, the client or adapting person, the physician, and even the bureaucracy of institutions. The adaptation student nurse herself is the source of internal stimuli, which include her physiological being, maturational level, and unique set of perceptions. As the adaptation student nurse interacts with this environment, she experiences growth and change. When the adaptation process itself becomes part of her thinking (and, therefore, acting) she can be called an adaptation nurse, i.e., a practitioner who interacts with adapting persons to facilitate the interaction between the person's internal state and the environment. Her practice is based on the belief that the adapting person is a unique, competent, responsible individual who acts in partnership with the adaptation nurse for the maintenance or enhancement of his level of adequacy.

Having attained the status of adaptation nurse, the growth process continues and is marked by progressive changes, which ultimately result in the maturation of the practitioner of adaptation nursing. The developmental theory of Erik Erickson has been used to demonstrate this progression of the newly graduated adaptation nurse (adolescent stage) to experienced nurse (young adult stage) to specialized practitioner (generative stage). These stages are described in terms of tasks she performs, the regulator/cognator process, the health/illness continuum, nursing actions, health care, facilities, and common medical diagnoses.

The adaptation nurse in the adolescent stage of development is a nurse recently graduated from an adaptation curriculum. The tasks of this stage of development include selection of an appropriate model, separation from the influence of the educational institution, and establishment of her identity as an adaptation nurse. The adaptation nurse in this stage generally selects the coping stances of approach/avoidance, compromise, and inaction. As a result, she uses the strategies of fight, flight, suppression/repression, projection, substitution, denial, and very infrequently reaction formation and dissociation. Given the tasks of this stage of development as well as the adolescent adaptation nurse's regulator/cognator process, she usually selects the nursing actions of support and collaboration. The adaptation nurse in the adolescent stage of development interacts most effectively with clients in the middle of the health/illness continuum, clients experiencing disrupted wellness. Her skills are most suited to acute care facilities and clients with medical conditions that include acute medical illnesses, illnesses treatable on outpatient basis or with short hospitalization, stable chronic conditions, and emergencies that do not require surgical intervention.

The adaptation nurse in the young adult stage of development has accomplished the tasks of adolescence and is striving to increase and solidify her role performance and acquire professional intimacy. The young adult adaptation nurse usually selects the coping stance of compromise, occasionally using approach/avoidance. However, she should have no need for the stance of inaction. She is also beginning to use the stance of self-enhancement. As a result, she uses the strategy of suppression/repression and is beginning to use confrontation and manipulation. The nurse in this stage of development seldom uses fight/flight, projection, or substitution, but she occasionally experiments with negotiation. Given the tasks of the young adult stage of development and her expanded regulator/cognator function, the adaptation nurse in this stage can skillfully use support and collaboration; furthermore, she is developing facility with teaching and enabling skills. She can interact with a client at any position on the health/illness continuum but is ideally suited for interacting with those on the second half of the spectrum, i.e., disrupted wellness and illness. She is perhaps the most employable and sought after adaptation nurse. She can be found in any clinical setting but is most prepared for working in critical care facilities and for interacting with clients with complex medical disruptions.

Finally, the adaptation nurse in the generative stage of development has completed the tasks of young adulthood and has acquired additional formal education beyond a basic degree. The tasks of this stage of development include increased productivity and care, growth and enhancement, and education and socialization of future adaptation nurses. The generative adaptation nurse selects the coping stance of self-enhancement almost exclusively and only occasionally uses compromise. As a result, she selects the coping strategies of confrontation, manipulation, and negotiation. Infrequently she uses suppression in combination with the self-enhancing strategies. Given the tasks of the generative nurse and the high level of her regulator/cognator process, she is especially skilled in the use of enabling and teaching. She uses support occasionally, rarely engaging in collaboration. The generative nurse can interact with the client at any position on the health/illness continuum. However, because of her orientation toward growth and enhancement, she is best suited for interacting with adapting persons on the first half of the health/illness continuum, i.e., wellness and the early stages of disrupted wellness. She is the most skilled adaptation nurse, qualified to work in any health care facility. She functions optimally as a practitioner in outpatient or alternate care facilities, interacting with clients who are anticipating potential threats to adequacy. As a consultant, teacher, or researcher she can be found in any facility interacting with clients in any stage of wellness or illness.

The process of becoming an adaptation nurse is a continuous, steady progression toward maturation. The adapting person first takes on the role of adaptation student nurse; then, as a new graduate, she progresses from adolescence to young adulthood, and finally to generativity. What implications does this process of maturation have for the practice of adaptation nursing?

IMPLICATIONS FOR NURSING PRACTICE AND GROWTH

First, identifying the progression from adaptation student nurse to generative adaptation nurse allows the nurse at any stage of development to set reasonable goals and expectations regarding her practice. For example, students of nursing often set unrealistic goals for themselves. They feel anxious anticipating what will be expected of them when they graduate. They deal with their anxiety by searching and planning varied collaborative experiences, or by becoming confused and disappointed with the psychological and sociological emphasis in the curriculum. The adaptation nursing student is no exception to this anxious experience, often fearing that she will be unable to meet her role expectations. Then, as a graduate, she believes that she is expected to function optimally, regardless of her experience or stage of maturation. Typically, she will express the resultant anxiety by using projection and being angry and dissatisfied with her work. The identification and acknowledgment of the maturation process should help both the student and the graduate define the scope of their practice.

Second, institutions and agencies that employ adaptation nurses most frequently wish to employ those who are in the young adult stage of development, because a nurse in this stage has experience, is skillful, and can function with a wide range of clients. However, even when the agency does employ an adaptation nurse in the adolescent or generative (rather than young adult) stage of development, the agency rarely changes its expectations for the position to fit the developmental stage of the nurse. Hence, the adolescent nurse is expected to function as a young adult nurse, and the generative nurse is expected to function as a young adult as well as a generative nurse. The agency experiences conflict, too. The facility must meet the needs of the client and cannot truly justify employing different developmental levels of nurses unless they can document the maturational process and its cost-effectiveness in the provision of health care.

In summary, recognition of the adaptation nurse's stage of development should allow the adaptation nurse and the employing agency to establish realistic expectations for her performance. The adaptation nurse should be able to describe clearly the developmental stage she is in at the time of employment. Based on this description she can identify the client population and the health care environment where she can function optimally, facilitating the client's level of adequacy as well as her own. With this assessment she can then present herself to the health care system without feeling anxious. Similarly, the health care system should be able to define the stage of development that the nurse must maintain to function successfully in a particular environment. This type of classification has the added advantage of providing criteria for documenting salary schedules and for budgeting to obtain nurses developmentally suited for specific client populations.

Recognition of the evolutionary nature of the stages of development leading to the mature practitioner of adaptation nursing allows the nurse and the health care system to set reasonable expectations of each other. If the developmental stage of the nurse, the health care environment, and the level of adequacy of the adapting person are compatible, both the adapting person and the adaptation nurse will maintain or enhance their levels of adequacy. This positive change in levels of adequacy has the secondary effect of increasing the effective functioning of the health care environment.

ADAPTATION NURSING PROCESS

The adaptation nursing process involves assessment, diagnosis, and intervention with adapting persons. It is a problem-solving process in which data are gathered, judgments and evaluations are made, a diagnosis is formulated, action is taken, and an evaluation is completed. The adaptation nursing process utilizes the procedures nursing has used for years; however, it is unique in its philosophical view, which asserts that the adapting person and the adaptation nurse significantly affect the manner in which the elements of the process are assembled and utilized. The adaptation nurse and the adapting person occupy complementary roles; together they interact in a shared environment for the purpose of maintaining or enhancing adequacy.

The adaptation nursing process is divided into three distinct steps. In step I behavioral observations are made and related influencing stimuli are identified. The relationships between the behavioral responses and the stimuli are identified. These relationships are hypothesized by classifying the behavior according to one of the four modes (physiological, self-concept, role performance, or interdependence) and identifying the causal significance of the stimuli (focal, contextual, or residual). The adapting person is an active participant in the first step of this process, validating or invalidating the nurse's perceptions. In step II the adaptation nurse engages in a variety of internal operations. Based on her assessment, which includes an understanding of the person's regulator/cognator process, she formulates judgments, assigns diagnostic categories, makes nursing diagnoses, and sets priorities. The adaptation nurse clearly expresses her understanding of the person's interaction with the environment by assigning the person to the first, second, or third diagnostic category and identifying his position on the health/illness continuum. Finally, in step III the adaptation nurse and the adapting person set goals, plan and initiate interventions, and evaluate the effectiveness of these interventions in the maintenance or enhancement of the person's adequacy. The nurse and the person use the judgments and the diagnosis formulated in step II as a basis for action in step III.

The adaptation nursing process is not a unique process; it utilizes the same procedures the nursing profession has used for years to assess, diagnose, and intervene with adapting persons. However, the adaptation process is unique in its philosophical view, which accounts for the unique thinking process that characterizes the manner in which the adaptation nurse and the adapting person assemble and utilize the process.

IMPLICATIONS FOR NURSING PRACTICE AND GROWTH

What implications, then, does the adaptation nursing process have for the practice of nursing? The adaptation nursing process represents an organized way of thinking about the massive amount of data the nurse collects during her interactions with adapting persons. This organized cognitive process allows the adaptation nurse to articulate her observations and their meanings to the adapting person. This articulation facilitates the partnership that exists between the adapting person and the adaptation nurse. In addition, the adaptation nursing process increases the adaptation nurse's ability to communicate in an organized manner with other health care providers.

Historically, the nurse assisted the physician. More recently, the nurse is assuming the role of facilitator, one who aids the client in coping with the impact of illness. The definition of adaptation nursing, which clearly specifies that the adaptation nurse and the adapting person interact for the purpose of maintaining or enhancing the person's level of adequacy, supports this recent perspective. The relationship between the adaptive models as well as the prominent focus on the psychosocial aspects of the adaptive person indicate the focus of adaptation nursing.

The adaptation nursing process has been altered by the delineation of the functions of the regulator and cognator, which has clarified the distinction between the physiological mode and the other three modes. Physiological behaviors that emanate from the regulator process remain largely outside the control of the adapting person and therefore outside the influence of the adaptation nurse. However, the self-concept, role performance, and interdependence modes are mediated by the person's cognator process; because these modes are under the control of the adapting person, they can also be influenced by the adaptation nurse. The adapting person's cognator does not affect the physiological mode. The cognator is responsible for the person's response to the physiological experience, but the cognator cannot terminate the physiological behavior. The cognator's response to physiological experience is predominantly expressed in the role performance and interdependence modes.

The practice of the adaptation nurse, then, is largely focused in the psychological and social modes. A knowledge of pathophysiology and the skill to perform collaborative activities have assumed a secondary position in the prescribed role behavior of the adaptation nurse. The facilitation of the adapting person's coping response has assumed primary significance, and the actions of support, teaching, and enabling are used extensively. The adapting person's response to illness or anticipation of illness has become the ultimate concern of the adaptation nurse.

Where do we go from here?

If the 1980s are truly the decade of the nurse and the adaptation nurse represents the practitioner of this decade, what changes should be expected in the performance of this adaptation nurse as the decade unfolds?

First, the generative adaptation nurse must assume responsibility not only for the education of future adaptation nurses but also for validating the impact of adaptation nursing practice on the adapting person's level of adequacy. This textbook raises many researchable questions; it is essential that these questions be addressed and that answers be utilized to develop further the constructs that support and define the practice of the adaptation nurse. The 1980s, then, should see an increase in clinical research utilized to explore and expand the practice of adaptation nursing.

Second, there exists in this decade the potential for a dramatic change in the adaptation nurse's role in the health care environment. The adapting person has many needs that are unmet in the current system. Economic, social, and political stimuli are causing the client to question present systems and demand alternative forms of health care. These demands include the client's desire for more personalized service and more autonomous functioning. In addition, the adapting person is requesting help to deal with his response to the complex scientific and technological advances of modern medicine. The practitioner of adaptation nursing is prepared to meet these needs. She views the adapting person as a unique, competent, and responsible individual. Defining her role in the health care environment as that of a facilitator, she assists the adapting person to maintain or enhance his level of adequacy. Finally, she is especially skilled in dealing with the problems of adequacy that arise out of the experience with or anticipation of illness. The adaptation nurse is prepared to meet the health care needs of the adapting person of this decade. However, the adapting person's demands, the economics of health services, and the short supply of qualified nurses will result in a vastly different method of delivery of these adaptation nursing services.

This is the decade of the adaptation nurse, the independent practitioner who can clearly articulate her beliefs about the client, her relationship with that client, and her special areas of knowledge and skills for interacting with particular types of clients. In recent years professional nurses have entered the arena of private practice. The adaptation nurse of the 1980s is prepared to expand the scope of private practice to include the nurse in the adolescent, young adult, and generative stages of development. Each of these nurses has specific, essential skills to offer the adapting person. The 1980s should see the adaptation nurse forming an individualized contract with the adapting person for the purpose of effectively maintaining or enhancing his level of adequacy. The adaptation nurse of this decade will be self-employed, a professional who contracts for a fee with the adaptive person, the health care system, or another health care professional to provide a service for which she is especially qualified or prepared. In so doing, she will provide the client with individualized care that facilitates his own ability to cope with the multitude of triggering events associated with the anticipation or experience of illness. The hope, as well as the task, of the adaptation nurse of the future is to move from the function of taking care of ill persons to the more exciting process of forming a partnership with clients who recognize and accept a vital role in maintaining or increasing their level of biopsychosocial adequacy.

Glossary

Adaptation nurse The adaptation nurse enters into a partnership with a person to help the person maintain or achieve a sense of adequacy and security. She believes that people are constantly vigilant, open, living systems who are constantly striving for survival, growth, reproduction, mastery, and autonomy in a give-and-take relationship with the environment. She also believes that people utilize the adaptive process to transact with the environment. The adaptation nurse interacts with a person to facilitate the interaction between the person's internal state and the environment. She utilizes a specialized body of knowledge in combination with specific strategies for intervention and a variety of nursing skills.

Adaptation process Encompasses *all the activities* engaged in by the person in his *striving for adequacy*. This process is represented by the *give-and-take relationship* between the *transaction* and the *influencing stimuli*. The ultimate effect of this process may be to maintain, increase, or decrease the level of adequacy.

Adaptive mode The channel of energy for the behavioral activity or response in which a person engages for the purpose of maintaining or enhancing his level of adequacy.

Adequacy The *state of balance or equality between the person and the environment*, which he constantly strives to achieve and maintain. This state of balance is experienced as a feeling of competence in relationship to the stress experience.

Adolescent stage of development The developmental stage of the adaptation nurse who has recently graduated from an adaptation curriculum. The tasks of this stage of development include selection of an appropriate model, separation from the influence of the educational institution, and establishment of her identity as an adaptation nurse.

Behavioral assessment The systematic gathering of information or observations about the person's observable or measurable activities or actions. These actions are assigned meaning and classified according to the adaptive mode.

Behavioral responses Observable or measurable activities in which the person engages in an attempt to achieve or maintain physiological, psychological, and social adequacy.

Category I diagnosis Is represented by congruence between both nursing judgments. The coping stance and strategies are congruent with the triggering event, and the behavioral response is maintaining or enhancing the level of adequacy. In the physiological mode this diagnosis occurs when the behavioral response is maintaining adequacy.

Category II diagnosis Occurs when the behavioral response is ineffective in maintaining adequacy. The coping stance and strategies and the triggering event are congruent. There is incongruence between the behavioral response and the level of adequacy.

Category III diagnosis Is represented by a lack of congruence in both nursing judgments. The coping stance and strategies are incongruent with the influencing stimuli; as a result, the behavioral response does not maintain adequacy. In the physiological mode this diagnosis occurs when the behavioral response is ineffective in maintaining adequacy.

Change The process of altering, varying, or modifying. When a person or situation is changed, it is said to be made different. This difference may be perceived as positive or negative and is evaluated by the person's experience of comfort or discomfort.

Client   The adapting person who interacts with the adaptation nurse in a health care setting for the purpose of gaining support, assistance, or knowledge regarding his level of adequacy.

Cognator   The person's *conscious* and *unconscious adaptive mechanism* that, when signaled by the regulator, *labels, clarifies, defines, and initiates a behavioral response*. This mechanism *alters the stress experience* and terminates the activity of the regulatory mechanism by affecting the relationship between the person and the environment.

Collaboration   The behavioral activity the nurse employs in cooperation with other caregivers for the purpose of maintaining the person's physiological adequacy.

Coping stance   The intellectual or emotional posture assumed by the adapting person when he transacts to process a triggering event.

Coping strategy   The careful plan or method the person will behaviorally employ to master his relationship with the triggering event.

Contextual stimuli   Identifiable internal or external factors that noticeably influence the person's adaptive response to a triggering event.

Development   The progressive changes in adaptive functioning. Development is a process that focuses on the dynamic, unidirectional elements of change, an integration of constitutional and learned changes that make up the person's ever-developing professional role performance.

Diagnostic category   The organized grouping of nursing judgments. This grouping must reflect the degree of disruption in the person's level of adequacy and the quality and quantity of nursing interventions required.

Disrupted wellness   Refers to adapting persons who demonstrate behavior in the second diagnostic category in at least two modes or in three or more components of a single mode.

Enabling   The set of complex behaviors the nurse engages in for the purpose of strengthening, maintaining, or giving power to the adapting person.

Evaluation   The judgment process the nurse uses to reassess the person's behavioral response to nursing interactions and methods of intervention. This judgment process is based upon evaluative criteria reflective of the diagnostic categories, and goal statement.

Evaluation criteria   Reflect the goal of the adapting person to achieve an optimal level of adequacy. Therefore, the criteria for effective nursing intervention concern whether the adapting person maintains or achieves a higher level of adequacy.

Environment   The *constantly changing* but often *predictable* composition of *people, places, and objects* that surround the person.

Focal stimuli   Environmental stimuli that provoke the person's behavioral response and cause a change in his level of adequacy. In this text a triggering event is always a focal stimulus.

Generative stage of development   The developmental stage of the adaptation nurse who has accomplished the tasks of the young adult stage of development and has acquired additional formal education beyond a basic degree. The tasks of the generative stage of development include increased productivity and care, growth and enhancement, and education and socialization of future adaptation nurses.

Goal   A precise and positive statement about the adaptive person's behavioral activities in which he must engage in order to reestablish, maintain, or enhance personal adequacy. The goal statement must reflect the cause-and-effect relationship defined in the nursing diagnosis.

Health/illness continuum   A graphic representation of the possible range of levels of adequacy the adapting person may experience. The levels of adequacy are arranged in a progression from growth and self-enhancement to an absence of adequate functioning.

Illness   Refers to adapting persons who demonstrate behavior in the third diagnostic category in two or more modes.

Influencing stimuli   The *elements* that affect the person's *ability to achieve adequacy*. These stimuli include the person's *internal state* and the *environment*.

Interdependence mode   The channel of energy for the behavioral activities in which the person engages to maintain or enhance his social adequacy. This adequacy depends upon the person's nurturing and supportive relationships with others, which provide meaning to his being and acting. The cognator mediates these behavioral responses.

Internal state   Comprises the person's physiological make-up, maturational level, and unique perceptions.

Intervention   A specific behavioral activity engaged in by a person or persons for the purpose of achieving a previously stated goal. There are four methods of nursing intervention that help maintain or increase the adapting person's level of adequacy. These methods are support, teaching, collaboration, and enabling.

Nursing diagnosis   The summary statement of a nursing judgment. It clearly indicates the cause-and-effect relationship between the person's behavioral response and the influencing stimuli. This summary statement must reflect the relationship between the person's level of adequacy and the triggering event as well as the relationship between his cognator response and coping strategy.

Nursing judgment   Two statements formulated during step II of the adaptation nursing process. This first statement defines the coping stance and strategies the person is using and identifies the congruence between coping behaviors and the environment. The second statement defines the threat to the level of adequacy and identifies the effectiveness of the behavioral response.

Nursing process   The problem-solving process applied to nursing situations. The elements involved in the nursing process are assessment, analysis, planning, implementation, evaluation, and modification.

Person   An *open*, living system who uses *adaptive mechanisms* to meet needs for biological, psychological, and social *adequacy*. This level of adequacy is influenced by the person's unique physiological make-up, maturational level, and perceptions.

Physiological mode   The channel of energy for the behavioral activities the person uses to maintain or enhance his biological adequacy. This adequacy depends on the person's biological function and regulatory behavior necessary for the maintenance of life. The regulator is the source of this behavioral response.

Priority setting   The ongoing process the nurse uses to make critical decisions about the timing of her interactions with the adapting person as well as the immediacy and importance of her nursing intervention.

Problem-solving process   Is based on the scientific method developed for the purpose of logically and systematically searching for the cause-and-effect relationships in specific or predetermined situations. The elements of this process include data collection, problem identification, formulation of a hypothesis (cause-and-effect relationship), validation of the hypothesis, and the actions taken to solve the problem.

Reality shock   Intrarole conflict experienced when there are contradictory expectations (role prescriptions) from the profession and the institution that employs the person.

Regulator   The person's *physiological adaptive mechanism* for responding to an environmental impact. This mechanism *alerts* and *mobilizes* the neural and hormonal systems to produce a *continuous, universal, physiological* response. It is also responsible for the body's specific physiological response to a physical, chemical, or infectious triggering event.

Residual stimuli   Internal or external stimuli that appear to influence the person's adaptive response to a triggering event. These require validation as to their actual level of influence.

Role change   The process a person goes through in order to enter a new or previously relinquished role. This process involves incorporating society's role prescriptions and the environmental influencing factors with a person's unique self.

Role performance mode   The channel of energy for the behavioral activities in which the person engages to maintain or enhance his social adequacy. This adequacy depends on the person's knowledge of who he is in relation to others so he can act. The cognator mediates these behavioral responses.

Role prescription   Actions which society ascribes to a role.

Self-concept mode   The channel of energy for the behavioral activities the person employs to maintain or enhance his psychological adequacy. This adequacy depends on the person's sense of self so he can know who he is in order to be or exist. The cognator is the mediator of this behavioral response.

Stimuli   Internal and external influencing factors provoke or influence a person's behavioral response.

Stimuli assessment   The systematic gathering of information or observations concerning the internal and external stimuli that provoke and influence a person's adaptive response to a triggering event. The stimuli are then evaluated and classified according to their level of influence on the adaptive response.

Stress   Any *change* in the level of adequacy experienced by the person any time he is touched or penetrated by the environment.

Student nurse role   Encompasses all the activities engaged in by the student nurse as she strives for personal and professional adequacy. This adaptive process is represented by a give-and-take relationship between herself and the environment, which includes classroom and clinical settings, persons who direct her learning experiences, and persons who need her professional service.

Support   The behavioral activity the nurse uses to approve, sanction, or validate the person's adaptive behavior.

Teaching   The behavioral activity the nurse utilizes to impart or clarify knowledge, information, and cognitive or psychomotor skills.

Transaction   The process whereby the person *alters* his *stress experience*. This alteration, expressed as a behavioral response, is achieved by the regulator and cognator and may be said to have maintained, increased, or decreased the level of adequacy.

Triggering event   Occurs whenever the environment touches or penetrates the person and causes a change in his level of adequacy.

Wellness   Refers to adapting persons who demonstrate a category I diagnosis in three of four modes or all but two components of a single mode. In addition, the mode or two components demonstrating incongruence between the judgments must be a category II level.

Young adult stage of development   The developmental stage of the adaptation nurse who has accomplished the tasks of the adolescent stage of development. The tasks of the young adult stage of development include increasing and solidifying role performance and acquiring professional intimacy.

Index

Self-concept mode, 44, 51-55
  behavioral response in, 53-54
  behaviors in, 51-52
  definition of, 42
  diagnosis in, 70
  diagnostic categories in, 68
  evaluation criteria for, 85
  goal setting in, 75-76
  influencing stimuli for, 52-53, 54
  interventions in, 82
  judgments in, 66
  nurse/client interaction in
    cardiac distress, 193-195
    developmental delay, 229-231
    pediatric experience, 149
    postnatal experience, 249-250
    well child, 256-257
  nursing care guide for, 55, 87
    anxiety reaction, 158-159
    cardiac distress, 194-195
    chronic illness, 171
    depression and loss, 213
    developmental delay, 230-231
    well child, 256-257
  regulator/cognator transaction in,
    53
Self-consistency, 52
Self-enhancement, 9
  coping strategies associated with, 13-14
  in generative stage, 131-132
  in young adult stage, 127-128, 128-129,
    130
Self-esteem as internal influencing stimulus,
    30
Self-ideal, 52
Self-identity, 115
Selye, H., 5
Settings for adaptation nursing process
  for anxiety reaction, 151-152
  for cardiac distress, 178-179
  for chronic illness, 159
  for depression and loss, 196
  for developmental delay, 214
  for elderly grandfather, 262
  for pediatric planned surgery, 144-145
  for postnatal experience, 236-237
  for well child, 251-252
Social adequacy, 60
Sociological behaviors, 16-17
Solidarity in young adult stage, 126
Specialized practitioner, 116
Stamina, 117
Standards of Nursing Practice, 28
State of constant vigilance, 6-7

Stimuli, 26-29; *see also* Contextual stimuli; External
    influencing stimuli; Focal stimulus(i); Inter-
    nal influencing stimuli
  definition of, 42
  that influence development, 116-118
  interactional, 48
  residual, 46
    definition of, 42
Stimuli assessment, definition of, 42
Stress, 4, 5
Student nurse
  adaptation process of, 30-38
  influencing stimuli for, 35
  maturational level of, 29
  perceptions of, 30
  physiological makeup of, 29
  role of, 32
    definition of, 24
  senior, 34-36
    role of, 35
Substitution, 12
  in adolescent stage, 120-121
  in young adult stage, 127
Support, 78, 79
  in adolescent stage, 123
  definition of, 43
  in generative stage, 133
  in young adult stage, 128
Suppression, 12
  in adolescent stage, 120, 121
  in generative stage, 132
  in young adult stage, 126
Suppression/repression, 11-12

T

Teaching, 78, 79
  definition of, 43
  in generative stage, 133
  in young adult stage, 129
Terms
  for adaptation nurse, 24-25
    developmental stages for professional growth,
      114
  for adaptation nursing process, 41-43
  for adapting person, 4
  for health/illness continuum, 95-97
Tertiary role, 56, 57
Theory of development, 114-116
  experienced nurse, 115-116
  recent graduate, 115
  specialized practitioner, 116
Theory objectives
  for disrupted wellness, 141